Eaglebrook - 1950
Deerfield, Massachusetts

INSTRUMENTAL MUSIC
PRIZE

STEPHEN HENSLEICH WEDGWOOD

Music of the World

A History

Kurt Pahlen's

Music of the World

A History

Translated from the German by
JAMES A. GALSTON

With 400 Illustrations

Crown Publishers — New York
1949

Preface

CENTURIES ago, enjoyment of good music was the prerogative of a privileged few. The advent of printed music made it available to new classes. A similar widening of music's sphere of influence is taking place in our century. Mechanical means of reproducing music—phonograph, radio, sound films, television—are the pioneers that carry the hallowed names of Bach and Beethoven and the sound of noble music to the masses of the population. Let these much maligned means be given full credit for such a development and for having made practically the entire inhabited and civilized world into one realm of music.

As a consequence, a tremendous yearning for music has seized the world. Hundreds of thousands, millions, want to take it to their hearts, want to enjoy it, and be uplifted by it. It has been my privilege to talk about music to any number of audiences on both sides of the Atlantic and in many cities. This book is addressed to those whom I have been unable to reach. It is therefore almost a spoken book. In penning it I felt as if I were talking to friends, for all lovers of music are friends, are my friends, the world over.

I wish to communicate to them what I know and have experienced in the magic realm of music. So perhaps this book is a bit more personal than a history of music ought to be.

This, then, has been my guiding thought: "To be gripped and moved by music is more important than to be able to dissect a piece; for music is a matter of the heart . . ." That is how a wise friend of mine once put it. In that sense this book has been written. I place it in the hands of those who think and feel as I do. It may conceivably be their first book on music, the one that raises the curtain, as at a theatrical performance.

Mighty and momentous are the changes taking place in the world of today. Nobody knows whither they may lead. At any rate, youthful America is destined to play a leading part in world development. Here, in the land of still unlimited possibilities, a new civilization, a new cultural epoch, may crystallize and take shape. May it lead us back to the true sources of life. May music exercise its exalted mission in connection with the world's rebirth which we seem about to witness. Far, far back in human history, there were times when music stood in the center of life, when it was an intermediary between natural and supernatural phenomena, when it was the sister of religion and the corner stone of all education. And, ah, they were happy times . . .

There may be music without culture. But there can never be true culture without music.

KURT PAHLEN

1949

CONTENTS

Book One — THE ASCENT

Book Two — THE SUMMIT

CONTENTS

LIST OF HALF-TONE PLATES

ix

Book One

The Assent

It is more important to "feel" history
than to master its details . . . . .

(*Hendrik van Loon*)

1. Satyrs at wine press. Ancient example of work accompanied by music. Painting on a Greek amphora. Würzburg.

.1.

Music in Man's Life

ALL life is sound. We are constantly surrounded by sounds and noises produced by nature and everything astir in it. For thousands of years man has been speaking and singing and, thanks to his wonderfully constructed ear, perceiving sounds and noises, although they are but a small part of the inconceivable wealth of the sounds filling the universe.

Children everywhere and without exception are born with musical abilities, with voices, and with hearing. The difference lies only in what they do with these gifts. That varies according to temperament, upbringing, nationality, race, and epoch.

Nature itself is full of sound, full of music. Musical sounds existed millions of years before there was a human ear to hear them: the soft bubbling of the water, the roll of thunder, the whispering and rustling of leaves in the wind, and who knows how many other audible manifestations of nature. Perhaps the morning sunbeams sang as they caressingly warmed the awakening mountains, just as they sing today so mysteriously in the Egyptian Memnon Pillar. Since time immemorial the natural organ in Fingal's Cave has been sounding, long before the Celts gave it the name *Llaimh Binn*, Cave of Music, and still longer before a romantic composer, Mendelssohn, made a modern orchestra reproduce these sounds of nature in his *Fingal's Cave Overture*. And the strange "Ear of Dionysus" in Sicily amplified all sounds reaching it long, long before there was a human brain to fathom the miracle. The cracking of the youthful earth, the bursting forth of springs, the spouting of volcanoes, the rising up of mountains, the surging of the waters of the Great Deluge—what a mighty symphony of sound, unrecorded in the musical annals of mankind!

Man was born into a world of sound. Thunder filled him with fear and became the symbol of supernatural powers. In the roar of the wind he heard the voice of demons. Dwellers at the seashore judged the temper of the gods by the sound of the waves. The echo was a prophecy, animal voices were revelations. Religious rites and music were inseparable at the dawn of humanity.

The power of music over the human mind has been great ever since. Primitive man had but few words at his disposal. Only the things he saw had names. To give voice to his feelings, he had recourse to sound and so found his way to music. It enabled him to express his exaltation, his fondness for dancing, his mourning, his love, his warlike instincts, and his belief in a supreme power. Music became part of his life, from the cradle song to the death dirge, from the ritual dance to the healing of the sick. Melody and rhythm were his constant companion.

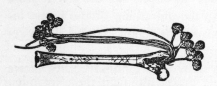

2. Flute from British Guiana, made from the bone of a jaguar.

In the course of thousands of years, the effect of music on man became weaker; still, the history of mankind, from ancient times to the very present, is full of examples testifying to the power of music. David played the harp to drive away King Saul's evil thoughts; Farinelli used music to cure Philip V's profound melancholy; Timotheus knew how to unleash the rage of Alexander the Great by a certain melody and to calm it again by another; Celtic priests taught the people by means of music, since it alone was able to exert an ennobling influence on their wild mode of life; Terpander was said to have suppressed the Lacedaemonian revolt by the playing of his flute. St. Augustine tells of a shep-

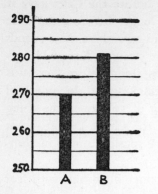

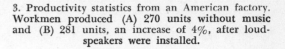

3. Productivity statistics from an American factory. Workmen produced (A) 270 units without music and (B) 281 units, an increase of 4%, after loudspeakers were installed.

herd whom the people made their ruler because of the sweetness of his melodies. The story of the Pied Piper of Hamelin is an eloquent example of the effect of music on man and beast. Modern literature has produced a number of profound psychological works ascribing to music the power to bring forth the strongest emotional manifestations. With the exception of Goethe's *Werther*, no other work has raised so powerful a wave of melancholia and suicides as Wagner's *Tristan*.

Music exerts its effect upon the individual as well as upon the masses, as proved in revolutionary times and in connection with war psychoses. Man has made a magical device of music. Its effects run the gamut from the rousing of the noblest sentiment to the unleashing of the basest instincts, from the most devout contemplation to raging excesses, from religious worship to brutal sensuality.

These brief remarks will serve to show how infinitely many facets music has. What a difference between a modern dance song and the solemn chant of monks in monastic seclusion, between a quietly hummed lullaby and a rousing march intended to put spirit into a body of attacking soldiers, between a love song floating on the air of a starry summer night and the gay and rhythmic airs coming from a loudspeaker to raise the production figures in a modern factory! [Ill. 3.]

Infinite indeed is the variety of music. Think of the tri-tonal and unceasingly repeated melody of the American Indian and the symphony of a great master; the temple dances of the Far East and modern operatic music; Gregorian chorals and jazz! And yet, they all exist at the same time, now, today, on our planet, and to all we apply the one word—music.

Still more striking becomes the difference when we follow music, as we intend to do, on its way through the ages: Egyptian temple melodies, Greek theater, early polyphony, guild and work songs of the Middle Ages, and then the great artistic awakening in the days of the Renaissance! And even from that day to ours, what a difference between Palestrina and Haydn, between Bach and Chopin, between Beethoven and Stravinsky, between Mozart and Debussy. . . .

All life is sound, we said. For life is motion, and sound grows out of motion. The science of acoustics, to be sure, differentiates fundamentally between two kind of sounds, tones and noises, depending on whether their vibrations are uniform or irregular. According to old precepts, music ought to concern itself only with the former. But it is not so simple to draw a clear dividing line. How many instruments play an important part in a modern orchestra, though they produce noises rather than tones. Triangles, cymbals, drums, tom-toms, castanets, tambourines! And he who has once listened to a Malay gong orchestra and its fantastic chiming will no doubt have received a strong musical impression, contrary to all musical teachings. We shall be told later how, in our very day, the tonal system which for centuries has formed the foundation of occidental music is being violently attacked. Many of these attacks are aimed at what actually is a sore point. It is that our tonal system, originally developed from the series of overtones, has become simpler by "tempering," but has at the same time become mathematically and physically impure, so that any connection between science and music is today merely fictitious.

Theory and science are not to bother us here. Let the number of vibrations be pure or impure, C-sharp be equal to D-flat or not, the half-tone be the smallest unit or not, the leading tone be an arbitrary institution or not, the twelve-tone system unwarranted or not—we are to concern ourselves only with the works produced by that system; we are to follow the development of music through the thousands of years of human history, from the primitive manifestations of life, from the instinctive urge, to the production of works representing art and humanity in their noblest and most sublime expression. We shall be able to observe a cycle, nay, a series of great and mysterious cycles, an eternal growth and decay and regrowth, a mystic way through life and death, through lands and continents and cultures and epochs.

Let us realize, above all, that of all the sounds round about us, in an infinite and inscrutable variety, only a small part finds its way to our ear and brain. A still smaller part reaches the place where it may rouse an echo: the spirit. And this small part is in itself again a whole world. . . .

What is music? When I was still quite young, a student surprised me by asking the question. I replied: To the prosaic, it is an acoustic phenomenon; to the theorists, a problem dealing with melody, harmony, and rhythm; and to those who really love it, the spreading of the soul's wings, the awakening and fulfillment of all dreams and yearnings. . . . Today, this is still my belief.

· 2 ·

Music in Ancient Times

MUSIC is as old as mankind. Together with the dance, it is the oldest of all arts, although primitive man was unable to conceive it as such because the term art was as yet unknown to him. Nevertheless, its history is the shortest and newest of all. We have monuments made of metal or stone, bearing testimony to vanished cultures. Thousand-year-old poems, legends and philosophies enable us to construe a mental image of far-off epochs. With music, it is different.

Not a sound has come down to us from vanished cultural epochs. The earliest manuscripts we are able to decipher, to transpose into modern writing, and thus to bring to life again, are of comparatively recent date. Everything else that came before, thousands of years of musical production in countless cultural epochs, is lost forever in the night of ages.

Once—I think it was in a book by an American author—I came across an ingenious comparison. Let us assume, the writer said, that the earth, from its first day until now, had not lived for millions of years but merely for a single terrestrial year, from some first of January to the last day in December. If we tried to indicate man's arrival on earth, we would have to select a point late, very late, in the year: on December 31, at 6 in the afternoon, the lord of creation appeared. But that would not by any means mark the beginning of historical times. More hours would have to pass. About a minute and a half before midnight, history began. . . . And now I should like to go a step farther to demonstrate the incredible shortness of musical history. It would begin about fifteen seconds before midnight of the last day of the entire long year lived by the earth. . . . Ought we to feel quite small and futile — or be proud of all the beauties produced by a mere fifteen seconds?

We know mighty little of the music of ancient times. To begin with, the most essential thing is missing: the music itself. We can read about it in old learned books on religion, philosophy, mathematics, astronomy, and aesthetics. Strange to say, music has an important part in all of

4. Egyptian harp players. From a mural in the tomb of Rameses IV, abt. 1150 B.C.

them. Old poems, fables, legends, and fairy tales of many nations mention it. The Bible speaks of it, it is found in the ancient tales of China, and in the traditions of the American Indian. There are references to its beauty, its magic, its power. What may it have sounded like? Nobody knows. Oceans of time lie between it and us, and there is nothing that can bring it back.

True, we are taken a step nearer by witnesses made of stone: monuments, monoliths, reliefs, plates, cups, urns. Not infrequently, musical scenes appear on them, pictures of instruments, of whole orchestras even. Measurements have to some degree ascertained the pitch of these instruments. The strings of lyres and harps have been counted, the openings of the wind instruments—precursors of our flutes, oboes, and trumpets—investigated, the effects of percussion instruments studied.

And, now and then, the instruments themselves were found in ancient tombs or on the site of lost cities. We could reconstruct their play and compare it with that of our day. But what had been their music? We do not know. Was it music for its own sake, for diversion, pleasure, joy? Or did it serve a higher idea? Or material purposes?

From discovered remnants and from what has come down to us through poetic sources we are tempted to reconstruct a picture essentially rather similar to that presented by the music of our day. Did the priests in the temple sing as they do today? Did a giant orchestra sound in honor of a victorious king, as suggested by an Assyrian relief? [Pl. 3]. Was the work of the Pyramid-building Egyptian slaves accomplished by music to lighten their arduous work, just as the Volga towmen still sing to the rhythm of their ponderous steps, or the Haitian Negroes chant under a broiling sun while carrying heavy bags of coffee on board an ocean steamer? The music whose joyful sound filled the old royal palaces, accompanied the dance, or delighted those partaking of a meal—was it not like that of our time?

5. Egyptian lute players in dance attire. From a mural in ancient Thebes.

Everything has been reconstructed. We know that there was individual and group singing, accompanied or unaccompanied by instruments. There was religious and secular music—just as today. And yet, we cannot imagine how it may have sounded.

Important discoveries have also been made in connection with ancient musical theory. We know, for instance, of a Chinese scholar, Lyng Lun, who, 2500 years before the birth of Christ, strung together five tones of oriental music, explained them, formed them into a system, and gave them strange names, every tone being called after a social stratum, from the emperor down to the peasant.

Five tones? Five only, as against the twelve comprising our present musical system? This pentatonic scale, to give it its Greek name, was found to have existed in all parts of the world: in Japan, America, Greenland, and even in Europe. Ancient China, we saw, formed it into a theory, and even today these five tones are characteristic of considerable parts of the Orient. Are 4500 years then of so little account to the East? Think of all the changes wrought in the musical systems of the Occident during that span of time! Is this five-tone music a beginning or is it already a step forward from the three-tone system found still to exist among some primitive races in Africa and America?

And how, from this primitive music, did the slowly moving chain of tone systems known to us develop? Was there a gradual addition of tones: from three, to four, to five; in Greece, to six and seven; and, in the Middle Ages, by the "raising" or "lowering" of tones to a much larger number, until we finally arrived, by tempering, at our twelve-tone scale? Was there actually a constant development? Had not the Indians, the Arabs, and perhaps even the Chinese known other musical systems thousands of years ago? Music with third- and quarter-tones? Could not a people have had two kinds of music at the same time, one for religious, and one for secular purposes? Or one for the upper classes, and another for the common people? Certain details would suggest such possibilities. Can there be a difference in auditory sensations according to races or epochs? Is there a development toward constant refinement, or a cyclic recurrence, or an indiscriminate up-and-down?

6. Assurbanipal's court orchestra in Susah. Fragment from an Assyrian relief, abt. 650 B.C. Brit. Museum.

Is it true—and here I am touching upon an essential point of all musical research—that polyphonic music was "invented" only in our Middle Ages and that throughout all the preceding thousands of years, throughout all the highly developed cultural epochs that had come before, only monotonic music was practiced? Just a single melody, without a counterpart, without harmony, and without accompaniment? Why, then, the large orchestras which existed at the courts of Ninevah, of Susah, and of Babylon? Why the huge wind choir in the great Temple of Jerusalem? And what about Greek tragedy, that theatrical ideal because of its profound wisdom and its amalgamation of all arts? Could such a presentation have been without polyphony, though it was framed in music, perhaps accompanied by it, and partly even sung? Is there any justification for denying the existence of polyphony, just because we cannot prove it? Is it permissible to underestimate the musical wealth of other ages, which in many respects were by no means inferior to ours, and in some respects even superior? Is it permissible to assume that we are richer in that respect? Is it not possible that during the many centuries between the flowering of Greece and medieval polyphony, any indications in old texts pointing to a deviation from monotonic practices were simply eliminated because they would have been incomprehensible? These questions may be suggestive, but they should not be considered assertive. I merely give utterance to what often goes through my mind, for it is a fact that in all realms of art there is an immeasurable amount of "forgotten" treasure from old cultural epochs.

Music is not like lyric or pictorial art. It sounds one moment, and is wafted away. And, before the invention of the phonograph, once it was gone, nobody could give it concrete form again. That is why this chapter is so full of question marks.

There are two ways to the understanding of the music of a past time. One is marked by details which come down to us orally. Some peoples actually succeeded in keeping airs alive for a long time. However, since folk melodies are not entrusted to anybody's care and protection, a few centuries would seem to be the limit. A longer survival would be possible only where such care and protection existed. They did exist in two exceptional cases that take us far back into the past: the Jewish temple chant which has undergone but little essential change in the course of three thousand years and, related to it, the

7. Old Buddhist musicians with mouth organ, traverse flute, shawm, lute, and harp. Mural in a Khan's palace in Chinese Turkestan.

early-Christian chant, of which more will be said later. These two musical forms afford a glimpse of ancient times. But it is only a single kind of music which we thus come to know, and we are hardly justified in drawing conclusions affecting other kinds. That would be as if musical science of the year 4000 were to try to judge the music of our day on the basis of the then still practiced Catholic ritual, or of Indian temple music, to mention but two examples which are timeless rather than characteristic of a certain epoch.

The other way to a comprehension of old music is marked by written notations. But, matter-of-course and simple though it may seem to us, it is beset with a great many difficulties and problems. To begin with, the transformation of sound into written signs does not so easily suggest itself as that of the spoken word. Neither is it so easy; for the height, length, strength, and expression of a tone, of a whole phrase or melody, must be indicated. We shall see that it took centuries until the perfection of our written music could be achieved. However, the difficulties to be overcome were by no means merely of a technical nature. Psychologically, the others are even more interesting. There were long periods during which the peoples *refused* to write down their music. Its care was entrusted to the priests, to whom it had been vouchsafed as a divine revelation, to be used in the temples for the glorification of the deity. To the people, it must remain a secret science, to be handed on by the priest only to his son or successor.

8. Indian woman with sitar. From an Indian miniature.

But once the will existed to write down music, it appeared that there were two means toward that end: by letter-like symbols or by a graphic reproduction. Let us consider briefly how this was practically possible and what were the respective advantages and disadvantages. In a letter-like reproduction, C-E-G may represent a three-tone melody. But there is nothing to indicate whether or not the melody rises, whether the E is above the C, or whether a lower E is meant. The same applies to the G. Let us assume that by the use of little direction-pointing arrows this objection may be overcome. The height of the tone would thus be determined, but not its duration and strength. This kind of written music is wholly lacking in clarity. The reverse is true in the case of a graphic reproduction. Here, a steadily rising line would clearly indicate a melody of a similar tendency, and so on. The clarity of this method is more than counterbalanced by its lack of interpretation. This style of written music was in use in a number of cultural epochs. Perhaps it had its origin in a chorus leader's practice to guide his singers by drawing in the air a line of the melody. Later, lest he himself forget it, he drew it on some material— the invention of paper lay still in the dim future. This may be the reason why this kind of written music, whose strange hieroglyphics were found all about the Mediterranean, got the Greek name *Neume*, which, roughly, means gesture or hint.

A third method for perpetuating music, the most ideal of all, does not belong in a chapter dealing with old music, but has its place at the very end, in the most modern part. We refer to the phonograph record, the recording tape, and the sound film—technical achievements of the twentieth century which all at once made it impossible for music ever to became lost again.

And now, after having filled the preceding pages with so many question marks and doubts, let us look at the established facts concerning the music of ancient times.

China, we said, produced the first musical theorist known to us. His name was Lyng Lun. He put into a system the five tones whose quality he had determined by carefully observing their vibration frequencies. The appellation of the tones according to social ranks— *kong*, the emperor, *chang*, the minister, *kyo*, the burgher, *tchi*, the official, and *yu*, the peasant—shows how deeply rooted in public life was music. There are references to music even in China's earliest history. The mythical "Yellow Emperor" who is said to have ruled about 2700 B.C. is assumed to have been the composer of the "Song of the Cloudy Gate," which was sung for centuries. Of his successor, Shun, supposed to have lived about 2250, Confucius [Pl. 9] says that his music was "consummately beautiful as well as consummately good." Finally, the great wise man accorded to music a prominent place both in education and in moral philosophy. To him, music was a culture-producing power. What a pity that we have only his words on music and occasional song texts collected by him, while the sound itself has been wafted away irrevocably. . . .

In India, we find traces of a remarkably early cultivation of music. *Sama-Veda*, a sacred book, tells of its significance. According to an ancient legend it was the god Brahma himself who gave to his people the *vina* which, in a great many varieties, has remained his favorite instrument to this day. To the Indian, music meant the same as "great world harmony," and was therefore considered the equivalent of religion.

The oldest instrument known to us was discovered on Ceylon. A legendary king of the island, called Ravana, invented it about 7000 years ago and called it Ravanástron. It was the archetype of all our string instruments, had two strings, and was played with a round bow.

Many a piece of sculpture showing musical scenes or instruments has been preserved from the rich cultural life of the Assyrians, Babylonians, and Persians [Pl. 3, Ill. 6]. A remarkably high level of musical culture seems to have prevailed in the land of the Samarians, sunk into oblivion in distant times. In the recently excavated ruins of *Ur*, the country's capital, near the Persian Gulf, a beautifully carved lyre was found, whose age is estimated to be about 5000 years.

That there was an exceptionally developed cultivation of music in ancient Egypt is beyond any doubt. It seems that the country had a real musical life, in our sense of the word, with religious and secular music, work songs, and dance tunes. Many carved likenesses of instruments have been found in tombs. They prove that the Egyptians were acquainted with wind, percussion, and string instruments. [Pl. 4 and 5; Ill. 4 and 5].

We also know of ancient bow instruments from Arabia, although they are of considerably more recent date than either the Ravanástron or some of the Egyptian or Chinese instruments. The kemantche [Ill. 10] of the Arabs makes use of a coconut shell for its resonance chamber. Here, too, the bow is a literal one, meaning that it is arched. Probably of more recent origin is the *rabab*, which the Moors brought to Spain in the year 711 of the Christian era. There it was called *viela*, and it may well be that the name of our viola, and that of its offspring, is derived from that ancient instrument.

Finally, we must refer to another Asiatic people responsible for a rich flowering of music: the Hebrews. They may be said to have

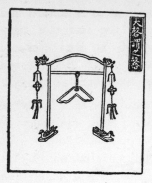

(1) Phonolite made of nephrite.

(2) K'in, seven-stringed zither.

(3) Se, a stringed instrument.

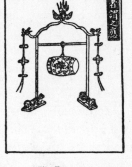
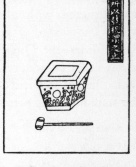

(4) Double flute.

(5) Drum.

(6) Rattle and mallet.

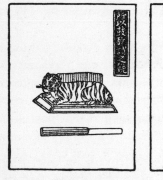

(7) Tiger-shaped spiculum.

(8) Mouth organ.

(9) Large bell.

9. Chinese musical instruments. From a Chinese dictionary.

represented a transition from the music of ancient times to that of the early Christian era. Their scant inclination toward sculpture and painting may have been at least partly due to the fact that they were forbidden to fashion an image of their God. So they centered all their creative artistic power on writing and music. Both served religion to a high degree. Two of their kings have become symbols

10. Kemantche, a Bedouin bow instrument.

of this people's love of music: David (1000-960 B.C.), who always was depicted with a harp in his hand, and his successor Solomon, whose knowledge of art was so greatly appreciated all over the Orient that visitors—the Queen of Sheba, for instance—traveled long distances to his court to admire his treasures. The history of the Jews is replete with musical incidents, from the collapsing of the walls of Jericho at the sound of trumpets to the cultivation of music at the Great Temple

11. A touching duet. Japanese woodcut
caricature by Kiosai, 19th Cent.

at Jerusalem. When the latter was finally destroyed, in the year 70 B.C., and the dispersal of the Jews all over the world started, the influence of the Asiatic spirit upon many lands increased. New doors to the Occident were opened to oriental music. Spreading in many directions, it also reached the North. Its traces are found in many a Russian region, for instance, where it may have arrived by way of Byzantium.

It is not surprising that we are inclined to identify "ancient times" with Asia. The ancient world known to us and considered the cradle of civilization was an Asiatic one. Naturally, this does not mean that there were not other places in the world, long since obliterated and forgotten, where culture flourished and where music was known and cultivated. The writer has stood amazed at the Sun Gate of Tiahuanacu, on the Bolivian highland, near the shores of mysterious Lake Titicaca, and beheld on that last memorial of a cultural epoch vanished thousands of years ago the sculptured head of an Indian blowing a trumpet. Since all the decorative details of the Sun Gate may be assumed to represent religious symbols, the conclusion is justified that in all ancient countries with a highly developed culture music went hand in hand with religion, the synthesis of wisdom, beauty, kindness, and solace.

12. Dionysian procession with music and dancing. From a sarcophagus at the Brit. Museum.

. 3 .

The Hellenic World

IN Greece, the culture of the ancient world shone forth in all its splendor. Although according to present-day geographic definitions Greece is part of Europe, its flourishing must be considered the last period of glory of an Asiatic world and not, or only with many a reservation, the beginning of an occidental one. Europe as a center of culture and a symbol of musical achievement was not to emerge for some time to come.

The ancient history of Greece covers a span of nearly two thousand years. Greece was almost a world in itself. It is obvious that in so immense a space of time uniformity could not have existed, that there must have been times of ascendance, of flourishing, and of decline; that both crises and periods of progress must have occurred before the rich heritage finally fell into the hands of other peoples who, ignorant of the deep roots of such a culture, were unable to preserve it.

It seems but logical that, as in all times, music was bound to be a reflection of the culture and civilization of Greece, faithfully mirroring both the country's glory and its decline. Unfortunately, we are still faced with the question marks and doubts of the previous chapter. We know very little of Hellenic music, especially since its main ingredient is missing: its sound. But there is nothing to justify an assumption that Greek music was less great than the country's architecture, its sculpture, and its literature. That such an assumption would be incorrect is also vouched for by the close interrelation of all art—and of art and life—a fundamental characteristic of all Hellenic culture. Is it therefore really true that the Greeks knew nothing of polyphony?

It is probable that the *Iliad* and the *Odyssey* were originally presented in musical form, perhaps in a recitative-like manner, the words

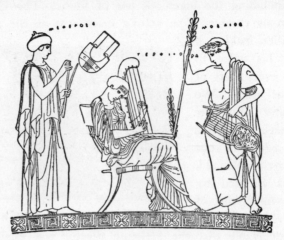

13. Greek musicians with flutes, harp, and lyre.
From an Attic vase of the 5th Cent. B.C. Brit. Museum.

being supported and colored by the chords of an instrument, as was the case in the medieval days of the bards, the troubadours, and the minnesingers. The rhythm inherent in many of the verses even suggests singing, which in many languages is a direct outgrowth of declamation, separated from it only by a difference in degree.

Somewhat later, in the sixth, fifth, and fourth centuries B.C., Athens became the spiritual center of Greece. Within its walls lived men like Aeschylus, Sophocles, Euripides, and Aristophanes, whose works surely were often surrounded and accompanied by music. Below the Parthenon Temple of the Acropolis stood the immense Dionysus Theater, able to accommodate about 30,000 spectators. An integral part of the musical spectacles which were everyday occurrences there was the chorus. Both as a declaiming and a singing body, it played a highly important part in the Greek drama.

Here, for the first time, we come face to face with a theater devoted to art. We shall meet it again, many times, as the scene of opera, operetta, ballet, pantomime, and oratorio. The theater may have had its inception in man's desire to disguise himself, to put on a mask, either to deceive or placate an angry god or to escape from the wearied self and be able to do things which otherwise would have been prohibited. This original idea, which we shall meet again in medieval drama, had been developed to the utmost artistic perfection in Greece, including the ingenious use of music. The Greek theater was an open-air theater. The actor's mask was at the same time a

sound amplifier making it possible for his voice to be heard in every part of the enormous arena. We shall see later how the idea of open-air theaters took roots again in our epoch. Another Greek practice was adopted by the modern world: that of festival plays.

14. Greek comedy scene. From a vase design.

It is conceivable that the Hellenic theater was established upon the basic idea of festival plays. As far back as the eighth pre-Christian century, they admirably expressed the unity of the life of those days by an ideal combination of religious ceremonies, sport contests, spiritual tournaments, and artistic presentations. The oldest and most venerable of these festivals were those at Olympia, whose origin has occasionally been connected with the figure of Heracles. Beginning in 775 B.C., they were held every fourth year and achieved so great an importance in national life that time was measured by four-year spans, the Olympiads. The term is familiar to us. It is applied today to the games which, unfortunately, are dedicated solely to sports, to the exclusion of spiritual and artistic endeavors.

According to chronicled reports, the theater as such seems to have made its first appearance in the year 535 B.C. At that time, recited odes were changed into dramatic action by the advent of the actor. This first actor, a producer-manager named Thespis, became the symbol of the theater. At first, he assumed a number of consecutive disguises and put on a number of masks. His counterpart was played by the chorus which, singing, speaking, or acting, was charged with a great variety of tasks. It served as counselor to the acting person, may have represented a divine voice or human conscience, contributed incidental music, and filled the intermissions with song. Finally, it may also have assumed the role of the narrator, telling the drama's antecedent story and explaining details not revealed by the action. It is interesting to note that the part of the narrator recurs in many dramatic works of our day.

15. Papyrus fragment of the "Orest" score of Euripides (verse 330 f.) with musical note indications above the text.

Theaters rose in Greece and in all countries within its sphere of influence. Their relics are to be found in Sicily, in southern Italy, and in North Africa. They were usually located in charming scenic surroundings. So good were their acoustics, that some of them can be used even in our day.

We have some knowledge of Greece's theory of music, thanks mainly to the work of Pythagoras, who lived in the fifth pre-Christian century and received his education in Egypt. It is therefore probable that Greek music, in its theoretical foundations, was a direct continuation of the musical science in the realm of the Pharaohs. Like all musical scientists of ancient times and the Middle Ages, Pythagoras was a mathematician. His theories of vibration frequencies, overtones, and intervals have never lost their validity.

The written music of Greece was not uniform. There were times when the letter system was adopted [Ill. 15], others when the neume was resorted to. Besides, different

16. Apollo with lyre. From a Greek vase design.

systems seem to have been applied to vocal and instrumental music. The Greeks knew eight scales, which deviated essentially from ours in the important fact that they employed different tonal progressions. The Greek scales are rather to be compared to our major and minor in their distinctive character. Each one of the eight Hellenic *modi* had a character of its own, because its structure differed from that of the others. And since to each was ascribed a special effect upon the human emotions, their application, too, was different. To Plato, the Lydic scale was "wailing," the Ionic "mellow and sensuous, suited for drinking bouts," the Doric "militant," and the Phrygian "peaceful, expressing free resolution." Just as in our music the lighter major is preferred for the expression of bright moods and the more somber minor for the characterization of sadness and melancholy, there was a similar differentiation in Greece. But it went much farther. Secular music required this *modus*, while sacred music had to be performed in that. The cult of one god required not only a different key but also instruments different from those used for the cult of another god. The cithara, a kind of lyre, was the national instrument [Pl. 12, Ill. 16] and, because of its mellow sound, was reserved for serious music. The mythological singer Orpheus used it to accompany his melodies which moved not only human beings and animals, but even rocks and trees. When his wife, Eurydice, died, he descended into Hades and so moved its master by his singing that he gave him back his wife under the condition that he never look back to gaze at her. This cruel condition was beyond the singer's strength [Pl. 15]. In the Orpheus legend, the realization of music's power may be said to have assumed its most beautiful form. We shall meet this enchanting subject again and again in connection with opera.

The counterpart of the cithara was the aulos, a double-reeded oboe introduced from Asia and producing excitingly sensuous sounds. It was used for the impassioned cult of the god Dionysius.

Slowly the Hellenic world declined. The onslaught of Rome, the new world power, was too much for Hellas to withstand. But it was not the conqueror who forced his culture upon the vanquished, but, on the contrary, the higher culture of the defeated was taken over by the victor. Thus Greek music and the Greek theater reached Rome, Italy, and Central Europe. However, a culture cannot be plucked from its native soil and transplanted into a realm whose fundamental conditions of life are wholly different. Rome, with the materialistic aspect of its civilization, could not understand the culture it had taken over; nor could it appreciate the depth of the spiritual roots anchored in a world which was so alien to its own. Lofty spiritual flights sank to the level of trivialities, sublime thoughts degenerated into mere entertainment. The contemplative, perhaps deeply mystical, chants intoned by devoutly believing Greek crowds assembled at the hallowed spots dedicated to their Oracles, became sensuous fanfares introducing the bloody spectacles at the Circus Maximus [Ill. 17] and were intended to drown out the agonizing cries of the tortured. Or, they were turned into the roll of drums, to the sound of which the victorious legions marched to the borders of the known world. The scope of the games mounted immeasurably. Hundreds of thousands attended the chariot races and gladiatorial contests which had taken the place of the noble Olympiads.

17. Tuba, horns, and organ accompany the gladiatorial combats at the Roman circus. From a mosaic in Zliten (Tripolis,) abt. 70 A.D.

The Romans invented no new instruments. They imported them all from whatever new territory was joined to their empire by their armies. They had a special liking for the flute which they used both at solemn religious services and at the Bacchanalia—distant precursors of the carnival. Theatrical spectacles, too, were introduced. The year 336 B.C. marked the first Roman performances of Etruscan pantomimes, successors to the Greek plays with continuous music. Gradually, Rome developed a theatre of its own, although it was mainly given to the performance of either satirical pieces or those which pandered to a low popular taste [Pl. 17].

And so the Roman world empire, imposing in its political and military organization and power, became the capstone of a cultural epoch. Music played the degrading part of accompaniments to sensual feasts and cruel spectacles. No wonder that the early Christians abhorred music, since they knew it only in its lowest form. And yet, they of all people were to be the ones to collect the musical remnants of ancient times and lead the way to new heights.

18. Circus games announcement on Pompeian wall: The gladiatorial group of the Aedile Aulus Suettius Cerius will fight in Pompeii on the eve of the June calends (May 31). There will be beast baiting, and protective cloths (against the sun) will be stretched.

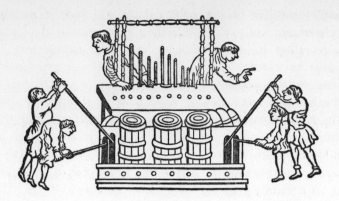

19. An organ with 2 organists and 4 bellows attendants.
From the Utrecht psaltery, abt. 860.

.4.

A Cultural Epoch Vanishes and A New One Begins

EVER since man began to inhabit the earth, countless cultural epochs have pursued their mysterious course, growing slowly, reaching a culminating point, and sinking back into nothingness. Rarely, however, was the decline of one cultural epoch and the beginning of another so centered in space and time that the phenomena could be observed in one city. Such was the case in Rome during the early Christian centuries.

"All roads lead to Rome." In the musical history of ancient times, too, this assertion is justified. The thousand-year-old Asiatic currents, which formed the subject of our previous observations, took us to Rome. There came the disintegration and end of a gigantic cultural epoch, of whose musical aspects we had, alas, so very little to say.

Now, in Rome, we are to witness the rise of a new and entirely different culture, the culture within which we have been living for nearly two thousand years. Viewed from a musical standpoint, many

of the early centuries of this new culture still have a merely introductory character. Only with exceeding slowness did the veils of the
past lift, revealing to us the first decipherable manuscripts, the first
melodies that have come down to our day, and the first creative musicians whose works actually speak to us.

In the brilliant metropolis of Rome, in its sumptuous streets and
squares, in its palaces, places of amusement, barracks, and slums the
old world slowly expired, and hardly anybody who lived in those
days was aware of it. At the same time, in the bowels of the city, in
the mysterious corridors of the catacombs, a new era of the human race
was born. A steadily growing number of disciples of the Master of
Nazareth assembled there. At first, they abhorred music. It was known
to them only as warlike fanfares or trumpet calls used to drown out
the death groans of their brothers in the arena. It was known to them
also as voluptuous dance music or as an accompaniment to heathen
worship. But every true revolution needs music. Even Christianity,
the greatest revolutionary human upheaval in many thousands of
years, could not do without it. The earliest believers, joined in the
gloomy catacombs, tried to lift up their hearts in songs of praise to their
new God. But they knew no melody to express the purity of their
thoughts, no sound to lend wings to their fervid prayers.

Then Christians from the Near East came to Rome. They taught
the young Christian community how to pray, illumined their nocturnal
meetings by the delivery of strange airs, filled with an austere beauty
and a chaste enthusiasm. These were oriental airs, surely quite old
and closely related to Jewish temple chants. The revolutionary group
in the catacombs found in them all they had been looking for. Age-old
melodies became imbued with a new spirit.

This chanted music had come to stay for many long centuries.
For a thousand years, it was to fill the entire history of music, most
closely joined to the growth of the Christian religion and to its triumphant spread all over the world. The missionaries used it in converting heathen peoples, carrying to them not only a new religion
but also a new music. The music was actually quite old, and yet it was
new and alien to the peoples of Europe and, a thousand years later,
to those of America.

These chants—and the word chants (and not music) is used ad-
visedly, for many centuries were to pass before an instrument accompa-

nied the sung melodies—went through a development of their own, adapting themselves, eliminating some things so as to be able to include others. They survived long interruptions and are to this day used by the Catholic Church. Their name perpetuates that of the Pope who collected, registered, and filed all the melodies then in use at religious services: Gregory the Great (540-604) [Pl. 21]. For many centuries the large book representing his life work was attached by a chain to the altar of St. Peter's Cathedral. The Catholic Church is greatly indebted to him for the uniformity, still maintained, of its religious music. St. Ambrose, too, must be mentioned here (340-397) for the great service he rendered to the development and preservation of occidental church music.

While we are talking of Rome and the early martyrs, the name of St. Cecilia should not be omitted, the patroness saint—and according to an old manuscript the "inventress"—of music. Others ascribe to her the invention of the organ. She died a martyr's death on November 22, of the year 230, a date which is still celebrated in many countries as "Music Day." Her figure became the subject of many pictorial representations of music, especially in the days of the Renaissance.

Christianity became the official state religion in the year 323. Its music emerged from the catacombs and made its entry into the churches. Soon, however, dissension and disputes arose among the clerics occupied with musical questions. Congregational chanting was violently attacked. Music was to be the exclusive prerogative of the clergy. At the Council of Chalons, in 650, women were forbidden to sing in church. The struggle between an oriental tendency, advocating the use of the complicated and convoluted melodies of the East, and a Western one, which would tolerate only simple and unassuming chants, was never to cease entirely. In those early centuries, music played a considerably more important part in the Catholic Church than today. The very fact of the unsatisfactory solution of the musical question furnished a vital point of attack to the Protestant reformers who proposed to let the masses participate increasingly in musical exercises. An especially protracted and violent dispute concerning the church use of musical instruments took place, and it was quite some time before at least the use of the organ was permitted.

But in spite of all dissension, music, as we said, formed a highly essential part of the fast developing missionary and converting activities.

Whenever the priests' words were ineffective, be it because the natives knew no Latin or the missionaries were unfamiliar with the language of the land or those clinging to old beliefs refused to listen to the preaching of newcomers, music wrought veritable miracles. It is quite likely that the spoken word and music shared equally in bringing new converts into the fold.

In Rome and in other cities, there were schools, called *scholae cantorum*, where missionaries received their musical training. The spreading of these schools all over Europe brought in its wake the foundation of monasteries in which musical instruction played an important part. Many of these monasteries became famous for their cultivation of music, as for instance the one founded in Kent by St. Augustine, the first Archbishop of Canterbury, upon his arrival in England.

Slowly the political power of Rome began to wane. The year 476 is generally considered the historical turning point, at which the old world definitely faded and the dawn of the new era began. So essentially different is this new era, not only from the preceding one but also from our own, that it appears to us confused, mystical, strange, and full of fanaticism and acts of violence. Still, we would do well to consider these developments in the light of evolutionary necessities without which the way to the new occidental ascent and flowering could never have been prepared.

Few and quite unsafe were the roads and highways of the Europe of that time. The routes over which Christianity—and with it literature and music—was able to spread were not many. In some instances, the large rivers, like the Danube and the Rhine, had to be used, in others Alpine passes. Settlements were founded, their central point always a monastry, such as the famous Abbey of St. Gall, whose history goes back to the year 720. It was one of the important centers of education of the world of that day. Within its walls lived the most learned monks of the Middle Ages, as for instance the poet Notker Balbulus (830-912). He is said to have been an accomplished musical theorist and the composer of the melody *Media Vita* which, usually in Martin Luther's arrangement, is sung to this day. It clearly expresses the essence of monastic existence with its assumption that in the midst of life we are surrounded by death. This was symbolic of medieval thinking which, it seems, was always directed toward the beyond. It follows that the music of that time, too— the Gregorian chorale—could express nothing else.

There was another Notker, called Labeo (950-1022), whose versatility matched that of his namesake. He translated the works of Latin and Greek writers, Aristotle for instance, into German. He was the author of the first German-language treatise on music and of a manual dealing with the building of organ pipes.

It is highly interesting to cast a glance at the library of the monastery of St. Gall. As early as the year 850, it contained more than 400 volumes, a considerable number in those days. Musical works occupied an important place among them, especially a codex of sacred chants, from which, on Pl. 13, a page with the picture of the musician Luither is reproduced. These manuscripts make us realize with what exceptional strictness art was treated at that time. But they also convey to us the fact that music, thus deprived of every contact with the people, had changed into a petri-fied, dry science which had turned its back on the free development and the soaring flight without which a true flowering of art is impossible. Great, to be sure, was the theoretical progress made by music in those centuries, but its development as an art was practically at the zero point. In the next chaper, dealing with the minnesingers, we shall have occasion to observe the reaction.

A third musical personage of those centuries must be mentioned here, Guido of Arezzo. He is perhaps the most important of all. A wealth of musical innovations is ascribed to him: considerable progress in music writing [Ill. 20], practical exercises for intonation—called the

20. Italian neumes with F-line. Manuscript, abt. 1100. Vaticana.

"Guido Hand"—and the invention of the musical alphabet, which is still valid today in many parts of the world, the Do-Re-Mi-Fa-Sol-La-Si.

Guido of Arezzo, who lived from 995 to 1050, was a man of many ideas. In order to find suitable syllables for his intonation exercises, he used a hymn to St. John, sung by the choir boys, imploring the Saint to preserve them from hoarseness. In that melody, every phrase started a tone higher than the preceding one. It ran as follows:

UT queant laxis	That servants we
REsonare fibris	With loosened voice
MIra gestorum	Miracles and power
FAmuli tuorum	Of thy deeds may praise,
SOlve polluti	Take heavy guilt
LAbii reatum	From defiled tongues,
SAncte Joannes . . .	Saint John!

Guido used for the key tone the syllable ut; for the next following tone re; and so on. It soon appeared that ut was rather unsuitable for singing, since it did not end in a vowel, and so it was replaced by do. The musical alphabet of the Latin countries was born.

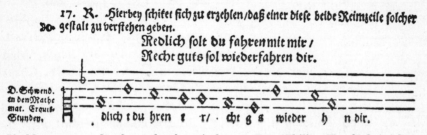

21. Memory game for the study of musical notes. From Philipp Harsdörfer's "Conversation Games," Nürnberg, 1644-45, with notes added by Gottlieb Stader. The missing syllables represent the names of the notes, re-sol-fa, etc. The key signature of C (ut) on the first line.

What happened to the music of the countries into which the missionaries brought the Gregorian chorale (for it is common knowledge that there is no people in the world without a music of its own)? The music of the European peoples seemed to the Romans "barbarous, ugly, and jarring," or so we are told in many a chronicle. Julius Caesar said so of the Helvetians, and the biographer of Gregory the Great confirmed this opinion, as it concerned the Europeans generally. We should not be greatly bothered by this, for it is difficult to argue about what is beautiful and ugly in the realm of music. There can be no doubt, however, that in its artistic qualities the Gregorian chant was far superior to the folksong-like airs and dance tunes of the European tribes. Thus, the impression made upon the primitive Europeans by these chants was quite a powerful one. Although the music was wholly foreign to their nature and understanding, they endeavored to master it. At the same time, they withdrew with their own musical creations to places inaccessible to missionaries. And from these places, as we shall soon see, the reaction against the Gregorian chant was to set in.

For the time being, however, it was wholly triumphant. It was Europe's only visible musical form for a thousand years. Its distinguishing marks are easily expressed: it is pure vocal music without the support of instruments; and it is strictly monophonic, without counterparts and without accompaniment. But it is also music without rhythm, as we understand the word today; and the melody, too, greatly differs from present conceptions. It is difficult to paint a word picture of a music that is so fundamentally different from ours. And yet, there are two ways to make this old music comprehensible: he who steps into an orthodox synagogue on one of the great festival days hears age-old sounds which take him back to the epochs described in these pages; and, by the same token, there are a number of Christian churches in which the Gregorian chant is being cultivated and where we may expose ourselves to the strange effect of the austere beauty of an unworldly music. Mention may be made here also of recordings made by the Sistine Chapel musicians and the monks of Solesmes. They, too, afford an opportunity for being carried back to the epoch whose description is here attempted. Almost without noticing it, we have passed from the prehistoric to the truly historic time of music having its beginning in our knowledge of music itself. But it is still in a preparatory stage, developing only slowly and gradually into that flowering period which necessarily must form the principal part of any book on music.

22. 11th Cent. bow instrument. From a relief. France.

23. Concert with organ accompaniment. From a Pesaro library manuscript.

. 5 .

The Picturesque Time Of Minstrelsy

FAR behind us lie the temples which were our guideposts through the cultural and musical history of the ancient world. Fallen into ruins are the open-air theaters of Hellenic civilization. Turning from the monasteries of the early Christian centuries, we are faced with a new and important change.

European civilization was in danger of attack everywhere. The Mohammedans in the south, the Normans in the north and west, the Huns, Tartars, and Slavs in the east were threatening to overrun and subdue the weak young continent. The man of God had to step into the background and cede precedence to the man of arms. Feudalism and knighthood came into being.

Art, including music, has in all epochs been a faithful reflection of the times which gave it birth. It is therefore obvious that so fundamental a political change must bring in its wake a complete change also in the realms of art and music. The ideology of the knight was necessarily wholly different from that of the priest. Although the former's piety was still profound and great his fear of an accounting after death, worldly matters were irresistibly coming to the fore: friendship, warlike adventures, experiences in far-off lands, and, especially, love. These were the themes that filled the knights' life; they sang of them, and wanted to be told of them as they sat round the campfire or in the lofty halls of their castles on long winter evenings, surrounded by their families. The castle towered over the land. It guarded roads and rivers and furnished protection to the small peasant huts timidly clinging to the foot of the hill.

A knight-errant is staying at the castle as a guest, and in his honor the nobles of the district have congregated. In the evening, long after he has unbuckled his sword, he takes up the lyre, the small harp he carries with him, and begins to sing. The men listened to him tensely, for he sings of what they have all experienced, or will some day experience: of fighting and the journey to the Holy Land, of the beauty of dark-hued women, of the solemn wedding at a regal castle, of betrayal and death in battle, of a friend's supreme loyalty, of mysterious potions causing love or forgetfulness, of single combat, of destruction. The women in their finery listen even more tensely than the knights themselves, for a strange and undreamt-of world opens up before them. The knight-errant recites in a tender voice. His words are partly poetry, partly song; a mixture of both at times, a melody at others . . . And when he has finished late at night, his host's daughter presents him with a precious flower, and he feels richly rewarded.

Of many elements was the knight's song composed. There were in it folk tunes of his country and melodies from all the oriental and occidental countries he had crossed in his wayfaring. Throughout the land, the new song was heard and appreciated. It may be that the bards, the Celtic professional singers, were its first representatives. In Ireland, Wales, and Scandinavia, the bards were still members of the priesthood, but they roamed far and wide, living chroniclers of what they saw, changing into song what they experienced. More and more did they develop into a true caste of musicians. Among them were harp players boasting of the title "Doctor of Music," bestowed on them after long study and rigorous examinations. The bards met every third year for the conferment of such titles, ranging from simple "Skilled Apprentice" to a "Professor of Poetry and Music."

Enjoyment of
sic and singing
the innate
operty of chil-
n the world
r. [*Photos,
der and Bau-
ister]

2. The Lanjala, the Bard of the North, wanders from village to village in East Finland, singing to the sounds of his home-made Kantele age-old songs collected in *Kalewala*.

3. Assyrian Army Band. Zither, cymbals, and dulcimer accompany the soldiers' rhythmic forward and rearward steps. Detail from an alabaster relief of the 7th Cent. B.C. [*Louvre*]

4. Egyptian musicians with harp and traverse flute. Detail from the Mastaba of Akhuthotep. Fifth dynasty, abt. 2700 B.C. [*Louvre*]

5. Sacrificing Egyptian priest and musicians with harp, traverse flutes, and lute. Relief from the tomb of Patenemhab. 18th dynasty, about 1350 B.C. [*Leyden, Rijksmuseum*]

6. Egyptian harp with carving. [*Brit. Museum, London*]

7. Lute players before an enthroned prince. Persian miniature from the book by Raschid-ad-Din, school of Tabris, abt. 1400. [*Bibl. Nat., Paris*]

8. Minnesinging in Persia. Painted gilt plate from Kashan, 12th Cent.

9. Confucius playing the zither. In company with a musician, he contemplates the inner meaning of music. 16th-Cent. woodcut after Ku K'ai Tshi.

10. Japanese woman with gekkin, a lute-like stringed instrument.

11. Samisen, a three-stringed Japanese plucked instrument.

Greek cithara
player. Vase
painting on an
earthen jar from
an Athens tomb.
Probably depicts
the youthfully
deceased at his
favorite occupa-
tion. Second half
5th Cent. B.C.
[*Louvre*]

13. Pandora player. The
pandora was a mandolin-
like plucked instrument
with 2 or 3 strings. Tana-
gra figurine, 8″ high. 3rd
Cent. B.C. [*Louvre*]

14. The Nine Muses. Hel-
lenistic relief from a sarcophagus found near
Rome. At left, Clio, muse
of history, followed by
Thalia, muse of comedy
(with mask). At extreme
right: Urania and Mel-
pomene, muse of tragedy
(with mask tilted back on
head). The other five are
Calliope, Terpsichore, Er-
ato, Euterpe, the muse of
music, and Polyhymnia.
2nd Cent. A.D. [*Louvre*]

ZETVS   ANTIOPA AM HION

15. **Orpheus and Eurydice.** Orpheus (right) has just turned back to look at his wife, when Hermes seizes her hand to lead her back to Hades. Roman copy of a lost Greek relief from the 5th Cent. B.C. (The wrong names were inserted later).

[*Louvre*]

16. The music of Etruscans (double aulos and cithara) was strongly influenced by the Greeks. Tomb mural of the 5th or 4th Cent. B.C.

17. Comedy scene in ancient Rome. Accompanied by a woman flutist and supported by a slave, the young man at right totters back from a carousal. At left, a friend restrains the irate father from rushing at the wastrel. Roman relief.

[*Naples*]

. Choir accompanying church
ual. Ivory book cover. 8th or
10th Cent. A.D.

. (upper right) King David and
sicians. Ivory book cover. 8th
Cent. A.D.

. Two musicians, one with
ger-hole horn, the other with
ked cymbals and Panpipe.
om an Anglo-Saxon psaltery of
the 11th Cent. [*Cambridge*]

21. Pope Gregor, divinely inspired by dove perched on his shoulder, and 3
scribes. 9th or 10th Cent. Ivory relief. [*Museum of Art, Vienna*]

22. 12th Cent. musical manuscript with neumes, showing the monk Luither offering to St. Gallus the gradual mass chants. [*St. Gallen Monastery Library*]

23, 24. Pages of the Manesse Manuscript dedicated to Klingsor von Ungerland, depicting the Singers' Contest at the Wartburg and Tannhäuser in white cloak of the Knights of the German Order.

25. Angel sounding Day of Judgment trumpet. 12th Cent. sandstone sculpture at Gallus Gate of Basel Cathedral.

26. Impersonation of music with chimes, fiddle, and psaltery. 12th Cent. sculpture at King's Gate, Chartres Cathedral.

27, 28. Bagpiper and fiddler. Two 13th Cent. niche figures from Musicians' House, Reims Cathedral.

From the eleventh century onward, in the south of France, we meet the troubadours, the majority of whom were knights. At first they still recognized the supremacy of the Church. But ere long the sacred images had to give precedence to combat descriptions, while the Virgin cult was superseded by worldly love songs. The Latin language, too, gradually disappeared and was replaced by local idioms understandable to all. Poetry and music thereby gained a new popularity, a quality never achieved by Latin ecclesiastical chants. The center of troubadour activities was in Provence, the cradle of the Languedocian dialect. Toulouse, the capital, rose from the sunny soil of that province. There stands one of France's oldest cathedrals, at whose portals, as

24. Watched by a lady, the knight (Robert, the Devil) puts on his helmet. Woodcut from the novel "Robert le Diable," Nat. Bibl., Paris.

early as the eleventh and twelfth centuries, flower plays with music were performed at which the queen of the festival presented to the victor a single wondrously beautiful flower.

Many melodies from the days of the minnesingers have come down to our day, although probably with certain changes. We can still feel in them the expression of a noble high-mindedness, a sense for dramatic effect, and fine poetic taste. Manuscripts of these songs reveal to us considerable progress toward the modern way of writing music. There were no lines to establish the height of a tone. On the other hand, we have no written record of accompanying voices or of chords, so that we must assume that these were left to the skill or taste of the executor in a manner still practiced by folk singers of all lands. The troubadours and minnesingers seem to have furnished their

25. 13th Cent. troubadour song.

own accompaniment on ancient fiddles, called gigas, on vielles, or on one of the other stringed instruments making their first appearances in Europe at the time, after having originally been introduced by the Moors in Spain. But perhaps the troubadours also used some harplike instruments, which would suggest the thought that they knew a harmony of chords, albeit a primitive one, long before it was embodied in a theory.

In southern France we had the troubadours—in the north they were called *trouvères*. The movement also spread beyond the Pyrenees, throughout Spain and Portugal. And even at places where popular airs had undoubtedly existed at a much earlier time, the upper social classes now took up musical activities and produced many notable artists. Let us mention in this connection Alfonso the Wise, King of Castile and Leon (1221-1284), a highly gifted composer and poet, author of the famous "cantigas." There was also Don Juan I of Aragon, who found-

26. The troubadour. Title woodcut of "Carcel de Amor," by San Pedro, 1547.

ed a musical institute in Barcelona and, after the pattern of Toulouse, organized poetic-musical festival plays. They are performed in various parts of Spain to this day.

From the north of France, the movement found its way to Flanders and England. Here music was cultivated intensively. Here, too, there were troubadour kings. A famous old legend tells of one of them. Richard the Lion-Hearted, who had been proclaimed King of England in 1189, became the prisoner of his foe, Duke Leopold of Austria, on his return to Europe from a crusade to the Holy Land. Leopold put him in the gloomy dungeon of Fortress Dürnstein, on the banks of the Danube. The legend recounts how Blondel, Richard's loyal friend, went in search of the missing king and sang night after night a song before one of the numerous castles along the Danube, until one evening the king's voice answered with the second verse.

The knightly song also spread toward the east, to the countries now called Austria, Germany, Switzerland, and Holland, where at that very time a German written language was slowly coming into existence. While these musical knights were called troubadours or *trouvères* in France, minstrels in England, and *trovadores* in Spain, Germany gave them a name derived from the principal theme they glorified in song. It called them minnesingers, *Minne* being the Old German word for love.

The minstrels began to include in their songs legends which later achieved the status of a national possession. This is true especially of the Nibelungenlied which, along with the Nordic Edda and the Spanish Cid, may be counted among the oldest works of European literature; of the tale of Tristan and Isolde; of Parsifal and the Holy Grail. These themes will have to be discussed in detail in connection with Richard Wagner's works.

It was Wagner, too, who introduced in his *Tannhäuser* one of the customs of that epoch: a singers' contest. He presented a gathering at the Wartburg of the most famous minnesingers of their day: Biterolf, Tannhäuser, Wolfram von Eschenbach, and Walther von der Vogelweide. The event is not historic, in spite of the fact that a mural painting at the

Wartburg ascribed to it the date of July 7, 1207. Wagner's opera as well as the description of the event in the most beautiful and famous song collection of that time, the Manesse Manuscript [Pl. 27], are based on a Tannhaüser tale in verse from the thirteenth century. Needless to say, the actual life of the minnesinger of that name [Pl. 28], who died in 1270 or thereabout, did not run so romantic a course. Thus, although Wagner did not recount historical events but only gave new form to medieval

27. St. Martin, as a 15th-Cent. knight. Title woodcut of French mystery play with a cast of 53.

songs and legends, his *Tannhäuser* nevertheless furnishes a vivid and colorful picture of the time of knights and minnesingers.

Slowly, as their political importance waned, the castles fell into ruins. Europe became more densely populated. In 1287, Adam de la Halle, called the "Last of the Troubadours," died. He was the author of a strange musical drama, *Robin et Marion*, which strikes us as an anticipatory attempt at opera. Finally, in 1305, came the death of the last royal minnesinger, Wenceslas II of Bohemia. Some of his melodies have been preserved—witnesses, and at the same time precursors, of a bustling musical life on the banks of the Moldau.

The art of the troubadours and minnesingers represents the first penetration of European folk music into artistic music, an unconscious reaction against Gregorian chants. It also marks the birth of European music and the beginning of the long and tortuous way leading to the "Golden Centuries" of classicism and romanticism.

Again, after a long pause, towns came into being. And the burghers settling in them took over from the knights not only their power but also their music. But they changed them both most thoroughly, as will soon be demonstrated.

28. Round psaltery. After a 12th-Cent. description.

29. Music in the garden. Woodcut by Hans Burkmair, 16th Cent.

.6.

The Cities and Their "New Art"

IN the course of many centuries, throughout the ancient times, the towns and cities had become the intellectual and political centers of the world. This development reached its spiritual apex in Athens, its political one in Rome. At the time of the great migrations, and when the Roman world empire began to crumble, the towns disappeared. They were ransacked, burnt, destroyed, depopulated. In the Middle Ages, political and spiritual leadership was assumed by the monasteries, the princely courts, and the knights' castles.

But the towns grew up again. At the foot of the castle hill and under the protection of the powerful knights, peasants and artisans settled. Their houses grew more numerous, the inhabitants more self-assured, until one day the positions were reversed. The newly arisen and strengthened towns raised walls of their own, and the knights, weakened and impoverished by constant feuding among themselves, found themselves in need of protection. The towns kept growing, the castle became in-

creasingly unimportant, and the townspeople, who now called themselves burghers, "burg dwellers," felt secure in their own strength and
grew rich, proud, pretentious, and conscious of their importance.

The towns changed the face of the world entirely. A new spirit
filled the Europe of those days, a consciousness of collective power, a
new joy of living. He who looks for this spirit's formative expression
will find it clearly and plainly in the architectural wonders of those centuries, in cathedrals and palaces and castle gates and fountains. The
burgher, once his material needs were satisfied, started dreaming of
great works which were to launch his glory into space and time. He invented the art of book printing, he equipped ships for trading with far-
off continents, and even for voyages of discovery. His power was based
upon the spirit and upon money. The arts began to flourish as they had
not flourished for long epochs. Not only had the material foundations
been provided, but the intoxication of grandeur provided a powerful
stimulus and an inexhaustible source of new themes.

It is clear that in the midst of so great a change man, too, must have
changed. The new joy of living stirred timidly at first but powerfully
surged to the surface at last. The thought began to take root that it
might be possible to strive for the fulfillment of at least some of one's
wishes while still in this world. The Gregorian chants which had so
faithfully mirrored the monkish ideal of the blissful life beyond with-

30. Musicians at the Ark of the Covenant. Old Testament woodcut (I. Chron. 16) by Hans Holbein jr., abt. 1525.

31. Paul Hofhaimer, the organist, at the positive organ. Woodcut by Hans Burkmair, from "Triumph of Emperor Maximilian I." Abt. 1516.

drew more and more into the monasteries, there to be preserved for all time to come. The new music of the towns and burghers was a still stronger affirmation of worldly things than the minnelied had been. In spite of that, its themes were not infrequently of a religious character for man did not cease to believe in God just because his mundane life had become better, happier, and more secure.

The technical side of music now underwent a decided change which, so far as is known, has nowhere and never been causatively explained. It was brought about by the invention and introduction of polyphony. Naturally, this could not have happened from one day to the other. Let us review the circumstances leading up to this development.

It is presumed that, up to that time, man's knowledge of music, both vocal and instrumental, did not transcend the teachings of strict monody. In a musical tract written by Hucbald, a St.-Amand monk who lived from 840 to 930, there appeared the first hint of polyphony, called by him diaphony. He cited examples and let two differently pitched voices run a parallel course—in fifths, mind you, an interval which by following centuries was considered the most acute dissonance imaginable. But let us leave aside these relative and rather unimportant questions of consonance and dissonance—unimportant because of the very fact of their spatial and temporal relativity—and observe the further development of this vital subject. Other prominent theorists began to occupy themselves with the theme. There was the aforementioned Guido of Arezzo and, after him, John Cotton (1050-1130) who offered the following explanation: "Diaphony is a combination of different sounds. It is appropriately executed by at least two singers in such a manner that, while one sounds the main melody, the second colors it with other tones. At every point of rest the two meet either in consonance or in the octave. This kind of singing is usually called organum."

This proves not only that a primitive polyphony actually existed but also that its use was not particularly familiar since it required so detailed an explanation. The beginnings of polyphony, like so many other things in the realm of musical science, are thoroughly obscure. Why did it suddenly emerge? Why did it become the ruling tendency? We shall try to find answers to these important questions.

Primitive life produces a primitive art; simple, soil-bound life a simple, soil-bound art; mystical life a mystical art; pious life a pious art; knightly life a knightly art. The Gregorian chant could be, had to be, monophonic, for it expressed a collective ideal: precisely the same for everybody. The new town life became more complicated. We all know that, for we live in the ultimate stages of complication in the large metropolises. It became complicated by the growing demands upon life, but also by steadily increasing expansions and distances, and by the multiplicity of human interrelations. Above all, it became complicated by a growing individualism, by ever mounting specialization, and by an increasingly noticeable nervousness.

This is not a psychological study, but simply an explanation of the musical development in the centuries marked by the growth of towns and the bourgeoisie. We may find here even an explanation for the birth of polyphony. When, after the day's work was done, the burghers congregated for entertainment and diversion, music played an important part. Mind you, we already speak of entertainment, when but a short time before music was solely a matter of devotional exercises and edification. No longer did a solitary person tell of heroic deeds to the accompaniment of a lyre, while the others listened breathlessly. Hardly

32. The Flute Serenade, by Urs Graf. Traverse pipes and drums were used for
lansquenet marching. Pen drawing, 1523.

anyone in the congregation of burghers had ever traveled far or had had experiences which differed essentially from those of the others. Nobody wanted to take a back seat, nobody wanted to be inferior to the others. If they had all sung the same thing, like the monks in the Gregorian chant, it would hardly have satisfied their individualistic tendencies. And so they invented a number of vocal lines running a parallel course and assigning to each executant an individual and interesting task. It may be that the technical foundations of polyphony were laid at an even earlier time, but the psychological moment—which in the last analysis is of decisive importance—had come only now. The middle classes were bound to find their way to polyphonic music.

It made its early appearance in Paris where, under the name of a "new art," *ars nova*, it forged its first weapons. Let us mention here the names of two important musicians: Leoninus and Perotinus, pioneer contrapuntists of the twelfth century. Part-songs, called motets, came into being, and the singing of canons, too, became fashionable. The latter were subsequently to lay the foundation for the fugue, the most highly

33. Dance from a 15th-Cent. Burgundy manuscript. Below the text line, the dance steps are indicated by letters. Brussels.

developed form of polyphony. It has been averred, not without some justification, that the building style of those days reflected the new music. The wonderful Cathedral of Notre-Dame in Paris seems eloquently to support this contention. The dissolution of compact masses into moving rhythms, the mystical expansion of space, the pleasure in ornamentation, in fine details—all this may be found in the architecture as well as in the music of that time. The magnificent church edifices are in fact the very objects to act as guideposts on our way through the music of the polyphonic age and finally to lead us to the grandiose epoch of the Italian Renaissance. Winston Churchill once said very wisely: "Man forms the buildings, but thereafter the buildings form man . . ."

As a logical development, the centers of the new music formed where the currents of intellectual and political activities met, a phenomenon which we shall have occasion to observe more than once. And so, after the relatively brief prelude in Paris, Flanders became the focal point of musical events for several generations. From there, the new style spread all over Europe. Flemish masters were the leaders also of European painting at the time [Pl. 29]. The spiritual seat of Flemish music was the town of Cambray, but its representatives busied themselves at the courts of Munich and Innsbruck, in Paris, Italy, and Spain, where the new music met up with one of the world's most positive political epochs, resulting in a rich flowering, unmatched for many centuries to come. The preponderance of Flemish music is comparable only to the absolute and worldwide hegemony of Italian opera two hundred years later. Let us mention the names of the great masters of that school, men who in their era may have had the importance of a Bach or a Beethoven and who to us are now merely a historical memory: Guillaume Dufray (1400?-1474), Jan Okeghem (1430?-1495), Josquin Deprés, or Despres, or des Prets (1450?-1521), Adrian Willaert (1480-1562), Jan Pieter Sweelinck (1562-1621), and, pre-eminently, Orlando di Lasso (1530?-1594).

Within a brief time, polyphony had developed to such a degree that its cultivation could no longer be left in lay hands. What had begun as an evening's entertainment of the burghers had grown to be the highest and most complicated of all musical forms. Here the amateur was clearly out of place. But the people's enthusiasm for music had been awakened and was not to subside again. Let us here again refer to Richard Wagner who, in his *Die Meistersinger von Nürnberg*, afforded us a picturesque insight into that epoch of the art-loving middle classes by making us ac-

34. Invitation to a Nuremberg Mastersingers' meeting. Late 16th Cent. Central picture represents the 81-year-old Hans Sachs.

quainted with the honorable musical institution of the "mastersingers" in the German towns. They were burghers of the most varied vocations: notaries, tailors, bakers, or cobblers; but in the evening hours they devoted themselves enthusiastically to art, cultivating it with a pure will, with a sacrificial spirit and ambitious striving, and thus creating the type of the amateur artist, so unjustly looked down upon in our day. They formed regular schools of music and established strict rules governing the text as well as the melody, and even paying attention to the manner of delivery. All the rules were embodied in the *Tabulatur*, a kind of constitution of the guild of mastersingers. Wagner used the masters' conservative and faithful adherence to these rules to bring about the dramatic conflict in which Junker Stolzing finds himself involved and which almost causes his downfall. The man who comes to his rescue is a historical figure, a great poet and musician of the working class: Hans Sachs. A shoemaker in Nuremberg, he was also the head of his town's mastersingers, in the year 1554 [Ill. 34]. At that time, the mastersinger idea which had originated in Mainz was already about three hundred years old. It is difficult fully to appreciate what these men did to arouse and cultivate the people's love of music, in spite of all formalism and pedantry, and in spite of the fact that the caliber of their music was at all times so widely different from that of the great masters of polyphonic art.

The flourishing of the towns brought about also a change in the status of the itinerant musicians. For many centuries, they, together with vagabonds, beggars, and animal tamers, had been consigned to the lowest social stratum. They played at peasant weddings and occasionally became camp followers of some group of soldiers. Now, their services were increasingly in demand. The many balls in the cities required musicians. It was the custom, too, among the well-to-do young men to hire singers or musicians to serenade their inamorata. Picturesque details of these itinerant makers of music may be found in many an old chronicle. There were times when they became a public nuisance. They would come into a town and play before the houses of the councilmen and the burgomaster until board and lodging was granted them. Soon they also demanded to be paid. It was then that the city fathers decided to give them steady employment—it would be cheaper in the end. City bands and orchestras were formed. The municipal band of Bern, in the year 1426, consisted of the following musicians: three pipers, two trumpeters, one singer, and one organist. Soon these groups grew through the in-

35. Church choir accompanied by sacbuts and trumpets. Woodcut from H. Finck's Practica Musica. Wittenberg, 1556.

. 47

clusion of guitars, harps, violins and violas, bagpipes, trombones, timpani, and drums. The musicians began to organize. The "Nikolai Brotherhood," founded in Vienna in 1288, may have been the world's first musical union. It continued to exist for five hundred years and was headed by so-called *Spielgrafen*. In France, in 1330, the *Ménestrandie* was organized, whose members were regularly licensed. Their leader assumed the title *Roy des ménestriers* and ruled over a motley crowd of jugglers, itinerant musicians, and the last of the minnesingers.

In medieval Zurich, a rather modern-sounding decree was issued, according to which only regularly organized musicians were permitted to play. In 1397, Basel forbade the musicians to carry shield and spear, an interdict plainly aimed at the last troubadours . . . *Sic transit gloria mundi*. To be sure, thirteen years later, the same Swiss city forbade the musicians to wear trousers, the latest city style, to distinguish them in some manner from "regular" burghers. But even at that time the land register of many cities contained the names of musicians who had come to be the owners of fine houses.

The social position of the great composers was one of eminence. They were the friends and confidants of the princes and leaders of their day, were generally honored, and had a substantial income. We are now approaching the Renaissance with its almost inconceivable flowering of all arts.

.7.

The Theater in the Middle Ages

BEFORE bidding farewell to medieval music, we must mention one of its most attractive and important features: the theater.

The sad decline which the theater had experienced in the Roman Empire after its great flowering in Greece became even more pronounced during the early centuries of our era. It was like a reversion to the most primitive forms, which paid no heed to the deeper meaning and the ethical idea that had predominated during the Hellenic epoch.

The Church militated against these popular plays for a long time, but without success. Too deeply rooted was man's passionate liking for the stage which, during the early Middle Ages, supplied one of the very few popular entertainments. Realizing the futility of any attempt to uproot it, the Church decided to profit by the people's inclination. A dramatization of the miraculous life of Jesus was begun. The history of the Saints was another subject, until this finally led to the performance of plays in the squares in front of the churches, when abstract ideas in the form of persons were introduced in an effort to influence the mind and conscience of the beholder. Some of these symbolical figures may occasionally be seen even on a modern stage: Death and the Devil, beauty, kindness, love.

And so the medieval theater was changed into a Christian theater by a process similar to the one that had affected music. We may say that it started at the very steps of the altar; for, fundamentally, the mass is a dramatic action. This was further emphasized by the responsive chanting between priest and congregation, a musical dialogue with a genuinely theatrical effect. In the eleventh century, this dramatization of hallowed rituals reached its culminating point through the inclusion of church singing. The oratorio had come into being.

In addition, and independent of the Church and its edifices, theatrical plays amply provided with music made their appearance. They were plainly the precursors of opera. We know the names of some that were performed in that century both in the Netherlands and in France: *The Prophets; The Good and the Evil Virgins,* a symbolical drama with Gregorian music; and *Daniel,* in which, it seems, there were already parts which were either sung or played by instruments.

The liturgical dramas were naturally written in Latin. Soon, however, as had previously been the case in the purely musical realm, the language of the people came to the fore. One of the most important forms of the medieval theater, the mystery play, gradually developed. It tried to dissociate itself from the Church by moving first to the courtyards and then to the principal squares of the cities [Pl. 35]. In the thirteenth century, the lay theater had become fully developed and highly popular. It offered a mixture of religious and secular actions, of serious

36. The Fool and the bagpiping Devil. Woodcut from a Basel Death Dance, 1590.

and gay scenes [Pl. 32 & 33]. The part assigned to music in the mystery plays, which were also called miracles or, in Spain *autos sacramentales,* varied, depending on the theme as well as on respective local circumstances. The influence of these medieval theatrical presentations on the literature of later centuries was considerable. Their symbolic meaning and profound mysticism captivated Calderón de la Barca, inspired Gabriele d'Annunzio to write his *Martyrdom of St. Sebastian* with music by Débussy, and induced Hugo von Hofmannsthal to give new shape to the old legend *Everyman.* This "Play of the Death of a Rich Man" was performed every year, from 1924 to 1937, within the framework of the Salzburg Festival Plays under the inspired direction of Max Reinhardt, revealing to modern man his deeply and mysteriously anchored relationship to the same problems that had agitated the minds of the Middle Ages.

It seems to be an innate trait of humanity to make fun of its own creations. So, the serious theater soon had its parody counterpart. Plays of a satiric, ludicrous, and frequently extremely shameless character were performed and attained great popularity, even with the clergy. One of the more famous of these comedies, the *Festival of the Insane*, was performed in the church itself, in spite of the fact that it included the obscene parody of a mass. No less inconceivable, because it literally shrank from no profanation, would seem the *Donkey Festival*, celebrated annually at the Notre-Dame Cathedral of Paris [Pl. 34]. The Church tolerated these excesses and, one is almost tempted to say, furthered them because of the psychologically clever realization that medieval man, forced to live under strong pressure, had to be given a chance during a few precisely measured-out days to unleash his baser instincts so as to be able to be a good citizen and a devout Christian for the rest of the year. Naturally, the satire also included music. That which served to edify in the serious play or was used to invoke Death or the Day of Judgment was relentlessly ridiculed or, by a change in text, turned into grotesque obscenity.

¶Miracle de noftre dame de la marqſe de la Gaudine qui par faccufemét de ſonefe de ſoŋ mari auqſ ſoŋ mari ſauoit cómiſe a gar8er fu con8ampnce a ar8oir/Dont Antheno: p ſe cómañ8emẽt ð Poſtre dame ſeŋ combati a ſoneſe et ſe deſconfit eŋ cħamp. Et eſt ſe dict miracſe a. φ8ii. perſonaigcs. Jmpzime nouueiſſemét a Pario.

37. The marchioness on the way to the stake. Title page from a French miracle play of the 16th Cent.

Only in the days of the Reformation did these plays, heretofore tolerated by the Church, disappear, lest the adversary be furnished with a powerful weapon. But the people could no longer be made to give them up entirely. At carnival time, they may to this day be witnessed in many localities.

Slowly, all European countries built up their own theaters. A Spanish manuscript of the eleventh century has been preserved, being a dra-

38. From "The Fools' Shop," a satirical poem on the follies
and foibles of that time by Sebastian Brant, 1494.

matization of the story of The Three Magi and providing for several
changes of scenery, a large number of acting persons, and a wealth of
musical adornment. The famous Elche Mystery Play, which is performed to this day in the beautiful village of that name in the Province
of Venecia, dates back to the year 1226. It is a dramatization of the
death and assumption of the Virgin and is accompanied throughout by
music.

The religious theater in England started with the Christmas Plays,
whose essential features were the Christmas Carols. They had counterparts in any numer of other countries. In Germany, for instance, they
were called *Weihnachtslieder*, in France *Chansons de Noël*, in Spain *Vil-
ancico*. These were medieval man's first attempts at dramatic performances.

From the soil of Switzerland, where music had been intensively cultivated throughout the Middle Ages, grew the first Passion Play in German verse. Its first performance took place at the Muri Monastery, in
1250. The entire Passion of Our Lord was rendered in Basel, in 1377,
and repeated in Lucerne [Pl. 35]. The first drama dealing with the birth
of Christ was performed at the St. Gall Monastery, in 1400.

In Germany, Latin church performances of religious plays took
place far into the thirteenth century. Later, keeping pace with the

gradual loosening of church ties, scenes and songs of a more popular type intruded, performed by persons using the country's language. There followed the *Fastnachtsspiel*, the carnival play, among whose most successful authors was the previously mentioned cobbler-poet Hans Sachs.

A similar development took place also in other European countries. Countless were the forms of the medieval theater, and great was the enthusiasm displayed by a city's entire population in the enjoyment of this entertainment. This phase is particularly interesting because to it may be traced all the modern forms of the musical theater: the *opera seria* and the *opera comica* or *buffa;* the operetta; the *Singspiel;* the *zarzuela;* the oratorio; and the Passion Play. And many details of popular and folk music may be explained and understood through a study of those faraway medieval beginnings.

39. Drums and pipes furnish the 15th-Cent. dance music. Woodcut, Germany.

.8.

Toward the Modern World

THE polyphonic style had come to reign supreme in the Flemish cities. It pervaded all musical forms. Although, in the twenties of the thirteenth century, a polyphonic canon had made its appearance in England, ("Sumer is i-cumen in," called the Summer Canon), we are justified in considering the *Mass of Tournay*, written for three voices in 1350, the first documentary evidence of a great musical form in the polyphonic style. The mass composed by Guillaume de Machault for the coronation of Charles V of France, in 1364, was for four voices. From then on, the style became increasingly unfettered, but also increasingly complicated. Absent as yet was the feeling for harmony, which we may define as the simultaneous rendering of different tones agreeably combined. Polyphony, the many-voiced style, was perceived and comprehended exclusively in horizontal form, as the synchronous unfolding of several melodic lines developed in parallel manner and in accordance with strict contrapuntal rules. Listening today to specimens of that early polyphony with its multiplicity of simultaneous melodies sounding austerely together, without as yet forming chords in our harmonic sense, there rises within us a strange, and yet somehow gripping, yes, even magnificent, picture of a mightily striving mystical time.

The Flemish masters, as we said, ruled the musical life of all Europe. One of them, perhaps the most important, Orlando di Lasso [Ill. 40 & 43], came to occupy an influential and prominent position at the court of Munich. Heinrich Isaak (1460-1517), one of the first song composers in the history of music, and thus a distant precursor of Schubert, was active in Austria. To him we are indebted for the composition, or at least the written perpetuation, of the famous song "Innsbruck, I must now leave thee."

40. Orlando di Lasso. Woodcut. 1585.

The Flemish school reached the apex of its importance through its penetration into Italy. The forward-looking cities of the peninsula were becoming more populated and influential from day to day. Trade with the Orient, contacts with other peoples and races, the favorable climate, the centuries-old historical background—all these circumstances combined to award to the Italian cities the leadership in European affairs and cultural developments. Venice, toward the end of the fourteenth century, had 200,000 inhabitants. No city, since the de-

41. Palestrina presents to Pope Julius III his first book of masses.
Portrait-like woodcut, 1554.

cline of Rome, had been so large. Venice's musical center was the beautiful church of St. Mark, proud witness of a thousand-year-old Byzantine culture. Its organ, on which the great masters of the time had played,
had gained wide-spread fame. All these musicians had already adopted
the new polyphonic style that had come out of the North. To facilitate
the performance of these many-voiced works, requiring a multiple division of choirs and instrumental groups, a second organ was built in the
year 1490, so that each of the two main naves now had its own organ
and its own choir with orchestral accompaniment, affording the opportunity for magnificent combined effects.

Soon, Flanders provided not only the teachings, but the teachers themselves. In 1527, Adrian Willaert became the organist at St. Mark's. His influence on the musical atmosphere of Italy cannot be appraised too highly.

For the last time, the Church rose to the pinnacle of its might and glory. The Popes in Rome became the patrons of art, causing painters, sculptors, poets, and musicians to live within the walls of the Eternal City. Many of the latter came from Venice, pupils of Willaert, the Fleming. Among them were the two Gabrielis, uncle and nephew, and the great Frescobaldi, one of the finest organists of all time. Finally, Rome gave to the world the most important musician of his day, in whose work all the loftiness of medieval music was embodied for the last time. His name was Giovanni Pierluigi, called Palestrina after his native place.

Palestrina's life is woven round with legends. Until lately, the year of his birth was variously given. Some said it was 1514, some 1529. According to most recent research, 1525 seems to be most probably accurate. The date of his death, on the other hand, is firmly established: February 2, 1594. One of the most important discussions concerning church music occurred during his lifetime: the Tridentine Council. Many of the Palestrina legends are connected with that Council which in many of its sessions, lasting from 1545 to 1563, dealt with music's place in religious services. Secular, and at times even dance-like, melodies and distracting superficial details of a virtuoso-like nature had insinuated themselves into religious airs, to the confusion of the believers. As legend has it, a group of cardinals demanded the exclusion of all music from the church. Another group, however, succeeded in having a commission given to a musician who, by a work of both genuine piety and musical mastery, was to prove that not music itself but its abuse had led to the deplorable conditions. That musician was Palestrina. The legend goes on to tell how in the quiet of the night the angels descended from Heaven into the musician's poor study, high above the roofs of the Eternal City, near the Cathedral of St. Peter, and how they sang for him the wonderful many-voiced work which his trembling hand needed only to write down.

The mass actually exists. Palestrina called it *Missa Papae Marcelli*, in honor of his greatly revered deceased patron. It is said that the impression made by the work was so profound and lasting that the attacks on the use of music in the churches were silenced. (This mixture of history and legend furnished Hans Pfitzner with the material and music for his fine opera *Palestrina*.)

Palestrina had started his career as a church musician in his home town. When he was summoned to Rome, in 1551, he took over the direction of the boy choir of the Julian Chapel and subsequently became leader of the orchestra at St. Peter's. Three years later, in 1554, he dedicated the first book of his masses to Pope Julius III [Ill. 41] and was appointed to the Sistine Chapel. There he stayed, even during the brief incumbency of Marcellus II, one of the first critics of his time's church music. In 1555, however, Pope Paul IV dismissed a number of musicians, Palestrina among them, because in his opinion married life was incompatible with so spiritual a position. This severe blow was hardly softened by Palestrina's appointment as organist of San Giovanni de Letran and, later, of Santa Maria Maggiore. However, his fame as a composer grew so steadily that Pope Pius IV made him "Composer of the Vatican Chapel." Finally, in 1571, he returned to his old position at St. Peter's, at the steps of whose alter he was laid to rest, in 1594.

Palestrine embodied not only the utmost of purity in the realm of church music, but his work, both religious and secular, became one of the most treasured possessions of humanity. In him, polyphonic music reached its summit. But as always, once the summit is reached, the decline is not far away. Polyphonic music had outlived itself. Only a genius like Palestrina had been able to still fill it with the breath of real life. The works of most of the other composers remained mere theory and paper music. Technical details grew to gigantic proportions. Masses with twenty, thirty, and more different voices were nothing

42. Ascertaining pitch of natural tones. Woodcut from the Theorica musiae by Franchino Gafori, Milan, 1492.

out of the ordinary. Their scores looked wonderful, but the music lacked vitality and inspiration. There was in them as much life as in an arithmetical problem. Works were composed with more than ninety different voices, within which any number of playful tricks were used, such as themes to be read in a mirror, meaning that they proceeded in a reverse manner, from end to beginning. And there were hundreds of other such trivialities.

Polyphony had grown to be less of an art than a mechanical ability and had become so complicated that the people turned away from it more and more. Toward the turn of the century, its supremacy was threatened, and its downfall became imminent. And as it always happens when a principle has reached its apex of development, reaction set in and carried to victory the very opposite principle.

We have come to a decisive turning point in the history of music, and it is plain that it was bound to coincide with an exceptionally important epoch of political history. We are on the threshold of a new world. A new spirit had awakened in the peoples of Europe. Humanism made its entry into the universities. The demise of the Byzantine Empire was at hand when the Turks took possession of Constantinople, in 1453. And so disappeared the last witness and direct descendant of the Hellenic world.

At the same time, the desire arose all over Europe to learn more of that happy and highly developed world and, if possible, to emulate it. The modern age may be said to have begun in the decisive year of 1492. Columbus expanded the world in an unexpected and intoxicating manner. The same year marked the death of Lorenzo, the most brilliant of the Medici, the tyrants of Florence. And the same year also marked the ascension to the Papal See of Alexander Borgia, the most worldly of all Popes, the friend of artists and patron of arts.

A spirit of regeneration pervaded the Italian cities. They talked of a rebirth, and so this brilliant epoch was called Renaissance. The new music, reaction against polyphony, triumphed in these cities, in Venice, Rome, Milan, and especially in Florence. The harsh lines of counterpoint became pliable and formed the new harmony, over which, simple and song-like, the new melody arched. It may be symbolical that the counterpoint had come into existence in the rougher North and that harmony was now born under the more southern sun of Italy.

The new songs revealed a certain, though distant, relationship to the music of the troubadours and a broadly popular foundation. At first, purely vocal compositions predominated, but soon they were accompanied by instruments. Everybody played an instrument, be it the lute, the cembalo, or one of the wonderful old precursors of our modern string instruments. While in the churches polyphony still tried to preserve its domination, the new melodies were already sung in the palaces and the homes of the burghers. In Italy they were called *madrigale*, later

43. The Bavarian Court Orchestra under Orlando di Lasso, 1568. Musicians tuning their instruments, pitch being indicated by portative organ. Segment of engraving by Solis.

sonetta or *canzonetta*, in France *chanson*, and in Germany *lied*. At the same time, one of the loftiest musical genres was born, one that was to inspire many great masters: chamber music.

Florence was the cradle of the Renaissance. This illustrious city had many other claims to fame and immortality. It was the home of Dante, Petrarch, and Boccaccio, of the painters Uccello and Botticelli, and of the architect Brunelleschi who built the famous cupola of the Cathedral. What was more, it enriched the world immeasurably by giving it, in the sixteenth century, three men of truly heroic stature: Leonardo da Vinci, Raphael, and Michelangelo. It was Florence, too, within whose walls the strangest of all musical forms first saw the light of day. Many pages of this book will be devoted to the history of that strange musical form, for it has succeeded in moving the mind of man more than any other form. We refer to opera.

The sixteenth century represents an age of musical transition. The old and the new existed side by side. Future developments, however, became more clearly defined all the time. Music ceased to be subservient to other ideas. It rose to the rank of an art. Individualism and nationalism found expression in it. Religious and worldly elements had come to a parting of their ways, and while liturgical music withdrew farther and farther into the background, its worldly counterpart succeeded in capturing salient positions in artistic life. It took the place of the plastic arts which until then had been the faithful expression of the spirit of the times and of popular sentiment. There came a division between vocal and instrumental music, although there will always be forms in which both are united. National borderlines of music were drawn. Only now was one able to speak of Italian, French, or German music. National characteristics were to become accentuated in the course of time, only to grow blurred again in the end.

To the revolutionary invention of Gutenberg must be conceded a decisive influence on musical development. The first printed music made its appearance about 1500. Petrucci, in Venice, was responsible for that. What had formerly been available in only a few and frequently faulty manuscripts and to a small circle, could now be made to sound simultaneously in countless places of the world. Only the invention of the radio, in the twentieth century, may be compared to this event in importance to musical history.

Let us mention an additional number of prominent musicians of that transitional period, either the last representatives of a fading epoch or the precursors of what was to come. Reference was already made to the German Mastersingers, whose activity coincided with the flowering of the Renaissance. Nuremberg, the city of the immortal Dürer, was the center, although there were many other important points where this art flourished.

In Switzerland, there lived an interesting musician, Ludwig Senfl (1492?-1555), whose beautiful songs gained great popularity.

England was enjoying a particularly fruitful era of artistic creativeness. In the sixteenth century alone, which introduced the Elizabethan days of splendor, the following prominent masters were born: William Byrd (1543-1623), Thomas Morley (1557-1603), John Dowland (1563-1626), John Bull (1563-1628), and Orlando Gibbons (1583-1625). They were contemporaries of Shakespeare, an enthusiastic admirer of music, which he praised in many passages of his work.

William Byrd, the greatest English composer of the age, is famous for three fine masses, in which he combined the styles of polyphony and homophony, and instilled the spirit of the madrigal into the hitherto severe church style. The original book of Byrd's *Cantiones Sacrae* (in which Tallis collaborated) was the first printing in England of Latin motets. The counterpoint of the vocal work was a precursor of Bach's work. Byrd's music for the Great Service of the English Church is considered his finest liturgical achievement. But he is famous also for collections of madrigals, written to texts of Sidney, Ovid, Ariosto, and others; his development of the song, which he arranged for solo voice and string quartet; chamber music for strings; and keyboard music, for which he evolved the variation style.

Thomas Morley, a student of Byrd, was perhaps the leading English madrigal composer. He published not only his own compositions, but music of his contemporaries. John Dowland was a song-writer of historical importance, and also a lute virtuoso and singer. John Bull, another skillful musician (on the harpsichord and organ) composed vocal pieces which showed a unique mastery of counterpoint—even for the celebrated Elizabethan group. Orlando Gibbons, best known for church music, wrote chamber music for strings. He composed about forty keyboard pieces, as well, for he too was an outstanding performer, on the virginal and organ.

Spain, too, was experiencing a period of bloom. In the days of the great writer Cervantes, there lived a number of musicians of exceptional caliber, among them Tomás Luis de Victoria (1514-1611), a pupil of Palestrina, and Antonio de Cabezón (1510-1566), a blind organist and clavichord player at the courts of Charles V and Phillip II, a veritable Bach of the sixteenth century, whose name has unjustly fallen into oblivion.

We are now standing at the threshold of the musical epochs which we have learned to call classic and romantic. Far behind us lie the musically prehistoric times through which we had to feel our way by relying on uncertain data and extra-musical documents. What now follows is the repertoire of our musical life. One thing alone remains to be done before we can start discussing the classic masters: we have to attend the birth of opera.

And so, while bidding a final farewell to medieval art, let us cast a last glance at it. In its greatest creations it was dedicated to God. From that fact it drew its strength, that *was* its strength. Inspired by thoughts of the divine, it pondered eternity. Modern art is dedicated to man. His emotions and passions are its motive power. That is why it can never be greater than man himself. But even that is much—very much.

44. Italian stage with standees. Woodcut, Venice, 1552.

.9.

The Birth of Opera

Florence: A Mistake Brings Forth the Most Popular of Musical Forms

"OPERA is impossible!" That has been the cry of philosophers, theorists, and even musicians, who have despised or hated it from the very day of its birth. Opera has been attacked throughout its existence. It has been declared dead, exposed to ridicule, and made the object of every conceivable argument. What could make so much nonsense bearable? When have the most banal phrases of everyday life ever been sung? What makes people listen to the endless repetition of the same words in an aria? How can two mortal enemies, before attacking each other with the sword, join in singing long and fine-sounding duets? Who ever heard of a fatally wounded person rising up once more to launch an intricate coloratura aria? Why do people, pursued by the enemy, sing endless musical scenes which make them not only lose ground to the pursuer but actually seem to summon him into their presence? These are some of the objections to opera. Others are not directed against its logic (which, after all, is a logic wholly its own) but against its aesthetics. But nothing has been able to keep opera down. The "impossible" opera keeps on living, living better, more persistently, with considerably more splendor, and acompanied by more sensational acclaim than all other varieties of music taken together. Most modern European cities have houses specially dedicated to it. For more than three hundred years, operatic singers have been among the most extolled artists in the world. Their earnings are fabulous, their fights and intrigues unbelievably romantic. And operatic melodies have hardly their equal in popularity.

Opera—magic word! Harmony of all arts, all-encompassing masterpiece, feast for the eye as well as for the ear and the spirit! Poetic, dramatic, and musical delight! Field of activity for poets, composers, conductors, impresarios, musicians, painters, stage designers, directors, dancers, supernumeraries—a whole army of people! And behind them, another invisible army: tailors, dressmakers, hairdressers, shoemakers, machinists, electricians, prompters . . . They toil and they labor, but theirs is not the glory. The glory is reserved for but one, for one only: the singer! And to make his triumph secure, he needs just three things, if we are to believe Rossini who ought to have known what he was talking about: Voice, voice, and once more, voice!

To understand the origin and growth of opera, we must once more be carried back to the Florence of the Renaissance. We witnessed in that city the awakening of a spirit which considered the return to Greek artistic ideals a most desirable goal. It was therefore not surprising that a group of highly cultured and educated men dedicated their efforts to a resurrection of the Greek tragedy, the most sublime artistic expression of the old world. But the cultured men of Florence had an experience very similar to that of the seafarer Columbus who had set out to find a new way to an old goal and discovered something new and wholly undreamt-of. The Florentines wanted to revive something old, the Greek drama, and discovered something new and wholly unprecedented: opera. At any rate, it may be mentioned that opera is the only form of music (and, likely, form of art, generally) that did not have to pass through long stages of development. Rather, it was the result of theoretical experiments, a homunculus produced in a retort.

In musical language, opera was the result of the advent of the new forms of music mentioned before. It would have been unthinkable without melody and harmony. Spiritually, it was the expression of a richly flowing middle-class life and a newly arisen joy of living. And finally, it was a true daughter of Italy. Only by keeping that in mind shall we be able to comprehend it.

What has been said makes it understandable that opera—like a person, and not like a species of art—had a definite place and date of birth. The place: the palaces of Florence, and particularly the remarkably beautiful Palazzo Pitti [Pl. 42]. The date: 1594, when, for the first time, the results of theoretical research were collected in a little "musical action." Of course, it was not as yet, and would not be for a long time, called opera. According to the then prevailing taste, its theme was a pastoral one. Its title: *Dafne*. Unfortunately, the music, by Peri, has not been preserved. Three years later, an interesting work made its appearance. It was called *L'Amfiparnasso*, and still was not an opera, but a series of madrigals arranged in three acts, with a preface. In it, the composer, Orazio Vecchi, drew illuminating comparisons between Renaissance painting and the new musical ideas: just a few leading persons in the foreground, and a large number, descriptive of the milieu, filling the background. And that is exactly the idea of opera.

We have come to the year 1600, which by many is considered the real birth date of opera because in that year intellectual Florence witnessed the first performance of *Eurydice* [Ill. 45] at the Palazzo Pitti. This is the oldest opera extant, the work of the poet Rinuccini and the two composers Jacopo Peri (1561-1633) and Giulio Caccini (1550?-1618). Naturally, the subject was a Greek one, the story of the mythological singer Orfeo and his wife Eurydice, whose fate was to be sung again and again on the operatic stages.

No sooner had opera outgrown its first childhood than a prominent master was ready to take care of it. He was to lead us to the second stage of its picturesque history, to Venice, where many a surprise awaited us.

Venice: Enter Their Majesties, the Public

Claudio Monteverdi (1567-1643) had, since 1613, been the organist at St. Mark's, where, for more than a century, the period's prominent musicians had been active. Monteverdi was one of the most prominent

45. First edition of Caccini's opera "Euridice," Florence, 1600.

of them all. A brilliant church musician, he was at the same time an enthusiastic champion of the new opera, in which he thought he could detect the noble origin of Greek tragedy. Beginning with *Orpheus* and ending with *Incoronazione di Poppea* (1643), he wrote a series of operatic masterpieces, deeply expressive of noble sentiments and revealing a remarkable progress in instrumentation. Monteverdi must undoubtedly be counted among the most noted pioneers of that art. Much in his works makes us think of Gluck and Wagner, although the form of his operas was essentially different from that of modern works. It was rather a cross between opera and oratorio: allegories, scenic pictures almost without action, long recitative-like singing, but no musical ensembles.

How, then, did opera take the decisive step that made it into what it is today? How—if we may be permitted to use the metaphor—was the fine young lady of the Florentine palaces changed into the *enfant terrible* with whom we shall soon become acquainted? A change in locale was primarily responsible: circumstances made it necessary for the young lady to attend a village school. There, unfortunately, she failed to exert an ennobling influence on her companions. On the contrary, she picked up a lot of new, and not always admirable, qualities.

The village school which young Miss Opera had to attend was the theater. But rather than describe this course of development, the writer would prefer to explain the confused and grotesque events by relating the action of a modern opera. It is *Ariadne auf Naxos,* words by Hugo von Hofmannsthal, music by Richard Strauss.

At the palace of a wealthy bourgeois in Vienna, two groups of artists await their cue. They have been engaged to entertain the guests until the time when fireworks are to end the festivities. One of the groups is composed of singers prepared to give the first performance of a young composer's serious opera. The opera is called "Ariadne auf Naxos" and is written in the style of the early operas just described: very noble and full of profound ethics, but to an average public, and especially at a summer festivity, rather boring. The other group ready to perform is composed of dancers and popular comedians, the very kind of whom we had a few words to say when speaking of medieval theatrical affairs. There is Harlequin and Columbine, and the other stock figures of the gay and light-hearted *Commedia dell' Arte* [Ill. 46]. For some reason, the beginning of the festivities is delayed, and the wealthy man's major-domo appears to inform the artists that, because of lack of time, the comedy only is to be performed and not the serious opera. Shattered seem the hopes of the young composer who had written with his heart's blood the long mournful songs of the deserted Greek woman on the lonely island. The prima ballerina who likes the looks of the disconsolate composer (no artistic motives are thus involved) makes him a strange proposition. There is little time for consideration and discussion, and so the grotesque suggestion becomes a fact: the two performances are given at the same time, and so, while Ariadne mourns her loneliness, the dancers come on stage and amuse the public. . . .

Let us now return from this enchanting opera to the reality of the seventeenth century. In the year 1637—an historic date!—the first theater was opened in Venice: San Cassiano. Two years later, it was joined by a second, called SS. Giovanni e Paolo. There followed the San Mosé Theater, in 1641, and fifteen others before the century was over [Pl. 44]. Take note, if you will, that the Venetians named their theaters after the nearest church.

These theaters, then, were the scene of the grotesque juxtaposition

46. Six Commedia dell' Arte figures. France, last
16th-Cent. quarter.

described in the story of the Strauss opera. No sooner had the impresarios realized that the serious and solemn style of the early operas was unable to attract and hold the attention of the new public, the people, than they tried their luck with comic intermezzi during the intermissions. Well, that was more to the Venetians' liking, but now they would arrive at the theater just in time for the intermezzo and leave immediately it was over. So, the intermezzi had to be made more elaborate all the time, at the expense of serious opera, until one day the two seemingly so heterogeneous elements were fused into a whole. Opera had gone through its great metamorphosis. There were now three different kinds: the serious, or *opera seria* (though even that kind had gained in elasticity, dramatic tension, and sprightliness), the comic, or *opera buffa*, and, dwelling between the two, the *opera semiseria*, a mixture of serious and gay scenes. Many masterpieces belong in the last category. To mention but two typical examples from different centuries: Mozart's *Don Giovanni* and Puccini's *Turandot*.

For the first time, mention was made in this chapter of "the public." A matter of course though it is to us, it was quite a novel and revolutionary institution to the art of the seventeenth century. Fomerly, music had been confined to private circles; or it was heard by members of the same social stratum: by the knights in the castle, by the monks and their believing flock in the churches, by the mastersingers in their schools, by the aristocrats in their palaces, and by the people at large in the convivial places providing music and dancing. From now on—what an extraordinary change!—there was a common music for all. It embodied elements of the aristocratic song as well as of the popular dance.

The creation of the "ticket of admission," that bit of pasteboard available to all who were able to pay the price, had undreamt-of consequences. Above all, this "democratization" led to a simplification of music to make it comprehensible to all. The text, too, had to be more "low-brow." The director of a theater, by many considered a person to be envied, became the victim of a double slavery. He—and lamentably also the text writers and composers—were tyrannized by the public as well as by the singers, who in turn seemed to be the only ones able to impose their will on that unpredictable, fickle, and dangerous mass of people, the public. All this led to weighty conflicts, resolved only—and then but partially—when a state, a city, or a true Maecenas stood ready to assume responsibility.

And so we come to the third period in the life of opera. It takes us to the city of song, to Naples.

Naples: The Triumph of Bel canto

It is understandable that a form of art whose history of development was so confused (we could describe but a small part of it here) should give rise to a vast number of problems. What was to be the predominant ingredient: the text or the music? Dramatic expression or the sung melody? These questions provided the main conflict at all times, and every epoch solved it according to its own aesthetic ideas, every country according to the character of its public. The Florentines had made the drama, the word, their fundamental starting point. But only a few decades later, during the third period now to be discussed, the other extreme was reached, the complete victory of the sung melody. This was wholly in keeping with the character of the Neapolitan people, almost all of whom, burghers and workmen, fishermen and market women, seemed to have been blessed with fine singing voices. Thus came about

47. Venetian engraving by Giacomo Franco, 1610: "Daily entertainment offered to people of all nations usually gathered at St. Mark's Square morning and evening."

the triumph of bel canto, of the sweet, tender, intoxicating melody which put entirely into the background everything else: sense, text, logic, dramatic action. It was in Naples that opera took the decisive step which made it into what we call today "Italian opera." It was created by the gay and sensuously-inclined southerners and acclaimed with an enthusiasm never witnessed before.

We know of modern metropolises with two, and in two exceptional instances even three, opera houses functioning at the same time. In late eighteenth-century Venice and Naples (and in other Italian cities, too) as many as eight stages gave performances every night. This makes us understand the regrettable fact that, because of the enormous demand, the artistic level sank to an unprecedented low point. Few of us have any conception of the number of existing operatic works. Recent statistics enumerating only the musical dramas of all kinds actually performed revealed the startling number of—42,000! How many more which had never seen the glare of the footlights?

To satisfy the enormous demand of the opera-struck population of Italy, every conceivable expedient had to be resorted to. It actually happened that parts of different operas—a love aria, a vengeful duet, or a great chorus—were supplied with a new text and made into a "new" work. Writers and composers, bound by contracts which demanded of them a yearly output of a certain number of works, could not afford to be particular in their choice of subjects and actions. A comparison with the modern cinema is not out of place, where both the excessive demand and the exigencies of business interests also militate against the maintenance of a high artistic standard. And yet, both there and here, it would be unjust to let the litter of mediocre works make us forget the glorious existence of so many masterpieces.

The early history of opera is studded with the names of important composers. In Venice, in addition to the great Monteverdi, there lived Francesco Cavalli (1602-1676) and Marc Antonio Cesti (1623-1669), musicians whose fame spread all over Europe. Of the Neopolitans, mention is due Alessandro Stradella (1645?-1682), a truly lengendary figure as a musician, singer, and romantic adventurer, who finally fell victim to an avenging dagger (a Flotow opera and other works made him their hero), Alessandro Scarlatti (1659-1725) [Ill. 48], and finally one of the greatest geniuses of them all, Giovanni Battista Pergolesi (1710-1736), who died in the prime of his youth. His *La Serva Padrona* is a shining example of *opera buffa*, greatly admired by such men as Verdi and Puccini.

A few words should be said about the public of that epoch. Its behavior in the theater was almost beyond belief. Woe to the singer who failed to find favor in its eyes, or rather, its ears! The fruit venders peddling their wares in the aisles would do a rushing business. This rather radical manner of expressing one's displeasure remained in vogue

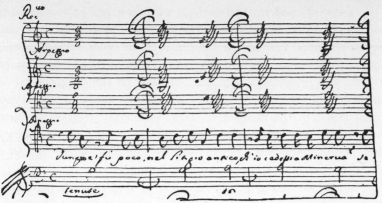

48. Neptune's recitative from Scarlatti's opera "Telemaco," in the composer's handwriting, 1718.

until comparatively recent days. On the other hand, the artist who knew how to grip his audience was fortunate! Extravagant as was the people's disapproval, their enthusiasm was equally so. Every beautifully sung melody, yes, every successfully produced high note, was received with thunderous acclaim. The singer became the idol of the masses who, for the first time since the decline of the Greek drama, were given the opportunity to attend an artistic theater. The enthusiasm of the gallery gods was shared, although to a more moderate degree, by the "upper" classes filling the orchestra floor. This orchestra floor was fundamentally different from that of the modern theater. It was bare, had no seating facilities [Ill. 44], and those who wished to listen to a performance in comfort had to bring along their own seats. Everything from stools to chairs to portable sofas, on which fine ladies were carried into the theater by their servants, was in evidence. There were even tables. They were used for card playing or dice throwing, if some of the cavaliers present felt so inclined. However, printed libretti had also made their appearance, and there were those who would follow the action by reading them in the light of candles. Many modern museums still own a yellowed specimen or two of old opera texts with spots made by dripping candle wax.

Before the rise of the curtain, everybody talked in a loud voice. Well-known politicians propounded their views to a circle of the curious, courtesans received the attentions of their admirers; while all the events of the day, the dress styles, and the market prices formed inexhaustible

. 73

subjects of conversation. Even the beginning of the performance often made little change in the prevailing commotion. It took the entrance of a favorite singer or the start of a popular air to change the noisy crowd into a raptly listening community—until the thunder of applause broke loose and threatened to bring down the walls of the house.

We owe the birth of an important musical form, the overture, to this undisciplined attitude of the public. At first, it consisted of little more than a vigorous trumpet blast, which was to apprise the gossiping, smoking, and gambling crowd of the impending rise of the curtain. Soon, however, it became customary to anticipate the most popular airs of a work and play them to the audience in a sort of medley. If these airs had become genuinely popular, the crowd would enthusiastically join in singing them, and the purpose of drawing attention to the stage was accomplished. Present-day operetta has adopted similar tactics by embodying the principal melodies of the piece in the prelude and the between-the-acts music.

Opera succeeded in drawing all social strata within its magic circle. Its influence was not confined to the theater but was felt also in daily life. We shall soon have occasion to mention a revolution that broke out after an operatic performance. Chronicles tell of a rebel who escaped capital punishment because he was also a popular composer of operas. We shall hear of street fighting between adherents of different operatic tendencies. Kings, princes, cardinals, aristocrats, and burghers were either patrons, composers, poets, impresarios, critics, amateurs—or simply

49. Dancer and comedian, with stage in background. Engraving by Jacques Callot from "Balli di Sfessania," abt. 1516.

members of the audience. The singers alone were in a class by them-selves—and what a class it was!

Naples became the city of the world's most famous singers and the home of operatic music, just as Cremona became the home of the violin, Vienna that of the waltz, and Argentina that of the tango. In Naples, looking down upon the eternal blue of the bay, stands the tomb of Enrico Caruso, like the mausoleum of a true king. There, in a crystal coffin, rests the great singer, embalmed and in full dress. And every three years, the dress suit is changed for one of the very latest cut. What more striking symbol could there be for the triumph of bel canto, of the lyric art, and of opera?

The Conquest of the World

No sooner had the rule of opera been established in Naples, than it started to conquer the whole world. Not only Europe, but America, too, was soon flooded with operatic works. They were accompanied on their travels by conductors and singers who in the theaters springing up in all the cities of the world created little Italian islands whose social and general influence soon assumed dimensions wholly out of proportion to their importance.

Italian musicians were received with all honors at the courts of Europe; and it was not long before their position in international musical life had become dominant. For more than a century and a half, they were the supreme masters of music not only in the theaters, but also in the palaces, and at times even in the churches. They crowded to the wall a man of Beethoven's stature, to say nothing of Bach and Mozart.

To be sure, this absolute rule of Italian opera also brought national resistance movements to the fore in many countries. Some of these aimed at fighting the "operatic monster" which threatened to devour everything, while others were animated by the feverish desire to supplant the all-powerful Italian opera by works of a nationalist character. There should be a French, a German, an English national opera!

The history of German opera had an early beginning. In 1627, a good musician, Heinrich Schütz (1585-1672) [Pl. 48], wrote the opera *Daphne,* using a German translation of Rinuccini's Italian text. The opera *Seelewig* by Sigmund Staden (1607-1655) also belongs in this early period. Thereafter, opera houses seemed to be shooting out of the ground all over Germany. (Prior to the Second World War, Germany had the largest number of permanent opera houses of any country in the world.) Soon, however, two irreconcilable tendencies began to manifest themselves. The Catholic South, ready to follow the Italian school, had erected in Vienna a veritable fortress for Italian opera, while the Protestant North insisted upon its national ambition to be German in spirit as well as in word. Hamburg became the center of this musical North, and Reinhard Keiser (1674-1739) its foremost composer. At the Prussian court, it was Frederick the Great himself who furthered music and offered a home to national opera. He was the author of several operatic libretti, among which was *Montezuma*, dealing with a phase of the American conquest. The music was written by Frederick's court composer, Karl Heinrich Graun (1704?-1759).

German opera had a checkered career. There were times when it seemed to disappear entirely under the victorious onslaught of its Italian rival. Finally, however, the positions were reversed. Weber and, to a still larger degree, Wagner seriously threatened the survival of bel canto music. A notable detail deserves to be mentioned here: three composers of the German tongue represented in their operatic works the art of other countries: Handel that of England, Gluck that of France, and Mozart that of Italy.

50. Title page of Heinrich Schütz's opera "Daphne." Typical baroque title with effusive dedication. Breslau, 1627.

In France, it was an Italian, Lully (1632-1687) [Pl. 28b], who must be regarded as the founder of a national school which, from the beginning, chose the ballet for its medium. Plays at court were staged with so much pomp that they put in the shade even the splendor of Italian opera. Later, Jean Philippe Rameau (1683-1764) [Pl. 96] became the most prominent figure of French opera. His fame in all musical arts and sciences was extraordinary. The grotesque struggle which began in the theaters and was continued in the streets and drawing-rooms occurred during the last years of his life. In 1752, an Italian company had been granted permission to give performances in Paris. It was tremendously successful, especially with its production of *La Serva Padrona*. This fact called to arms the nationalists, and soon the entire city was divided into two hostile camps: that of the "buffonists," avowed admirers of the Italian comic opera, and that of the "anti-buffonists," who held aloft the banner of the young French opera. After two years of violent struggling, the Italians were forced to leave Paris, but their influence did not entirely wane for a long time to come. We shall once more come face to face with it in connection with the struggle which was to rage round the person of Gluck, and we may also recognize its survival in many a French institution, such as the Opéra Comique.

Before the beginning of an almost barren period of two centuries, musically speaking, England produced a genius in the person of Henry Purcell (1658-1695) [Pl. 51], who must be considered his country's most prominent operatic composer. Among his fifty-four stage works there were some that were based on Shakespearean texts, like *Richard II* and *A Midsummer Night's Dream*. His most mature work—he died at a very early age—was *Dido and Aeneas*, in which he tried to adapt the noble style of the early Italian operas to the highly developed English theatrical activities. Purcell's successor was Handel, the German versed in the Italian school, with whose struggle on behalf of English national opera we shall soon become acquainted. Here, however, we want to mention a

51. Beginning of Purcell's "Golden Sonata," in composer's handwriting, 1683.

curious work, performed in London in the year 1728 and, a most remarkable fact, in New York in the year 1750. It was parody, a multiple parody, we may say. Under the pretext of aiming a dart at the exaggerations and absurdities of Italian opera, a grim social satire of the times was launched [Pl. 52]. The success of the *Beggar's Opera* was so pronounced that Handel was forced to close his opera house. He was unable to withstand the competition of this popular, ballad-like, and frequently quite aggressive music, which mercilessly parodied his own melodies and secretly made fun of his public. And, by the way, exactly two centuries after its birth, in 1928, this curious work was modernized by two Germans, Bert Brecht and Kurt Weill, whose *Dreigroschenoper* came near being even more successful than its prototype, the *Beggar's Opera*. The name of the author of the older work was John Gay (1685-1732) and that of the producer Rich, which gave rise to the pun that "Gay became rich, and Rich became gay."

Before closing this first chapter on opera, we want to make special mention of a man whose name was indissolubly connected with baroque opera. He was not a musician, but a librettist: Pietro Metastasio (1698-1782). Again and again it will be pointed out that an opera hardly ever represents the work of one individual but requires the highly artistic cooperation of two persons: the writer and the composer. Not infrequently it is the librettist who points the way and guides the musician by the convincing force of his style, his language, and the either more lyric or more dramatic character of his work. Let us not forget one thing in connection with opera as well as with the artistic song: In the beginning was the text!

Two generations of operatic activities bore the stamp of Pietro Metastasio. A Roman by birth, he displayed at the early age of ten a remarkable aptitude for improvising, which quite suited the taste of his time. His original name of Trapassi he changed into Metastasio. That, like many of his contemporaries, he also adopted a title, that of Abbate, was probably no more than a matter of form. The year 1724 witnessed the performance of his first opera book, *Didone Abbandonata*, with music by L. Vinci. So uniformly successful were his works that he was summoned to the court of Vienna by Charles VI and made Court Poet. While in that city, he wrote more than fifty operatic texts in addition to the words for cantatas, oratorios, and other works which were set to music by the most prominent composers of his epoch. Some of his books served as libretti for more than ten different operas. Hasse, a man who was rather famous in his day, boasted that he had set to music all of Metastasio's fifty libretti. Among those who availed themselves of his texts were Pergolesi (*Olimpiade*), Gluck (*L'innocenza giustificata*), Haydn (*L'isola disabitata*), Mozart (*La Betulia liberata, Il re pastore, La clemenza di Tito*), and even Rossini, representative of an entirely different period, in his *Semiramide*, fell back upon one of the prolific Roman's books. Metastasio's works were the expression of the purest baroque art, his figures were not men but types—abstractions of an idea—and his verses a sounding-board for the broad melodic arches of his time. His was a monumental art, one which occupied an important place in the early history of opera, and which was abandoned only in the Age of Enlightenment and the French Revolution. Today, Metastasio is almost forgotten, and few of his works have survived him. Nothing but the name of a quiet little street in the central part of Vienna reminds us of him, and a memorial plaque on the wall of the house where he had lived for more than half a century in the glamorous imperial city.

Soon, however, we shall have to devote a whole chapter to a musician who, poor, young, and unknown at the time, owed his discovery and considerable financial assistance to the world-famous Metastasio: Joseph Haydn.

First Intermezzo

At this point, our book changes its course somewhat. So far, it has dealt with epochs and tried to have them rise up before us as pictures, expressive of the musical atmosphere of their day. From now on, we shall place into the foreground the musical creators themselves, their life, and their work. Historical and stylistic problems will be augmented by psychological ones. But, on second thought, it is not a change at all, for every creative man mirrors his time and surroundings. And every one of them is indissolubly connected with his epoch: he is its son, or its slave.

We are about to enter upon the greatest era of our musical history, the era which, for certain stylistic reasons, is called the classic, and the romantic. I have given to this second book the title "The Summit." This summit is the apex of our history of music. What has gone before, no matter how magnificent, slips from our consciousness. It is too far away from us. Here, in truth, begins what constitutes "our music", begins what lives and breathes in us and round about us. The European middle-class culture, the mighty rise of which we witnessed in the last chapters, reached is culminating point in the eighteenth and nineteenth centuries. Music accompanied it, becoming its expression and its noblest spiritualization.

52. 16th-Cent. girl playing angled-neck lute. After Tobias Stimmer.

History is always unjust. Written by humans, it cannot be otherwise. And so we, too, may be unjust in calling the two golden centuries ahead of us the summit. A time may come when another period will be considered the towering point, other works called classic, other musicians immortal.

A very brief technical summation may prove an aid to the reader's comprehension. The material equipment of music has gradually grown in the course of its slow development, spread over centuries. Now it is to form the foundation for all those who are to dwell on "the summit."

The writing of music, the problems of which were discussed, had reached its ultimate perfection. Bach already wrote his music as we would write it today, with but trifling deviations. We generally use only two clefs now: the violin, or G, clef and the bass, or F, clef; and two additional ones for certain instruments, while Bach still used at least six of comparatively equal value.

The printing of music by means of movable characters, invented by Petrucci in Venice about 1500, is now so familiar a practice that the world-wide distribution of music has become as easy and almost as much a matter of course as that of books. That invention alone has made it possible for musical creations to spread unhindered over time and space. It has furnished the foundation for a truly international musical life.

The musical system had reached a stage which is still used as the platform upon which students are taught today. The two musical genera, major and minor, had been clearly defined, the new scales and chords had become firmly established, and so the human ear grew accustomed to the new system, which had dislodged the old "church tones." It had become the foundation of the new musical aesthetics.

The two fundamental principles of our music, too, had become quite clear. Polyphony, with its contrapuntal style, was to reach its apex in the works of Bach, while homophony, the single-voiced melody with harmonic accompaniment, was to become the dominating power for the remainder of the two "golden centuries."

The principles of all forms of composition already existed. Vocal music had found expression in the opera, the oratorio, the chorus, and the solo song. Instrumental music practiced the fugue, the tripartite forms which were to lead the way to the sonata and the symphony, the contraction of short, and generally dance-like, pieces into the "suite," and the free forms represented by the fantasia and by improvisations.

Finally, the instruments, too, had almost reached their present stage. There were four groups, separated from one another by differences in technique and use, but harmoniously joined in the steadily growing orchestras: strings, winds, percussion instruments, and keyed instruments. Among the latter, only the most important was still missing: the piano, which was produced by the Italian, Christofori, in 1711.

FIRST INTERMEZZO

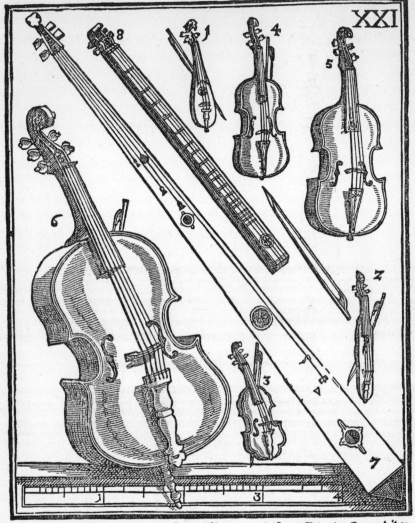

XXI

𝕰. 2. Kleine Poschen / Geigen ein Octav höher .   3. Discant-Geig ein Quart höher.
4. Rechte Discant-Geig. 5. Tenor-Geig. 6 Bas-Geig de bracio. 7. Trumschеit.
8. Scheidtholtt.

53. Early 17th-Cent. string instruments. From "Syntagma Musicum" by the
Thuringian composer Michael Praetorius, 1620.

*These, broadly, are the technical aspects. The psychological ones
are not so easily defined. All artistic creation borders on the miraculous,
every creator represents a world of his own, nearly always incomprehensible to those about him. Therein lies the cause of the clashes, the*

82 .

misunderstandings, and frequently the sorrows which no creative person is able to escape.

Each of the great musicians we are to meet is by temperament and character different from each of the others. To one, creation is joy, to the other, torture and struggle. One will carefully consider each note, change it, correct it a hundred times, while another will write as if in his sleep, with a dreamlike assurance which forever makes the changing of even a single note unnecessary. The creative power of one will find stimulation in travel, in the sight of landscapes, in feasts, in adventures. Another will be visited by the Muse in a wretched suburban garret from which he hardly ever stirs.

Artistic creation is mysterious and miraculous. Did not Mozart write his gayest operas when poor and ill? Did not Beethoven in a state of the most profound depression compose the hymnic jubilation of his "Ninth?" Did not Schubert in his songs depict thousands of things which he never really saw in his brief life?

The question may occur to some why the history of music, of art, and of literature tells almost exclusively of men. Were there no creative women? There were, and there are. But how was it possible for woman to maintain a place of equality at the side of man at a time when she was considered to be intellectually far below him? At a time when public life was the exclusive domain of man? Mozart's sister may have been no less gifted than he himself, and Mendelssohn's sister seems to have been as talented as her famous brother. But both had to resign themselves to a place in the background because the social order of their day demanded it. Only now, in the age of woman's emancipation and when woman's equality of rights has been duly recognized, does the history of the arts begin to produce eminent women.

54. Monochord, from an engraving by Bracelli, abt. 1615.

Book Two

The Summit

To send forth light into the depths
of the human heart—the artist's task.

(*Robert Schumann*)

55. Bach manuscript. Beginning of E-flat major prelude in the "Well-Tempered Clavichord," Part II, No. 7.

. 10 .

Bach: or Faith

IN the year 1740, when Bach was the organist at St. Thomas in Leipzig, a German newspaper published a list of the ten best musicians of the country and time. (Strange, that even in those serious days people should have entertained such an idea.) Bach was accorded seventh place. First place was given Telemann, the most famous musician of his time, although today his name seldom appears outside the pages of a history of music. Handel was assigned a place prominent enough to be acceptable to us. But all the others are entirely forgotten.

Exactly two hundred years later, in 1940, an American paper submitted the same (insoluble) question both to a group of experts and to the public at large, although the question was expanded to comprise musicians of all times and nations. The public voted for their great favorite Beethoven and put Bach in second place. The experts, however, reversed this judgment and declared Bach to have been the greatest musician of all times.

A strange case, this, of a composer who, two hundred years after his death, was not only held in higher esteem than at the time of his bodily existence but was felt to be thoroughly "modern." Had the unassuming St. Thomas organist been so far ahead of his time? Or are we yearning so much for the mysticism and profundity expressed in his works?

Bach made the spirit of religious polyphony surge up once more, and for the last time, completing the grandiose picture started by Palestrina. He was at home not only in the polyphonic music and the linear counterpoint known to the Middle Ages, but also in the new harmonic music which was taking possession of the world at an ever increasing pace. Hardly any other musician could have thoroughly comprehended and mastered two styles that were fundamentally so different from each other. At a turning point in the history of music, he embodied both a synthesis of the past and the essence of things to come. No sooner had he died than the scene changed completely. His own sons joined the revolutionaries. At the time of his death, Hadyn was already eighteen years old. Six years later, Mozart was born. In the works of these two, the new style, homophony, the "chivalrous" music which had its origins in feudalism, reached its finest flowering.

Fifty-eight giant volumes contain the mighty work left by Bach to a world able thoroughly to comprehend but the least important part of him—the mortal organist. His immortal creative genius is still not fully appreciated. Thumbing through these volumes, we come upon presentiments, or direct anticipations, of almost all the musical styles which have since placed their imprint upon the history of music. His all-encompassing spirit mastered not only the great forms of oratorios, masses, and Passions, but also the small, the smallest, ones, such as instrumental pieces, dances, and comic songs.

Bach's music is frequently called "absolute." This is an apt description, especially in contrast to program music, to illustrative and descriptive music, which tries to put extra-musical thoughts into sound. (In this connection, it seems significant that when Walt Disney undertook a pictorial interpretation of famous musical pieces, in his beautiful film *Fantasia,* he confined himself to colors and forms as an accompaniment to Bach's *Toccata and Fugue.*)

And now we must give some heed to the status of the German music and musical life from which Bach emerged. Above all, we must keep in mind that a summit, like Bach, could never have sprung from a low plain. In all realms, the great creators are like the highest points in a tall mountain massif. The higher the general level, the higher the pinnacles. The mountain massif is the entire cultural level of the time. How high did the musical level of the time have to be to bring forth a Bach as its crowning point? Let us mention here but a few of the prominent musicians: Schütz, Schein, Scheidt, Telemann, Pachelbel, Buxtehude. They formed the mountain massif from which Bach, the crowning head, towered into eternity.

Some of these masters would deserve a chapter of their own. Their art was great and pure, their influence on the German music of coming centuries powerful. A few words about the one who was perhaps the most important of them. He was Heinrich Schütz. Born exactly a century before Bach (1585), at a time when Palestrina and Lasso were still alive and active, he composed madrigals and polyphonic motets, until he reached the glorious maturity of the "Evangelical Histories," without which many a work by Bach might have remained unborn. It took the miracle of the latter's monumental *St. Matthew Passion* to equal and surpass in musical significance Schütz's work on the same subject. Schütz died in Dresden, in 1672.

During the second half of that century, Germany started to attend to the wounds inflicted by the Thirty Years' War (1618-1648). The land had been broken up into hundreds of small feudal states ruled by kings, princes, dukes, and margraves. Although most of them were politically unimportant and their territory so small that a modern express train would traverse it in a few minutes, they were nevertheless all filled with the desire to make their capital a center of culture. The life of the German musicians of that time was fundamentally different from that led by their Italian colleagues, whose field of activity was the whole world. They had not as yet achieved the status of free artists, such as Beethoven was to have for the first time, a hundred years later. They were merely employees who, like lackeys, wore the livery of their master. Their life took its course within the narrow confines of those tiny countries, in their palaces and churches. They were either organists and choir masters, with the title "Cantor"; or they called themselves "Kapellmeister" when the palace could boast of a small orchestra; or they were "Chamber Musicians" who were active in small ensembles at concerts and festivities. In addition, they often had to perform the duties of a schoolmaster, and not only in connection with music.

Within so narrow a scope and so limited a horizon Bach lived his life. The breadth of his thinking and the universality of his world-embracing music thus becomes doubly inconceivable. In tracing the various stages of his life, we are surprised by the man's simplicity, his profound morality, his noble kindness, and the even tenor of his character. A single passion ruled this exemplary life: the passion for music.

Johann Sebastian Bach [Pl. 54] was born in Eisenach, a small Thuringian town, in the year 1685. His cradle stood at the foot of the Wartburg, where the country's most famous minnesingers are said to have met, in 1207, and where, three hundred years later, Luther translated the Bible into German (1521), an event that was as important to the development of music as it was to that of religion. Bach thus grew up in a center of Protestantism. It was the faith of his family and became one of the most potent inspirations of his music. The choral, the ideal expression of Evangelical church music, was one of the main pillars of Bach's work. Whatever Bach created in the realm of religious music was a typical manifestation of his faith, and there is hardly a more striking proof of the universality of his art than the fact that today members of all religions, without exception, humbly bow their heads before the majesty of his music, and the further fact that his Whitsun and Easter works are heard today both in Protestant and in Catholic churches.

The Bach family was a family of musicians. It represented a most extraordinary case of hereditary transmission [Ill. 56]. Scattered over many places of Central Germany, the name Bach had actually become a synonym for musicians. And the chain was by no means broken by Johann Sebastian. His sons upheld the tradition. Among them were men of considerable talent, like Wilhelm Friedemann, Carl Philipp Emanuel, and Johann Christian. The latter was one of the musical revolutionaries of his time. He made fun of his father, the "old peruke," moved to Italy —which was tantamount to going over to the archenemy, became a Catholic—which meant the forsaking of sacred family traditions, and wrote operas—an activity which the Bach clan must have considered the devil's work.

Bach's youth was filled with musical impressions. The family reunions especially were annually recurring festival climaxes, when all the Bachs from near and far gathered and actively devoted themselves to the joint playing of music for days on end. Johann Sebastian began his musical career at the age of eighteen as a violinist in the orchestra of the Duke of Weimar. He was thus able to live in one of Germany's most cultured cities, a place made doubly famous later by harboring the great poets Goethe and Schiller, and a place, moreover, to whose musical fame

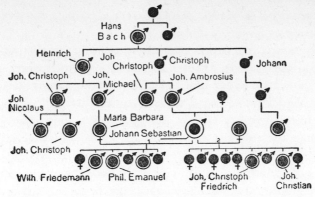

56. Genealogical table of the Bach family. Striking example
of the hereditary property of musical talent. There were 17
musicians among the primogenitor's 32 descendants.

Liszt was to contribute considerably. However, Bach remained in Weimar but a short time. From the days of his childhood, all his yearning had been for the Queen of Instruments, the organ. And he would not rest until this yearning was appeased.

It was in the little church of Arnstadt that he was first active as an organist. His desire to perfect himself prompted him, in 1705, to set out on a strange journey. He traveled on foot to the Hanse town of Luebeck, just to hear Buxtehude, the greatest organist of that time. The profound impression made by so perfect an art intoxicated him anew day after day. Bach became lost to the world about him, forgot that his duties called him back to Arnstadt, and forgot, too, that he had been granted but a brief vacation by his superiors. His "unseemly transgression" and other offences, among which was his taking a young girl to the organ loft (she was his future wife), cost him his position. He found a new field of activity in Mühlhausen, in 1707, but there, too, his stay was not of long duration, mainly because of an awkward religious dissension among the believers of that town. This was bound to affect the life and professional activity of a church musician.

Once more it was Weimar whither Bach guided his steps (a turn of speech which could be taken literally, since lack of funds frequently compelled the young man to do his traveling on foot). This time, he advanced to the position of Court Organist and Chamber Musician to the Duke. In 1714, he was promoted to the desk of the First Violinist, which at that time meant a kind of leadership within the ensemble. According to then prevailing standards, the orchestra was quite sizeable, having at times as many as twenty members.

At the same time, Bach's fame as an organist kept growing rapidly. This is eloquently attested to by a curious event occurring in 1717. In that year, a French organ and cembalo virtuoso, Louis Marchand, performed at the Court of Dresden and claimed that he had no superior in Europe. It took Bach's friends and admirers a long time before they could induce the reserved and almost timid man to enter into a contest with Marchand. When he finally consented and arrived in Dresden to compete with Marchand, the Frenchman took "French" leave without even having met his rival. Telemann, the famous Hamburg composer and critic, wrote at that time: "Nobody can surpass Handel's organ playing, unless it be Bach."

Cothen, in the Duchy of Anhalt, became the next stage in the life of Bach, the only one to keep him entirely from religious music. There he was conductor of the Court Orchestra. To this activity the world owes the major part of his secular musical works, whose importace is all too frequently obscured by the gigantic proportions of his religious music. In spite of this fruitful activity, there was no power in the world that could have kept Bach from his beloved organ for any length of time. In 1723, he entered the list of those who wished to compete for the vacant position of Cantor of St. Thomas' in Leipzig. He did not entertain great hopes, for he had recently been cheated most shamefully out of a similar job in Hamburg. This time, however, everything was fair and square, and so Bach came to live in the city which was to witness the longest period of his artistic activity, the birth of his most important works, and his death. Here he worked with unflagging zeal, here he was happy—in his home, and at his organ [Pl. 56]. No striving for worldly honors spurred him on, or caused him any bitterness. Few people sensed his true greatness and importance as a creative musician. Even those who unreservedly admitted his mastery of the organ frequently failed to recognize his creative genius. Among his staunchest supporters was Frederick the Great, who invited him to Potsdam, in 1747, for a series of organ and cembalo recitals.

Only during the last years of his life did his world fame assume commensurate proportions. Travelers in increasing numbers, on their arrival in Leipzig, inquired about the "great Bach," wanted to see and hear him. What they found was a man withdrawn from the world, indefatigably

Clavier Ubung
bestehend in

Præludien, Allemanden, Couranten, Sarabanden, Giquen,
Menuetten, und andern Galanterien;

Denen Liebhabern zur Gemüths Ergoezung verfertiget
von
Johann Sebastian Bach,
Hochfürstl Anhalt-Cöthnischen würcklichen Capellmeister und
Directore Chori Musici Lipsiensis

Partita V.

In Verlegung des Autoris
1730

57. Title page of the first edition of Bach's partitas.

devoted to his musical work and living a truly happy life in a home abundantly blessed with children. After the death of his first wife, he had married again, and he was lucky in having chosen once more a woman who was an ideally understanding companion and a competent head of his household. He composed one work after another, until his diminishing eyesight made the writing of music difficult. He died on July 28, 1750, at the age of sixty-six, and was buried in the crypt of Leipzig's St. John's church.

The last notes he wrote were part of a fugue in which he used the letters of his name—B-A-C-H (B being our B-flat and H our B-natural)—for the formation of the counter-subject. At that point, Death intervened —Death, of which he had sung so often, not with terror or fear, but with the deeply religious faith that had been his lodestar throughout life. This last manuscript shows a remark in the hand of Philip Emanuel: "While working on this fugue, which reveals the name BACH in the counter-subject, the composer was overtaken by death."

A century and a half later, Anton Bruckner dedicated his last and greatest symphony "To the Dear Lord." It is probable that Bach, without expressing it, dedicated all his works to God. His manuscripts are prefaced by the letters J. J. (*Jesu juva*) and concluded by S. D. G. (*Soli Deo Gloria*), surely more than merely a meaningless matter of form to the great believer, all of whose strength came from God.

The physical size of Bach's work was mentioned before—fifty-eight stout volumes. It would be extremely difficult to arrange his compositions according to their worth. First place may be due his oratorios.

A few explanatory lines must be interpolated here concerning this form of art which occupied an important place in the creations of Bach as well as of Handel and of many subsequent composers. The oratorio stems from the medieval forms of the Passion and Mystery Play and is thus a twin brother of the opera. And as is so often the case with twin brothers, they have much in common but also many points in which they are different. The oratorio and the opera have a common fatherland, Italy, and approximately the same birth date, about 1600. Of the two, the oratorio was the first-born. The name is traceable to the *Oratory* of St. Philip Neri. It owes its development to several prominent composers, often of Roman descent, such as Emilio de Cavalieri and particularly Giacomo Carissimi (1604-1674). The oratorio is not necessarily a form of religious music. There also exist worldly types, although they are never so worldly as opera and always reveal a certain solemnity as their basic element. What opera and oratorio have in common are the approach, the fact that they are sustained by a number of characters, the inclination toward an alternation of solo and choral numbers, the occurrence of vocal forms (arias, duets, etc.), the orchestral accompaniment, and the interspersion of independent orchestral pieces (overture, intermezzi, marches, etc.). It is not surprising that the early stages in the life of twin brothers opera and oratorio should have run a parallel course and been quite similar to each other. But it is also natural that differences should have appeared later, rivalries even. Opera captured the popular stage, while the oratorio was ready to do without footlights, without costumes and scenery, in a word, without everything that smacked of the theater. Dramatic conflicts there were, but they frequently assumed a lyric-contemplative character, and they were always presented in a concert-like manner. To preserve the necessary continuity, the oratorio introduced the figure of the narrator, the speaker, who connected the musical numbers, usually in the semi-musical form of the recitative.

The oratorios occupied a prominent place in Bach's life-work. In

[Facsimile of a handwritten letter in German]

58. Letter written by Johann Sebastian Bach to Councillor J. Fr. Klemm, in Sangerhausen, asking him, as a "faveur," to give consideration to a "subjject very close to his heart," in the appointment of an organist.

view of the life led by the St. Thomas cantor and his natural inclinations, their religious character cannot surprise us.

Foremost in this category are the three extant *Passions*, that of St. Luke, that of St. John, and the monumental masterpiece of the *St. Matthew Passion* [Pl. 53]. Bach performed this work but once, on Good Friday of the year 1729. When it was received coolly and seemingly without comprehension, he abandoned the idea of further presentations. Fully a hundred years later the score was unearthed by a young musician of genius, Felix Mendelssohn-Bartholdy, who gave back to mankind this inconceivably magnificent work. Bach's paternity of the *St. Luke Passion* has been increasingly questioned of late. While the original score is in his own handwriting, there are many reasons why it is not likely to be the child of his creative spirit. The *St. John Passion* was written in 1723, that is, before Bach entered upon his Leipzig duties as cantor of St. Thomas'. But he subjected it to two quite comprehensive revisions, in 1729, and in 1738. This rather infrequently occurring dissatisfaction of Bach with a work once finished probably had its main reason in the text. Bach had been his own librettist, shaping for his particular use an outline written by the Hamburg Councillor Brockes and set to music before by Handel, Mattheson, and Keiser. Instead of the the bombastic baroque verses of the outline, Bach chose the original text of St. John, although aria-texts by various authors are interspersed. The backbone of every *Passion* is formed by the narrative of one of the four Evangelists, while arias, choruses, and chorals are inserted into this recitative-like account. Under Bach's treatment, the *St. John Passion* became a magnificent synthesis of spirtual purity and gripping realism hardly ever witnessed before in the entire history of music. The judgment scenes describing the raging mob's demand for the Saviour's life could not have been formed more realistically by any modern composer. The wonderfully heartfelt chorals which interrupt the evolvement of the momentous events are by no means a breach of style. They are, on the contrary, lyric climaxes wholly integrated with the dramatic procedure, whose stirring effect they enhance.

Of no less a magnitude are Bach's other religious works, like the Mass in B Minor, the Christmas Oratorio, the numerous cantatas, and his simple, yet deeply felt, chorales.

Pre-eminent among Bach's secular works are two of superlative dimensions: *The Well-Tempered Clavichord* and *The Art of the Fugue*.

The former is a collection of preludes and fugues in which, for the first time, our whole musical system of major and minor keys is traversed from one boundary to the other. Uniform pitch or "tempering" had been established but a short time before by Andreas Werckmeister, representing an equal division of the octave into twelve half-tones. In his other great secular work Bach occupied himself with his favorite musical form, the fugue. This happened shortly before his death, so that the masterpiece, an inexhaustible source of information for students of polyphonic music, could not be completed. His Brandenburg Concertos were written in the orchestral style of his time, with several movements. We must not overlook, either, a number of highly important concertos for a solo instrument and orchestra. To enumerate all of Bach's works would go far beyond the scope of this book.

59. Scene from Handel's opera "Julius Caesar in Egypt," 1724. This anonymous caricature is wrongly ascribed to Hogarth.

. 11 .

Handel: or The Power of Will

BACH and Handel, the two great geniuses of German eighteenth-century music never met in the long course of their life, although they were born within a few weeks—and not many more miles—of each other. A century later, Beethoven's and Schubert's paths were not to cross, although they walked the same streets every day. Wagner and Verdi, too, were to remain strangers to each other, another half century later.

In almost every respect, Handel's life was the very opposite of Bach's. His represented the triumph of a fighter who had to contend with obstacles of many kinds, with resistance and intrigue, with envy and malice, and who finally emerged victorious thanks to his iron will and his indomitable energy.

29. Angels, either singing or playing positive organ, harp, and square fiddle, as shown on side wings of the Gent altar, the work of the brothers Jan and Hubert van Eyck, 1432. Such angels, and later human beings, were favorite subjects of Renaissance art.

30. In *Little Eden*, a small Upper-Rhenic painting (abt. 1420), the mysticism and strict religiosity of Gothic art is already softened by mundane sensuous enjoyments. Like a king's daughter, Mary enjoys the serenity of her walled garden, while St. Cecilia teaches the Christ child to pluck the psaltery strings. [*Städelsches Institut, Frankfort*] ....

31. Roundelay to bagpipe music. Carved side of minne-casket, 14th Cent. *Haarlem.*

32. The *Passion of Christ* by Hans Memling unites the various stages of the Passion in one large painting, thus providing a clear picture of the enactment of the mystery plays and dramatic processessions of that time.

33. Scenes from a mystery play. Miniature from *Miracles de Notre Dame*, chronicled for the Duke of Burgundy. [*Bibl. Nat., Paris*]

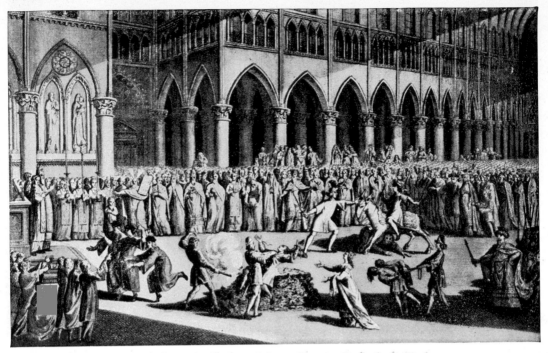

34. Donkey Festival at Notre Dame Cathedral, Paris.

35. Model of the Lucerne wine market (abt. 1583) with stage setting and scene of the Lucerne Passion Play. [*Theatermuseum, Munich*]

36. King David with psaltery, followed by musicians playing the lute, vielle, and chimes. Miniature of the Wenzel Bible. Early 15th Cent.

37. Angels singing and playing music. Section from *The Birth of Christ* by Piero della Francesca, abt. 1485. [*Nat'l Gallery, London*]

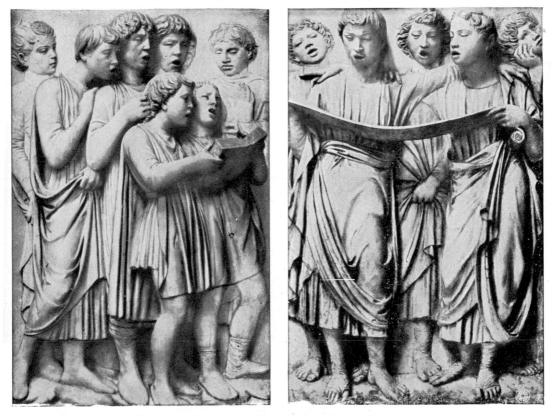

38. Boy singers. Two sections from the relief by Luca della Robbia, at the choir chancel of the Florence Cathedral. Abt. 1435.

39. Angel with lira da braccio. Mural by Melozzo da Forli in the choir of
Santo Apostoli, Rome, 1481. This instrument with five finger strings and two
off-the-board bourdon strings forms the link between the medieval fiddle and the
viola da braccio.

40. Madonna with Child and angels by Giovanni Boccati da Camerino, abt. 1460.
Upper left: Angled-neck lute, timbrel, and cymbals. Upper right: rebeck, bagpipe, and harp. At bottom: portable organ and dulcimer.

41. Segment of the *Adoration of the Christ Child* by Bartolomeo Suardi, called Bramantino (1475-1536). The figure at left holds aloft the monochord, usually placed on the ground. This medieval instrument, also called Mary's Trumpet, consisted of a long sounding board and a single string.

42. The Palazzo Pitti, Florence, where Caccini's opera *Euridice* was performed, in 1660. *Engraving by J. S. Müller*. The event marked the historic beginning of a form of art which, 37 years later, moved from the palaces to the operatic stages.

43. Sea battle staged by Buontalenti, Lord Marshal of the Court of the Medicis (abt. 1598), in the courtyard of the Palazzo Pitti, one of the pompous and technically ingenious spectacles of the Renaissance period which, accompanied by music, were the precursors of opera.

44. The Teatro Fenice, Venice, after an 18th Cent. engraving.
45. The ideally constructed Italian Renaissance stage: the Teatro Olimpico, in Vicenza, built by Andrea Palladio, begun 1579.

46. The cloud-supported Palace of Virtue descends upon Parma. Stage setting of Giuseppe Tosi's ballet prelude for a festival performance at the wedding of Duke of Parma, 1690.

47. Stage design for an early-Rococo opera. French. 18th Cent.

48. Heinrich Schütz (1585-1672).
[*Portrait*]

49. Jean-Baptiste Lully (1632-1687).
[*After Mignard*]

50. The Italian comedians depart. [*Engraving after a Watteau painting, 1697*]

51. Henry Purcell (1658-1695). [*Portrait by Kneller*]

2. Third-act court scene from *The Beggar's Opera* by Gay and Pepusch, 1728. [*Engraving by W. Blake after the painting by Hogarth*]

abermahl laut und verschied.
Choral
Wenn ich einmahl soll scheiden
Evang.
Evang.
Und siehe da, der Vorhang im Tempel zerriß in zwey Stück von oben an
bis unten aus.
Und die Erde erbebete und die Felsen zer-
rißen
und die Gräber thäten sich auf, und
stunden auf viel Lei-be der Heiligen die da schlie-

53. Death scene of Jesus in Bach's manuscript of the Passion of St. Matthew.

54. The youthful Johann Sebastian Bach (1685-1750).]*Anonymous portrait at the Erfurt Museum*[

55. The house in Eisenach where Bach was born.

56. The Bach organ in Leipzig's St. Thomas' Church.

Bach's family was one of musicians. There was not a single musician in Handel's. This makes us understand his father's strong objection to the young man's "strange" choice of profession. Even though music had come to represent an occasionally well-paying occupation—many Italian operatic composers had succeeded in amassing a considerable fortune— there still existed a wide-spread prejudice against professional musicians, who by many were relegated to a rather low social stratum.

George Frederick Handel [Pl. 57 and 58], born in Halle, in 1685, first proved the strength of his will by overcoming his father's opposition. In the very year in which Bach began his career in Weimar and Arnstadt, Handel, a young man of eighteen like the other, turned to Hamburg, whose importance to German opera was mentioned before. Soon, his first two operas were performed there. From Hamburg, Handel found his way to Lübeck, more easily, to be sure, than Bach, since he did not have so far to go and had at his disposal considerably more funds. He, too, was most deeply impressed by Buxtehude's mature art. There were those who urged him to marry the famous organist's daughter, a union which according to prevailing customs would have automatically made him his father-in-law's successor. But Handel's temperament made him shrink from marrying and taking root at so early a stage in his life. To him, as to so many artists, traveling was a vital necessity. He wanted to gather impressions, for he felt that they would heighten and enrich his creative abilities. In this respect, too, he was the antithesis of Bach (and also of Schubert and many another musician) who apparently stood in no need of inspiration from outside to enable him to conjure up a whole universe of sound. Handel, like so many other German artists, felt drawn toward the sunny South. In the very year that witnessed Bach's going to Mühlhausen, Handel was on his way to Italy, where he submitted enthusiastically to the seductive embrace of opera.

After having stayed for some time in Venice, Florence, and Rome, he settled in Naples, whose musical ideas, represented by Alessandro Scarlatti, then dominated the world. Three years later, Handel returned to his native land, a perfect Italian operatic composer. He was appointed Kapellmeister in Hannover, but again his restless temperament would not let him stay. He may instinctively have been looking for a larger field of activity. His travels took him to the North, and there, in England, he found his second, his real, homeland.

Handel started out as an operatic impresario, supplying his own

60. From Handel's manuscript of "Salve Regina," 1751.

works, of which he wrote an incredible number. He had to struggle against a powerful opposition, directed partly against himself, partly against the school he represented. He finally succumbed, without however, relinquishing the idea of establishing a national English opera, though with a Neapolitan imprint. His second enterprise struggled along, as had the first, until the *Beggar's Opera*, mentioned before, brought about its collapse.

The blows of fate had embittered Handel. Besides, his health had suffered because of excessive work, and he had become partially paralyzed. He went to Aachen, though the doctors advised against the use of the powerful baths. But a hardy nature like Handel's was not amenable to the laws applicable to average mortals. He took three times the number of baths usually prescribed and was cured. No sooner did he feel again in possession of his strength than he hurried back to England. He was the true fighter who never gives up the struggle as long as there is still a vestige of hope. In addition, he felt that he was actually bound to the country of his adoption. And this time victory was his.

But it was not opera that helped him gain it. Handel had turned to a new realm, that of the great popular oratorio—theatrical, and yet fundamentally religious. At the age of fifty-six, from August 22 to September 14, 1741,—within twenty-four days!—he wrote his master-piece, *The Messiah*. So great was his creative power that he immediately went to work on another opus, *Samson*, which he completed on October 29.

Handel, having little confidence in the London public which had twice forced him to close his theater, entrusted the first performance of the *Messiah* to Dublin, the capital of Ireland. Only after the prodigious success scored there, in 1742, did he produce the work in London in the presence of the King and his court. When the orchestra and chorus started the final exultant *Hallelujah*, the monarch, deeply moved, rose from his seat to pay homage to so magnificent a work. It has remained customary to this day for English audiences to stand while listening to this last part.

From that moment, nothing stood in the way of Handel's fame and the popularity of his music. He could hear his melodies while walking through Vauxhall Gardens, where an orchestra used to play in summer, and where his statue stands today. He also heard them on many a trip on the Thames when he accompanied the King on mild summer evenings and the orchestra played the *Water Music*, composed for this very purpose.

One day, he stopped work on a new manuscript with the words: "I have come thus far; I cannot continue, for I have lost the sight of my left eye."

Was the moment as terrible for the indefatigable fighter as it must have been for Beethoven at the first foreboding of impending deafness? Nine years later, when Handel was totally blind, he felt tired for the first time and entertained thoughts of death. A legend has it that he expressed the desire to die on a Good Friday. He who had achieved everything he had striven for had his last wish fulfilled. The night of Good Friday, 1759, was about to give way to dawn when the eyes that had long ceased to see the light closed forever. He was buried with great honors and put to rest in Westminster Abbey's "Poet's Corner" at the side of England's great masters.

Handel's abiding place among the world's immortals is not due principally to his operas, although there, too, we find music of exceptional beauty, as for instance the famous *Largo*, which occurs in *Xerxes*, and

61. The so-called "Handel Choir" singing the oratorio "Judith," by W. de
Fesch. Satirical engraving by Hogarth, 1731.

the aria *Lascia ch'io pianga*, which he used no less than three times: in
the operas *Almira* and *Rinaldo* and in the oratoria *Il trionfo del tempo*.
This is interesting for another reason, too, since the latter belonged in
the category of non-religious oratorios which, in keeping with medieval
principles, dealt with abstract ideas, like truth, beauty, or time.

Handel's light shines most brightly in his magnificent oratorios.
They make no secret of their family relationship with opera; quite the
contrary. Every one of his oratorios could be played on the stage, just as
every one of his operas could be performed on the concert platform.
Most of his oratorios are based on the Bible. They reveal a considerable
change from previously used forms; they are works intended for all the

people and designed to produce an immediate mass effect. The large choruses employed lend to his style a monumental character. Handel's oratorios have greatly influenced generations of composers, from Haydn to Schumann, to Liszt, and to César Franck.

A place of equal importance is occupied by his instrumental compositions, especially the *Concerti grossi*. Here, too, his music is colorful, monumental, and broadly spread, obviously planned for large orchestral masses. While Bach had had to petition the Leipzig Town Council to grant him an additional two men for both the chorus and orchestra—augmenting them to fourteen and sixteen, respectively—Handel had at his disposal large masses of sound for the realization of his artistic dreams. Hundreds of schooled choristers—England has always been the land of excellent choruses—collaborated enthusiastically to make some of the most beautiful passages in the Holy Writ come to musical life.

Madame de Staël said of Michelangelo that he was the painter of the Bible. Handel was its composer.

62. Last lines of Handel's testament.

· 12 ·

Vienna Becomes the Musical Center

THE death of Bach and Handel occurred at a time of transition, both general and musical. Polyphony, which had been dealt a severe blow by Italian opera, was breathing its last. Even the purely instrumental forms would have no more of it. The new style—monotonic music with harmonic accompaniment represented the era of the feudal rococo. A few decades more, and the world would be transformed by events of cataclysmic force: the French and American Revolutions. But for the time being life at court was at the zenith of its splendor.

It was not the purpose of music at the palaces to move people, to lend depth to their feeling, or to purify their ideals. It was a mere pastime, amiable but trivial, and must never give offense. The name given to the music of the aristocratic salons seems highly significant. It was called the gallant, the chivalrous, style. Its musical form was expressive of court ceremonials. Everything was so scrupulously prepared and measured that the formulas stifled the content. Even a genius able to transform into sound the trembling of the soul and the dim conception of the infinite would not have dared to lay hands on the form. It always remained "gallant" and elegant, always aristocratic. Sentiments and passions may have been no different from those of the closely impending days of the bourgeoisie, but how different was the form in which they were expressed!

For more than a century, opera had unquestionably been the ruling musical power, in spite of all the important figures in other realms, in spite of Bach and his sons, and in spite of Handel and some eminent Italian composers, like Tartini, Vivaldi, and Corelli, whose chamber-music style was a virtuoso-like admixture which both affected and was affected by the works of the German masters. But it was a fact that opera had been the most tangible musical form ever since the year 1600. It was left to future generations to cast many operatic composers into

104

oblivion and to replace them by masters whose work in their lifetimes had been overshadowed by the glamour of the opera.

Now, in the middle of the eighteenth century, Italy, the land of opera, lost the hegemony which it had been able so long to maintain. At the same time, other cities rose to prominence and became cultural and musical centers, gathering within their walls the leading spirits of their time and, temporarily at least, attracting the attention of the world. It was stated before in these pages that it is never mere chance which determines the gathering point of a certain epoch's spiritual forces and causes them to bring about a rich flowering of the arts. After the Flemish cities, came the flourishing towns of the Italian Renaissance. And now it was Vienna which became the spiritual and artistic center of Europe and the undisputed musical heart of the world, a distinction it was not to relinquish for almost a century and a half.

The history of that beautiful city goes far back into ancient times, probably into pre-Roman days. Its geographical position places it at the crossroads of European traffic. Peoples of Teutonic, Romanic, and Slav origin met there. Dominating the thousand-year-old Danube route, it had from time immemorial been a prominent trading center and a junction point of considerable political importance. It was a veritable fortress, against whose stout walls all Asiatic invasions had been dashed to pieces. For more than two hundred years it had been threatened or besieged by the Turks. When, in the year 1683, these invaders were definitely crushed, Vienna's rapid rise set in. The city received its first charter in 1137. A bare hundred years later, in the days of the minnesingers, it had already become the most important center of Central Europe. The great influx of international artists and scientists began in the eighteenth century. All of Europe's nations contributed to the development of the truly cosmopolitan character of the city. Here French gracefulness mingled with Italian gaiety, tempered by Slav melancholy. German thoroughness lived side by side with Hungarian pride and Spanish chivalry. He who minutely examines Vienna's music, be it the "classic" compositions of its great masters or the popular pieces of its princes of the waltz, will have no difficulty in finding traces of all these influences—and of many more, all of which formed the ingredients of what came to be known as the true Viennese character.

In 1750, the Italian style still predominated in the Danube capital, but the proverbial musical enthusiasm of the inhabitants had led to a certain division. While previously the opera had been practically the only point of attraction, instrumental music now started to occupy a prominent place. The aristocratic and the well-to-do middle classes, the ambition of the latter being to imitate the former as much as possible, increasingly cultivated orchestral music. Many palaces had their own ensembles in which the master of the house and members of his family frequently played side by side with musically accomplished servants. Chamber music, too, enjoyed a growing popularity. On a balmy summer night, the gardens would resound with serenades. Significant for those days were the numerous newspaper advertisements in which the services of "a cook, who plays the viola" or a "valet, who is an accomplished flutist" were required in aristocratic or bourgeois palaces.

For a period of a hundred and fifty years, there was to be hardly a single composer of any importance in the world who did not in some manner become affiliated with Vienna. This is not to say that these affiliations were always of a pleasant kind. On the contrary, there are many bitter pages in the musical history of that city. In spite of everything, however, no musician coud quite escape Vienna's magic spell.

63. Chorus from Gluck's score of "Feste d'Apollo," 1769.

64. Gluck's manuscript of "Alceste," Act III: "Grands dieux, soutenes mon courage."

Gluck was one óf the earliest of these. Christoph Willibald von Gluck [Pl. 60] was born in thc Palatinate, near the Rhine, in 1714. He was at first active in Prague, briefly in Vienna, and then set out on the Italian pilgrimage still considered obligatory for an operatic composer. There, in 1741, his first work was performed. It was to be followed by a hundred others in the long course of his life. Summoned to England, he wrote three operas for the Haymarket Theater—the same in which Handel had been active,—all of them in pure Italian style. Europe's most prominent theaters performed his works [Pl. 63]. In 1750, Empress Maria Theresa summoned Gluck to the Vienna Court Theater. It was the year that witnessed the death of Bach and the beginning of the brilliant career of a poor eighteen-year-old lad, Joseph Haydn. Now, at the height of Gluck's fame, a singular change took place in him. He began to reflect upon the undeniable crisis of the opera and to turn away from the trivialities of its routine. It suddenly dawned on him that the salvation of musico-dramatic art must start at the text.

Monteverdi's pronouncement had been: "Let the word be master of the melody, not its slave." That was the point to which Gluck wished to return. Besides, he wanted to imbue opera with a profound ethical meaning, make it more human, more moral. Gluck found an ideal collaborator in Calzabigi, a man whose poetic talent was able to grasp and realize the composer's basic ideas. These two men now began their great work of reform. A century later, a single man, poet and musician all in one, was to complete it: Richard Wagner.

It is not surprising that the two operatic reformers reached back to Greek tragedy in direct opposition to prevailing operatic tendencies.

Orpheus—the theme set to music so frequently—and *Alceste* formed the first stages of the reform movement. But the public failed to grasp the idea. It was still too filled with the melodic bliss of the Italian style. This made Gluck decide to go to Paris, where Lully and Rameau had already tried to shake off the yoke of the belcanto. And now the city on the Seine witnessed a renewal of the two-party fight, buffonists and anti-buffonists formerly, and now Gluckists and Piccinists, (so called after Piccini, chief protagonist of the Italian tendency). Again France was split into two camps, whose dividing line was not without its piquant details: on Gluck's side stood the King and Madame Pompadour, a fact which in itself was enough to make the Queen and Rousseau espouse the cause of the other party. The battle raged for many years. A significant detail was furnished by a letter from Rousseau, who enjoyed an enormous prestige as a writer, although he was little more than a mediocre amateur in musical matters. Rousseau said in that letter: "The French have no music of their own, they cannot have any, and if one day they were to succeed in creating one, it would be a calamity...." It is quite impossible to render even an approximate account of the intrigues accompanying the fight. We shall confine ourselves to mentioning the fact that bloody street fighting occurred between Gluckists and Piccinists.

Two of Gluck's masterpieces—*Iphigenia in Aulis* and *Iphigenia on Tauris*— finally enabled him to triumph over his exceptionally gifted rival. When he returned to Vienna, in 1780, he was able to note a great progress in the city's musical life. Regularly recurring orchestral concerts had been established, concerts such as had come into being in London a full century earlier. In Paris, where they had been introduced in 1725, they had become quite famous by the name of "Concerts spir-

65. Closing lines of a Gluck letter to the poet Klopstock, June 24, 1775.

ituals." The Vienna orchestra had acquired the new Mannheim technique. Active at the time in that culturally prominent city of Germany were a number of "modern" musicians who worked unceasingly at the development of the orchestra and of symphonic forms of composition. Their spiritual head was a highly gifted Bohemian conductor, Johann Stamitz (1717-1757). The contribution of the Mannheimers to the development of the sonata and symphony, as well as the revolutionary introduction of the orchestral crescendo in place of the formerly used abrupt change from piano to forte, made possible in many respects the ultimate perfection given to the orchestral style by Haydn.

Keeping step with all these improvements, the taste of the Viennese had also become more mature. They respected Gluck's reforms, although they did not quite agree with some of their details. At any rate, whenever they wanted to have a good time, they unashamedly went to hear some Italian opera. Gluck died in 1787, the first great musician to lay the foundation to Vienna's fame as a city of music.

In that year, Haydn, steadily rising to fame, was already fifty-five, Mozart thirty-one—but he had only four more years to live. Most clearly mirrored in the music of these two is the aristocratic-gallant style of the time. Both, however, have furnished irrefutable proof of the fact that even the most profound human suffering and the emotions of a whole world may be expressed in this occasionally superficial style.

Five years later, a revolutionary genius was to enter Vienna's musical life: Beethoven. Coming from his Rhenish homeland, he was never to leave Vienna again. And ten years later, in a wretched suburb of the same city, the divinely gifted creator of the Lied was to be born.

For thirty-one years, Franz Schubert was to walk through the streets of Vienna, an unknown, practically, to the day of his premature death.

Vienna happened to experience one of the most brilliant theatrical epochs at the time of Beethoven and Schubert. The Kärntnertor Theater was subsidized by the court, as was its successor, the Imperial Opera. (Much later, it became the State Opera.) In 1822, Barbaja, one of the cleverest theatrical men of Europe, was summmoned to Vienna. His had been a fantastic career: waiter—circus director—theatrical impresario. At one time, he was General Manager both in Vienna and at the Scala of Milan. In spite of his Italian orientation in operatic matters, Vienna and the German-language musical drama were indebted to him for the launching of a number of important works. He commissioned Weber to write his *Euryanthe* and Schubert his *Fierrabras.* At the rival "Theater an der Wien," too, (since the destruction of the State Opera in 1945, it has been the scene of Vienna's operatic activities) highly important first performances took place. Among them was Mozart's *Magic Flute* (one of the old theater's doors is still known as "Papageno Gate," after that opera's most popular figure) and Beethoven's *Fidelio* during the time of the French occupation; Spohr's *Faust;* Rossini's world-electrifying *Barber of Seville* (1819); an early Meyerbeer (1820); Spontini's *Fernand Cortéz* (1823); and finally, hardly more successful than *Fierrabras* at the other house, Schubert's *Rosamunde.*

Old chronicles have rather curious things to report of Vienna's concert activities. As credible a witness as Hanslick—the same who later so fiercely, and yet in so scholarly a manner, attacked Wagner and Bruckner while at the same time making Brahms his idol—stated that in the days of his boyhood rehearsing for orchestral concerts was an almost unheard of procedure. Just think of a work like Beethoven's "Ninth," which today must be accurately rehearsed over and over again by professional orchestras, having to be played at sight by amateurs. We are told, for instance, that weekday concerts were given in the Prater—at seven in the morning, and that it was a most rare occurrence to find an entire symphony on a concert program. The first movement of one symphony was often followed by the last of another, and preferably divided by an Italian coloratura aria. And today we have become so strict that we do not even permit applause between the movements of a symphonic work!

The Vienna musicians became organized as early as 1771. They formed the *Tonkünstlersozietät* (Musical Artists' Society). As always when artists band together, they outbungled even the most case-hardened bureaucrats. Mozart, for instance, could not be admitted because of his inability to furnish a long-lost baptismal certificate. Lanner, co-creator of the Vienna waltz, was coolly blackballed because of his "association with the dance." And Haydn? The most famous musician of his day had to wait a long time for his admission. Later, it was only through the annual benefit performances of his oratorios that the chronically anemic exchequer of the *Sozietät* found some sustenance.

Ever since the days of the famous Congress, which put an end to the Napoleonic wars and which, according to the assertion of a contemporary, "danced, but made no progress," Vienna was engulfed in a giant wave of popular music. Starting in the suburbs, it slowly but surely captured even the "genteel" center of the city. Its reign was to last almost a hundred years, and the name of its dynasty was Strauss. Stopping but briefly, or remaining for a longer stay, almost all the masters of romanticism passed through the gay city: Weber, Schumann, Chopin, Liszt, Wagner. There the last of the great symphonists settled: Brahms, Bruckner, Mahler. There, at the turn of the century, Hugo Wolf sang his unhappy songs; and there, for quite some time, lived Richard Strauss.

In Vienna there was a concurrence of all the factors which, in their blending, make a city into a real cultural center: giftedness and idealism on the part of the people, an attitude of understanding and generosity on the part of the leading class, and intelligence on the part of those who ruled. Throughout all upheavals and changes, through the time of the French Revolution, the French Empire and the Napoleonic Wars, the foreign occupation, the Congress, the period of political reaction, the revolution of 1848, the age of the machine and increasing materialism—throughout all this, Vienna as a musical center remained unaffected, for a century-and-a-half. So saturated with melodies did the air seem that foreign journalists, musicians, poets, philosophers, politicians, statesmen, and business people found but one expression to characterize Vienna: the city of music.

· 13 ·

Haydn: or Serene Tranquillity

MUCH was said in the preceding chapters about Vienna's palaces, and about the city's gallant music. But now, when we are about to speak of the composers usually called the "Vienna Classics," we must mention the considerably more modest buildings in which these masters were born and in which they lived while their music lent enchantment to the life in the palaces. Joseph Haydn was born in a farmhouse in the Burgenland province, while Mozart came into the world in the home of a rather humble musical official in the old Episcopal see of Salzburg. Beethoven's home surroundings in Bonn can hardly be called other than poor, nor were living conditions in Schubert's parental home any better.

Not one of these geniuses lay in the cradle of luxury, and it may be asserted generally that but few great musicians were born into wealth and a carefree existence. But perhaps the very fact of having to struggle through life enabled them to experience their inspirations and to achieve the clarity of their immortal works.

The first of the Vienna Classics was Haydn, born in the year 1732. The general public did not consider him an "interesting" musician. He was no child prodigy, like Mozart, to make the world marvel; no fighter, like Beethoven, who frantically tugged at the gates of fate; no tragic personality, like Schubert, who dwelt in obscurity throughout his life. And yet, the story of his existence reads like a fanciful tale, an eloquent example of what forces in the human mind may be called awake through the pursuance of a lofty ideal. It was a long and rocky road, for Haydn owed his rise solely to his own character, his work and talent.

Joseph Haydn was born in Rohrau, a small village near the Austro-Hungarian border [Pl. 65], not far from another village, Raiding, where, three-quarters of a century later, Liszt was born. Folk-like traits of both races mingled in that section. Haydn's work revealed traces of this fact, although they were not nearly so clearly defined as those which

112

characterized Liszt's music. Haydn was a true child of the people. His simple manner, free from all vanity, gained him sympathies everywhere. His father was a wheelwright and a great lover of music; his mother, a cook who had a fine voice. Music and singing thus sounded at the cradle of Joseph and of his brother Michael, who also became an excellent musician.

Haydn received his first schooling at Hainburg, a small town on the Danube, where a relative lived. But the man's educational method seemed to have consisted more of blows than of music, and so it was a deliverance when one day the head of the Vienna Boy Singers passed through Hainburg, heard little Haydn sing, and forthwith took him along to the glamorous capital of the Empire. For a number of years, then, Haydn sang in the choir of St. Stephen's or participated in palace concerts. He heard a great deal of music, and was happy. However, a boy's voice has but a brief natural life. Adolescence not only deprived young Haydn of his livelihood but of the very roof over his head.

It was a lonely lad of eighteen who wandered through the streets of the big city and started to take up the fight, not so much for his daily bread, which was a secondary consideration, but for his ideal to become a musician and composer. He managed to earn a little money by copying music, and by playing the violin at suburban dances. Slowly, very

66. Kyrie eleison from Haydn's manuscript of the "Missa brevis."

slowly, his material circumstances improved. He finally succeeded in gaining the confidence of a distinguished Italian vocal teacher, Porpora by name, whose pupils he was permitted to accompany on the cembalo. As ill luck would have it, he happened into the home of Keller, a suburban barber, while hunting for a room. It was not his ill luck that he fell in love with the man's daughter, but that—out of sheer gratitude, it was said —he married her sister. Rarely are chronicles as uniform as in the case of Anna Maria Haydn, who is reported to have been the worst imaginable shrew a man could have married. He bore with her for forty long years.

Hadyn obtained his first position as a musician at the Bohemian castle of Count Morzin. There he composed his first symphony, the first of more than a hundred. It is frequently, and erroneously, assumed that a genius is born a master. No, Haydn's youthful works, like those of most novices, plainly showed his immaturity. He was lacking not only in routine but also in theoretical knowledge. But Haydn was one of those who never rest. Since there was nobody in sight to teach him counterpoint and harmony, there was nothing he could do but learn them by himself.

This he did so thoroughly that, as early as 1761, one of Europe's most famous amateurs and patrons of the arts, Prince Esterhazy, summoned him to join his private orchestra in Eisenstadt. Haydn's position was that of assistant conductor. He was to live the major part of his life in the livery of the Esterhazys. In 1776, he was made first conductor and so became the leader of one of the best European orchestras of that time. To his guidance were entrusted about thirty musicians. For them he composed work upon work—in accordance with his contractual obligations. He himself copied out the voices, took charge of the rehearsals during the week, and, on Sundays and holidays, conducted the festive concerts attended by invited guests from near and far. Among them were the leading personages of the realm, foreign potentates, and at times even the Empress from Vienna. They were all astounded by the high standard of the music presented to them at the Esterhazy palace, and the Prince himself was not a little proud of his conductor who could write all those beautiful overtures, symphonies, concertos, suites, minuets, and serenades, yes even the little operas produced in the castle's theater [Pl. 69], to say nothing of the hundreds of compositions written for the personal use of the Prince who was an excellent performer on the barytone, the name given to the noble-sounding precursor of the cello.

It is thus understandable why the number of Haydn's compositions is so stupendously large and, by the same token, why they cannot be expected to be of uniformly high quality. He who has to work at someone's behest and not because of an inward urge cannot always be inspired. The exact number of his works is not known. Much, undoubtedly, has become lost, mainly because Haydn did not affix his signature to works written for a particular occasion, since he could not have foreseen their future importance.

The Esterhazy Castle Orchestra was dissolved after the death of Prince Nikolaus, in 1790. Haydn received a pension and was permitted to retain the title of a Princely Conductor, Composer, and Chamber Musician. He decided to spend his declining years in Vienna. There, a surprise awaited him: without knowing it, he had become a celebrity. In the course of the almost thirty years of his activity at the Esterhazy Castle, so many visitors had become acquainted with his work that there was hardly a place in Europe to which his fame had not penetrated. The Imperial Court and the public paid him marked respect and reverence. European capitals demanded his presence. He dedicated six new symphonies to Paris and also accepted an invitation tendered by England, where honors were heaped on him. The venerable University of Oxford conferred on him the unusual title of "Honorary Doctor of Music." But when the Dean referred to him as the greatest living composer, he declined this distinction gravely, but with conviction. There were others, he said, as great as he, and especially one who was far greater. His name was Mozart, and he, too, lived in Vienna. The English took this as the expression of a great man's modesty, having long since forgotten the child prodigy who, twenty-five years before, had been so loudly acclaimed in their country.

Hadyn, at the age of sixty, was at the height of his creative power. His *London* and *Oxford* symphonies, which he had just then dedicated to the English, were truly admirable. Returning to Vienna by the Rhine route, he passed through Bonn. There a youth was presented to him who submitted to the master some of his musical attempts. Haydn encouraged him, thought that the compositions showed talent, and added that, should the young man ever come to Vienna, he would gladly reveal to him the secrets of composition. How could he have foreseen that this moment would change the course of a human life, perhaps even that of musical history? Soon the young musician actually journeyed to Vienna,

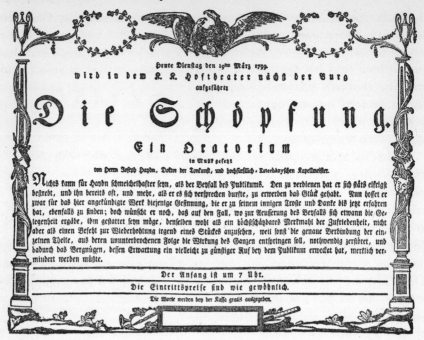

67. Announcement of first performance of Haydn's "Creation," March 19, 1799. The composer requests that the public refrain from insisting that any number be encored, lest the continuous flow of music be interrupted.

but his studies with Haydn were of short duration and rather unsatisfactory. Two worlds, two generations, clashed, and one could not understand the other: the world of Hadyn and that of Beethoven.

In 1794, Haydn paid a second visit to England. His success was even more pronounced, if that were possible. But only after he had returned to his homeland did the most important works of his life, the oratorios *The Creation* (1798) and *The Seasons* (1804), mature in the mind of the aging master. This was a veritable miracle, vouchsafed to but a very few of the great: not only to have preserved one's creative power, but, at the age of three-score-and-ten, to be able to tread new paths instead of repeating old successes. While the former of the two great works still clung to the Bible, the latter consciously entered the realm of the secular oratorio. Unmistakable is the deep impression made on Handel's *Messiah* in London.

We are approaching the end of a rich life. Haydn's figure had become popular in Vienna. The man who had once been a poor peasant child, the son of a wheelwright, now received the homage of the great of his day, had a house of his own in the capital, and a modest fortune, too. He was, by the way, the only one of the Vienna Classics who had known how to solve his financial problems. Mozart died in abject poverty, Beethoven's life was a constant financial up-and-down, and Schubert never had the faintest idea of the value of money.

Haydn, a most zealous Austrian patriot, the man who had given to his country its magnificent national hymn, had to witness, in the evening of his life, the capital's occupation by the French and the exile of the Emperor. But the Corsican who drove out the aristocrats bowed to the genius: he placed an honor guard at the gate of Haydn's house.

On March 27, 1808, Haydn once more appeared in public. He witnessed a performance of his *Creation* at one of the so-called "Cavaliers' Concerts" given at the University and attended by the heads of the Empire. Prince Esterhazy sent his own carriage for him. It drew up before the University building, and it seemed as if everybody of any importance in the

A V V I S O.

Oggi Venerdì 8. del corrente Gennajo la Sigra. Maria Bolla, virtuosa di Musica, darà una Accademia nella piccola Sala del Ridotto. La Musica sarà di nuova composizione del Sigre. Haydn, il quale ne sarà alla direzione.

Vi canteranno la Sigra. Bolla, la Sigra. Tomeoni, e il Sigre. Mombelli.

Il Sigre. Bethofen suonerà un Concerto sul Pianoforte.

Il prezzo dei biglietti d'ingresso sarà di uno zecchino. Questi potranno aversi o alla Cassa del Teatro Nazionale, o in casa della Sigra. Bolla, nella Parisergasse Nro. 444. al secondo piano.

Il principio sarà alle ore sei e mezza.

68. Announcement of a Vienna concert of the year 1796, in which Haydn and Beethoven are to participate.

country had assembled to receive him, including musicians—Beethoven among them. Yet Haydn was able to listen to but part of the concert. When, supported by friends, he had to leave the hall, all those near him kissed his hands. They seemed to realize that they would not see him alive again.

The French were still in the city when Haydn died, on May 31, 1809. At the funeral ceremonies the immortal requiem was sung which, eighteen years before, had been given to the world by the genius whom

Haydn himself had pronounced the greatest living musician: Mozart.

If we are truly to understand Haydn's music, we must—as always—put ourselves back into the epoch which gave it birth. It was the time of the powdered wig, of the irreproachable form, of the strict ceremony governing every motion. It was therefore also the time of precisely measured music, whose symmetrical proportions must never be shattered by the great outbursts of passion which, shortly thereafter, were to form the chief characteristic of the romantic style. And yet, especially in the lyric parts, we feel the beat of a compassionate heart to which no human woe was alien.

Haydn outlived his time. His life and work still belonged to the pre-revolutionary epoch. In spite of the numerous and important innovations revealed by his music, he was by no means a revolutionary. He could not, would not, be one. He had grown by a process of slow and steady development, had placed stone upon stone, had now and then dimly foreseen romantic ideas, had set against absolute music many a programmatic page dealing with the description of natural scenes and the like, and had been the first to give in many of his scores musical expression to a sunny sense of humor. But all without revolution. And at the very last, he had in his oratorios entered a realm already permeated with the spirit of a new era. Without violating any of the old laws, these oratorios went far beyond palace music and formed the first bridge leading to the people.

Soon, quite soon, there was to come one—he already lived in the same city—who would tear to pieces the musical laws, just as the Revolution had torn the social laws. A giant was to fling open the gates of a new century: Beethoven.

69. Visiting card used for his intimates by the aged Haydn: "Gone is all my strength, Old and weak am I."

70. From Mozart's London Sketchbook.

· 14 ·

Mozart: or The Divine Spark

ONE day, the gods felt whimsical. They centered all the qualities of genius, of sublimity, of gloriousness, in a child, lifting him and leading him by mysterious paths to perfection. They used him to spread an immeasurable amount of happiness over generations. The whim was magnificent, and cruel at the same time. For it included the granting to the chosen one of but a few—ah, how very few!—years of life. It permitted his sensitive soul to experience all the trials and tribulations of the world and let him be consumed by his own flame.

Mozart's earthly existence lasted thirty-five years. These thirty-five years sufficed to let him run the gamut from nothingness to glory, and from glory to debasement; and they sufficed to give to a world which did not understand him eight hundred works, every single one of which was superlative in its realm, be it opera, symphony, instrumental piece, chamber music, or religious work. Probably no other master of such versatility has ever existed.

He had hardly reached the age of six when the wondrous wellspring of his art began to flow, and only death could make it run dry. In other lives, whose span permits sufficient time for an organic development, periods of creation, of tension, and of inspiration are relieved by those of tranquility, of relaxation, and of preparation. But in a meteoric life, such as Mozart's, Schubert's, Bizet's, and Purcell's, some secret organ, sensing an early death, seems to bring about a forcible synchronization of the body with the restless spirit until everything has been created that a superior power wants in so mysterious a way to bestow upon the world.

People have wondered about the puzzle presented by the child prodigy. Whence comes this perplexing strength, this strange maturity? Once only did the writer hear an explanation. It was given him by a wise man from the Orient and, in the absence of literal explanation, it may be mentioned here. Every man has an immortal soul, the wise man said. It returns to earth after death, in search of another body, which it tries to carry a step farther on the road to perfection. During this time between death and re-birth, the soul forgets everything it knew in its previous existence. But sometimes, very rarely, the soul forgets to forget. Mozart's soul, in a former life, undoubtedly belonged to a musician, and it had not forgotten. . . .

Wolfgang Amadeus Mozart was born in Salzburg, the enchanting Austrian Alpine town, on January 27, 1756. The place represents a direct point of confluence of Romanic and Germanic cultures. Its population is cheerful and its melodies have the crystalline serenity of the mountain lakes and the sunny summits surrounding them. These facts account for one of the components of Mozart's work; the social conditions of his time account for another.

Mozart's father, Leopold, in addition to being an excellent violinist and the author of a violin primer, was one of the many people in the

71. Mozart at the age of 29. Silhouette by H. Löschenkohl.

service of the Archbishop, whose palace represented the cultural and political center of the town. Seven children were born to Leopold and his wife, but only two survived, Maria Anna, known as "Nannerl," and Wolfgang Amadeus [Pl. 68]. They grew up in the old house standing to this day near the bank of the Salzach. Early in their lives—(Wolfgang at three)—they revealed remarkable musical talents. When Wolfgang was six and Nannerl eleven, they undertook their first musical journey, to present themselves to the "great world" [Pl. 70]. That was in 1762.

Munich and Vienna were the first stages on this truly triumphal tour. Wolfgang played the cembalo, the violin, and the organ. He proved himself a masterful improvisor on any theme given him.

The child prodigy aroused enthusiasm in all music circles and attracted the attention of the Court. A "command performance" was a huge success.

In the following year the children journeyed to Paris, always guided by their father. On the way, they stopped for concerts at many towns and palaces. In Frankfort, the young Goethe was profoundly impressed by Wolfgang. (Nearly half a century later, he was to meet another musical prodigy who reminded him of the former: Mendelssohn.) Other stages of the journey were Stuttgart, Mainz, Koblenz, Aachen, and Brussels, extraordinary distances for a child, especially in the days of the mail coach. These exertions, combined with the constant high tension caused by concerts, receptions, festivities, and examinations, may have contributed to the undermining of little Mozart's health.

In Paris, the boy of seven published his first compositions. The title page stated his age and the place of his birth. Covered with glory, the Mozart family continued its journey to London, where new triumphs were reaped and where Wolfgang dedicated six sonatas to the Queen. They returned by way of Holland, Lille, Dijon, Bern, Zurich, Ulm, and Munich, arriving at Salzburg after an absence of three years.

Serious musical studies were continued under the guidance of Father Mozart. He made clever use of many advances he had observed in the course of their journeying, for he had come in contact with quite a

72. Mozart's "Bäsle" (cousin), Maria Anna Mozart, of Augsburg. Drawing by Mozart in a letter dated May 10, 1769.

number of "modern" composers, such as Johann Schober (1720-1767) in Paris—a man wholly forgotten today—and the exceptionally spirited "London" Bach, Johann Christian (1735-1782), the youngest son of the St. Thomas cantor.

The year 1767 found the Mozart family again in Vienna, where Wolfgang, at the age of eleven, had his first experience with human wickedness and professional envy. Calumnies and accusations were launched, and it took a long time to silence them. It was hinted that the father, and not the son, was the author of the compositions. Wolfgang had to pass through many a trial until he was believed. Nevertheless, the jealousy of his colleagues rose to further heights when the Emperor commissioned the boy to write an opera. It was not to be the last time in his life that bribed impresarios and artists purposely singing poorly tried to ruin his work.

After a brief stay in his native town, Mozart set out on the journey which was still considered the most important for a musician of his day: to Italy. There, too, the boy had to submit to rigorous examinations. The foremost musicians wished to convince themselves personally of his talent. Locked in a room, and kept in strict seclusion, he wrote any and all musical forms demanded of him and improvised on any given theme. The masters stood agape. Never had they seen anything like it.

Mozart was fourteen when his first grand opera *Mitridate, Re di Ponto,* was performed at the Scala of Milan. It was naturally written wholly in the Italian style, like most of his stage works. We should not expect this *Mitridate* to be a masterpiece in the sense of the modern opera, which requires considerably more than just beautiful melodies. How could a child have credibly set to music emotions with which he was not as yet acquainted? The Italian opera of that time did not stress psychological depth. Gluck's reforms had only just begun, and they never made much headway in Italy anyway. Mozart still had a long road to travel—not in his technical ability, which was exceptional even in 1770, but in vital experience—before he arrived at his masterpieces: *The Marriage of Figaro, Don Giovanni,* and *The Magic Flute.* The Milan performance was nevertheless a great success and created a sensation all over Europe. When further triumphs were added in Bologna, Rome, and Naples, Mozart's celebrity had reached its apex. Hasse, a prominent operatic composer of that time, said: "This child will cause us all to be forgotten . . ."

Mozart's return to Salzburg was marked by a humiliating experience. The Archbishop, irked by the boy's continued absence, tried to treat him as he would have treated a disobedient lackey. The ensuing breach with Salzburg was painful, but final. More journeys, more successes—but they grew less radiant, less enduring, as time went on. It is sad to observe how this life, which had started out with such unparalleled brilliance, gradually lost its luster now that a wonderful maturity was

73. Program of the first performance of "Don Giovanni" in Prague.

slowly taking the place of youthful exuberance. Soon, the very same cities which, but a few years before, had so jubilantly acclaimed him, hardly noticed his presence. The success of his works did not greatly differ from the more or less customary success of Italian operatic works in an age of mass production: praised today, forgotten tomorrow.

In Mannheim, Mozart fell in love with a beautiful young singer, but his father, still the counsellor and teacher of his children, advised against an early marriage. It was years later that Mozart married—the sister of his first love. A duplication, this, of the case of Haydn, although this time it turned out more happily. Constanze Weber proved herself a good companion to Mozart, though not an ideal one. But how could an ideal one have been found for a Mozart? The letters Wolfgang wrote to his wife from his travels were exquisite. They breathed tenderness and kindness and revealed a maturity attained by way of many disappointments. "To gain Heaven," he once wrote, "is splendid and sublime, but here on dear Earth, too, it is wonderful . . ." Fundamentally, in everything he did or said, he was gay, youthful, witty, and hopeful to the day of his death.

Another ten years, and the tragic event was to occur. But they were the years of his greatest works. Mozart now lived in Vienna whose musical life was governed by a small Italian clique. His financial circumstances grew worse from day to day. His *Abduction from the Seraglio*, that enchanting musical play which formed a milestone in the history of

. 123

the German opera, would not have been produced had it not been for the Emperor's explicit order. And in 1786, his *Marriage of Figaro*, the most ingenius musical comedy since the days of Pergolesi, became a noisy failure, mainly because the singers deliberately sang off-key.

Not until the opera was performed in Prague was the true value of this masterpiece revealed. In gratitude, Mozart dedicated to that city his next work, *Don Giovanni*, which also made a profound impression. [Ill. 73 & 74].

There followed the death of his father who, foregoing successes of his own, had dedicated his life to the service of his children, and especially of Wolfgang. His mother had died nine years before, while accompanying her famous son on a tour of Paris.

Shortly after the Prague performance, the Vienna premiere of *Don Giovanni* took place. It was another incomprehensible failure. Mozart

74. Luigi Bassi, the first interpreter of Don Giovanni at the initial performance in Prague, 1787.

had come to be considered second-rate by Vienna's musical circles, while others, whose names have long since been forgotten, were permitted to take themselves seriously and bask in the sun of success. One last journey was undertaken by Mozart, in 1789. He appeared at the Courts of Dresden and Berlin and rendered homage to the spirit of Bach by playing on the master's own organ in Leipzig's St. Thomas Church. The King of Prussia offered Mozart a leading position at his Court, but Mozart declined. It was the only befitting offer in Mozart's whole life.

Did he still hope for recognition in his own fatherland? Of the many musical positions available in the imperial city, at the Court, in theaters

75. Mozart's manuscript of the "Marriage of Figaro," Act II, finale.

and churches, Mozart could not obtain a single one. Insignificant titles and still more insignificant sums of money—that was all Vienna had to offer him. But his cup of humiliation not as yet drained, the worst was still to come.

His comic opera *Così fan tutte* had its initial performance in 1790. So Italian is it in its spirit that the original Italian title has been maintained to this day in all parts of the world. But it is typically Italian also with respect to its impossible libretto which only the incomparable brilliance and gracefulness of Mozart's music was able to vitalize. He dedicated his last Italian opera, *La Clemenza di Tito*, to Prague in the following year. The same year also witnessed the Vienna performance of the last stage work of his life, *The Magic Flute*. This German opera is extraordinary in every respect. Musically, it was a precursor of *Fidelio* and *Freischütz*. In text, it deviated from every accepted standard by using a libretto whose rather childlike figures and exceptional symbolism served to mask problems which only an initiated Freemason could possibly understand. No less a personage than Goethe was so enchanted by this ap-

. 125

parently childishly naive libretto that he contemplated writing a second part. The music of *The Magic Flute* is so full of graciousness and wisdom, of wit and human feeling, that it seems like a self-portrait of Mozart [Pl. 72].

The success of *The Magic Flute* was considerable, though it was due to its comic rather than to its serious parts. Mozart lived at that time in wretched quarters near the "Theater an der Wien" where the work was staged night after night. Only rarely was he able to attend a performance, since he was confined to his bed most of the time. But with childlike pleasure he listened to the accounts of his friends who called on him late at night to inform him which aria had been most liberally applauded and which numbers had had to be repeated.

Strewn about his sickbed lay sheets of music at which he worked with what strength was left him. It was his *Requiem*, the purest and most mature work he had ever written [Pl. 71]. He was not able to complete it. (His pupil, Süssmayer, added the final page.) On December 5, 1791, at a time when the success of *The Magic Flute* was still mounting and the librettist Schikaneder, who was both the manager of the theater and the opera's principal performer, was reaping a golden harvest, Mozart died in abject poverty.

They laid him to rest on December 8. It was a cold rainy winter day. Only a handful of friends accompanied the coffin to the church. From there to the cemetery not a single human being followed the miserable vehicle carrying to their last resting place the six plain boards enclosing the mortal remains of Mozart. Only a dog proved his loyalty to the last. He is plainly discernible on a contemporary picture as the lone mourner.

As there was no money for a private burial ground, Mozart's body was dumped into a common grave. It was some time before his widow, recovered from illness, could visit the cemetery. Furthermore, the attendant, who was the only person able to tell with certainty where Mozart had been interred, died in the meantime so that his grave has never been found.

But nobody is dead as long as his works continue to live. No sooner had Mozart died than humanity seemed to realize the irretrievable loss it had sustained. His works were collected, his life studied, his letters published, streets and squares named after him, statues were erected to his memory. Salzburg, his native town, organized the famous Festival

Plays in his honor. On the money spent there by a single visitor, Mozart could have lived a month without care and oppression.

Mozart's work is so gigantic that it can be touched but lightly here. The place of honor, at the side of his operas, must be accorded to his numerous symphonies, especially the later ones, and among these, again, to the three which, in the course of a single summer, that of 1788, he conceived as a magnificent trypitch: those in E-flat major, in G minor, and in C major, the Jupiter Symphony. His chamber music, too, must be counted among the rarest gems of this branch of musical literature; and in his *Requiem* he attained heights which few mortals have been permitted to scale.

"A genius, that is one who can be harmed by no teacher," Mozart once said. Let us add: And by no fate either!

76. Mozart's manuscript of the symphony in G minor, 3rd movement, minuet.

Beethoven: or The Lonely Rebel

NO artist, perhaps, has succeeded more in stirring the imagination of mankind than Beethoven. Why has his personality been able to rouse so extraordinary an echo?

Is it because in every sensitive person among us there is a string which is set to vibrating by his music? Because he expressed that which we all are yearning for? Because we admire the superhuman effort, the indomitable will, the superlative strength which enabled the ceaseless struggler to create his own laws of life? Or because we realize the abysmal tragedy which must have engulfed his melancholy existence?

It would seem that Beethoven's work makes one feel two things above all: freedom and loneliness. He had to be a rebel to fight his way through to freedom; and his heart had to be filled to overflowing with love of humanity lest he perish in his loneliness.

His works send forth the light showing the way into the labyrinth of his great soul. His letters, too, are revealing. We have moreover the staggering document represented by his "conversation pads": 11,000 pages, written from 1816 to his death; one thousand pages a year, one thousand pages by means of which he kept up the contact with the surrounding world and on which visitors and friends had to write questions which his ear had long ceased to hear. And finally there exists still another equally heart-rending testimonial from his own hand: his diary.

The deeper we delve into these sources, the more confused become our impressions, the more conflicting his personality. A man who carries the universe in his soul can never twice appear the same. The essence of genius, which to ordinary man seems unfathomable, is like a gem whose thousands of facets sparkle differently, depending upon the light that strikes them. Who dares say: I know him; I understand him?

It was Schopenhauer who expressed the cruel truth: "The inward agony of the genius is the womb of immortal works."

Ludwig van Beethoven was born in Bonn on the Rhine, on December 16, 1770 [Pl. 80]. He was the son of a mediocre tenor, whose vices greatly outweighed his virtues, and of a cook, whose tenderness and kindness were the light of his childhood. His musical impulses became apparent at an early age. It was in 1778 that his father first presented him to the public as a pianist. The announcements tell of his *Soehngen*—a dialectal diminutive of son—"of six years," although he had already reached the age of eight. It was evident that the shining example of Mozart would not let Beethoven's father rest.

Beethoven's first compositions were published in 1783. They were the result of serious studies with a good teacher, Christian Neefe (1748-1798), who revealed to the boy the then still rather unknown wonders of Bach's world and, in addition, taught him the works of Mozart, Haydn, and Clementi. The title page of this first edition shows the same "mistake" concerning the composer's age and it likewise found its way into a newspaper appeal published by Neefe in behalf of his pupil. The appeal was intended to raise the means that would enable the wholly destitute boy to make an educational journey.

77. Beethoven at 16, as "Electoral Cologne Chamber Musician." Silhouette by Nessen.

Bonn had a cultured society and a good theater. The proximity of France made possible a quick contact with the new ideas launched there. And so Beethoven was alive to the great revolution, which influenced his whole being. Rousseau's cry "Back to nature!" also made a deep impression on the sensitive boy. From then on, democracy was to represent his political ideal and to find its most profound expression in his music. For what he wrote was music for all the people, no longer for a certain class. He wanted to express in sound the emotions and the yearnings of all humanity. He was the first free artist, independent in his creative work from outward compulsion, no longer a musical employee of feudalism as Bach and Haydn had been. He reached the goal which Mozart's early demise had not permitted him to attain. He was the first to write purely subjective music and who, whenever he considered it necessary for the expression of his thoughts, did not hesitate to run counter to established theoretical rules. His works were inspired by deeply human problems, far removed from those which had agitated the age of the powdered wig.

His burning desire for freedom and truth found expression even in those youthful days in Bonn, when he stated in his diary the motto of his life: "Do good wherever you can, love freedom above everything, uphold truth even before the throne."

Neefe's appeal was successful, and so we see Beethoven set out on his first journey to the banks of the Danube, in 1787. We know that the

78. Beethoven's manuscript of his song "I love you."

Vienna of those days resounded with music, that orchestras and chamber music flourished in the palaces, and that the city had become the musical center of Europe. To begin with, however, Beethoven did not see much of all this. Before he was able to make any decisions concerning his future, the impending death of his beloved mother called him back to Bonn.

Home conditions now became even more unbearable, and the dream of an international career had to be abandoned. Beethoven had to make up his mind to accept some musical job in his native city. But fate had ordained for him something else, bigger and more painful at the same time. He met Haydn, and all the dreams and possibilities were once more awakened in him.

An Austrian aristocrat of noble rank and spirit, Count Waldstein, made possible another journey to Vienna. He gave him many letters of introduction—whose curious effect we shall soon see—and wrote him a few truly prophetic lines: "My dear Beethoven," they ran, "You are now going to Vienna in fulfillment of long entertained wishes. Mozart's guiding spirit is still mourning him. The inexhaustible Haydn has given him refuge, but no work. Through him (Haydn), he wishes once more to be united to somebody. By the exertion of unremitting zeal you will receive: *Mozart's spirit from Haydn's hands.*"

Was it Mozart's spirit for which Beethoven searched? He did not find it through Haydn. An abyss separated the two generations. Besides, the lessons given Beethoven by the aging master were but few.

Waldstein's letters of introduction caused Beethoven to be cordially received in Vienna's most distinguished homes. He was a frequent visitor at the palaces in which Haydn had rarely set foot, Mozart and Schubert never. The democrat, the revolutionary, the foreigner, the young man with a rather poor upbringing and an arbitrary and capricious disposition, gained the unconditional moral and material support of the highest aristocratic circles. More than that, he found in them true friends and devoted followers.

And yet, not for a moment was he untrue to his convictions. To his pupil, the Archduke Rudolf, he remarked: "Freedom and progress are the purpose of art and of all life." The great rebels were his idols. He dedicated an overture to Prometheus, considered a symbol by all revolutionary fighters for liberty. He inscribed his third symphony, the Eroica, to Napoleon but tore up the dedication in a rage when told of the imperial coronation: "Is he too nothing but an ordinary man? Now he too will trample underfoot all human rights and live only for his ambitions. He will place himself above everybody else and become a tyrant!" Strange words to be uttered in the Imperial City of Vienna!

But his aristocratic friends did not let him down. They tried their best to understand him and to further his purposes. They arranged concerts for him, seeing to it that all available tickets had been taken up beforehand, and they banded together to have his compositions published at once. In 1800, Prince Lichnowsky assured him of an annual stipend of 600 Gulden, the only condition being that Beethoven remain in Vienna and reject Jerôme Bonaparte's summons to the Court of Kassel.

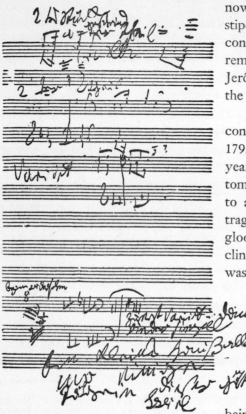

79. A characteristic page from Beethoven's sketchbook.

Beethoven had given his first concert in Vienna in the year 1795. But in the very following year, he noticed the first symptoms of the affliction which was to affect his whole future life, a tragedy that steeped in perpetual gloom a character naturally inclined toward melancholy. He was growing deaf! After the first crisis, which brought him to the brink of insanity and almost caused him to commit suicide, he took up the fight against fate, the heroic struggle against being drowned in despair. And he was vouchsafed a most glorious victory in his work. It seems inconceivable to us, but it is a fact: almost all of Beethoven's creations— with the exception of a few compositions of his youthful years—were the products of a sick man, a deaf man.

"I am happy only when I have overcome a difficulty . . ." he confided to his diary. And yet, his growing loneliness, rising like an invisible dividing wall round about him, was a horrible trial to him. Like all the great lonely ones, he felt the strong urge to open his heart to his fellow-man, to commune with him. In his soul rose a mountain of aimless love, of which the affecting "Heiligenstadt Testament" furnished eloquent evidence.

Beethoven, to whom the doors of Vienna's most brilliant salons were open and who was revered by the city's most cultured set, slowly, but steadily, withdrew from all social life. He became ever more unapproachable, more misanthropic. His was not the loneliness of Mozart, brought about by the shameful neglect of the world; not the loneliness of Schubert who lived forever in a world of dreams. "For you, poor Beethoven, there is no happiness from outside; you must create everything from within yourself, and only in the world of ideals will you find friends." Thus he wrote at one time.

How many attempts—too many!—have been made to penetrate into Beethoven's emotional life, to define his attitude toward the problem of the eternal feminine. He left us nothing to guide our steps; nothing but an entry in his diary (1817) in which he implores God to let him at last be happy in real love; nothing but the famous words of the "Immortal Beloved" contained in the dedication of one of his compositions; nothing but the three love letters whose addressee is unknown. There is much to support the contention that Therese Brunswick was the great love of his life, and not Giulietta Guicciardi, as was assumed for a long time. But neither of these two, and none of those others who may have had some connection with his life,

80. Beethoven in Vienna. Drawing by J. P. Lyser.

became a true companion. To none of them was it vouchsafed to bring balm to his pain-tortured body and his inconceivably great soul.

And like all the great lonely ones, Beethoven loved nature from the very depths of his soul. In many respects, nature, in his life, took the place of religion, whose meaning to him was so wholly different from that entertained, for instance, by Bach. He himself expressed it in the words of Kant: "The starry sky above me, and the moral law within me." That was what he believed in, although he did not for a moment question the existence of God. But his was a God who did not relieve man of mundane struggles and, even less, of the struggles with one's self. Once, when a copyist brought him the score of his *Fidelio* and he found on the last page the usual words "With the help of God!" he added, not without bitterness: "O man, help thyself!"

Long walks took him out into the verdant suburbs of the city where he found peace and inspiration. No sooner had summer come, than he would move from wherever he happened to live to some small house near a vine-clad slope or at the edge of the forest. Many of his works and also the Heiligenstadt Testament, of October 6, 1802, came into being at one of these summer residences [Pl. 79 & 81]. The Pastoral Symphony reflects his great love of nature in a descriptive manner quite novel in his time and day. But let us not forget that the voices of the forest, the murmur of the brook, and the song of the birds had ceased to be proximate experiences, cheerful impressions, but merely the memories of happier days when his ear was still able to communicate these sounds to him.

Some of Beethoven's biographers—like those of many another creative genius—have asserted that there is a close interrelation between life and creative work, in the sense that creations of an optimistic character are the product of a successful and healthy time, while the tragic works coincide with a period of mental depression, of impaired health, and of increasing material anxiety. I do not believe in so direct a reflex. Take Beethoven's Ninth Symphony. Never has more rapturous joy been set to music than in the last moment of that symphony in which, contrary to all rules and standards, the ecstatic human voice is made to join the jubilation of the instruments. And let us consider a deeply moving entry in his calendar of the year 1823. There, in the very days of June when he was likely to have been at work on his gigantic masterpiece, we read: "From June 1 to 6 . . . Beastly days . . . Nothing to eat . . ."

Beethoven's affliction grew worse from year to year, and his loneliness more pronounced. The Napoleonic wars wrought many changes in the life of Vienna. The high aristocracy had followed the Emperor into exile, and the depreciation of money, an unfailing aftermath of all wars, had an adverse effect on many old fortunes. Both these circumstances affected Beethoven's fate because of his connection with the high nobility. Death, too, had thinned out his circle of friends.

The newly rich—another result of turbulent times—could not

at once reach the cultural level occupied by the former leading class. The masses, more music-mad than ever—this, too, was a consequence of existing circumstances—either continued to be enraptured by Italian opera or became devotees of the new waltz that flooded everything with its swaying three-four time. Rossini called on Beethoven upon his arrival in Vienna. He found an embittered and tired deaf man who seemed to take offense at the very fact that his visitor was triumphantly acclaimed in the streets. And the local gods of the hour were Johann Strauss and Lanner . . .

Distress came to dwell in Beethoven's house. His notes tell a sad tale of the unreliability of copyists, of his constant dissatisfaction with the servants, hired and fired almost every week, of the unpleasant circumstances which burdened him with the guardianship of his nephew, of hundreds of vexations and difficulties, of his distrust of all who were about him, of financial annoyances, of housing problems, and of illness.

But the same hand that chronicled the disagreeable events of everyday life was also writing page upon page of musical sketches, in every one of which tradition was swept aside and new ways were explored. No longer could his ideas be expressed in the carefully measured forms of Haydn and Mozart. Beethoven's work was the bridge leading from the musical rococo, to which his early work obviously still belonged, to romanticism with its new content and its new forms. But it was even more than that. Beethoven was responsible not only for the expansion of the symphonic structure, for the inclusion of the human voice in what had until them been a purely instrumental form, for the creation of a new piano technique, for the arbitrary increase or reduction of the movements of a cyclical form, but, strictly speaking, he had also pointed the way leading to the abolition of fundamental musical laws that had been valid for hundreds of years. His last string quartets, messages already from another world, were the musical precursors of *Tristan* and of the thorough dissolution of harmony, melody, and rhythm in the twentieth century. Robert Schumann was one of the first to consider this chamber music, which even today poses grave problems, as the utmost limit so far reached by human art and imagination. He compared it, not without justification, to some of Bach's works, because there, too, "any explanation by words must fail." Bülow was another who somehow sensed the inward relationship of the two Titans when he said: "The *Well-Tempered*

Clavichord is the Old Testament, Beethoven's sonatas the New. We should believe in one as well as in the other . . ." And Wagner, who always considered Beethoven's Ninth one of the world's great musical achievements, once said: "I believe in God, Mozart, and Beethoven . . ."

Beethoven's manuscripts are perhaps the most interesting ever left by a great musician. The colossal and truly Titanic struggle Beethoven had to wage with himself on behalf of the expression of his ideas, the purity of his style, and the realization of so much that was well-nigh inexpressible, is demonstrated by the thousands of scraps of music that have been preserved. It is no exaggeration to state that Beethoven wrote, changed, cut, and corrected every one of his works twenty times over; that by the time the first sketch had ripened into the finished score hardly anything of the original form remained; that in his sketches whole

81. One of Beethoven's many sketches for the Dona-nobis-pacem part of his Missa Solemnis, with the remark: "Dona nobis pacem still in minor, since peace is asked for, hence peace individually treated, as if it had already come."

pages were at times ruthlessly condemned; and that much of what was left was erased, crossed out, or otherwise obliterated.

What to Mozart was a matter of inconceivable facility—he was able during the brief night hours in a mail coach to write the most perfect score without ever having to change a single note in it,—what to Schubert was like the dictate of a supreme power, was to Beethoven a struggle, a violent struggle, in which every foot of ground must be fought for relentlessly. Mozart composed with a smile on his lips, Schubert with the enraptured look of one lost to the world, while Beethoven had to flee the companionship of others, go into hiding, so that he might be alone with the raging torrent within him, that he might with a trembling hand and a pain-ridden face carry on the fight in which he must either conquer or be vanquished. His creative work was a mission as well as an obsession.

As late as 1814, Beethoven tried to keep his defective hearing a secret. In that year, with a superhuman effort, he gave his last piano recital in Vienna. It was eight years later that the terrible incident took place which was to weigh on his mind to the end of his days. It occurred in connection with his only opera *Fidelio*, whose very first performance, in 1805, had stood under so unlucky a star. On that occasion the audience was composed largely of French officers to whom both the idea and the language of the opera meant practically nothing. Beethoven, who never felt on secure ground where the operatic style was concerned, made a number of radical changes in his opera in the course of years. To these changes we are indebted for the three Lenora Overtures, and for the fourth, and final, one bearing the name of the work. It was the year 1822. Beethoven wanted to conduct the general rehearsal of the final version. The result was chaos. There was no contact at all between the stage and the orchestra. Uneasy and startled, everybody kept his eyes on the master who continued to conduct until, slowly, through the expression on the faces around him, the horrible truth began to dawn on him. His loyal friend Schindler (to whom we owe the description of the incident) sent him the following note: "I implore you not to continue. I shall explain everything at home." But no further explanation was necessary. A broken man, Beethoven sank into a chair, unable for many hours to rise . . .

The winter of 1826-27 came, and Beethoven felt the end approaching. But he spoke the proud words: "My work is finished . . ." The death throes started on March 24, 1827. Two days later, in the afternoon hours, while a blizzard was raging which suddenly—at the very moment of death—was accompanied by a flash of lightening and a mighty roll of thunder, the lofty soul left the tortured little body forever.

Beethoven's funeral was the very opposite of Mozart's lonely interment. All Vienna was afoot. Many thousands lined the streets, troops paid the last tribute to the honorary citizen of Vienna, and eight prominent musicians acted as pallbearers. Austria's greatest poet, Grillparzer, had written the funeral oration. It was delivered by a famous actor.

Among the solemn crowd there stood a young man who was seen frequently to wipe his eyes behind the lenses of his spectacles. But few there were in the immense cortège who knew him, and nobody realized that his yearning, the great dream of his life, had vanished: to meet Beethoven and to tell him how deeply he revered him, he the little suburban musician, Franz Schubert.

"My work is finished!" How wonderful to be able to say that at the end of a life whose motto had been: "There is much to do in this world, tarry not!"

Beethoven was thirty years old when his first symphony was performed. It was in Vienna, on April 2, 1800. In its form, it still observed the Haydn tradition. Nevertheless, here and there a new idea flashed forth, considered revolutionary by the contemporary critics. What would they have to say of his later symphonies? The four-movement rule had become universally accepted. The symphony had now reached maturity. As we have said, instrumental music first came into play as accompaniment to vocal music. Gradually it attained greater importance and composers created works exclusively for the instruments which were achieving more and more popularity. There then developed the tripartite form, called the sonata form, which in turn led to the sonata proper and symphony. The tripartite form consisted of contrasting themes, repeated alternately, and a coda or finale.

The sonata proper is a series of related movements. The symphony is really a sonata for orchestra. There must be a sprightly first movement, gay at times and heroic at others, sharply profiled in rhythm, agitated by driving forces. This first movement always had for its foundation the above-mentioned sonata form, a rather strict and complicated construction. While the masters of the eighteenth century were content at times to use only two different themes for the construction of the sonata form, it was always three-themed with Beethoven. According to the natural rule of contrast, the three themes used in the first movement of a sonata or symphony were to be as different as possible from each other. The structure of the sonata movement, established in broad lines already by Haydn and Mozart, was not essentially changed by Beethoven. This was the formula: statement (of the three themes)—development—recapitulation (or restatement)—coda. The dimensions only were considerably shifted, due to Beethoven's dramatic temperament. He favored those parts which permitted a larger amount of constructive freedom (the development, and even the coda) and accorded to them a broader space within the work than they had had before. The second movement of the symphony had no fixed form. There were those who again used the sonata form, while others preferred the simpler lines of the song. The character of the second movement within the cyclical works, comprising, as we just said, the sonata, the quartet, and the symphony, was generally maintained by Beethoven. Compared to the first movement, it represented its tranquil counter pole. An essential innovation, however, was introduced by Beethoven in the third movement of his symphonies, and the same may be said of his sonatas. He replaced the courtly minuet with the more dramatic and lively scherzo. At times, he retained the old three-four time of the minuet, at others he changed it even to two-four time. And finally, the last movement, the fourth. It was the fastest moving of all, quite agitated, at times rather gay. Its musical form was often that of the rondo, in which a principal theme, interrupted by contrasting episodes, returned again and again. There were instances where even the fourth movement was composed in the sonata style.

So we see that, by and large, Beethoven kept to the rules of the game as far as the outer skeleton of the form was concerned. To be sure, in the Ninth, he interchanged the second and third movements. He made the minuet into a dramatic scherzo whose contrasting themes nullified any dance-like quality. Above all, however, he was responsible for a shifting of the equilibrium within the structure. While in the compositions of Haydn and Mozart certain proportions had predominated, this was no longer so in the case of Beethoven. He might determine, for the sake of a dramatic idea, to make the formerly small and unimportant coda the most essential part of the sonata movement, and let the development become larger than the statement and recapitulation combined. Some of his symphonies started with a slow introduction which had nothing to do with the actual statement of the themes, or this statement was prepared in a different, and frequently highly exciting, manner, as in the Ninth. The entirely new element in Beethoven's symphonies was their content. In that respect, we are in many instances justified in speaking of veritable "musical dramas without words."

The First Symphony, apart from minor details, does not as yet reveal the master's hand to be found in Beethoven's later works. In spite of all his impetuosity, a first attempt could not very well have carried him beyond the advanced standards established by his predecessors. Every artist, even the genius, must start where his predecessors left off. The First Symphony is a brief piece. Its performance takes less than twenty-five minutes. It is written in C major, and Beethoven gave it the number

21 in his works. There has been some talk recently of a "Symphony No. O," ascribed to Beethoven. It is also referred to as the "Jena Symphony" because the manuscript was discovered in that town. The case is not clear. Beethoven himself did not include it in the series of his symphonies, which he numbered from One to Nine in his own handwriting. It may have been a product of his youthful days in Bonn. At any rate, it is of no great importance in relation to all of the master's work.

The Second Symphony is a product of the year 1802. It is written in D major and carries the opus number 36. That year was one of the saddest in Beethoven's life. It was the epoch of the Heiligenstadt Testament. Much of the yearning expressed in that document may be found in the music of the Second. But, taken as a whole, it, too, is still transitional. It was first performed on April 5, 1803, in Vienna. It may interest the reader to learn something of the later course taken by Beethoven's symphonies. The First was performed outside of Vienna as early as 1801, at the Leipzig Gewandhaus. Then came Paris, in 1807, although the executants were merely pupils of the conservatory. The first regular Paris concert performance did not take place until 1830. The London performance, in 1813, was a pronounced success. The Second was played in London in the same year, on the occasion of the founding of the Philharmonic Society. It was considered so complex that the audience was granted half an hour's intermission before the remainder of the program was performed. Paris produced it for the first time in 1821. It had a mixed reception. Berlioz was the only one to praise it rapturously.

Some say that the "real" symphonic Beethoven made his appearance with his Third, called *Eroica* by himself, in E-flat major, Opus 55. Its original idea may go back to the tragic October of the Heiligenstadt Testament. Beethoven did sketch theme notes for the *Eroica* at that time, although he was still at work on his Second. Toward the end of April, or the beginning of May, 1803, he finished the monumental structure of the Third. In it he walked entirely new paths, enlarging the dimensions and for the first time giving the whole symphony a programmatic foundation. After two orchestral blasts, the work immediately begins with the principal theme—without the slow introduction used by the composer in both the First and the Second. The second movement is the famous funeral march, given the Italian superscription *Marcia Funebre* by Beethoven. And yet, it seems to me as if it were not a march at all, but rather a death prayer, a deeply moving plaint, a self-contained symphonic poem (although this descriptive term did not as yet exist at the time). The third movement is a phantasmally onrushing scherzo, rhythmic through and through; and the finale is a short forceful theme with grandiose variations played against a jubilant background, which gives way once more to a contemplative mood. The first Vienna performance was a private one, on April 7, 1805. Two years later, the work was heard in Leipzig, in 1814 in London, and in 1828 in Paris. The Third was the first of Beethoven's symphonies to be given a public performance in Russia in 1833. Not until 1866 did Italy hear it. The audience, on that occasion, included Liszt.

The Fourth Symphony, in B-flat major, opus 60, was composed in 1806. A slow pensive introduction is followed by the statement of an almost playful main theme and a rather short developing part. It seems as if Beethoven, after the unprecedented irruption of the *Eroica*, did not wish to burn all his bridges behind him. At any rate, the Fourth is not nearly so stirring as the Third or the Fifth, a fact which has of course nothing to do with its musical worth. An adagio such as the one occurring in this symphony is a rarity even with Beethoven. The initial performance took place in Vienna, in 1807. The work was received with considerably more understanding than the Third. Its duration of hardly more than half an hour seemed to be more to the public's liking than the fifty minutes of the *Eroica*, surely the longest symphony produced up to that time.

And now we have come to the Fifth. It is today perhaps the most frequently played of all. For the first time, Beethoven chose a minor fundamental key for a symphony. This one is in C minor, opus 67. It seems that no sooner had Beethoven finished his Third than he immediately thought of the one bearing the number Five today. It may have been due to a sudden impulse that he interpolated the shorter and sweeter Fourth between the two monumental works. Beethoven composed the Fifth toward the end of 1807 and the beginning of the following year. Its first performance took place in Vienna, on December 22, 1808. The program, incredibly overcrowded according to our ideas, included not only two of the master's new symphonies, the Fifth and Sixth, but also a piano fantasy, the great fantasy for chorus, piano, and orchestra, parts of a mass, and some arias. The success was rather lukewarm. This faulty judgment was soon set aside by the Leipzig Gewandhaus, in 1809, and thenceforth the popularity of the Fifth grew more rapidly than that of any of its sisters. The introductory measures of the Fifth have become world-famous, those unison orchestral blasts which, as Beethoven himself is reported to have said, thunder against the gate like the blows of destiny. The second movement, the "andante con moto," contains variations on a beautifully noble melody. The third movement, superscribed simply "allegro" but according to its character a dramatically charged scherzo, contains one of the master's most brilliantly conceived passages: the transition without pause to the finale, a slow uninterrupted crescendo whose merging into the C-major ecstasy of the final movement produces an overpowering effect.

How wholly different is the Sixth! Beethoven called it the *Pastoral* and, in addition, superscribed each of its parts with a program title. The first movement is called *Awakening of Pleasant Emotions on Arriving in the Country*, but this pattern is not permitted to infringe upon or change the formal structure of the movement. Beethoven proceeded similarly in the second movement, the idyllic andante, entitled *Scene at the Brook*. The birds which sing in it—Beethoven even indicated their names at the respective places: nightingale, quail, cuckoo—do so in a wholly unrealistic manner, the sound being emotional rather than imitative, as Beethoven himself said. *Merry Peasant Gathering* is the title of the third movement, in which the composer returned almost imperceptibly to the old dance character of the third symphonic movements. Without interruption, Beethoven continues with the agitated part entitled *Thunderstorm, Tempest*, as if the dance had been interrupted by a natural upheaval. And, again without pause, the stormy weather ebbs away. The symphony closes charmingly and peacefully with a *Shepherd's Song*, to which the composer gave the subtitle *Feelings of Joy and Gratitude after the Storm*. Beethoven's ardent love of nature was expressed in tones that were new to his day and new in his creative work. New, too, was the form here used: five movements, for the first time! Beethoven himself was never to return to this innovation, and a long time was to pass before any of his successors did. New, above all, was the idea of an extra-musical program. Eventually, in the course of succeeding decades, this led to the symphonic poem. The first performance of the *Pastoral* took place on the occasion of the concert mentioned before (December 22, 1808). London heard it three years later, Paris in 1829, New York in 1853.

The Seventh Symphony, in A major, opus 92, was called by Wagner the *Apotheosis of the Dance*. As a matter of fact, none of the master's other symphonies contains such a wealth of light-gaited themes and rhythms. They set in in the very first movement after a slow introduction, pause but briefly in the beautiful second movement, to give way again to a pleasant striding, to a stormily rushing along in the scherzo—marked "presto"—and terminate in a veritable orgy in the finale. It is understandable that this symphony had the least difficulty in finding favor with contemporary audiences. Its initial performance took place at the Vienna University, on December 8, 1813. At the time of the Congress, in 1814, it was repeated twice, was played in Leipzig in 1816, in London in 1817, in Paris in 1829, in Russia in 1840, in Spain in 1866, and in Italy in 1874.

A few months only separate the Seventh from the Eighth Symphony. In the latter, Beethoven returned to the key of the *Pastoral*, F major, and the opus number immediately follows that of the Seventh: 93. Likely to surprise the listener most in this Eighth Symphony is its cheerful fundamental mood, its amiable charm, and its sense of humor. There can be no doubt that the Eighth represents a rare case in the life of Beethoven. None of his other great works had required so few notations and sketches; and we know how bitterly the master had to struggle for the attainment of his goals. In other respects, too, the Eighth is an exception. Not only are the melancholy, and frequently tragic, aspects of most of the other symphonies conspicuous by their absence, but the Eighth also lacks in lyric expansion. It is the most compact and also the shortest of all. Perhaps the most remarkable movement is the second. It is ingenious, humorous, and wholly unsentimental. Its knocking rhythm is imitative of the metronome, and its theme had its origin in a jocose canon which Beethoven had dedicated to the inventor of that apparatus, his friend Maelzel, who had also constructed a number of hearing aids for him. In spite of the "ease" with which the work can be comprehended, its success was not a striking one. The first performance in Vienna, on February 27, 1814, was followed by one in 1818 in Leipzig, as always the first German town to produce a Beethoven symphony, in 1826 in London, in 1832 in Paris, and in 1846 in St. Petersburg.

And then, like a stroke of lightning—no, rather like an earthquake or a great deluge, came the colossal Ninth. It would seem as if the Eighth and the Ninth could not possibly have been written by the same man. Between Beethoven's next-to-last and last symphonies there is a long interval, the longest to separate any of his symphonic works, eleven years. In November, 1822—it was the year in which Rossini, the most fêted composer of his day, came to Vienna and was so coolly received by the master—the London Philharmonic Society sent Beethoven the sum of fifty pounds, in return for which he promised a new symphony for the following year. But Beethoven needed considerably more time for its writing. The various chronic afflictions besetting him had been augmented by an attack of conjunctivitis. The gigantic work was finished about the end of February, 1824. The first copy bore the title: "Grand Symphony, written for the Philharmonic Society of London." But the final manuscript was dedicated to the King of Prussia. He gave it the opus number 125. The key of the work is D minor, the only minor symphony besides the Fifth. Here, in the Ninth, Beethoven broke almost all the bonds of tradition. Its performance takes considerably more than an hour. He put the scherzo in second place, the slow movement in third place. He shifted the proportions within the movements for the sake of a grandiose dramatic effect. And a crowning touch was supplied by something that had never been done before: the inclusion of the human voice, of soloists and choruses, in the structure of the symphony. The Ninth has called forth an immense amount of commentary. The most prominent musicians, Wagner among them, have tried to interpret and explain the work. And all of them without exception have placed the human content before the musical. That is to say, here the step was taken from a work of pure and absolute music to the expression of an idea. That idea could not have been a loftier one: Humanity, Brotherliness, Love, Faith—and all expressed in the one word: Joy! Schiller's *Ode to Joy* supplied the textual fundament for Beethoven's inspiration. As shown by a sketch, Beethoven had been thinking of letting a solo voice sing the introductory words: "Let us sing the ode of our immortal Schiller!" But in the final version he succeeded in producing an exceptionally dramatic effect: the orchestra intones, one after the other, the principal themes of the preceding three movements, only to interrupt them, to discard them, as it were, until the bass sounds the words: "O brothers, these tones no longer! Rather let us join to sing in cheerful measure a song of joyfulness!" And presently the solo voices and the mighty chorus echo the exultant cry: "Hail thee, Joy, from heav'n descending, Daughter from Elysium . . . !"

The initial performance of the Ninth came very near getting away from Vienna, but once more all of Beethoven's friends united to prevent this. And so Vienna may claim the enviable distinction of having been the scene of the first performance of all of Beethoven's symphonies. The Ninth was played and sung for the first time on May 7, 1824, and, in contrast to some of its predecessors, was enthusiastically received. Beethoven, stone-deaf by that time, had to be informed by the conductor, Umlauf, at the end of the movements, that the people sitting behind him were applauding rapturously. London, for which the work had originally been intended, heard it in 1826, Paris in 1831. In 1842, Nicolai, the founder of the Vienna Philharmonic Society, arranged for a performance in which 750 singers and 450 musicians participated, as against the hardly more than 80 and 70, respectively, at the initial performance. Russia became acquainted with the work in 1836, Italy in 1878 (although the first three movements had been individually performed there before), while New York listened to the Ninth for the first time in 1846.

The master's sonatas would deserve almost as much space as his symphonies. If we include only those numbered by Beethoven himself, there are thirty-two of them. Here, the variety and colorfulness is still more abundant than in the case of his symphonies. They frequently represent a most personal avowal on the part of Beethoven. With regard to form, their list includes every possible variety, from scholarly, short, and almost sonatina-like pieces still written in the style of Haydn, to grander compositions in which form is entirely disregarded and an approach made to the free fantasy. The number of the movements varies, and so does their sequence. Many of them have names, like the *Pathétique*, the *Appassionata*, and *Les Adieux*. On the other hand, the popular name *Moonlight Sonata* applied to opus 27 No. 2, which bears the title *Quasi una fantasia*, represents a subsequently adopted and somewhat questionable designation.

And what might not be said about Beethoven's only opera *Fidelio*, a glorification of wifely love and an outcry against tyranny! This work, whose ethical content places it far above the average run of operas, truly was Beethoven's child of sorrow. In spite of many years of arduous labor, it gave him but little joy. And what about the wonderful score of the *Missa Solemnis*, so far from being doctrinal, and yet so deeply religious? Beethoven's superscription may well be applied to his entire creative work: "From the heart—May it find its way to the heart!" There is also his chamber music, including those last quartets which sound like a greeting from another world, incomprehensible almost and appalling in the utter loneliness they reveal. There are furthermore his five piano concertos, in whose sequence the same course of development is noticeable, from the classic to the romantic, from the writing of music to the expression of ideas, an advance into unexplored territory by which many a future generation was to be benefited. And finally, I should like to mention but one other piece of music by Beethoven, because it is particularly dear to my heart; a work more world-removed and farther from all terrestrial and material things than almost any other manifestation in the wide realm of art: the second movement of the violin concerto.

. 16 .

Schubert: or The Unreal Life

AN interesting experiment was made a few years ago in a school in
Buenos Aires. A symphony was played to the children, twelve and
thirteen years old, who were then asked to write down their impressions.
As always in such cases, the results were surprising because of the children's receptivity and their ability to grasp the meaning of the music.
This is how one of the little essays began: "A profound sadness must
have reigned in the soul of this composer . . ." That composer, whose
name the children had not been told, had himself said 120 years before:
"I am at times seized with an inexplicable melancholy . . ." The work to
which the children had been listening was the Unfinished Symphony,
and the composer with the "profound sadness" Franz Schubert.

And while we are talking about that work, this melancholy may
also explain why the famous symphony remained unfinished. It may
well be said that it is unfinished only from the standpoint of style which
required of every symphony of that epoch four movements. The first
was to be vigorous, cheerful, or at least rhythmically quite agitated; the
second, slow, lyrical, very melodious, and frequently melancholy. Up to
this point, the Unfinished more or less follows the classic norm, although
even the first movement reveals a strong dose of melancholy. And now
a third was to have followed, gay, dance-like, a minuet in almost every
instance. The fourth movement should have been the most agitated of
all: turbulent, onrushing, sweeping along, not unlike, in a certain sense,
the *stretta* of an Italian opera. (Not until Tchaikovsky wrote the profoundly sad and slowly solemn final movement of his Pathetic Symphony
was this rule broken.)

Schubert composed the first two movements at the age of twenty-
five. After that outpouring of melancholy he felt unable to add to the
sorrowful work a minuet and a cheerful finale. He left it as it was, "unfinished," and sent it to a friend in Graz. Many decades after Schubert's
death, it was discovered among that man's effects. Only then did it find

SCHUBERT: OR THE UNREAL LIFE

its way to the public and became a great favorite in spite of its formally unfinished state.

Had Schubert been a revolutionary, like Beethoven, the work might have been "finished" in some original manner. But Schubert was anything but a rebel. He fought no demon in his soul and no fate in this world. His life may have been the most tragic of all, but he was not aware of it. Haydn, Mozart, and Beethoven had their triumphs and were permitted, at least temporarily, to live without material cares. Hadyn and Mozart experienced love. Schubert never had a home of his own, never a position, never money, never was loved in return when he loved, and never—unless it were in the most intimate circle of friends—tasted of the invigorating draught of success.

A kind Providence had given him two lives: one, earthly and poor, but cheerful; and another, super-earthly, or unearthly, and rich, but melancholy, dwelling in the nocturnal land of his dreams and fantasies that poured into his soul so infinite a wealth of melodies.

Gluck, Haydn, Mozart, and Beethoven settled in Vienna, attracted by the charm of the city and held fast by its cultural and musical atmosphere. Schubert was born there. And perhaps his work can be fully understood only by him who is able to go back in spirit to the Vienna of 1820, whose people, like no others in the world, knew how to combine melancholy and cheerfulness. Schubert's every melody is a piece of that city, of its old little streets, and of its green hills, of which Grillparzer wrote:

"If once from the Kahlenberg you've looked at the land,
What I've been and have written you will understand."

That was true also of Schubert. The city on the Danube was to him everything: cradle, home, grave. True, not for him were the fashionable streets in the center of the city, nor the palaces in which dwelled Beethoven's friends and patrons. It was far from such scenes, way out in the suburbs, that Schubert was born and lived the short years of his earthly existence.

In his terrestrial life, Schubert was a true child of his city: gay in the circle of his friends—a Bohemian, harmless, witty, and exceedingly good-natured. He was affectionately called "Franzl," or "Bertl," or "Schwammerl," the latter word meaning "little mushroom," and having reference to his short stoutish figure surmounted by a large head. Among his friends were artists, like Moritz von Schwind, small officials given to writing poetry in their spare hours, singers, and plain citizens. But what united them was an exceptional enthusiasm for art and a worshipful affection for Schubert, in whom, with the instinct of those touched by the Muse, they sensed the genius. During festive and gay evenings, enlivened by music and dancing, would come the solemn moment when Schubert sat down at the piano to play his latest melodies. Everybody who was privileged to attend, his friends, the more affluent burghers of the suburb, and the pretty girls who had put on their Sunday-best for the occasion, had the same name for these evenings: "Schubertiades" [Pl. 85]. How gay the Sundays, when the cheerful company drove out to the Vienna woods and when, in the sunny open, melodies and poetry blended so happily with the magic spell of a summer day and the laughter of unburdened spirits!

82. Schubert, Schwind, and some friends, serenading. Drawing by Moritz von Schwind, from the 12-meter-long "Lachner Scholl," presented to their mutual friend, Kapellmeister Lachner, in 1862.

Thus passed the inconceivably short years of Schubert's life on earth. Thirty-one years! But how different, how wholly different was his other world! Suddenly he would be in a far-away sphere, borne there on the wings of music into an unknown distant realm full of all the things real life was unable to offer. There he would find the sea and the sunny slopes of the South, snow-clad mountains and lonely hardly accessible castles, distant continents, colors and intoxicating scents, adventures and travels. And there would be thousands of other things which never existed, never could exist, in real life. So it came about that a small assistant teacher from the Vienna suburb of Liechtenthal, poor and unpretentious, was able to depict in tones everything that is beautiful, great, and lofty in this world. Inconceivable, with what force, with what violence, Schubert's creative power hewed its course! What an unbelievable wealth of creations! One single year—1815—witnessed the birth of two

. 149

symphonies, two masses, four stage works, more than 140 songs, one string quartet, two piano sonatas, chorals, church music, and a great deal more.

All artistic creation is a mysterious act, a miracle. And Schubert's creative work is perhaps one of the greatest miracles of all. Now he would be talkative, in good spirits, waiting in the circle of his friends for a waiter to bring him what he had ordered—and in a single moment he would be carried away, as by a supernatural power, into his other, his unreal, and yet much more real, life. Everything around him would sink away, and he himself became a changed man: his eyes would begin to shine, his rather commonplace snubnosed face seem to be bathed in an unearthly brilliance, a brilliance poured over him by his goddess: Music. Melody upon melody surged up from his soul, picture upon picture was created in his mind. His hands would grope for a piece of paper—it may have been a bill of fare. Soon its prosaic statements would be covered with a maze of notes . . . When Schubert was himself once more, eating and chatting, he had forgotten everything, even the paper. A friend usually picked it up, and that was how mankind came to know the music. It may have been the *Serenade*, known and loved today all over the world. Similar occurrences dotted his teaching activity. In his father's little suburban school he was supposed to teach the children the three R's. Suddenly, he would be wholly lost to his surroundings. There would be the same surging up of music, and also the same indifference to its fate once it had been committed to paper. To him, happiness lay in the creative act itself. Of far less importance was recognition by a world which forever remained strange and forbidding to him.

Schubert manifested greater ambition when striving for goals which were rather beyond him. He greatly yearned, for instance, to have his operas performed on a stage. But the libretti were too feeble to make success possible. Besides, his genius was more elegiac and lyrical than operatic, in spite of many a song of breath-taking dramatic force.

Once, a friend let him see one of the sketchbooks of Beethoven, his idol. It made him exclaim with touching simplicity: "If composing is so arduous a task, I'd rather not compose!" To him, however, the production of music was far from an arduous task. His creative spirit was comparable to that of Mozart's. "Just as it's in me, so I let it come out, and that's all there is to it!" That was his own characterization of his creative process. In the course of the few years of his maturity—he had not been

Einladung

zu dem Privat Concerte, welches Franz Schubert am 26. März, Abends 7 Uhr im Locale des österreich. Musikvereins unter den Tuchlauben N° 558 zugeben die Ehre haben wird:

Vorkommende Stücke

1. Erster Satz eines neuen Streich. Quartetts, vorgetragen von den Herren Böhm, Holz, Weiß und Linke

2. a) Der Kreutzzug von Leitner
   b) Die Sterne von demselben   } Gesänge mit Begleitung des Piano Forte vorgetragen von
   c) Der Wanderer a. d. Mond v. Seidl   } Herrn Vogl k. k. pensionirten Hofopernsänger
   d) Fragment aus dem Aeschylus

3. Ständchen von Grillparzer, Sopran Solo und Chor vorgetragen von Fraulein Josephine Fröhlich und den Schülerinnen des Conservatoriums

4. Neues Trio für das Piano Forte, Violin und Violoncelle vorgetragen von den Herren Carl Maria von Boklet, Böhm und Linke

5. Auf dem Strome von Rellstab Gesang mit Begleitung des Horns und Piano-Forte vorgetragen von den Herren Tietze und Lewy dem Jüngern

6. Die Allmacht, von Ladislaus Pyrker, Gesang mit Begleitung des Piano Forte vorgetragen von Herrn Vogl

7. Schlachtgesang von Klopstock, Doppelchor für Männerstimmen.

Sämtliche Musikstücke sind von der Composition des Concertgebers

Eintrittskarten zu f 3 W. W. sind in den Kunsthandlungen der Herren Haslinger, Diabelli und Leidesdorf zu haben.

83. Invitation to Schubert's only concert at the hall of the Society of Friends of Music, in 1828. The place was crowded, and the event netted almost 800 Gulden —but the critics ignored it entirely.

a child prodigy, like Mozart—he created about 1,250 works of all kinds. His operas which, in spite of all criticism, contain valuable fragments, were mentioned before. He left to the world eight symphonies. Work on a ninth was interrupted by death. His piano music, his pieces for violin, cello, and other instruments are truly inspired. Of the highest rank is his chamber music: the wonderful quartets and quintets, and a masterly octet. His profound religious music is pure sentiment and filled with a childlike simplicity of faith. Pure sentiment—and seemingly without technique. And that is the very point at which his critics have attacked him at all times: they reproach him with "too-much of melodies" and "too-little of contrasts;" Schumann, however, referring to Schubert's music, spoke of "heavenly" length. A Viennese wit put it more crudely: "Jesus had a hard job bringing Lazarus to life. Schubert puts him to death again and makes him sing for ever and ever . . ." (That was a reference to Schubert's oratorio *Lazarus*.)

The crowning glory of Schubert's work was his songs. In this most intimate, and seemingly so simple, form the whole magnitude of his vision is crystallized. It is quite impossible to analyze here even a small number of his six hundred songs. He wrote them all—at times several in one day—between the fourteenth and thirty-first years of his life. Not all of them are based on verses by great poets. At the side of Goethe, Heine, and Shakespeare—the inspirers of the most magnificent Lied compositions of the entire nineteenth century—stand other names which are today known and remembered only by virtue of this association with Schubert's music.

Two of Goethe's poems, *Der Erlkönig* (The Erl-King) and *Gretchen am Spinnrade* (Gretchen at the Spinning Wheel), first inflamed Schubert's boyish imagination [Pl. 86]. He set them to music and sent them to Weimar. But it seems that the songs and their most humble dedicatory line did not merit the thanks and recognition of the Prince of Poets.

Many of Schubert's songs are collected into cycles: *Die schöne Müllerin* (The Fair Maid of the Mill) and *Winterreise* (Winter Journey). In the latter, he gave expression to a first premonition of impending death. It also sings of unrequited love and is full of overwhelming sadness. Everything seems to be enveloped in snow and loneliness. When his friends heard these songs, they felt as though an icy finger had touched them. Perhaps, for the first time, they sensed how far away and in what gloomy realms dwelt the soul of their gay "Schwammerl."

The piano part, which his predecessors had used merely as a support of the voice and which had had no life of its own, gained decisive importance in the works of Schubert and became an equal partner of the singing voice. In these accompaniments, in hundreds of variants, he depicted the murmur of the brook, the rustling of the linden-tree leaves,

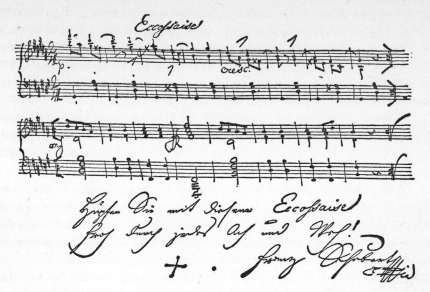

84. "Album Leaf," by Schubert (1823 ?) intended for Seraphine Schellmann.

the gentle splash of the oars in the quiet evening water of the lake, the jubilant blare of the postillion's horn as the mail coach enters the little town, the monotonous humming of the spinning wheel, the soft twanging of the guitar, the sublime tranquility of the starry night, melancholy, yearning, love . . . To the instrument he entrusted the majestic chords gently calming the maiden's cringing fear at the approach of Death, the expression of the immeasurable loneliness of the wanderer looking in vain for happiness, the spectral atmosphere created by the gruesome and ghostlike figure of the *Doppelgänger* (Haunted Man) in the night-covered street, the hopeless despair at the sight of the inexorable way pointed by a fateful guidepost . . . All this—and so much more!—is contained in the piano part of Schubert's songs. He had at his disposal hundreds of different tone colorings which he used with so consummate an art for the depiction of sun and spring, autumnal storms, snow, rural loneliness, summer evenings, forest quiet, and—again and again—the water, which mystically attracted him, be it a brook, a river, the sea.

No wonder that many of his songs have attained the status of national possessions, for they had grown from the people, from the soil of his homeland.

We have so far spoken mainly of Schubert's "unreal" life, of that existence which gave to the world 1,250 works. But we have said little as yet of that other, the real, life which, to be sure, had in his case lost much of its reality. It ran its course in unbelievable simplicity and came to its end with fearful speed, seemingly little more than the vehicle for his mysterious creation. "It seems to me at times, as if I did not belong in this world at all." These were Schubert's own words.

Schubert was born on January 31, 1797, in Liechtenthal, a poor but cheerful suburb of Vienna. Hadyn was then already a famous composer, Mozart's death had occurred five years before, and Beethoven, a self-willed young man, was the sensation of the aristocratic salons.

The house in which Schubert was born, the school in which his father was active and in which he, too, taught with so little success, and the parish church in which he played the organ and in which, when he was still quite young, took place the initial performance of his first mass —all these buildings may still be seen today. And à propos of his mass, a pretty girl of the neighborhood, Therese Grob, sang the soprano part so beautifully that Schubert fell head over heels in love with her. But she soon married a prosperous burgher, and Schubert could not put her out of his mind to the day of his death.

In the central part of the city there still stands the old Jesuit church with its annex, the monastic school, to which Schubert's exceptional musical accomplishments and his fine singing voice had gained him admittance on a scholarship. There he was, the son of a poor suburban teacher, among the children of the wealthy. In his letters from school, Schubert asked his father and brother for two things: for some money, that he might not have to go to bed hungry while the others, thanks to their pocket money, were able to add considerably to the frugal monastic fare, and for some music paper . . .

Hardly another great musician did as little traveling as Schubert. There is not in the story of his life any account of triumphal concert tours, of honorable invitations to other cities and to princely courts. A famous singer of the Vienna Opera, Vogl, who was aware of Schubert's talent once took him along on a trip into the Austrian mountain country, where they even gave occasional concerts. And another little journey took him to Hungary, to the estate of the Esterhazys, relatives and descendants of the prince who had founded Haydn's fame. But Schubert was not an orchestral leader or a palace composer there. He was merely the teacher of the young countess, to whom he gave piano lessons.

"If I wanted to sing of love, it turned into pain. And if I wanted to sing but of pain, it turned into love. And so I am torn between love and pain." Could the tragic rôle played by love in Schubert's life and work be more plainly and touchingly revealed than by these, his own, words?

In 1827, it looked as if one of Schubert's most burning desires was to be fulfilled. He was to spend the summer at the home of friends and in company with Beethoven. How feverishly he looked forward to the moment when he would be face to face with the Titan! Perhaps he would be able to show him one of his works, woefully insignificant though they were. Perhaps the master would even repeat the words he was said to have uttered at the sight of a Schubert manuscript: "That fellow has the divine spark!" But the meeting never took place. Spring of the year 1827 was not yet over when Beethoven died.

85. From Schubert's diary: "On this day I first composed for money." The mentioned cantata "Prometheus" performed under Schubert's direction on July 24, 1816, has been lost.

In the following year, Schubert fell ill. Slightly delirious, he is said to have called for Beethoven, pronouncing his name yearningly, as if he were looking for him with restless anxiety. The end came on November 19, 1828. He died in the prime of life, at the age of thirty-one. His family provided the money to fulfill his most ardent wish: in death at least he was near Beethoven. He was laid to rest a few steps from the latter's grave.

If someone had told Schubert in the last days of his life that the twentieth century would count him among the greatest masters of all time and peoples, that his melodies would lead an immortal life on the lips of millions, and that his songs would be on almost every singer's program, he would, I think, have given one of his quiet smiles, a little happy, a little timid, and a little incredulous. And perhaps a little surprised, too, as he was when a young girl once asked him: "Tell me, Herr Schubert, are you really writing nothing but sad music?" and he had answered softly:

"Why, is there any other?"

86. Dancing master with pochette (pocket
fiddle). French fashion drawing.

. 17 .

The Waltz of the Empire –
The Empire of the Waltz

THE dance is one of the primordial sources of music. Its history starts
with the beginning of mankind and will end only with its extinction. In the course of centuries folk music assumed various positions in
art, according to the prevailing social order. There were times when the
two currents, which we may call folk music and art music, approached,
and even touched, each other. At such times, dance music and serious
music traveled a common road for a while.

Throughout long centuries, at the end of the Middle Ages and at the
beginning of modern times, the rift between folk music and art music was
very deep, as deep as it was between the dances of the people and those
of society. The gavot and minuet [Pl. 73 & 87] were still formal society

dances, and many great masters—we have made the acquaintance of several—wrote music for them with the same seriousness they would have applied to operas or chamber music. They even introduced these dance forms into suites, sonatas, symphonies, and quartets.

On the other hand, folk dances do not appear in the history of music. As late as the eighteenth century, they were at best the subject of study indulged in by individual scholars, but they aroused little general interest. It was still the time when history knew and said much of the few, and very little of the many. To put it in the words of the *Beggar's Opera* of 1728, or rather its modern edition of 1928, *Die Dreigroschenoper*: "Many people stand in darkness and the others in full light; Those we see are but the latter, and the rest are out of sight."

The French Revolution radically changed the world order. Those who had formerly stood in darkness came into the light. Democracy was on the march, carrying folk music and folk dances into the drawing-rooms. They found their way even to the concert platform and the theater. The wall dividing society dances and folk dances began to crumble. The gavot and the minuet were followed by three dances of purely folk origin: the polka, the mazurka, and the waltz. And the latter became the symbol of a whole epoch.

The waltz is part of Vienna's folklore. In it the Viennese soul found its embodiment. This round dance was like a symbol of happy days, of a city wholly given to the enjoyment of life, of perhaps the last idyll in European history. Its revolving motion expressed the blending of social classes, merging into one another to the sound of the new and enchanting rhythms and melodies. Not for many centuries had the dance been so genuine a manifestation of the age. Everybody swayed to the same three-four time: the aristocrat and the workingman, the artist and the burgher, the Second French Empire [Pl. 48] and the budding American democracy, the revolutionaries of 1848 and the young Queen of England. Among the masters of the Vienna waltz we find prominent musicians, among its admirers all the great composers of the century.

The two Slav dances, mentioned above, had a similar, though somewhat modified, experience. They, too, penetrated into all strata. Great composers, like Chopin and Smetana, opened world-wide artistic perspectives to them.

The Viennese had always been inordinately fond of dancing. An English actor said in 1786 that they appeared to him "seized with a dance mania." Reference was made before to the famous Congress, which attracted Europe's most brilliant personages, and whose distinctive marks were the gorgeous festivities which gave rise to the saying that it was the "Congress which danced."

87. Marquis X, waltzing.
Caricature by Bertail.

In speaking of the fathers of the waltz, we must not overlook Schubert and Weber. The latter's *Invitation to the Dance*, published in Dresden, in 1819, was a dance suite with introduction and coda and therefore, in its forms, an anticipation of the future Vienna waltz. A number of Beethoven's dances, too, sound like a premonition of the waltz and, like those of Schubert, gave an idea of its course of development. It had its origin in the *Ländler*, a Tyrolian slow dance, and the "german." At that very time, two musicians came to the fore who guided the rage for dancing and the musical enthusiasm of the Viennese into new paths. The two masters who began to raise the new waltz to the level of a work of art were Lanner and Strauss.

Joseph Lanner (1801-1843) was a quiet man and a fine musician, but he entertained no ambitions that would carry him beyond Vienna. His dance orchestra held forth in the garden restaurants through the summer months and soon became as popular as his compositions. One day, a young man called on him, giving the name of Johann Strauss (1804-1849) and asking to be taken on as a violinist. He was hired, but the collaboration did not last long. The restless, and at times violent, disposition of the younger man was not amenable to discipline. Johann Strauss resigned and organized his own orchestra. There was something gypsylike in his violin playing and something in his outward appearance that struck the Viennese as exotic. It may have been attributable to his alleged, but

88. Baron Z., waltzing.
Caricature by Bertail.

never wholly proved, Spanish origin. He forged to the front rapidly. The Viennese grew enthusiastic about his waltzes, and soon other cities and countries began clamoring for him. He was enthusiastically received in Germany, France, and England. Berlioz, the composer-genius of Paris, and a dreaded critic, wrote: "We had no idea of the perfection, the fire, the intelligence, and the fine rhythmical feeling possessed by the Strauss orchestra. Listen well to what I am saying! I am speaking of rhythm! All Italian composers, and ours too, have always maintained a wrong standpoint with regard to rhythm. The number of possible rhythmic combinations is almost as large as that of the melodic ones . . ." He went on to compare Strauss to Gluck, Beethoven, and Weber. (It is a strange fact that even the most severe critics were disarmed by the waltz: Hanslick, Wagner's implacable enemy, was to be an enthusiatic follower of Johann Strauss, junior.)

While Strauss was touring foreign countries, was celebrating extraordinary triumphs, and was playing his waltzes at the coronation festivities of the young English Queen Victoria, three sons were growing up in Vienna. They gave early indications of exceptional musical gifts. From afar, their father, who had private reasons, too, for not wishing to return home, thundered against their taking up a musical career. But when he finally got home, it was too late to keep at least the eldest, whose name was also Johann, from devoting himself to music. Inward compulsion was not to be denied, and when the father definitely left his home to take a new wife, the son was able to steer a straight course toward his goal. The day came when he organized an orchestra of his own and made his debut. His father and his father's friends had done all they could to prevent this. But now the son stood on the platform of one of the smartest establishments of Vienna, a pale, well dressed, youthful leader, swinging his bow and urging on his musicians, while thousands of eyes were riveted on him, thousands of ears were listening to judge, or to condemn. The date was October 15, 1844. On that day began the career of one of the most brilliant composers in the history of music: Johann Strauss the Younger, called the "Waltz King."

The younger Johann was as sparkling a fiddler as his father, a still better conductor, and an incomparably more gifted composer. His works are as popular today as they were during his lifetime. Indeed, it would not be surprising if a world-wide poll were to reveal that there is no piece of music more generally beloved than his *Blue Danube* waltz. Oddly, this very waltz had but little success when it was first heard in Vienna; so little success that Strauss said: "To hell with the waltz; it's the coda I'm sorry about!" That coda revealed his gifts as a composer, just as the

89. A page from Johann Strauss's manuscript of the "Gypsy Baron," 1885.
Stadtbibliothek, Vienna.

introductions and concluding parts—the codas, that is—of many of his
other waltzes demonstrated that he was not only a melody-maker of
great genius but also a consummate symphonist. One is moved to admire
and envy an era which, in the serious as well as in the lighter art, was
able to produce that blissfully perfect symmetry, inherent only in that
which is truly great. The *Blue Danube* waltz has made the round of
the world ever since it was enthusiastically acclaimed at the Paris World
Exposition of 1867, much to the surprise of its creator who had considered it rather as a filler-in on his programs. Even more than its innumerable brothers and sisters it has become the symbol of an epoch, a
city, a world.

Johann Strauss, the younger, wrote hundreds of waltzes, many of
which have become tremendously popular, like his *Voices of Spring*,
Roses from the South, *Artists' Life*, *Wine, Woman, and Song*, and *Em-*

peror Waltz. Most of the titles were merely a product of the composer's imagination and had no bearing on the work itself. In the case of some others, however, the occasion of their first performance was of deciding importance. There is also outright program music in some of the Strauss works, as in the introduction of his *Tales from the Vienna Woods*, which almost deserves to be called a miniature pastoral symphony.

When Johann Strauss was at the height of his fame and glory—the city of Boston paid him $100,000 to conduct a number of monster con-

90. Vienna caricature of Strauss and Offenbach. Offenbach: "What if you do outweigh me! All the more am I the representative of the 'light' Muse!"

certs—he was seized with a new passion—for the theatre. Jointly with gifted composers like Ziehrer, Millöcker, and Suppé, he became the creator of the Vienna Operetta. Among his immortal contributions to the theater are *The Bat, Gypsy Baron*, [Ill. 89], and *A Night in Venice.* The Vienna operetta is kin to the French musical farce, whose creator was Offenbach, and to some degree also to the Spanish *zarzuela*. Both of these forms will be discussed presently.

The world fame of Johann Strauss unjustly put in the shade the masterly waltzes of his brother Josef, whose *Village Swallows from Austria* must be accorded a high rank among musical pieces of this kind. In the composition of the charming *Pizzicato Polka* the two brothers collaborated. When Josef died at an early age, the third brother, Eduard, took over the direction of the "Strauss Orchestra," since Johann had retired from the post to devote his time to composing.

To the general popularity of Strauss's music is joined the high esteem in which it was held by almost all the great composers of his and a later day. Schumann, Mendelssohn, Liszt, and Chopin sang its praises. To

57. George Frederick Handel (1685-1759). [*After T. Hudson, 1749*]

58. The Haymarket Theater, the scene of Handel's first London activity.

59. Covent Garden, London. At left, Covent Garden Theater. [*Painting by B. Nebot, 1735*]

60. Christopher Willibald von Gluck (1714-1787). [*Painting by J. S. Duplessis, 1775*]

61. Performance of Gluck's *Armida* at the Opera in rue Saint-Honoré, Paris. [*Painting by G. de Saint-Aubin*]

62. Vienna's old Burgtheater on Michaeler Place, opened 1778. [*Engraving by Karl Postl*]

63. Ballet pantomime *Le Turc Généreux*, with music by Gluck (?), performed for Count Durazzo in Vienna, April 26, 1758. [*Engraving by Belotto, called Canaletto, 1759*]

64. Franz Joseph Hadyn (1732-1809). Wax plaque which Haydn himself considered his best likeness.

65. House in Rohrau, Lower Austria, where Haydn was born.

66. Grand concert at Prince Esterhazy's, led by Haydn. [*Painting by J. Schmid*]

67. Final scene from Haydn's *L'Incontro improviso* at the Esterhazy opera house, 1775. The 13 strings and 2 flutes seated at one long desk. At the cembalo, Haydn himself. At left, 1 cello, 2 contrabasses, 1 bassoon.

68. Wolfgang Amadeus Mozart (1756-1791). Unfinished portrait by Joseph Lange, 1872. [*Mozarteum, Salzburg*]

69. The Mozart family, abt. 1780. Painting by J. N. de la Croce. [*Mozarteum, Salzburg*]

70. Mozart's father with 7-year-old Wolfgang and 11-year-old Nannerl (Marianne). [*Engraving by Delafosse after a watercolor by Carmontelle, painted in Paris, November 1763*]

71. Mozart on his deathbed. Friends and pupils play and sing the finished part of the Requiem. [*After a contemporary drawing*]

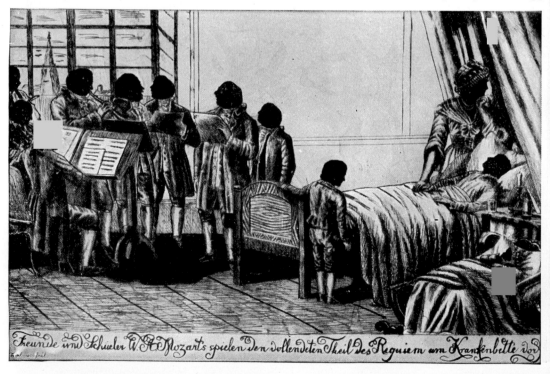

Freunde und Schüler W. A. Mozart's spielen den vollendeten Theil des Requiem am Krankenbette vor

72. Palm forest. Stage scene, Act III, from *The Magic Flute*, executed by Karl Friedrich Schinkel, Berlin, 1815.   73. The Minuet. [*Painting by Joh. Zauffely*]

74. Beethoven's manuscript of the Spring Sonata, op. 24. Marginal remark: "The copyist who inserted the 3 and 4 here was a jackass."

75. Beethoven's piano.

5. Beethoven, part of a
painting by Waldmüller,
1823.

7. Beethoven. [*Engraving
by Hoefel, after L. Le-
tronne's drawing, of 1814*]

8. Beethoven, (l o w e r
right). [*Lithograph by
Fischer, after A. v. Klöbel,
1817-1818*]

79. View of Heiligenstadt at Beethoven's time. [*After a colored engraving by Jos. Kohl*]

80. House in Bonn where Beethoven was born. [*Photo Rumpff*]

81. Courtyard of the Beethoven House in Mödling near Vienna.

82. Franz Schubert (1797-1828). [*Portrait by W. A. Rieder*]

83. Schubert at the age of 16. [*Drawing by Leopold Kupelwieser*]

84. Katharina Fröhlich. [*Drawing by B. Heinrich*]

85. A Schubert soirée at Joseph von Spaun's. At Schubert's side, the opera singer Vogl. [*Drawing by Moritz von Schwind, abt. 1868*]

86. Schubert's manuscript of the song *Gretchen at the Spinning Wheel*, from Goethe's *Faust*.

87. 18th-Cent. dancing school. [*Engraving by Dequevauviller, after a gouache by Lavreince*]

88. Ballet at the time of Louis XV, with the famous dancer Marie Gallé (1711-1756). [*Engraving by N. Larmessin after a painting by Nicolas Lancret*]

89. French family. Drawing satirizing the dance craze, by Thomas Rowlandson (1756-1827). 90. Society dancing makes for brilliant film scenes. A Paris soirée in the days of the Second Empire.

Wagner, it meant "the best he had heard in Vienna." And Brahms, the profound and serious symphonist, felt irresistibly attracted by the floating cheerfulness of that music. He himself composed a cycle of *Love Song Waltzes* for a vocal quartet and piano and once inscribed the first measures of the Danube Waltz on a young girl's fan with the melancholy dedication: "Unfortunately not by me. Johannes Brahms."

The list of composers who drew inspiration from the waltz is quite impressive. Chopin used it in his dreamy, romantic manner; Gounod and Delibes imbued it with their French esprit; Tchaikovsky showed his liking for it in the broad melodic sway of his *Nutcracker Suite*, in his *Serenade for String Orchestra*, and even in his Fifth Symphony. Mahler, one of the last great symphonists, at times put a waltz in place of the old minuet. Richard Strauss adopted the waltz as the fundamental idea of his *Rosenkavalier*. And Ravel, the French late-impressionist of our century, evoked a somewhat cruel portrait of Vienna in his *La Valse*.

Johann Strauss died in 1899, at the age of seventy-four. Perhaps he did not care to greet the twentieth century which was to sound the death knell of his world. The words "Strauss" and "Vienna Waltz" make a vision of days gone by rise up before our eyes. Having withstood all revolutions, the inroad of jazz, and the ever growing materialism of the world, the waltz appears today like a sturdy old rock in a seething sea. It is a memento of a happier epoch, long since become history and beginning to assume the character of a fairy tale: Once upon a time . . .

91. Cello Player. Drawing by Bernard Picart, 1701.

. 18 .

Concerts and Virtuosos

LET us leave briefly the march of events and cast a glance at the musical life of the epoch. It is but natural that musical creation and musical life should constantly act and react upon each other. We must realize that our present form of musical life has come into existence so gradually that even the term "the public," so familiar to us today, is of comparatively recent origin. We saw the public make its appearance for the first time in the days of the early Italian operas and witnessed the revolutionary effect this had.

Opera paved the way, and then instrumental music reached "the public." As we have said before (Chapter 12), there was a tremendously increased cultivation of orchestral and chamber music, and this brought about another broad development in musical life: a third element between the composer-creator and the listener-public, the performer. The demands in music became greater from day to day and the repertoire became larger all the time through the constant inclusion of new works, while the older ones, too, thanks to the printing of music, were not so quickly forgotten as before. New instruments, rapidly perfected, spurred the players on to the attainment of ever new effects; because of the expansion of the philosophical, sociological, and geographical world picture, the choice of musical themes became ever wider; the rivalry between the constantly increasing number of musicians grew keener all the time; the idea of "art," which is newer than one is inclined to think, demanded ever greater perfection of its disciples; and, finally, purely musical progress with relation to new harmony, formation of melodies, orchestral technique, and many other points became more rapid from day to day.

A division had necessarily to be made among the functions of the musicians. At first, the professional musician was frequently creator and interpreter at the same time. His every "appearance" meant a production of his own works. But the progressive mechanization of life and the division of labor—an essential symptom of modern economic existence—demanded of the artist, too, increasing specialization. He had to choose the most conspicuous of perhaps several talents and, by sacrificing all others, strive to bring the one to the utmost possible perfection. He had to specialize as a performer, or as a composer.

Today, we have perhaps reached the end of this development. Specialization has reached its culminating point in the virtuoso, and the technical mass idea in the formation of our present-day gigantic orchestras. We shall refer again to this present condition in a later chapter. What we wish to discuss here are the problems and questions engendered by this development in its beginnings. A cleft had opened between the executants and the public. No longer was an arbitrary interchange of parts possible. But greater than this cleft was the veritable abyss that separated the creative musician from the public. The troubadour had been creator and interpreter in one person. How could the same be asked of the virtuosos of our day? Does not our public insist upon the very opposite? That the virtuoso play the works with which he has been able most thoroughly to identify himself? This means that musical life has gone through the same process of development as economic life. To express it prosaically: between the producer and consumer a middleman has appeared—the dealer or distributor in business, the interpretative artist in music. Are we at all aware what a wealth of problems this has evoked?

Is the work as it reaches the listener identical with what the composer had created? What is to be the attitude of the re-creative artist (the very term is interesting!) toward the work? Objective? What does that mean? Is there such a thing as strict objectivity? If so, the interpreter would be hardly more than a machine. Subjective? Would not that do violence to the work? If these questions present difficulties in connection with the works whose interpreters and creators are of the same generation, perhaps of the same cultural circle, how insoluble does the whole complex become when works of a past epoch, wholly different from ours, are invovled? Is it at all possible today to interpret Bach, Palestrina, Mozart, or any of the great masters of the past according to their own intentions? How often do we read in the newspapers that Mr. X interpreted the music of the seventeenth century with a great fidelity to style? How does the writer know that? A great deal of ink has been used up in connection with the question of musical interpretation. From "utter faithfulness to the work" (which is impossible) to "individual conception" (which is interesting, but dangerous), everything has been defended or attacked.

Our present musical life must deal with a treasure representing almost three centuries of creative work. That is why the interpreter was bound to become the center, the axis, of that musical life. He occupies the place which in days gone by had been held by the composer. Today, the composer has almost entirely lost direct contact with the public, while the re-creative artist has succeeded in gaining the favor of the public to such a degree that the different conceptions of a work, as presented by different virtuosos, are at times more interesting to the listeners than the work itself.

Let us be done now with theories, with criticisms and controversies, which cannot possibly change existing conditions. Let us rather rejoice in the wealth and the undeniable magnitude of modern musical life and give a passing thought to its historical growth.

The fourteenth and fifteenth centuries were the great age of the organ. Rarely, however, could its sound be heard outside of religious services. The organ concert, slow in developing, consisted for centuries mostly of improvisations. Among the world's prominent organ virtuosos, the blind Florentine, Francesco Landino, (1325?-1397), may have been one of the first. He was followed by masters, of whom some were mentioned here in connection with Venice's church of St. Mark. Foremost were the two Gabrielis and Claudio Merulo, until an unsurpassed master arrived on the scene: Girolamo Frescobaldi (1593-1643) [Ill. 92]. He was in every respect an extraordinary musician. More than 30,000 listeners are said to have gathered for his concerts in Rome. The art of the organ flourished to no less a degree north of the Alps. Active in Nuremberg was Konrad Paumann (1410?-1473), blind as had been Landino, and Johann Pachelbel (1653-1706). There was Jakob Froberger (1616-1667) in Vienna, Paul Hofhaimer (1459-1539) [Ill. 31] in Innsbruck, and finally Dietrich Buxtehude (1637-1707) in Lübeck, at whose feet sat two young musicians: Bach and Handel. The leading organist in Flanders was Jan Pieter Sweelinck (1562-1621). And from what was said before it is clear that these masters were also—or rather, foremost—creative artists, composers. The di-

92. Girolamo Frescobaldi (1583-1643). From an engraving by Cl. Mellan.

viding line between the creative and the re-creative artist had not as yet been drawn.

The waning Middle Ages witnessed the European spread of an instrument which was to occupy a leading position for a long time. The Moors, overrunning Spain, had brought it from the Orient, where the Arabs, since time immemorial, had known it by the name of *El oud*. In Spain, the name was changed to "el laùd," the etymological root of our word lute. That beautifully sounding instrument, equally suited to the rendition of intimate song accompaniments and difficult polyphonic phrases, quickly became a favorite with the social set of those days. There was hardly any Renaissance palace within whose walls it was not heard. The pieces for lute were recorded—as were the organ works—in so-called "tabulatures." A rich literature from the fifteenth and sixteenth centuries has thus come down to us, so that our ears may still enjoy the delights of that music. For many centuries following, the lute was used as a concert instrument, until the mounting popularity of the guitar and, above all, the increasing size of the concert halls put an end to its prominence in the musical life of Europe.

The seventeenth century witnessed the rise of the string and bow instruments. What was accomplished at that time through a perfect blending of manual skill and diligence and inspired ingenuity has never been equaled since. Sufficient to mention three great names: Amati, Stradivari, Guarneri. They are more than individual names, for there are instances where they represent sequences of generations, family traditions, and hereditary knowledge. The instruments from that period have to this day preserved the full nobility and richness of their sound, and no modern technique has been able to fathom their secret. Amati, Stradivari, and Guarneri del Gesù all lived in one city: Cremona. But in Brescia, too, in Mittenwald, and in the Tyrolian Absam masterly instruments were built, occupying an important place in musical history. Had it not been for these instruments, the development of violin virtuosity as well as of the entire string literature would have been impossible.

Again, the mention of great violin virtuosos is tantamount to that of great creative artists. Let us begin with Arcangelo Corelli (1653-1713) [Pl. 97], who was called *maestro dei maestri* and whose remains lie interred at the side of those of Raphael. He was followed by Antonio Vivaldi (1680?-1743) and Giuseppe Tartini (1692-1770), both of whom added considerably to the violin technique, and a large number of other virtuosos, like Giovanni Battista Viotti, who made quite a stir as a violin-playing child prodigy at the very time when the brilliant star of the child Mozart ascended over Europe. The style of the compositions of these old-Italian masters is characterized by a truly wonderful nobility of sentiment. Beautiful in sound and profound are these works, although the beginnings of virtuosity were responsible for an occasional display of outward effects. Close relations existed at the time between the virtuoso activities of Italy and Germany, and between both and those of France. The latter country produced men like Pierre Rode and Rodolphe Kreutzer, the latter having gained immortality through the Beethoven sonata bearing his name.

And then came the greatest master of the fiddle, a fascinating personality (1782-1840) [Pl. 95]. So demonic was the impression he made on his contemporaries that a pact with the Devil was in all seriousness suspected. He invented a wealth of new effects, perfected the playing of double-stops to a bewildering degree, and was known to have finished

93. Sketch of a Paganini capriccio, dated May 24, 1832.

an exceedingly difficult piece on a single string, after the other three had snapped in the course of a performance. His adventurous life, which in all probability will never be wholly clarified and which, according to the observer's viewpoint, makes him appear either as a large-minded noble person or a petty schemer, took him to all the cities and countries of the Europe of that time and brought him into contact with all the prominent minds and musicians of his day. It seems, too, that Paganini was the first virtuoso ever to play a concert program entirely from memory, a practice which later became a matter of course. His weirdly interesting virtuoso figure—disheveled black hair, closely fitting black tail coat, and a pale face with thrillingly brilliant dark eyes—makes us forget at times that Paganini, like almost all the virtuosos of his day, was also a prolific composer, to whom we are indebted for many fine works. Just as the entire work of Chopin, his contemporary, was dedicated to the piano, so Paganini's sprang from and was intended for the violin. Musical history has frequently recorded the contemporaneous existence of masters of the same genre in Italy and Germany. Here it happened once more: the fabulous Genoese had a worthy, if less picturesque, northern counterpart in Ludwig Spohr (1784-1859), likewise both a virtuoso and a composer.

The keyboard instruments finally surged to the fore with irresistible force. At first it was still the cembalo at which the early virtuosos presented themselves. In France, it was called *clavecin*. A number of prominent composers and performing artists therefore called themselves "clavecinists." First mention is due here François Couperin (1668-1733), called

On voit dans ce Portrait le Célèbre Rameau,
Fils cheri d'Apollon, Rival de l'Italie.
Et qui par un Chemin nouveau
A sçu nous découvrir les Loix de l'Harmo.

94. Rameau. Engraving by Fayet.

le grand, an extremely rare appelation with musicians. He was the typical representative of the gallant, courtly art, a master of the musical miniature. He was followed by Jean-Philippe Rameau (1683-1764) [Pl. 96], whose importance was pointed out before. In Italy, there was Domenico Scarlatti (1685-1757), Alessandro's son, a brilliant cembalo virtuoso. And now we ought to mention once more all the great masters whose lives were recorded in the preceding chapters: Bach and Handel were not only great organ virtuosos but also exceptionally fine cembalo artists. Mozart and Beethoven, too, were masters of that instrument, and almost every old chronicle makes special mention of their astonishing skill at improvisation, one of the essential qualifications of all virtuosos of that time.

Today, the art of improvisation has disappeared from the concert hall. We meet it occasionally at organ recitals but never at the piano or violin concerts, which form the majority of virtuoso performances at present. There are several reasons for this. To begin with, a good improviser must first of all be a good composer, and we have seen that this is hardly ever the case with contemporary virtuosos. Then again, the concert programs of our day consist of works that are not the creations of the performer, so that improvising within these works would be out of place. Furthermore, improvisations have lost most of their popularity and are hardly appreciated at all in our day. And yet, how magnificent must have been that art!

Among the earliest piano virtuosos were Liszt and Chopin. We shall presently speak of them in detail. They represent our popular conception

95. Barcarole. Drawing by Grandville.

of the virtuoso, that king of the concert hall who travels from city to city and whose superlative technical ability is taken as a matter of course. Countless are the names of Liszt's and Chopin's successors. Those of a more recent day (with few exceptions, such as Rachmaninoff, Paderewski, and Kreisler) merely continue the line of re-creative, and not of creative, artists. The fact that the composer concentrated upon his creative work and the reproductive artist upon his concert activities gave the latter sufficient time to keep his fingers constantly in practice. Thus he was able to reach heights of technical perfection of which, a hundred years ago, but a few chosen ones dared to dream.

One of the inevitable consequences of the indicated course of development was an enormous increase in the production of pieces for concert use. As a further consequence of the flourishing state of concert activities, even works not originally intended for the concert hall (simply because there were no concert halls) found their way to the platform. It seems that Liszt and Clara Wieck, Schumann's wife, were the first to give concert performances of Beethoven's sonatas. The master had originally intended them for use in private homes, just as Schubert had intended his songs for merely a small circle of intimates. But the song, too, made its triumphal entry into the concert hall. And finally, chamber music, whose very name indicates the intended home cultivation of music, also left its narrow confines. Public performances of string quartets were first given in Vienna in 1804, in Prague in 1808, and in Paris in 1814. Public concert activities increasingly dominated musical life, and the salons of the well-to-do cultured classes, the successors to the aristocrats and their palaces, all but disappeared. Music attracted ever larger crowds, penetrated ever more deeply into the interior of the country, into medium-sized and small towns, and added to the ranks of its followers from ever new strata of the conquered localities. Radio, the miracle of the twentieth century, of which much will have to be said, hastened this development.

The most eloquent proof of the technical progress of musical life and of its development from the narrowly confined amateur art practiced in the Renaissance palaces is furnished by the history of the symphony orchestra. What a tremendous rise from the small ensemble, numbering hardly more than a dozen musicians and but a few varieties of instruments, to the giant orchestra of today, with its 120 performers and its inexhaustible reservoir of sounds and effects! Keeping pace with this development has been the step-by-step elevation of the conductor, in both a figurative and a literal sense. At first, his activity was confined to the playing of supporting chords on the cembalo. Later, he was promoted to the desk of the first violinist who, seated, and subsequently standing, indicated the pitch and gave the starting cue. Now, he has come to be the controlling power of the mighty orchestral apparatus, towering high above it, a veritable ruler.

However, observations such as these have made us anticipate the historical course of events. Let us return to the point at which we stopped our contemplation of musical activities: the dawn of the nineteenth century.

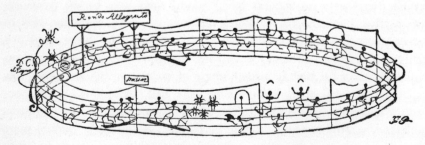

96. Rondo. Drawing by Grandville.

19

The Opera In Full Bloom

THE subject matter of the past few chapters has made us lose sight of the *enfant terrible,* called opera. That is not to say that in the age of the great masters the opera was outshone or obscured by the figure of a Bach, the symphonies of a Haydn or Mozart, the sonatas of a Beethoven, or the songs of a Schubert. Far from it! Beethoven, no matter how well-liked and admired he may have been in Vienna, never for a moment was able to achieve the popularity of a Rossini, not even of a Cherubini. It was left to history to mete out justice—here, at least—and to establish approximately correct proportions.

The historical course of opera is so full of contrasts and piquant details that it would seem to be a theme for the novelist rather than for the coolly observing historian. If I were poetically inclined, I would spin out the picture which compares it to a girl. She has now matured into a woman, an interesting and generous woman, a woman with charms and attractions for every taste and temperament. Ready to assume any number of different forms, she is capricious and erratic, but always driven by the insatiable desire to enslave everybody and everything she comes into contact with. She appears in countless disguises: as a *grande dame,* when she wants to enthrall the upper classes; as a simple girl, when she addresses herself to the people; as Cinderella, when she wishes to arouse our pity; or as a queen, when she wants to impress us with her majesty. She may be aristocratic or revolutionary, realistic or dreamy, serious to the point of tragedy or gay and ironic to the point of the grotesque. She may cause us to laugh or to weep, be philosophical or commonplace, complicated or simple . . .

To begin with, three varieties of the species have to be discussed separately: the Italian, the French, and the German opera, each having its characteristic marks and its own history. While English opera had ceased to exist, there will soon be new offshoots, as new peoples enter the history of music. And a little sister, too, has appeared on the scene.

We have met her under the name of Vienna Operetta and shall make the acquaintance of her French and Spanish counterparts. When, in a later chapter, we speak again of the opera, she will have outgrown her childhood and youth and be revealed in all the spendor of her beauty and maturity.

THE ITALIANS

The two hundred years of Italian opera lying behind us had no uniform line of development. Flourishing times gave way to epochs of decadence. It was during one of the latter periods that Mozart appeared, a man who according to his operatic style must be numbered among the Italian composers, although in his *Magic Flute* he also proved himself a pioneer of German opera. But while even the most commonplace situations in his operas reveal the beating of a warm heart, similar scenes composed by his Italian contemporaries seem cold and hackneyed by comparison. They show nothing but technique; a great deal of technique, to be sure, for the technical side of the profession had been perfected to such a degree that, for long stretches in a score, the work of a mediocre composer could not be distinguished from that of a good one. Operatic composition had become as impersonal as, say, some of the figures at the court of Louis XIV. Besides, it had actually become the practice of prominent and busy masters to have all the recitative parts in their works written by pupils or by other less famous musicians. How, then, could the operas be other than cold and impersonal?

In spite of all this, the rule of the Italian opera was still undisputed. What a triumph was scored in Vienna, in 1792, by *The Secret Marriage!* All the world spoke of the composer, Domenico Cimarosa (1749-1801); nobody spoke of Mozart who had died but recently. Cimarosa, composer of buffo operas in the purest Neapolitan style, found that his fame later served his practical needs well when no judge dared to convict him, though his participation in a revolt was an established fact. But fame did not outlive him. Neither did it outlive his competitor, Giovanni Païsiello (1740-1816), the composer of more than a hundred operas, and a favorite of Napoleon. So popular was his *Barber of Seville* that Rossini's work of the same name, unquestionably the greatest achievement in the line of *opera buffa*, was unable to hold its own against it when it was first performed, in 1816.

However, that was one of the uncommonly rare failures in the life of the singularly lucky Gioacchino Rossini (1792-1868) [Pl. 102]; and besides, it was one which was quickly turned into the very opposite, into a sweeping world success. Rossini was one of the most singular and brilliant figures in the history of music.

On the night following the unquestioned failure of his *Barber of Seville*, Rossini did not go to the Teatro Argentina. The fate of the second performance seemed of little concern to him. Suddenly, in the middle of the night, he was torn from his sleep by a great commotion in the street. To the glare of improvised torches, the enthusiastic Romans were paying homage to him. Rarely has a faulty judgment been amended so quickly.

When Rossini was but twenty-one, all the theaters of Italy knew him. He wrote musical dramas and comedies—at times as many as six in one year—with incredible facility. It took him only thirteen days to write his *Barber*. His presence in Vienna, in 1822, set all minds a-whirl. Within the space of five months, he earned a fortune in England. Paris offered him the highest position in its musical life.

97. Rossini's Score of the first-act quartet of his "Elisabetta."

Up to that point, his career was extraordinary, but not unique. But what he did now was really unique. In the year 1829—he was thirty-seven and had written an equal number of successful operas—he suddenly felt bored, tired of the colorful game, weary, perhaps, of the new public that somehow had lost contact with the old style, although it crowded the theaters and acclaimed him vociferously. It was after the triumphant first performance of *William Tell* that he suddenly decided to withdraw from all musical activities.

The first thing he did was to return to his native town, made immortal by the surname given by the world to its great son: "The Swan of Pesaro." When the Revolution caused unrest even there, he went to Paris, where he stayed until the still far-away end of his life, occupying himself with everything but music. Only twice did he break his strange vow. First, when he wrote a cantata for the World Exposition; and second, when he once more came forth with one of his important works. A new opera? Serious? Gay? Nothing of the kind! The great satirist gave to the world a religious work, his *Stabat Mater*.

Today, only a small portion of his entire output is still alive on the stage. But that is attributable to a change in style rather than to his work. The *Barber*, in which he gave expression to all the genius and temperament of his race, is an exception. It still forms an integral part of the international standard operatic repertoire. Now and then, in Italy, people still listen with pleasure to his *Thieving Magpie, Cinderella,* the *Italian Woman in Algiers,* and *William Tell*. The overtures to these operas are heard to this day quite frequently everywhere. Rossini also wrote an opera to Shakespeare's *Othello*, but it was put in the shade by Verdi's great work.

In addition to Rossini, two other stars shone on the firmament of Italian opera, which at that time experienced the most brilliant epoch of the belcanto style: Vincenzo Bellini (1801-1835) and Gaetano Donizetti (1797-1848). Of the latter's works, *Lucia di Lammermoor* still lives, thanks mainly to a masterful sextet and a number of fine arias. Also unimpaired is the vitality of some of his comic operas, such as *The Elixir of Love, The Daughter of the Regiment* [Pl. 103], and *Don Pasquale*. Four survivors out of an original family of sixty-four! Bellini's best-known operas are *La Sonambula, I Puritani,* and, above all, *Norma*, with its magnificent aria *Casta Diva*, whose difficulties are beyond the reach of almost all present-day sopranos. Much in Donizetti's and Bellini's operas is unquestionably valuable, nobly conceived, and written with a perfect understanding of the human voice. If another belcanto era were ever to occur, these works would again come to the fore and enrapture the melody-loving listeners as of yore.

Very little of Luigi Cherubini (1760-1842) has come down to us, hardly more than his name and the fact that Beethoven esteemed him highly. His chief work, *The Water Carrier*, is forgotten today, and so are all his other operas which, though profound and noble, are as lacking in dramatic impact as those of Schubert. Who would ever recall him to-day, had he written nothing but operas? How many people would know the name of Beethoven, if operas had been his only means of musical expression? Cherubini, too, was lacking in "stage instinct," a quality so essential to operatic success.

But there were others. Who today knows anything of the works of Gasparo Spontini (1774-1851), although he had plenty of that instinct, and although he was a sort of musical dictator in his day? His two operas, *The Vestal* [Pl. 105] and *Fernand Cortéz*, were tremendously successful in Paris. Napoleon was quite enthusiastic about the latter, even though his admiration was due more to the opera's violent anti-Spanish tendency than to his love of music. The King of Prussia, who wished to make Berlin the operatic center of Europe, summoned Spontini to his capital. But although no effort was spared, Berlin found it impossible to compete with Paris which, second to the Italian centers, was then the main bulwark of opera in Europe.

Rossini retired into silence after his *William Tell*, in 1829. Bellini died at the age of thirty-four, in 1835. At his grave wept Chopin, foreseeing his own premature death. The same old trees of the Père Lachaise cemetery threw their shadows over their last resting places until, on the centenary of Bellini's birth, his remains were taken to Catania, his Sicilian home town. And a few years after Bellini's death, Donizetti, too, retired into silence. But his retirement was due to the distressingly sad circumstance that his mind had become deranged. This was the end of belcanto, the end of vocal ecstasies, the end of the widely arching and profusely ornamented phrases whose only aim it was to be melodious. Italian opera seemed deserted, vulnerable once more to the attacks coming from Germany. There, Weber was triumphant. His simple and folk-like romanticism smoothed the way for the great man who was to follow him. That man was Richard Wagner, and he had the power to deal a decisive blow to his southern rivals. But Italy's opera proved invincible. A new genius rose up in its behalf. His name was Giuseppe Verdi. And the more violent the attacks,—compared to them, Gluck's reforms were mere child's play—the stronger grew the defense.

THE FRENCH

The year 1752 had witnessed the coming to Paris of the buffonists, the Italian opera company responsible for so violent a conflict that its expulsion became necessary two years later. Gluck's arrival in Paris was the signal for the reorganization of the former adversaries: they became Gluckists and Piccinists.

The Italian comedy-opera *Serva Padrona* had left behind a profound impression. The wish to follow in its footsteps had been responsible for the birth of the *opéra comique,* the French comic opera, whose cultivation became the chief task of a number of prominent Paris theaters, pre-eminently of the one bearing its name. It has to this day remained one of the centers of French musical life. Soon thereafter, the history of the French operetta began. The first theater devoted to it was directed by Offenbach and revealed in its very name, *Bouffe,* its descent from the *opera buffa* of Italy.

The early composers of the *opéra comique* shared the fate of all precursors: honorable oblivion. Their names were Egide Duny (1709-1775) and Pierre Monsigny (1729-1817). The libretti, with their lower-middle-class milieu, are wholly uninteresting today. Spurred on by the Revolution, the librettists tried to turn modern, to dramatize the events of the day, and to glorify the Republic. The composers, too, wanted to march with the times. All they lacked was talent. It was not an easy matter to write revolutionary lyrics or music that could outlive the Revolution. Beethoven was in fact the only true musical interpreter of the French Revolution.

André Ernest Grétry (1741-1813), one of the best musicians of that epoch, clearly recognized the danger and raised a warning voice: "It seems that ever since the storming of the Bastille only music with the roar of cannon in it has been composed in France. This is a tragic mistake, as it undermines the inventive talent, the taste, and truthfulness of melodic expression. Unless we proceed with care, the ear and taste of the people will soon be corrupted, and a few years hence there will be nothing but musical noise makers. No doubt, this monstrous 'art' will be the death of true art . . ."

The latter part of the eighteenth century seemed to have produced nothing but musical mediocrities. The works of that period are wholly forgotten today, and no coming generation will ever be able to unearth them. In a romantic opera, Grétry sang the fate of the royal minnesinger, Richard the Lionhearted. He was followed by Etienne Méhul (1763-1817), a rather famous man in his day. He wrote *Joseph in Egypt*, perhaps the first opera without a female part in it. Closer to our perception—but still rather far away—were François Boieldieu (1775-1834) [Pl. 104] and Daniel François Auber (1782-1871). Boieldieu became tremendously popular through his *La Dame Blanche*. Auber's *Masaniello* (*The Mute of Portici*), on the other hand, was responsible for the unleashing of the Belgian revolution of 1830. The masses, carried away by the opera, which symbolically depicted the oppression of the country, mounted the barricades and achieved their independence of Holland. Auber also set to music the same subject that later served Verdi for his *Masked Ball* and was the first composer to write a *Manon*, long before Massenet and Puccini. None of these composers' works is played today, unless it be Auber's graceful comic opera *Fra Diavolo*. Equally unknown in our day is the

98. Scene from Auber's "The Ambassadress," end of Act III.
From "Album des theatres," 1837.

opera *Zampa* by Louis Joseph Hérold (1791-1833), though it was quite successful at the time. The overture to *Si j'étais roi*, by Adolphe Adam (1803-1856), is still heard occasionally, and his *Le Postillon de Longjumeau* may be dusted off now and then, if a tenor with an exceptionally high range wants to bring down the house wtih the aria that was the delight of our grandfathers.

Although history has pronounced so negative a judgment upon the French composers of that day, Paris nevertheless succeeded in establishing itself more and more firmly as an operatic metropolis. The numerous works by the above-mentioned composers were at least temporarily successful. There were other contributing factors. Democracy and liberty were on the march. New strata of the population found their way to the theater, while many a prominent European musician felt induced to settle in the city on the Seine. As a matter of fact, almost all the great operatic composers lived there at the beginning of the nineteenth century, each trying to outdo the other. Here is but a small excerpt from the list of first performances in that city: Boieldieu's *La Dame Blanche,* 1825; Auber's *Masaniello,* 1828; Rossini's *William Tell,* 1829; Bellini's *Norma,* 1831. And the same year witnessed the production of a work by a new man, Giacomo Meyerbeer (1791-1865), who had come from Germany but a short time before. His schooling was Italian, but he soon became acclimatized in Paris. The opera's name was *Robert le Diable.* Like almost all productions of that time, it was a rousing success.

Meyerbeer was considered by his contemporaries the most famous operatic composer of his day and a true regenerator of his art. All the more sad was his downfall from that pinnacle to the rank of a second-rate striver for cheap effects, a rank accorded him by many of our generation. But just as surely as his time overestimated him, ours errs in the opposite direction. His was a truly dramatic talent, his inventive gift for melodies was considerable, and so was his skill of instrumentation. The blame for the adoption of huge proportions, the striving for pomp, and the exaggerated sentimentality must not be placed entirely at his door. He merely did what the era of the Restoration and his contemporaries demanded of him. His greatest successes, played for decades on all stages and still occasionally heard, were *Les Huguenots* (1836), *Le Prophète*

(1849), and *L'Africaine* (1865). Many fine pieces of music may be found in these and his other works. His technical mastery was never disputed and had an admirer even in Wagner.

Two other names appear at the side of Meyerbeer: Jacques Halévy (1799-1862), who scored a considerable success with his *La Juive*, and Berlioz, of whom we shall soon have more to say in connection with other matters. His gifts, to be sure, were symphonic rather than theatrical, and his romanticism was closer to Germany than to his own country. He was a Meyerbeer in reverse. The lack of understanding with which almost all of his works met while he was alive applied to his operas *Benvenuto Cellini* (1838) [Pl. 111], *Beatrice and Benedict* (1862), and *The Trojans* (1869).

Just as it had been a German-born composer who gave France her *grande opéra*, so it was another German who gave her the operetta. He was Jacques Offenbach (1819-1880) [Pl. 106]. From the very beginning, the French operetta contained a goodly dose of satire and parody, and in this respect Offenbach was an unsurpassed master. His rhythms were brilliant, his melodies electrifying. These attributes frequently made one forget the depth of feeling inherent in folk-like little airs scattered almost unnoticed in his works. Hardly anybody could have imagined that he, undisputed king of the Paris operetta, the man who had launched such sparkling works as *Orpheus in Hades, La Belle Hélène, Engagement by Lantern Light, Fortunio's Song, The Isle of Tulipatan, Bluebeard, The Girl from Elizondo, La Vie Parisienne, The Princess of Trebizond, Périchole,* and countless others, was at the same time a yearning and melancholy romanticist. These characteristics were proved when there was heard the score of his last opera, which turned out to be a gem of the purest water. After so much satire, unfettered gaiety, and terpsichorean élan, how unexpected were the noble strains of true love, poignant sorrows of death, and mysterious play between dream and reality in his *Tales of Hoffmann!* This is the opera with the famous Barcaroll, whose origin is woven round with a wreath of legends. They may, or they may not, be true, but one thing is certain: hardly any other work was so much pursued by ill luck as this opera—from the death of its creator, who had not quite been able to finish it, to the horrible fire at the Vienna Ring Theater on the evening of the *Tales'* first performance, an inexplicable sequence of tragic events tried to dim the luster of one of the most romantic love melodies known to the world. *Belle nuit, o nuit d'amour . . .*

THE GERMANS

Chronologically, the German opera should be put in second place. For a long time, however, German operatic composers were little more than local celebrities, while the three greatest masters of the eighteenth century inclined toward other styles: Gluck wrote his finest operas in the style of France, while Handel and Mozart were adherents of the Italian school, the former in England, the latter in Austria.

We must nevertheless take Mozart as our starting point in the contemplation of German opera during its greatest century, the nineteenth. We know that among his many stage works were some in the German language. Two of them must be specially mentioned, because they were German not only in language but also in spirit: *The Abduction from the Seraglio* and *The Magic Flute*. As was customary in those days, Mozart did not call them operas but *Singspiele*, a name indicative not only of the simplicity of the action but also of that of the musical style and of the interpolation of spoken dialogue between the musical numbers—a breach of style unbearable to the Italians. (That is why, in their works, the intermediary texts are sung in recitative form.) But the Germans maintained the dialogue and so arrived at an opera type which was wholly eliminated only by Richard Wagner. In the operetta, on the other hand, this stylistic symptom is maintained to this day. It may be remarked in passing that France, too, used the spoken dialogue between musical numbers in many of her operas, among them the original version of Bizet's *Carmen*.

Mozart's *Magic Flute* undoubtedly scored the greatest success of all his works. It would nevertheless be an exaggeration to date the independence of German-language opera from the year 1791. For many years to follow, Italian opera remained the absolute ruler in German lands also. Neither did Beethoven's *Fidelio*—a further step in that direction—change the situation. Schubert dreamt of the romantic opera, of the form, that is to say, in which German-language opera actually became victorious. It was explained before why it was not vouchsafed to him to write it successfully.

The goal was attained by Mozart's contemporary, Carl Maria von Weber [Pl. 108], who was born in the North German town of Eutin, in 1786. His restless, and seemingly forever breathless, life and his pain-wracked body were in strange contrast with the quiet glow of his melo-

182 .

100. Weber's manuscript of the "Sword Song" after a poem by Theodor Körner, dated Sept. 13, 1814, Tonna.

dies and the robustly folk-like lyricism of his works. He succeeded in finding musical expression for the romantic yearning which the finest German minds of the day envisioned as the true spirit of the people. The world of his tone pictures was populated by fairies and legendary figures, showed sun-flooded forests, and was filled with genuine folk scenes in which both faith and superstition abounded.

After long years of wandering through Germany and Austria, Weber settled in Prague as an operatic conductor. There he led the first production of Beethoven's *Fidelio* outside of Vienna. The young musician had already finished three operas of his own, but his fame was not due to them. A single evening, that of July 18, 1821, made him a brilliant star in the German musical firmament. It was the day, memorable in the history of German musical dramas, when his *Freischütz* had its first performance and was jubilantly acclaimed. Overnight, Weber became Germany's leading operatic composer, whose further production was looked forward to eagerly. But while, in his *Freischütz*, he had been able to set to music a genuine folk-like, though rather naive, libretto with a wealth of musically effective scenes, he happened, in his *Euryanthe* and

. 183

Oberon, upon libretti that were so weak and incoherent that even his
nobly beautiful melodies were unable to redeem them. Many of his innovations, especially his magnificent tonal depictions of natural phenomena, particularly in his *Oberon,* made Weber the direct precursor of Wagner. Weber died a premature death in London, in 1826. It was an occasion for great mourning to the young German-language opera.

The other composers of that school, worthy though they may be
individually, are but landmarks on the road leading to the master of
Bayreuth. Ludwig Spohr (1784-1859) was a highly gifted musician. His
Faust bears a greater affinity to Goethe's work than that of Gounod,
though the latter put his in the shade. Heinrich Marschner (1785-1861)
wrote a successful, though now forgotten, opera, *The Vampire,* and
somewhat anticipated Wagner's favorite motive of redemption through
love in his *Hans Heiling.* Once in a while, there appears on our stages
Friedrich Flotow's pretty opera *Martha,* whose style wavers between that
of France and Germany, and which makes use, in Wagner's leitmotif
manner, of Ireland's beautiful song "The Last Rose of Summer." The
sparkling and highly ingenious comic opera by Otto Nicolai (1810-1849),
The Merry Wives of Windsor, still retains its vitality, in spite of the magnificent *Falstaff* written by Verdi on the same subject. Forgotten, how-

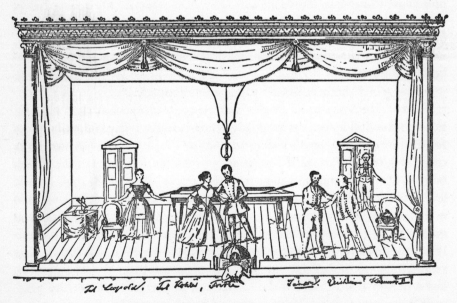

101. Billiard scene from Lortzing's "Poacher." After a contemporary drawing.

ever, is his *Allessandro Stradella,* in which the life of the early-Italian composer is depicted. The same fate has befallen *Das Nachtlager in Granada* by Konradin Kreutzer (1780-1849), the cloyingly sweet *Trompeter von Säkkingen* by Nessler, and many other operas of that period.

Special mention may be due Albert Lortzing (1801-1851), a musician with a fine sense of humor and a gift for simple, folk-like melodies. He was both the librettist and the composer of the successful opera *Zar und Zimmermann, Undine, Der Waffenschmied, Der Wildschütz,* and a number of others which, though they could gain no more than local fame, were immensely popular in Germany.

THE SPANISH ZARZUELA

The zarzuela is the Spanish sister of the French and Viennese operetta. In its more pretentious forms, it clearly approaches the comic opera, just as had been the case in Paris and Vienna. But its history, practically unknown outside the Iberian peninsula, is considerably older than that of its Central and Western European relations. It may have had its beginnings in the famous *Eglogas* by Juan del Encina who was a contemporary of Columbus and Magellan. The next stage of some importance in the early history of the zarzuela is represented by the drama of the great poet Lope de Vega, *La selva sin amor* (The Forest without Love), which was performed in Madrid, in 1629, with music written by an unknown composer.

The word zarzuela has a curious etymology. It stems from a country seat of the same name in the vicinity of Madrid, used by Philip IV as a summer residence, about 1634. Groups of artists used to come there for the performance of short musical works. These festive occasions were called *Fiestas de Zarzuela,* simplified into zarzuela later. It seems that, both as literature and music, these works occupied a rather high artistic level. What took place at that country seat may have been similar to the events at the Palazzo Pitti of Florence, of which a detailed account was given. A new genre was being created for the gratification of a culturally advanced class. At any rate, one of the first works of which there is a record *El golfo de last sirenas* (The Bay of Sirens), had for its author no less a person than Calderón de la Barca. For the first time in this singspiel, (the genre to which it may most nearly be compared) a national subject was joined to the folk music of the country. It was a strange piece, a mixture of courtly and popular elements. As time went on, the latter trait became more predominant. Ever more plainly was the music taken from the many and abounding sources of Spanish folklore. Choruses and dances were interspersed, scenes dealing with fishermen, seamen, peasants, and the many popular customs from all parts of Spain, especially from Madrid and Andalusia. But perhaps this occurred only after the zarzuela was transplanted from a courtly milieu to a public theater and thus had an experience similar to that of the Italian opera. It soon became the declared favorite of the whole people. Its melodies have at all times been no less folk-like than those of the homebred Italian operas. The zarzuela adopted as a distinguishing mark a division into two acts. Only much later was a third act added. Like the operetta, it presented a mixture of serious and comic figures, of songs and dances, of the sung and the spoken word. But while the operetta loved to lay its scenes in far-away countries, those of the zarzuela were Spanish without exception.

Calderón de la Barca, who, next to Cervantes, was Spain's greatest poet of the classic epoch, was quite active as a librettist. He wrote regular operatic books, although the word opera neither occurred in nor was applied to them. This international word appeared in Spain only in 1698. All the same, many works performed in the traditional theaters of ancient Madrid prior to that year really belonged in the realm of opera rather than of the zarzuela. Rising popularity made the zarzuela stray from the straight path. It went through a period of decadence that lasted until far into the nineteenth century.

In spite of all, however, it remained the most generally beloved form of Spanish music. Neither the opera nor concert music were able to dislodge it from the people's heart. It may well be asserted that there has not been a Spanish musician within the past centuries who has not tried his skill in this species, including even Isaac Albéniz and Manuel de Falla.

Let us, in passing, recall one of the most characteristic musicians of the peninsula. He was Vicente Martín y Soler, whose work coincided with that of Mozart. Born in Valencia about 1756—which happens to be the year of the great Salzburger's birth—he devoted himself to Italian opera, like all ambitious musicians. He wrote—he, too!—an *Iphigenia in Aulis*. But his greatest success was scored with a comic opera, performed in Vienna, in 1786. It was entitled *Una cosa rara* (A Strange Affair), and its success put in the shade Mozart's concurrently produced *Figaro*.

Nevertheless, there is nobody today who would ever think of that "strange affair" were he not reminded of it at every performance of Mozart's *Don Giovanni*. For in the last act of that work, which chonologically followed *Figaro*, Mozart lets the stage orchestra playing the dinner music strike up a melody from *Cosa rara*. It has become almost traditional for Leoporello, the opera's comic figure, to launch at that place a question across the footlights at the conductor: "*Che cosa rara?*" ("What's strange about it?) or: "Why not let us have some Mozart instead, maestro?" A little musical tit for tat! But the *Cosa rara* was remarkable also for another reason. There occurs in it a little dance piece in three-four time, graceful and swaying, a distant anticipation of the waltz, many decades prior to its definite appearance. And from Spain!

In the year 1778, one of Italy's best musician's, Luigi Boccherini (1743-1805), joined the ranks of the zarzuela composers. He had a greater success with *Clementina* than with his minuet, still played, and his beautiful cello concerto.

Among the nineteenth-century zarzuela composers, Francisco Asenjo Barbieri and Emilio Arrieta may be mentioned. The latter's *Marina*, first published in 1855, and made into a three-act opera in 1871, is still a big drawing card. There followed the greatest and most brilliant era of the zarzuela. It is linked with the names of some composers unknown outside of Spain and Latin America, although in these countries their works are esteemed as highly as, and have gained, if possible, an even greater popularity than, *The Bat* and *La Belle Heléne*. Let us name but five of the most important of those composers: Federico Chueca, Ruperto Chapí, Jerónimo Jiménez, José Serrano, and, foremost, Amadeo Vives (1871-1932). Among the latter's works are *Maruxa, Los Bohemios,* and *Doña Francisquita*.

Finally, we should like to add the name of an important Spanish musician whose activity embraced the zarzuela as well as the opera: Tomás Bretón (1850-1923). *Los amantes de Teruel* (The Lovers of Teruel) and *La Dolores* were his chief works in the realm of serious opera. They were, however, put entirely in the shade by the unparalleled success of his zarzuela *La verbena de la paloma* (The Dove Feast). This enchanting work was heard not only all over Iberia but, at about the turn of the century, played for many months in five theaters of Buenos Aires at the same time.

. 187

20

The Triumph of Romanticism

LIKE a mighty torrent, romanticism invaded the artistic life of the nineteenth century. Perhaps it started with poetry and its superlative ability to mirror life. "There must," said Emile Zola, "be a harmony between social evolution, which is the cause, and literary expression, which is the effect." He might have said: artistic expression, for all arts are but one. We should like to make another little change. Not: there must be harmony, but: there *is* a harmony, always and everywhere.

What had happened? Politically, a sweeping revolution had taken place. A new social stratum had come to the fore: the middle classes. A still newer one began to show signs of life: the proletariat. Fetters had been shed, dams burst, rules discarded, traditions made a laughing stock. From out a world that had seemed firmly constructed—with enjoyment for some and suffering for others, unchangeable in either case—a piece had suddenly been pried loose, and all proportions had been shifted. Everything had become unstable, for everybody. There began a struggle for new goals, new forms of life, new philosophies, new arts; a struggle which still continues and whose end nobody can foretell.

The old strict rules were replaced by a new freedom. Like every new freedom, it was still insecure, vague, and undefined. At first, that was quite novel, fascinating, and exciting. Everybody described it to everybody else, spoke of himself, revealed secrets which for centuries nobody had ever mentioned.

Thomas Mann once said: "Romanticism is the impulse to roam, and the tender desire to stay at home, all at the same time." Yes, it does indeed include the urge toward distant parts and a fondness for the native soil. For it is a yearning in its every form. Romanticism is all that, and much more beside. Romanticism is that which can never be explained to him who does not feel it.

What does that mean when referred to art? While in classicist times the firmly joined forms restricted and shaped the content, in romanticism, the idea, the inherent meaning of a work of art, burst all forms and shaped them anew. In every artist—perhaps even in every sensitive man—romanticism lives as something innate. And it may be that every genuine masterpiece reveals, in the last analysis, both components: the classicist, springing from a desire for noble form, and the romantic, representing his yearning for supreme expression.

Where, then, does romanticism in music begin? That, too, is difficult to say. Many things in medieval music impress us as being romantic. Romantic, for instance, may be Bach's mysticism and his brotherly intimacy with Death. Undoubtedly romantic, too, was Beethoven's closely identifying himself with Nature's om-nipotence, the cries of despair of his tortured soul, the most personal expression ever set to music. And according to E. T. A. Hoffmann, who was a prominent musical critic of romanticism, even Mozart's operas, schoolroom examples to us of classicism, are profoundly romantic. But as we said: every masterpiece is classic, and romantic at the same time. Of course, the mixture of the two components is proportionately not always the same. At the beginning of the nineteenth century there was an ever more clearly discernible inclination toward the romantic, until one day the last remnants of the classic spirit

102. The contrabassist dell' Occa.
Drawing by the musician-poet
E. T. A. Hoffmann.

of form had disappeared. But romanticism, too, came to the end of its road. We shall have more to say about this when discussing the twentieth century.

It is obvious that so strongly articulated an emotional art as the romantic was at times in danger of degenerating into emotional drivel. Just as a classicist style, when carried to excess, must suffocate in a plethora of forms, exaggerated or inferior romanticism is bound to become trashy. He who thumbs through old music or reads forgotten poems of the romantic era will come upon plenty of trash.

It is obvious that none of the "classics" of music could have considered himself classic. Only posterity put that stamp on him, expressing by it both a principle of form and an exemplary standard. The romantics, on the other hand, felt that they were just that. More or less consciously, they formed an actual school, a brotherhood. They were convinced that they were the heralds of a new art, for which they were ready to fight in polemic writings or by word of mouth and, above all, in their works. While between Haydn, Mozart, and Beethoven there existed but an extremely loose, an almost accidental, contact, and none at all between them and Bach and Handel, many of the most prominent romantic musicians were friends in the noblest sense of the word. Every one did all in his power to hew a way for the works of the others. Indeed, a rare epoch in the history of music!

Schubert may be said to have stood on the borderline between classicism and romanticism. The scales, which Beethoven had already set to trembling, were for the first time tipped in the direction of romanticism. But Schubert was not as yet aware of that. He only felt that his exuberant fantasy threatened again and again to burst the boundaries drawn by his predecessors. And yet, at the time of Beethoven's and his death, a genuinely romantic work had already been written: the *Fantastic Symphony* by Berlioz. With the advent of romanticism, descriptive, programmatic, and, I am tempted to say, pictorial music came to the fore, while absolute music, which had formerly ruled supreme, died away more and more. That is why the song, which played but a subordinate part in the classic epoch, became now, with the coming of the new art of tonal painting, one of the favorite forms of the new school. In the works of a Schumann, Loewe, Franz, Brahms, Wolf, Strauss, of the Russians and Czechs, of the French late-romanticists, the first to be tinged by impressionism, the song reached the heights to which the prophetic genius of Schubert had pointed the way. The connections between the arts became closer. New ties were established between music and painting, mutually inspiring each other. And music became fused with poetry not only in the song but also, to its ultimate limit, in Wagner's stage works. How close had become the tie that bound together these two arts in the romantic era is evidenced by the very titles of the musical works: the Symphonic Poem rivaled the symphony, while smaller forms were preferably called Songs Without Words, Ballads, Album Leafs, or Rhapsodies.

A chapter on romanticism would not be complete without a few words about that strange personality, briefly mentioned a little while ago: Ernst Theodor Amadeus Hoffmann (1776-1822). Although posterity quickly forgot him, he was nevertheless a highly characteristic figure of his epoch. He was a gifted painter, poet, and musician, all in one. He created the fantastic figure of "Kapellmeister Kreisler," the prototype of a romantic musician, in constant conflict with reality, a genius wavering on the brink of insanity. Many musicians discussed in this chapter and the following ones had something of that Kapellmeister in their make-up. Hoffmann's figure still lives in Offenbach's romantic opera *The Tales of Hoffmann,* in which three of the magic episodes of his adventurous life are recorded.

And now the romantic lives are to pass in review before us. How brief many of them were! Perhaps the dreamy, world-removed mental attitude of the romanticists was wholly alien to the iron energy displayed by a Handel or a Beethoven, men who triumphed over Death, the Devil, and their own hearts, or to the tranquil piety which served to prolong the life of a Bach, or a Haydn. True, there is no rule without its exceptions: Mozart, the "classic," only lived to be thirty-five, while Wagner, the romanticist, was a man of powerful vitality. No inflexible rule can therefore be established, but there is no escaping the sad fact that Schubert's life ended at thirty-one, Bellini's at thirty-four, Bizet's at thirty-seven, Mendelssohn's at thirty-eight, Chopin's and Weber's at thirty-nine, Hugo Wolf's at forty-three, Schumann's and Moussorgsky's at forty-six. And another point, still more deeply moving, comes to mind. Not a few of the romantic musicians stepped across that narrow borderline which the average man has drawn between normality and insanity: Donizetti, Schumann, Smetana, Wolf, Duparc. Many another came close to it, frequently at the very time of his most creative moods.

The curtain rises. Within the space of eight years, the great musicians were born who, continuing where Beethoven and Schubert had left off, were to give its final shape and content to musical romanticism: Berlioz, in 1803; Mendelssohn, 1809; Schumann and Chopin, in 1810; Liszt, in 1811. And two years later, in 1813, came Richard Wagner, who perfected it, crowned it, and exhausted it.

HECTOR BERLIOZ

The figure of a Frenchman emerges from the group of the earliest romantic composers. And what a strange man he was! Extravagant and overstrung, a real Kapellmeister Kreisler. His name was Hector Berlioz [Pl. 110]. He was born on December 11, 1803, in Côte-St. André, in the Dauphiné. Twenty-seven years later, after having overcome a great many difficulties in connection with his choice of profession, he gained the greatly coveted *Prix de Rome*, making possible a course of study in the Eternal City. What won him the prize was a cantata, *Sardanapale*, and not the *Fantastic Symphony*, which was the principal work he had thus far written and which had so excited the enthusiasm of the German romanticists. It bore the subtitle "Episodes from the Life of an Artist" and depicted in glowing colors love's intoxication and passionate dreams, the heaven and hell of an overpowering sentiment — exciting, torturing, cruel.

103. Berlioz. Caricature by E. Garjat.

With this youthful work, which undoubtedly was meant as a musical picturization of his own unbridled and passionate life, descriptive music took an important step forward. And when he sketched that symphony, mind you, Beethoven was still alive! Berlioz' art of instrumentation, too, struck out upon entirely new paths. His unbelievable imagination in the realm of sound led him to forsesee and essay new possibilities and combinations, of which none of his contemporaries dared even to dream. The masses of sound demanded by him were equaled

104. From the manuscript of Berlioz' symphony "Romeo and Juliet." Beginning of Juliet's mourning scene.

23 Benvenuto Cellini, opéra en
trois actes égorgé à Paris et qu'on
joue souvent en Allemagne. Jamais je
ne retrouverai la verve et le brio
qu'il y a là dedans.

24 La Damnation de Faust
Légende dramatique en 4 parties où
se trouvent les morceaux aujourd'hui
célèbres : Le chœur des Sylphes, le
ballet des Follets, La marche Hongroise,
la Romance de Marguerite et le
morceau fantastique la Course à l'abîme.

25 L'Enfance du Christ Trilogie
sacrée dont j'ai fait les paroles
et la musique.

105. From a Berlioz letter to an unknown addressee, enumerating his works.

only by such works as Mahler's Eighth Symphony, Schönberg's *Gurrelieder*, and a very few works of our—not his—century. His compositions required the cooperation of hundreds of musicians and singers, whose combined efforts—especially in his Requiem—produced exceptionally striking effects. There is full justification for calling Berlioz the father of the modern orchestra. His *Theory of Instrumentation* is still considered the basic work on orchestral knowledge. To bring it up to date, it had merely to be amplified (by Richard Strauss), not revised.

The life of Berlioz is one long chain of disappointments, both artistic and private, the latter mostly in connection with his passionate love affairs. His highly complicated character which, his contemporaries said, was "violent, naive, unreasonable, ungoverned, but, above all, sincere," allowed him but few moments that were tranquil and contented.

One of these extremely rare happy moments must have occurred when Paganini, who had attended a Berlioz concert, sent him a letter the next day, enclosing the prodigious amount of 20,000 francs, a veritable life-saver. Berlioz wished to thank the generous donor by the dedication of his charming work, *Romeo and Juliet* [Ill. 104], but Paganini died in Italy before the symphony could be completed.

None of Berlioz' compositions was successful in France during his lifetime. He was given a ridiculously small government position which, moreover, had nothing to do with music. On the other hand, his name steadily gained in reputation throughout the rest of Europe. Only after his death—he died in Paris on March 8, 1869—did his music come to be appreciated in his homeland. Those who had but recently cast stones at him, now burned incense on his altar, as a contemporary caricature very cleverly showed. People began to comprehend his work—not so much his operas as his symphonies and symphonic poems. They loved the beautiful and interesting legend *The Damnation of Faust* (which, by the way, contains the electrifying Rakoczy March) and grew enthusiastic about the grandiosely towering sounds of his Requiem.

Berlioz' influence upon the other romantic musicians was considerable. In 1860, Wagner sent him one of the first scores of *Tristan* with the significant dedication: "Dedicated to Romeo and Juliet by your grateful Tristan and Isolde." A strange move, this, on the part of Wagner, which, however, did not prevent Berlioz from criticizing Wagner most severely when the latter gave a concert in Paris. It was at that time that someone coined the apt phrase of "the two hostile brothers of the music of the future."

FELIX MENDELSSOHN-BARTHOLDY

Mendelssohn [Pl. 112] was born in Hamburg, on February 3, 1809. Two years later, his family—they were wealthy bankers—moved to Berlin. Felix revealed all the symptoms of a child prodigy. He reminds one strikingly of Mozart. In his life, too, there was a sister of exceptional musical talent. She might have become the first, and one of the very few, women in history with creative musical ability, had her father not convinced her of the soundness of the then prevailing opinion that, to a woman, music could be but an ornament and avocation, never a profession.

The name Felix seems to us like a symbol, for Mendelssohn's life was exceedingly happy. The intellectual elite of his time met at the house of his parents for weekly concerts. At one of them, the seventeen-year-old youth conducted his overture to Shakespeare's *Midsummer Night's Dream*, a most striking proof of his talent. The parental pocketbook permitted the young man to visit various parts of Europe and to study there. Musical notes and a wealth of drawn sketches of that period still exist [Pl. 113].

The impressions gained by Mendelssohn in Italy, and recorded in his *Italian Symphony*, were not particularly profound. Perhaps he was still too young to penetrate to the fundamental meaning of the Latin character. Everything he saw was flooded by sun and gaiety. His journey north left a considerably deeper imprint. The gloomy landscape of Scotland and the Palace of Holyrood in which the unfortunate Mary Stuart had breathed her last were musically depicted in his symphony called the *Scotch*. And the Fingal Cave, that natural phenomenon of sounding basalt pillars, suggested to him the beautiful overture of that name.

Mendelssohn wrote altogether four symphonies and one symphonic cantata. Among his finest compositions are the *Violin Concerto* and the *Midsummer Night's Dream Suite*, the overture to which was mentioned before. Its Scherzo, Nocturne, and Wedding March are to this day among the most-played works of the romantic literature. But the less familiar Fairy Dance, too, and the Funeral March are inspired pieces of music. Real depth—which is not present in all the creations of this perhaps all-too-happy life—is revealed in his great religious oratorios *St. Paul* and *Elijah*. He succeeded in writing many a beautiful song, expressed in a genuine, warmly felt folk style, a characteristic to be found also in his choruses. In these latter, he came to be a real singer of German romanticism, of the German forest, of wandering with a rucksack on one's back, of tarrying with the belle of the village . . .

Mendelssohn's activities as a conductor and organizer were of great importance. At the age of twenty, he proved his exceptional artistic farsightedness by re-discovering Bach's *St. Matthew Passion* and giving it back to the world. He became the head of the Leipzig Gewandhaus

106. A letter by Mendelssohn to his sister Fanny.

Concerts, in 1835, and succeeded in adding to their world fame. Eight years later, he founded the Leipzig Conservatory. Schumann was one of its first professors, and many prominent musicians studied there.

This life, free from great difficulties, from gnawing doubts, and from enervating struggles, but full of gracefulness, noble sentiments, and sincere sympathies, ended in Leipzig, on November 4, 1847.

ROBERT SCHUMANN

If Mendelssohn was felicity, Schumann was tragedy. Here we see an accumulation of all the enumerated symptoms of romanticism. An overflowing, morbidly sensitive mind, an infinite yearning, a distressing unrest, exultation, and despair. And then there was that crossing of the

. 197

borderline, that straying into the gloomy regions stretching out infinitely beyond the realm of normality. Schumann wrote his most inspired compositions between 1850 and 1854, already under the gruesome pressure of the mental debility that took him farther away from life from day to day. In that period he produced 250 songs, grandiose psychological musical studies steeped in abysmal sorrow.

And how strange! His life was not a sad one. It was lighted up by a wonderful star, he was ministered to by an angel, a Muse, an ideal companion such as is rarely vouchsafed to a creative—a struggling—man. Her name was Clara Wieck [Pl. 115]. How long he had to fight before he could call her his own! Father Wieck, a piano teacher, would not hear of the marriage, although he was sincerely attached to the young man. But love prevailed. Clara's heroism with which she stood by her husband when he was a prey to depressions, when his attacks frightened him and carried him to the brink of despair, would have secured for her a glorious place in the history of music even if she had not also been one of the most brilliant pianists of her century. When Schumann died, she had but one mission: in all the forty years that she outlived him she played to the audiences of the world's cities Robert Schumann's music.

Schumann's brief life was filled with a restless activity. He served his artistic faith by his works and his writings. The musical periodical edited by him was a veritable bulwark of romanticism. Schumann was largely responsible for the meteoric rise of Chopin and for the removal of many an obstacle in the path of Berlioz. It was he who, by a glorifying article, caused the wholly unknown Brahms to be received into the guild of romantic masters, who predicted for him severe struggles and wounds, but also final victory. Schumann's whole being was filled with his mission. In spirit and in deed, he served the brotherhood of the new music and repeatedly insisted that the struggle's main goal was the overthrow of Philistinism. He was David, and the brotherhood of romantic musicians the "Davidsbund," as he frequently called it, once even in the title of one of his works.

Schumann was born in the Saxon town of Zwickau, on June 8, 1810. After a brief period devoted to the study of law, much against his inclinations, he definitely turned to music, intending to become a pianist. But Fate willed otherwise. A paralysis of the fingers, the result of exaggeratedly complicated exercises, made him take up a composer's career.

The piano remained his favorite instrument, and a major part of his

works was devoted to it, beginning with his first twenty-three compositions. He may justly be considered a true regenerator of piano technique in that he always made the virtuoso subservient to the higher artistic idea. This is true to his *Papillons, Davidsbündler, Carnival, Childhood Scenes, Kreisleriana* (once more an allusion to E. T. A. Hoffmann's
fantastic figure), and above all, of his magnificent Symphonic Etudes.
The piano part of his songs, too, is more strongly developed than that of
any other master up to then and at times even outranks the voice in
importance. This dual singing opened to Schumann undreamt-of possibilities for the musical illustration of poetic expressions.

How fully conveyed is the profound and stirring poetic message of
Heine's poems in the song cycle *Dichterliebe;* how perfect a musical com-
plement is furnished for the beautiful Eichendorff verses in the *Lieder-
kreis;* how inimitably is Chamisso's noble ecstasy portrayed in *Frauenliebe
und Leben!* Only a few of Schuman's countless gems shall be mentioned
here: *Widmung,* with its soaring warmth; *Der Nussbaum,* with its masterly depiction of a mood; *Du bist wie eine Blume,* with its deep penetration into a heartfelt folksong-like text; *Mondnacht,* with its wonderful

107. Schumann's manuscript of "The Two Grenadiers," words by H. Heine.

. 199

expression of the soul's nocturnal yearning; *Volksliedchen*, with its charming archness; and finally the colossal painting of *Die beiden Grenadiere*: how from the lament of the two legionaires of the *grand armée*, destroyed in Russia, the magnificent vision of Napoleon emerges; how the ghostlike call of the Marseillaise, sweeping over the battlefields, makes the dead rise up again, armed and jubilantly ready once more to follow their Emperor. It is as gripping as it is weird, and yet electrifying.

Schumann wrote four symphonies. Their music is beautiful and noble, without, however, achieving the importance of that of Beethoven or Brahms. Impressive are his oratorios *Das Paradies und die Peri* and *Der Rose Pilgerfahrt*. Like so many other musicians, Schumann felt deeply impressed by Goethe's world of ideas. A few years before his death, he wrote *Scenes from Faust*. Exceptionally beautiful is his concerto for piano and orchestra, one of the most-played works in this category.

It was about 1840 that Schumann was seized with a melancholia that became more intense as time went on. He was subject to periods of horrible dread and anxiety and to inexplicable attacks of despair. In 1854, a fit of insanity made him plunge into the Rhine. He was saved—if it can be called salvation—and had to be confined in the lunatic asylum of Endenich, near the place where Beethoven, the man so ardently revered by him, was born. There, wholly insane, he died, on July 29, 1856.

His creed may be summed up in a single sentence written by himself: "Without enthusiasm nothing of any value can be accomplished in art." And there is another sentence from his pen which might serve as a dedication to all composers: "To send forth light into the depths of the human heart—the artist's task."

FRANZ LISZT

Franz Liszt [Pl. 117] was born on October 22, 1811, in Raiding, a village in the Austrian Burgenland province, that region between two cultures in which Haydn's cradle, too, had stood. But in the case of Liszt, the Hungarian admixture was considerably more pronounced. His Magyar temperament is revealed in many of his works, in spite of the fact that he hardly ever stayed in his homeland.

However, Liszt, the representative of his people, was not only a romanticist of the purest German school, but at the same time also a shining

108. Manuscript of the end of a piano composition by the 17-year-old Liszt.

example of the "world citizen." His life's religion was music, irrespective of the fact that in his advanced years he donned a priest's garb. The Emperor of Austria conferred on him a title of nobility. The women of Europe admired his splendidly virile figure, but his true beauty dwelt in his soul.

Liszt was the king of virtuosos. But he was more, too: a creative artist. His time was hardly aware of that. Wagner, who through Liszt had received glory, a wife, and not a few musical thoughts, put him in the shade, as he did everybody else. And Liszt, the unselfish champion of others, did nothing to further his own compositions.

Throughout his life, he was an indefatigable helper and counsellor to all who needed him, an effective promoter of the interests of not only the musicians of his intimate circle, but also of countless composers from beyond the border, of almost all the gifted of his time. He did much for Schubert's and Schumann's works, and put himself out to launch Smetana, Borodin, Moussorgsky, and Berlioz. There was something quite touching about his friendly relation with Chopin who, from a narrow-minded point of view, was a "competitor." How fine is the book Liszt published after Chopin's death about the Polish composer's life and works! Liszt became the discoverer of César Franck and the prophet of Richard Wagner.

The wealth and beauty of Liszt's work corresponds to the nature of his life. In both are mirrored love and kindness of heart. Countess d'Agoult was an ideal companion to him for many years. Her romantic passion for the great artist had made her leave her husband and accompany Liszt on his travels. In a quiet spot near one of the magnificent upper-Italian lakes, Cosima was born, a child of that great love, and Wagner's future wife. Years later, after the never wholly explained termination of his relations with Marie d'Agoult, Liszt found in Princess Caroline Sayn-Wittgenstein a high-minded companion, who had a decisive influence upon his life and work. It took a great deal of effort to bring about the Princess's divorce from her husband. After many years, the way to matrimony was clear. Too late! The aging artist had become Abbé Liszt.

In 1848, when he was already one of Europe's most famous musicians, Liszt undertook the direction of the Weimar Theater. This changed the old town of Goethe and Schiller into an important musical center. Liszt's clearsightedness was revealed in the choice of his repertoire. He was responsible for the first performances of *Tannhäuser* and *Lohengrin*. In the course of the concerts he gave, he conducted Beethoven's nine symphonies, Berlioz' *Fantastic Symphony*, and Schumann's Faust. At the same time, he championed these works in letters, articles and books, defending the tendencies of the young romantic school. He actually became a kind of rallying point for the young musicians of all countries, dedicating himself enthusiastically to the development of the rising musical generation.

In spite of all this, his own compositions were known to but few. By the time he left Weimar, his *Tasso, Hamlet, Dante, Faust, Mazeppa*, and *Les Préludes* had been written. They were symphonic poems with which, ideologically concurring with Berlioz, he gave final form to the new program music. Leitmotifs, too, began to appear in his work.

The coldness and indifference with which the public received Liszt's compositions, in spite of the unbounded enthusiasm he never failed to elicit as a piano virtuoso, made him gradually withdraw from concert activities. Among his songs there are some with great emotional depth. His oratorios *Christus* and *The Legend of St. Elizabeth* reveal true great-

109. A Liszt concert. Caricatures by Janko. Top: "Hamlet broods, Faust suffers, the keys tremble with sighs." Bottom: "Dante's Inferno; both the damned and the piano groan."

ness. Foremost, of course, stands his pianistic work. There are two piano concertos, the *Hungarian Fantasy*, the Rhapsodies, of which especially the second attained immense popularity, the Etudes, Legends, and other pieces written in free style. And let us not omit the Sonata in B minor, dedicated to Schumann.

Once, when Liszt, on one of his innumerable travels from one point in Europe to another, arrived in Geneva, he made the following entry in the hotel register:

Profession:	Musician-Philosopher
Born:	On Parnassus
Coming from:	Doubts
Going to:	Truth

Yes, he searched for truth indefatigably, practicing it wherever he could. There are few figures of equal nobility in the history of art. He died on July 31, 1886, in Bayreuth, the town of his great son-in-law, Richard Wagner.

21

The Musical Awakening of the Nations

WITH many nations, music remained in a primitive condition for long periods of time, without taking a decisive step on the road leading to art. That is why the contemplation of the past centuries has been confined to a rather limited territory: Italy, Germany, Austria, France. These were the nations in the foreground of the classic epoch. Let us put it this way: these peoples were the first players heard in the constantly spreading "concert" of Europe. In the course of the nineteenth century, other nations began to move in and occupy some of the still empty seats in this orchestra. Many of them were new arrivals making their first public appearance. Others—like Spain and England—merely returned after a long absence to take possession once more of their accustomed seats. It is obvious that not all of them could play the first fiddle. But, if we adhere to our simile, that was not at all necessary. In the modern orchestra, all instruments are important, not only the first violins, as was the case in former times.

This expansion of musical life can be traced to two causes, not counting a number of psychological reasons. One was purely material: railways, steamships, and somewhat later, telegraph wires brought the peoples in closer contact with one another. Cultural interchange became more brisk from day to day, and it grew ever more difficult for a people to remain artistically inactive while its neighbors were progressing rapidly all the time. The second cause was romanticism. We watched it become the spiritual banner of the century. It made age-old national possessions reappear: myths, customs, legends, and melodies that had slumbered since time immemorial in the people's memory were called to life again and cultivated. Romanticism devoted itself lovingly to the exploration of folklore. Its literature dealt with folklike figures, while its music made use of national melodic possessions, of popular rhythms, of simple harmonies in thirds and sixths, such as the girls in the fields and the lads at the dances used to sing. Nationalist tendencies came to the support of folklike art by making it a manifestation of the people's character. Social-revolutionary movements saw in it a weapon to be used in the conflict of the classes. The triumph of national over international music—represented in most countries by Italian opera—frequently was, consciously or unconsciously, an act of revenge on the part of suppressed peoples or a victory of the lower social strata over the ruling caste. But in a world constantly shrinking because of the ever more rapid means of communication, nationalism was no longer able to erect medieval barriers. The very case of music demonstrated quite plainly how nationalism was eventually superseded by internationalism.

And so, technical progress and romanticism's re-discovery of folk art smoothed the road for the new nations. In their entry into musical history they offered as credentials old national possessions, melodies and rhythms, that were so much part of themselves that their very sound instantly established certain associations of ideas. Europe had known practically nothing of all this. Now it had a sensational effect. Exoticism became the fashion and, like all fashions, was imitated everywhere. Soon there were Italians writing Chinese music and Frenchmen who yearningly embraced orientalism. Soon, too, new voices from overseas became audible. America began to make itself heard, timidly at first, like a countryman entering a city theater for the first time. But once he had been admitted, the twentieth century witnessed the growing of the European concert into a world concert.

A HANDFUL OF EARTH:

FREDERIC CHOPIN

There are creators of immortal melodies who fill us with respect and admiration; others to whom our heart goes out from the very first moment. Among these latter was Chopin [Pl. 119].

For centuries, Slav music and European music had led a separate existence. Until one day hapless Poland, the land of blood, suppression and cheerless history, produced a star whose brilliance attracted the eyes of the world and whose abrupt extinction left a romantic yearning in the hearts of millions. Frédéric Chopin became a symbol of his country, both as a man and as a musician. Liszt has described him to us, telling of the blue shine of his eyes, spiritual rather than dreamy, of the tender smile that never knew bitterness, of the fine transparency of his milky skin, and of the superlative harmony of his personality.

The songs of his homeland, the melancholy airs of the peasant girls, and the forceful rhythm trod into the ground by the high boots of the dancers had dwelt in his ears from the days of his childhood. For he himself was a true child of that soil, born in Zelazova Vola, a small agricultural place near Warsaw, on February 22, 1810. The days of his youth and studies coincided with one of his native country's most severe periods of suppression. And as his extraordinary musical talent asserted itself, so love of his homeland grew, and the desire to see it free.

Soon the European centers of music beckoned to him. But he hesitated; for he did not wish to forsake his friends who were preparing the struggle for liberty. He was finally prevailed upon to set out, accompanied by faithful Professor Elsner, the teacher to whom he owed so much. When the mail coach was about to leave the city limits of Warsaw, his friends handed him a small silver casket. It became his most treasured possession, from which he was never to be parted, not even in death. It contained a handful of Polish earth.

Vienna gave Chopin a pleasant reception, though it was not quite what his genius would have deserved. On the eve of his departure for London, he received news of his friends' rebellion, of their bloody barricade fights against the Russian oppressors, and of their heroic and desperate end. He knew then that he could never go back home, that now he must through his music carry on the fight in which his brothers had fallen, and that by his art he must win hearts for Poland and its just cause.

There was a brief entry in his passport, authorizing him to pass through Paris. But Paris became his second home, if such a term be permissible in connection with Chopin. Years later he remarked to some friends with a smile: "Why, I'm only passing through here . . ."

Chopin's success in Paris was complete. His concerts crowded the halls and drawing-rooms, his published compositions were greatly in demand, and the women adored him. In spite of all this, he was never cheerful, never happy. His mind dwelt in far-away realms, and at times he was tormented by frightening visions.

In a letter written as early as 1830, when he was but twenty years old, he said: "I seem gay, especially in the company of my countrymen, but I feel something within me that will kill me: gloomy forebodings, restlessness, insomnia, yearning, an indifference toward everything. One moment I am filled with the joy of living, but immediately there follows the wish to die . . ."

Melody upon melody came to him. The tunes seemed to flow from his fingers as he sat improvising at his beloved piano: melodies that were dreamy, tender, sad, yearning, but also revolutionary, rebellious, electrifying. Of these, Schumann said so aptly that they were "cannons hidden under flowers." The soul of Poland lived in his music.

The piano was the basis of Chopin's life and work. It sounds in all of his compositions, and most of them are written exclusively for it, like the ballads, mazurkas, waltzes, nocturnes, preludes, etudes, scherzos, polonaises, and impromptus, whose melodies have reached the far corners of the world. Even when Chopin added the sound of the orchestra, as he did in his two piano concertos, the piano always remained the dominant element. In it he lived, both as a virtuoso and a creative artist.

The more sensitive an artist, the more he longs for a female companion. But the more sensitive he is, the harder it is to find her. Chopin had left behind him in Poland a boyhood love. In Paris, he happened upon the woman who was to have the most important feminine role in his life. She was George Sand, the famous and extravagant authoress who knew how to attract so many men of genius. Was she Chopin's good or evil spirit? Nobody can answer the question with any degree of certainty. She was probably both, as so often happens in the case of a great love. She was independent, energetic, and perhaps egotistic. He was weak and ill, and therefore dependent, soft, sentimental. Could they possibly have understood each other? At any rate, they loved . . . The year 1838 saw them set out for the South. Chopin was entertaining hopes that his tubercular condition would be cured. But when they reached Valldemosa, on the Balearic island of Mallorca, and found shelter in the old monastery of La Cartuja, he grew worse. Everything seemed to oppress him: the thick, prisonlike walls pierced by tiny windows, the gloomy corridors, the ceaselessly howling winds, and the rains that came down without end. His terrifying visions increased. Often he would give a violent start and grow deathly pale when George Sand, in all her health and vigor, returned from one of her walks and unexpectedly entered the room where he was sitting at the piano, sunken in dreams. A gulf had opened between the lovers, and it yawned wider every day, every night. A buoyantly healthy woman and a miserably ill man—the one clinging to life with all her being, and the other dimly foreseeing death. Their love would have had to be all-transcendent to bridge so striking a contrast.

The final separation took place about 1847. Chopin tried to forget by striving for new successes. He gained a full measure of them in England, but the foggy climate aggravated his condition. He returned to Paris and died there on October 17, 1849. His remains were laid to rest in an idyllic corner of the old Père Lachaise cemetery, between Bellini and Cherubini, and not far from Heine, another exile to die in an alien land. It was he who had so aptly called Chopin the Raphael of music.

Over his coffin his friends sprinked the handful of Polish earth which had always accompanied him. They removed his heart and took it back to his fatherland. And so it finally returned after a long pilgrimage.

THE CZECH SOUL:

BEDRICH SMETANA

Another life full of sorrow, suffering, and tragedy, but infinitely rich and fertile in its art. In Bedrich Smetana (1824-1884) his nation had a bard who succeeded in attuning the richly flowing melodies of his native soil to European romanticism. His works truly embody the soul of his land, a land which for centuries had been singing and had always been the home of gifted musicians.

The melodies of the Czech people are less melancholy than those of the Poles, less mystical than those of the Russians. In keeping with the landscape, its green hills, its crystal brooks, its fertile fields, and its lovely villages, the country's songs and dances, too, are more pleasant and cheerful, although now and then we may hear one of the nobly mournful airs which seem to be the common property of all Slavs.

Smetana, a simple son of his people, set to music the history, the legends, the joys and sorrows, of his fatherland. He was the composer of one of the finest comic operas in existence, *The Bartered Bride.* In it, he managed to lift the folklike rhythms of the polka to the same artistic level that Chopin had found for the mazurka and Johann Strauss for the waltz. Unfortunately, his serious operas, like *Dalibor* and *Libussa,* are little known in other countries.

He poured forth all his love of home in the grandiose patriotic ode *My Fatherland*, a work consisting of six symphonic poems. The first, *Vysherad*, is a depiction of the times of Bohemia's ancient kings; the second, and best known, *The Moldau*, follows the course of the picturesque stream, gliding past festively decorated villages, listening to the nocturnal song of water sprites, and finally solemnly saluting the old Prague which, witness to a richly colored past, rises from its banks; *Sarka* takes us back to the legendary times of the bards; *From Bohemia's Fields and Groves* is a charming picturization of nature; *Tabor* gives sound to old Hussite motifs from the historical days of the religious wars; and *Blanik* gloriously rounds off the work like a hymn of victory and of faith in the rebirth of the Czech nation.

A striking contrast to this work is formed by Smetana's beautiful string quartet *From My Life*, a deeply moving picture of the composer's soul.

Smetana's life was a sad one. All the more admirable was the energy which made him overcome all difficulties and enabled him unflinchingly to pursue his way. The nationalist tendencies of his early works aroused the suspicion of the Austrian authorities who tried to suppress every symptom of Czech separatism. Outside of his country, there was but one man who did understand him; he who had a sense for everything that was great: Liszt.

Smetana left his homeland and settled in Sweden, in 1856. But it seemed as if his spirit continued to be active in his fatherland, for a change was taking place there: the whole people contributed toward the erection of a National Theater in Prague. And Smetana, who had dreamt of just such a thing, became its first director. The solemn dedication of the house took place in 1866. But the years of Smetana's happiness were brief. Both the tragedy of Beethoven and that of Schumann befell him. Deaf since 1874, he died in a state of mental derangement, in 1884.

Smetana's death, however, did not serve to extinguish the torch of Czech music, as had happened in the case of Polish music when Chopin died. Smetana himself had been the teacher of his famous successor, Antonin Dvořák.

THE INFINITE UNKNOWN EAST:

RUSSIA

Russia is a world in itself. Stretching limitless from Occident to Orient, it encompasses the thousand secrets of unfathomable Asia, the hoary mysteries of humanity. It is formed of hundreds of peoples, of languages and races, of manners and customs—a conglomerate, and yet, somehow, a uniform entity.

Many, too, are its musical sources, gushing forth from out of ancient rocks. Long before Russia became the possessor of artistic music, there existed folk music and religious music. The origin of the former is lost in the darkness of antiquity, while the origin of religious music is well known. The Russian Orthodox Church continued to develop what it had received from Byzantium. And so its music is related to the Gregorian choral, related, too, to the Hebrew temple chant, and related furthermore to who knows how many pre-Christian Asiatic melodies. Russian folk music, like that of all Slavs, reveals a deep sentiment, bordering at times on sentimentality. Symptomatic are its melancholy and its surden outbursts of savageness. The melancholy, characteristic of so many oppressed peoples, seems here, moreover, to be a reflection of the landscape, of the endless steppes, the giant rivers, the impenetrable forests and swamps, and the cheerless snowy solitudes. The songs of limitless plains are always sad.

The Russian native is profoundly musical. Music accompanies his life, constantly acting and reacting upon it. Full-throated voices are plentiful, especially basses of exceptionally deep range and organ-like quality. The folk dances are impelled by amazingly sharp rhythms, and frequently suggest a ceremonial action rather than a dance in the commonly accepted sense. Everything in Russia is different. Chopin and Smetana, though they, too, were Slavs, still represent the Occident. The Russians, however, of whose entry into the history of music we are about to speak, are Asia, the Orient and the Near East. Few are the bridges between the two worlds. Music may be destined to form one of the most important.

The nineteenth century witnessed the first emergence of artistic Russian music. As was the case everywhere else, it was in the beginning a reaction against a foreign product, the Italian opera, which, a century

110. Triumphal march and chorus from Glinka's "A Life for the Czar," in Glinka's handwriting, 1852.

before, had gained a firm footing in all the major cities. It was at the same time a reaction against the Court and the members of the aristocratic classes who gave their support to everything that was foreign and looked down with derision upon any attempt to establish a national music, contemptuously referred to as "coachman's music."

The first national-Russian musical work was an opera. It had to be an opera, either because the Italians must be beaten at their own game, or because there was no other available pattern. At any rate, Michael Glinka (1804-1857), animated by the desire "to write something that was genuinely Russian and would be comprehensible to every Russian," composed the opera *A Life for the Tsar* [Ill. 110], which was enthusiastically received, in 1836. In this opera as well as in the following *Ruslan and Ludmilla* Glinka made very clever use of Russian folk melodies, dances, and choruses.

Russia's musical awakening was facilitated and supported by the concurrent exceptional flourishing of national literature, whose most prominent representatives were Dostoyevsky, Gogol, and Tolstoy. Their works were frequently used as the basis for musical productions.

Glinka was flanked by another highly gifted man, Alexander Dargomyzhsky, who was also animated by a yearning for Russian national music. His best works were the operas *Rusalka* and *The Stone Guest*, the latter, as the title indicates, another treatment of the eternal Don Juan theme, based upon a text by Pushkin, to whom, by the way, we are also indebted for the libretti of Moussorgsky's *Boris Godounov* and Tchaikovsky's *Pique Dame* and *Eugene Onegin*.

Glinka and Dargomyshinsky were followed by a generation represented by a group which, both artistically and humanly, was equally interesting and attractive. It was composed of five friends, five music lovers: Alexander Borodin (1834-1887), César Cui (1835-1918), Mili Balakirev (1837-1910), Modest Moussorgsky (1835-1881), and Nicholai Rimsky-Korsakov (1844-1908). All of them were highly gifted; at least two were geniuses: Rimsky-Korsakov and Moussorgsky. The latter was one of the most vigorous musical creators of all time.

None of the five had originally been intended for a musical career. Borodin, the eldest of the circle of friends, was a physician and chemist who liked to refer to himself ironically as a "Sunday musician," a modest estimate of the creator of three highly interesting symphonies, some beautiful chamber music, finely conceived songs, the brilliant *Polovetzian Dances* from *Prince Igor* [Pl. 126 & 128], and the no less brilliant symphonic poem *On the Steppes of Central Asia*. The predilection for oriental themes greatly influenced his colleagues and, later, many European and American composers.

Cui, who rose to a high military rank, but was always passionately fond of music, wrote his first opera, *The Prisoner of the Caucasus*, on a theme by the fertile Pushkin. Subsequently, he chose subjects of a more international character, like *William Ratcliff* and *Henry VIII*. Little of his music managed to penetrate beyond the borders of his country (his beautiful *Oriental Air* did), but his influence within Russian music was quite considerable.

Balakirev, the soul of the group, was a good organizer in spite of his fiery disposition. When he arrived in St. Petersburg, in 1859, to study with Glinka, he formed a friendship with Cui, who at that time attended the Military Academy. Slowly he succeeded in gathering round him not only the group of the "Five" but also all the adherents to young Russian music. Best known of his own compositions are the fine symphonic poem *Russia*, which contains folk themes of great beauty, and *Thamar*, a piece with an oriental tendency, also evident in the same composer's successful and virtuoso-like piano piece *Islamey*.

And now we come to Moussorgsky [Pl. 124], one of the most interesting personalities in musical history. He might have been a figure out of a Dostoyevsky novel. Somebody once called him very aptly "the naked soul of Russia." After a happy youth, he entered upon a military career, the usual course followed by young members of the aristocratic set. He wore the gorgeous uniform of the Czarist army, had the entrée to the most fashionable drawing-rooms, and enjoyed great popularity because of his sparkling blue eyes and his exceptional pianistic gifts. Suddenly, he became aware of the hollowness and deceit of his life, the senselessness of his profession, and the thin veneer of a decadent society. There mounted within him the irresistible conviction that he must be a musician. More than that, he must give heed to the voice of the people, the oppressed, the poorest of the poor. He retired from service and abandoned everything that had made up his life and social existence.

Never having thoroughly studied music, he was greatly tormented by the realization that he was unable to give perfect artistic form to the abundant wealth of his ideas. Day and night he was haunted by visions, ceaselessly he heard mysterious sounds. He tried to jot them down, to sketch them, to elaborate them—and then in his despair sought refuge and oblivion in alcohol. For years, Rimsky-Korsakov lived with him. We have the latter's account of Moussorgsky's life, of his gradual drifting toward the abyss, and of his conceiving ever more sublimely ingenious ideas. Although the intervals between Moussorgsky's excessive drinking became shorter and shorter, they sufficed to conjure up from the wasting body works of inconceivable magnitude, melodies of a weight and greatness, of a warmth and melancholy beauty rarely equaled in musical history. In them there was a mixture of reality and dreams, of folk-like and artistic elements, of naive and mystic details, of dilettantism and the most sublime manifestations of genius.

In his *Boris Godounov*, Moussorgsky gave to his country and to the world of music a truly magnificent opera, a mass spectacle whose true hero is the people. There were furthermore the satanic and ghostly picture of *A Night on Bald Mountain*, the wonderfully plastic cycle of the *Pictures from an Exhibition*, originally written for piano, but later orchestrated several times (once by Ravel), the delightful *Nursery Scenes*, a number of other operas, splendidly conceived and containing beautiful melodies, like *Khovantchina* and *The Fair at Sorotchintsi*, the phantasmal *Songs and Dances of Death*, and a wealth of songs—a veritable treasure chest of inexhaustible riches, only a very small part of which has been comprehended and appreciated by Western Europe and America.

One day, in 1881, Moussorgsky was found lying in the street, wholly numbed by alcohol. He was taken to a miserable hospital and made to lie among the wretched and ragged figures for whose sake he had renounced a tranquil and successful life and to whom he had set in his music an imperishable memorial. He died on the forty-sixth anniversary of his birth.

Rimsky-Korsakov was the youngest, but also the most mature and disciplined, of the group of friends called "The Five" by history. In his capacity as naval officer, he sailed round the world several times and came into contact with many cultural strata. In spite of the undeniably Russian character of his music, he was at times somewhat more cosmopolitan than his friends, more akin in that respect to his compatriots Tchaikovsky and Glazounov. His work encompassed all musical realms. He wrote a number of fine operas, such as *Sadko, Czar Saltan, Snegourochka*, and the *Legend of the Invisible City of Kitesh*, symphonies, and a symphonietta, the *Russian Easter Overture, Christmas Eve Suite*, and the enchanting *Scheherazade*, in which all the fairy tales from the Arabian Nights came to life. He also composed quite a number of inspired songs.

This, however, does not tell the full story of Rimsky-Korsakov's musical work. He was the author of an interesting and valuable book on instrumentation. In addition, he spent countless hours in sifting and correcting the works of his friends. Borodin's Third Symphony, for instance, and his opera *Prince Igor* were found to be unfinished after the composer's death. (This gave Alexander Glazounov [1865-1936], who was quite young at the time, an opportunity to win his musical spurs.) Rimsky-Korsakov applied to them his exceptional art of orchestration. Countless works composed by his friends were retouched, polished, and instrumented by him, without his making any fuss about it. In one instance only did his unselfish action lead to protests and bitter discussions. It was in connection with Moussorgsky, his closest friend. It is undoubtedly true that the opera *Boris Godounov*, as the world knows it today, is essentially different from what is revealed in Moussorgsky's sketches. It may be that Rimsky-Korsakov's arranging hand did more than was necessary, that his more academic mind adapted to established rules too many of the unbridled expressions of a self-willed genius. But it is questionable, on the other hand, whether a performance would have been possible at all, had the original version been maintained; in other words, whether the work would ever have become known. And, by the way, this matter of "arrangements" forms one of the frequently discussed problems in the history of music and art. How rarely do the temperaments of the composer and the arranger harmonize! We shall soon learn of a parallel case in orchestral music in connection with Bruckner's symphonies.

Rimsky-Korsakov left to the world one other work, a document of great value. It is his autobiography, *My Musical Life*. In that book he tells us, simply and without any vanity, the touching story of that rare comradeship, that ideal friendship, full of the joys and sorrows, the work and dreams, the defeats and successes of the "Five."

THE HIGH NORTH SINGS OF ITS LONELINESS:

EDVARD GRIEG

Scandinavian folk music may be one of the oldest in Europe. Faintly only can we guess at its existence thousands of years ago, when the daring men of the North roamed the seas and probably got as far as America. The discovery of ancient wind instruments, the loures, which were excavated from Nordic soil, bear testimony to this people's love of music.

In spite of this, no Scandinavian of any importance to musical history had come to the fore until the nineteenth century. Niels W. Gade (1817-1890), a Dane, may have been the first [Ill. 111]. Unjustly, his

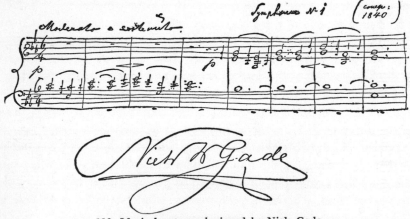

111. Musical autograph signed by Niels Gade.

216 .

112. Grieg's manuscript of "Wedding Day on Troldhaugen."

works are forgotten today outside his own country, although his name still adorns the annals of the Leipzig Gewandhaus where he was active for many years as a capable conductor at the side of Mendelssohn.

Scandinavia's claim to musical glory in the nineteenth century is centered upon a single figure, that of Edvard Hagerup Grieg (1843-1907) [Pl. 121], born in Bergen, a northern town of that most northern country, Norway. The possessor of an extremely elegant and supple European technique, his strength is most strikingly revealed by the masterly elaboration of his homeland's strange national airs. His music expresses the romanticism of lonely tracts of land, melancholy fiords, majestic snowy mountain tops. All the ancient folk tales of gods and heroes, of gnomes and trolls, come alive in melodies and rhythms such as nobody before him had ever put on paper. Grieg's principal work is the beautiful music to his compatriot Henrik Ibsen's drama *Peer Gynt*. Some of the melodious pieces in Grieg's suite, *Ase's Death, Anitra's Dance,* and *Solveijg's Song* have become popular the world over. Hardly less well known is his piano concerto, one of the most brilliant of its kind, a masterly combination of native melodies and universal technique. His "lyric pieces" have been collected in ten volumes. And how many beautiful songs he wrote! There is, above all, the world-famous *I Love Thee,* based upon Andersen's exalted words and written by Grieg for the woman who at the time was his fiancée, later his wife and companion, and who was so ideal an interpreter of his songs: Nina Hagerup Grieg. Hardly less popular are *A Swan* and *In a Boat.* But most impressive, perhaps, are his genuinely Norwegian songs. They are based on peasant texts, are therefore hardly translatable, and for this reason have been reserved mostly for home consumption.

When Grieg, after years of rather unsatisfactory studies in Leipzig, returned to Scandinavia, he settled first in Copenhagen and then in his own fatherland where he found an ever expanding field of activity and was able to devote himself to what he considered his real mission in life: to be Norway's musical herald. He was active as a pianist, conductor, and teacher, did a great deal of traveling and visited the principal cities of Europe as long as his rather feeble health permitted it. Aided at times by compatriot musicians, he was the founder of musical institutes and at one time, in 1898, organized a magnificent musical festival in Bergen. Having been granted a life pension by the Norwegian government, he was able to lead a quiet life and devote all his time to composing. He spent his last years in his native Bergen. There, following in his dreams the ships that sailed into the world, he died peacefully, a famous man.

A number of other Scandinavian musicians deserve to be mentioned, although none of them achieved Grieg's importance. There were the Dane, Johann Svendsen (1840-1911), and the Norwegian, Christian Sinding (1856-1941), both of whom have some reputation in the world of music. Halfdan Kjerulf was another extremely gifted Norwegian song composer, held in high esteem by Grieg. And there was Rikard Nordraak, one of those fascinating and tragic figures who seem to be quickly consumed by their own fiery brilliance. He died at the age of twenty-four, but left behind him proof of his exceptional musical gifts. His ardent patriotism (he was, by the way, the composer of the Norwegian National Hymn) is known to have strongly impressed Grieg.

113. "Tannhäuser." Wartburg scene from the performance at the Dresden Court
Theater, Oct. 19, 1845. Leipziger Illustrierte, 1846.

.22.

Wagner

MOZART, the divine spark; Haydn, the serene tranquility; Bee-
hoven, the lonely rebel; Chopin, a handful of Polish earth; Smetana, the Czech soul. . . . What term would be suitable for Wagner?
How define one in whom a whole epoch came to its climax and exhausted
itself? Sorcerer, prophet, tyrant? Philosopher, poet, musician? Or, to
put it all in one, universal genius?

Wagner's bibliography is even more voluminous than that of Beethoven. But while the latter, with but few minor exceptions, bears testimony to world-wide reverence, the former is still violently controversial.
Wagner gave rise to enthusiastic hymns of praise, but also to fierce chants
of hatred, both of a glowing intensity matched by no other figure in
musical history. He was one of those of whom it is possible to write in
every imaginable manner, except one: that of indifference.

Wagner was perhaps the world's most battle-scarred artist. Not only
were the public and the critics drawn into the fight raging about him, but

the entire era, including politicians and philosophers, found itself embroiled. His adherents saw in him a god, while his adversaries called him deceitful, egotistic, vain, and unprincipled. The battle about his work raged with unparalleled vehemence. Friends became estranged, barriers rose within families and towns, teachers and pupils were set against one another, new forms came into being in all arts. An impresario in Paris, wringing his hands in despair, had to implore the anti-Wagnerites in the audience to wait with their infernal yelling and caterwauling until the end of the performance; if they only do that, the master's adherents would agree not to insist by their applause on any number being encored. Decades later, the same city, the scene of *Tannhäuser's* ignominious failure and, generally, of many a violent outburst of passion generated by artistic struggles, was to witness actual bloodshed on the occasion of the first performance of *Lohengrin*.

Wagner's work, we said, represented the climactic point of an epoch. It was he who burst the last fetters that had still resisted Beethoven's revolt. He changed measured and symmetric melodies into infinite forms with neither beginning nor end, branching off like rivulets, disappearing at times almost entirely, spreading, growing more rapid, bypassing obstacles, and finally discharging themselves without really ending. But Wagner's work meant not only the fulfillment, but also the exhaustion, of an epoch. It was as if all musicians had been blinded by him. After his death, all roads seemed to be hopelessly blocked. His aftermath, like that of every dictator, was chaos.

All his works are still vitally alive, with the wholly insignificant exception of a few youthful attempts. A unique case, this, in operatic history. From *Rienzi* to *Parsifal*, the crowning glory of his work, all his operas, eleven great dramas, are on the repertoire of the theaters of all countries. They move us today as they moved those before us by the deeply stirring, genuine fervor of their music, and they captivate us now as before because of the eternal problems touched by them.

Wagner was both the author and composer of his works, and he was masterful in either capacity. So he towered above all other operatic composers, who had had to search laboriously for what came to him as a gift: artistic unity. Wagner probed into the most profound problems of humanity. What Beethoven had treated in the wonderfully abstract world of his tones was carried by Wagner into the three-dimensional theater. And it is strange indeed that he succeeded in gripping with equal force the amateur, who knows nothing of the technique of composing, by steeping him in a sea of poetic visions and musical harmonies; the loftily spiritual man able to envision beyond the colorful panorama and the ecstatic melodies the play of the sublime ideas that have agitated the human mind from time immemorial; and finally the expert who is compelled to admire the perfect mosaic of leitmotifs and infinite melodies created with matchless mastery by a genius.

To feel Wagner is easy; to understand him, difficult. The difficulty, to be sure, is caused least of all by the music, but rather by the basic idea and the language in which it is clothed. In spite of the monumental construction, a musical analysis is comparatively simple, since Wagner himself has smoothed the way by the use of the leitmotif, pointing the way to the ear and spurring on the mind. By leitmotifs, we mean the brief musical phrases indissolubly connected with certain persons, ideas, or things that play a part in the action. These phrases, which necessarily must be so simple that they may be recognized immediately when sung or played, occur with increasing frequency as Wagner's work matures. In *Der Ring des Nibelungen,* they constitute the ideologic-musical framework serving to keep together the gigantic drama. So, in addition to many others, there occur the following principal motifs in that work: motifs of Siegfried, Wotan, Hagan, Alberich, the Valkyrie; motifs for the ring, the fire, the gold, the gods' palace of Walhalla, the giants, the dragon; motifs also for the renunciation of love, the curse of love, the power of the law symbolized by Wotan's spear. These motifs, every one of them, are musically both simple and striking. By them, Wagner enables the listener who has grasped their meaning to follow the action; more than that, to follow the underlying idea of the action. Thus, understandably, the listener's mental processes are greatly stimulated. Let us cite two examples:

In *Die Walküre,* the second part of the great drama mentioned here, we listen to the conversation between Siegmund and Sieglinde, brother and sister, who are still ignorant of their relationship. Sieglinde tells the man, an unknown to her, of her sad past; how against her will she was forced to marry Hunding; how, during the marriage feast, a stranger suddenly entered, a mysterious old man who, fear-inspiring to all but her, drove a sword into the roof-supporting tree. Nobody knows the stranger, but at Sieglinde's words Wagner makes the orchestra sound a motif, smoothly and softly, revealing to the listener the identity of the mysterious stranger. He is Wotan, the god. And so the listener knows something that is still unknown to the persons of the drama.

The second is taken from the same drama, from the scene in which Siegmund is felled by Hunding's spear. The Valkyrie who, with an aching heart, has witnessed the event, now rushes up to the barely conscious Sieglinde, to save Siegmund's guiltily-guiltless sister and bride from the wrath of the god. Sieglinde, a thoroughly broken women wants nothing but death. But a single sentence of the Valkyrie makes her change her mind: " . . . the highest hero e'er known is borne in your sheltering womb. . . ." Months will have to pass before Sieglinde, alone in the forest, can give birth to her son; years, before the youth will receive his name from the lips of the very same Valkyrie: Siegfried. But the connection becomes clear to the listener the moment Brünnhilde sings those words, for heroically in the orchestra sounds the Siegfried motif. Only he can be "the highest hero e'er known" whose coming is foretold by the Valkyrie.

Countless other examples might be cited of this technique which, although it was not directly invented by Wagner, was elaborated by him until it formed the fundamental support of his musical dramas. I should like to compare this technique to a grandiose mosaic, the little stones of whose design are the leitmotifs. Like one who looks at a mosaic, the listener may admire the work in its entirety, or center his attention upon the minute details of which it is composed.

Richard Wagner was born in Leipzig, on May 22, 1813. His musical career began like that of any German orchestral conductor: activities at a succession of provincial theatres. The first profound impressions were made on him by the works of Shakespeare and Beethoven. They may have contributed toward making him feel the narrowness of his field of activity and the crushing dullness of his routine, which prevented the unfolding of his creative ability. And so, obeying a sudden impulse, he left his position in Riga, one day in 1839. He crossed the Baltic and the North Sea in a sailing ship, stayed in London a few days, and finally landed in France, penniless. The stormy voyages brought to maturity his first really personal work, *The Flying Dutchman*. Accident had put in his hands Heine's version of the old sailor's yarn telling of the ghostly ship condemned to sail the seven seas of the world to the end of time because of some misdeed committed by its captain. Heine, the romanticist, had added a deeply poetic detail. Wagner took it up eagerly. It was to become one of the favorite themes: redemption through love. The hapless voyager is permitted to set foot on land every seven years in search of a woman ready to love him though aware of his horrible fate. This be-

114. "The White and Red Lion," on the Brühl, Leipzig, the house in which Wagner was born.

came the subject of *The Flying Dutchman*. The accursed man meets Senta who in mystical expectation had been waiting for him. Believing her faithless, he hurries back to his ship and his roaming. But Senta, climbing a rock jutting into the sea, loudly and jubilantly calls out his name and hurls herself into the seething waves. The clouds are pierced by a bright light, and two blissful, redeemed figures are seen to float heavenward [Pl. 135].

Wagner feverishly started to set this drama to music. He invented for it a new tone language, from the overture with its thundering roar of the sea, to the gloomily ghost-like monologue of the Dutchman, to Senta's ballad, and to the final apotheosis. All this he wrote during the oppressive months in Paris, which were never to fade from his memory because of his financial distress, his artistic abasement, and the general hopelessness of his situation. But let us be fair: when Wagner came to Paris he was a wholly unknown young musician, hardly able to speak French, but expecting nevertheless that everybody defer to him. In common with many geniuses, he dimly foresaw his future greatness. But it was asking too much to expect others to sense what still lay dormant within him. All the same, he found a supporter in Meyerbeer. It was thanks to him that Wagner's *Rienzi* could be performed in Dresden, in 1842. This was his first striking success. The opera—we are justified in using a designation not applicable to any of Wagner's other works—had been written when he was still in Riga. It served to smooth the way for the *Flying Dutchman*, performed several months later at the same theater. Its success so fortified Wagner's position that he was able to leave his Paris exile and settle in Dresden as a conductor.

The first performance of *Tannhäuser* took place in 1845. In this drama, making full use of poetic license, Wagner combined two independent themes: the folk tale of Venus, the goddess of love, whose subterranean realm he moved to the Central-German mountains, and the previously mentioned contest of minnesingers at the Wartburg. In it once more we have Wagner's favorite theme: redemption through a woman.

Lohengrin was Wagner's next work, perhaps the most romantic of all. His sources were the old tales of the Knight of the Swan and of the Holy Grail, the vessel into which had flowed the blood of Christ on Golgotha.

While Wagner was at work on this drama, the agitated, crucial year 1848 approached. A revolutionary from the days of his youth, although

115. Warrant of apprehension for Richard Wagner.

more in an artistic than a political sense, and a convinced republican, Wagner gained admission to anarchist circles. When the rebellion was suppressed, Wagner had to flee.

For twelve long years he lived in exile. But no longer was he lonely: the prophetic eye of Liszt had discovered him. Liszt not only gave him sanctuary in Weimar, but also provided the financial means enabling him to proceed to Switzerland. In the meantime, Liszt took it upon himself to offer a home for Wagner's works in his theater. He was responsible for the lasting success of *Tannhäuser* and for the first performance of *Lohengrin*.

Wagner found more than an asylum in Zurich: a real home and a great love—Mathilde Wesendonck. This passion, blissful as well as tragic, inspired Wagner to the creation of the most magnificent musical monument ever erected to love: *Tristan und Isolde*. The subject is based on a Celtic tale given epic form by Gottfried of Strassburg, in 1210. Wagner made it into a paean of love, in which all reality becomes unreal and every yearning turns into melody. It depicts both love's most ecstatic de-

---

WAGNER

lights and its deepest sorrow; the symbolic clash of glaring daylight and the wonderful blue of the night; the painless transition from the vale of mundane affliction to the Elysian Fields of eternal love. The story of this drama may be told in a few lines, but no book is large enough to contain an exhaustive account of its beauty, its mystery, and its meaning.

Venice—an old palace on the Canal Grande. It was there that Wagner had completed his *Tristan* after the painful ending of the Wesendonck idyl. Minna, Wagner's wife, discovering the romance between her husband and Mathilde, had created an intolerable situation and Wagner fled from it to Venice. Mathilde had been his great, soul-stirring love, after the long years spent at the side of his first wife, before Cosima finally brought peace to his heart. Not only had Mathilde inspired Wagner and urged him on to new creations and thoughts—many of his most important theoretical writings came into being in those years—but she

116. A Wagner letter from Zurich, 1853.

226 .

91. Johann Strauss in Heaven. [*Caricature by Th. Zasche*] Listening to him, left to right: Haydn, Mozart, Lanner, Beethoven, Strauss the elder, Offenbach, Schubert, Brahms, Verdi, Wagner, and Bruckner.

92. Johann Strauss and his orchestra at at the "Paradeisgartl," Vienna.

93. *Auditus*. Musical group. Singing to the accompaniment of lute and viola da gamba. [*Engraving by Abraham Bosse, abt. 1650*]

94. Concert in the Trianon Park of Versailles, 1674. [*Engraving by François Chauveau, 1676*]

95. Niccolo Paganini (1782-1840), the violin virtuoso. [*Drawing by Ingres, 1819*]

96. (lower left) Jean Philippe Rameau (1683-1764). [*Portrait by Jean Baptiste Chardin. Dijon Museum*]

97. (lower right) Arcangelo Corelli (1653-1713). [*Portrait by Hugh Howard*]

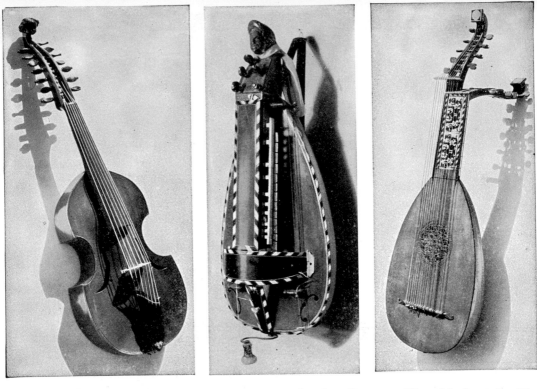

98. Viola d'Amour by P. Mantegatia. [*Milan 1767*]

99. Hurdy-gurdy by P. Louvet. [*Gerber Collection, Paris*]

100. Theorbic Lute by M. Tiefforbrucher. [*Venice 1610*]

101. 18th-Cent. clavichord. Like the viola and lute, it is at the Richard Wagner Triebschen Museum, near Lucerne.

102. Gioacchino Antonio Rossini (1792-1868). [*Photo Nadar*]

103. Festival performance of Donizetti's *Daughter of the Regiment*.

104. François-Adrien Boieldieu (1775-1834). [*Portrait by Louis Leopold Boilly, Rouen Museum*]

105. Stage scene by Karl Friedrich Schinkel of Spontini's *Vestal Virgin*, Act III. Abt. 1820.

106. Jacques Offenbach (1819-1880). [*Photo Nadar*]

107. The Melodrama. [*Painting by Honoré Daumier*]

108. Carl Maria von Weber (1786-1826). [*Portrait by Caroline Bardua. Nat'l Gallery, Berlin*]

109. Typical ballet scene from a French opera. Early 19th Cent.

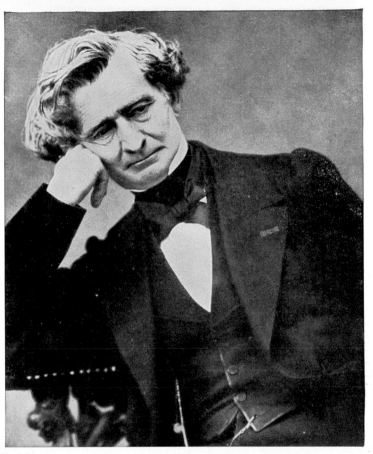

110. Hector Berlioz (1803–1869). [*Photo Pierre Petit*]

111. Scene from Berlioz' *Benvenuto Cellini*. [*After a woodcut, 1852*]

112. Felix Mendelssohn-Bartholdy (1809-1847). [*Pencil drawing by Bendemann, 1833*]

113. Mendelssohn was a gifted painter. He painted this water-color of the Ritzlihorn, near Guttannen, in 1847, on his last visit to Switzerland, shortly before his death.

114. Clara Wieck, Schumann's
wife, as a bride (1819-1896).
[*Drawing by Elvire Leyser,
1836*]
115. Robert Schumann (1810-
1856). Juvenile portrait.
116. The Schumann Room at
the Zwickau Museum, with the
piano used by Clara Wieck at
her first appearance at the Leipzig Gewandhaus, on Oct. 20,
1828.

117. Franz Liszt (1811–1886). [*Drawing by Devéria, 1832*]

118. An afternoon at Liszt's. At left, Kriehuber; right, Ernst; standing, Berlioz and Liszt's teacher Czerny. [*Lithograph by Josef Kriehuber*]

119. Frédéric Chopin (1810-1849). [*Portrait by Eugène Delacroix*]

120. Chopin's hand. A very sinewy variety of the sensitive type. Note the exceptional development, due to pianistic activities, of the after-wrist and the fingertips.

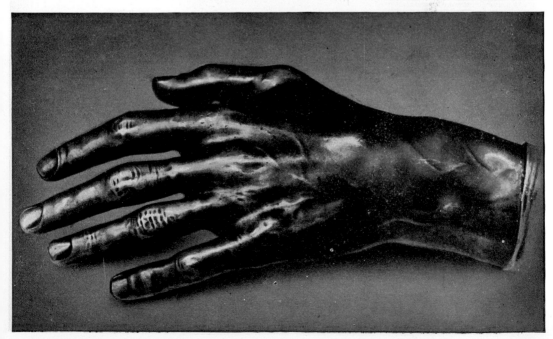

121. Edvard Hagerup Grieg (1843-1907).

122. In Norway, the land of the midnight sun. [*Photo Gardi*]

123. Nicolay Andrejevitch Rimsky-Korsakov (1844-1908). [*Photo Samur*]

124. Modest Petrovitch Moussorgsky
1839-1881). [*Portrait by Ilja Repin*]

125. Prologue from Moussorgsky's *Boris Godounov*, at a performance at the
Zurich Stadttheater.

126. Polovetzian Dances from *Prince Igor*, by Borodin. Ballet at the Grand
Theater of Moscow.

127. Ballet group from Rimsky-Korsakov's *Scheherazade*.
State Opera, Vienna.

128. The dancer Abramova
of the Russian ballet, at a
performance of Borodin's
Prince Igor.

even wrote the poems for Wagner's five songs which represent preliminary musical studies for his *Tristan*, and of which especially *Träume* and *Schmerzen* have gained considerable popularity.

Where to go after those creative years of exile? Paris beckoned to him. The Emperor himself ordered a performance of *Tannhäuser*. With a heavy heart, Wagner decided to take the advice of some friends and give heed to the Parisians' desire for a ballet by elaborating the opera's initial scene in the Mountain of Venus into a bacchanal. He who listens carefully to this second version, the so-called Paris version, will recognize the progress made by Wagner during the intervening two years. The bacchanal clearly bears the imprint of *Tristan* and even points the way to the *Ring*. But all of Wagner's endeavors were to prove in vain. Somehow, Paris and he seemed unable to get along with each other. To express it in trivial terms: the fine gentlemen of the Jockey Club who formed the main part of the audience at the Paris Opera refused, as a matter of principle, to put in an appearance before the second act, in the course of which every "worth-while" opera presented a ballet. The failure of *Tannhäuser* was as noisy as it was shameful.

What now? An amesty had been proclaimed in Germany. Wagner could return. But only disappointment and bitterness awaited him in his fatherland. No theater wanted to produce his works. His *Tristan* was declared unperformable. He did keep up the struggle for three years, until, grown hopeless, he considered himself definitely defeated. And at that moment, the miracle happened.

Wagner, as if in flight, was staying at a small inn at Stuttgart, expecting to leave again in the morning for an equally poor abode in some other town. There came a knock on the door. It was a messenger from Ludwig II, the young King of Bavaria. The aging Wagner was told that the romantically inclined monarch in Munich was dreaming himself into every one of his dramatic figures, was erecting castles on inaccessible mountain tops and was gathering round him on these Monsalvats a Round Table of medieval knights, although, to be sure, they existed only in his fancy. King Ludwig, the messenger added, entertained but one wish: to have Wagner, the creator of all his dreams, near him so that he might place at his feet whatever his kingdom had to offer.

Between evening and morning, a man vanquished and crushed became a triumphant victor. For the king, that handsome and enthusiastic king, kept his word, kept it against the opposition of all his counselors and ministers. And Wagner's demands were by no means paltry. He wanted theaters in which to produce his works with the best available artists and the largest orchestras. He also wanted the personal luxury for which he had always yearned: huge rooms with richly colored draperies and costly carpets from far-away lands [Pl. 133]. Wagner had an amazingly developed sense for colors and materials and was apt to give hours of thought to the minutest details. And perfumes! He needed them for his inspiration, used them lavishly, wasted them, had them brought to him from the four corners of the world, mixed them, tried them, and enjoyed them voluptuously.

Tristan was overwhelmingly successful in Munich. Wagner was already hard at work on his *Die Meistersinger von Nürnberg*, his only cheerful work. It affords a pleasant vision of the days of the Nuremberg mastersingers, with calls of the night watchman, a street scuffle and a brilliant festival procession and mass gathering on St. John's day. But it is much more than that. In the wonderful figure of Hans Sachs, Wagner had drawn himself, putting in his mouth many profound words concerning art, its rules, and its relation to the people. The *Meistersinger*, too, that most vigorously vital, most mundane, and most unproblematic of all his works, scored a brilliant success.

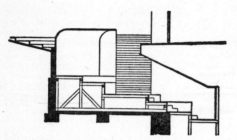

117. Cross section of the lowered and invisible orchestra pit at the Bayreuth Festival Playhouse.

Both the king and the artist were dreaming of even greater things. Ludwig II who, sobbing and lost to the world, the lone occupant of the theater while *Tristan* was played for him—this Ludwig was fully in sympathy with the idea of Wagner who wanted to have a Festival Playhouse far from the hubbub of the city; a theater to which people need not hurry, into which they need not bring their everyday cares, in which the orchestra pit was lowered and even the figure of the conductor invisible, so that nothing might mar the illusion [Ill. 117]; a theater which, like every sanctuary, would not be profaned by an admission fee and which every pilgrim devoted to art might enter.

An appeal was made to all German lands to contribute money for the erection of a National Sanctuary of German Art. The response was rather feeble. Again it was King Ludwig who made Wagner's dream come true. The Bayreuth Festival Playhouse [Pl. 132] came into being and was solemnly opened, in 1876, with a complete performance of the *Ring* and before an assemblage among which were quite a number of emperors and kings. It was a veritable world event. Liszt, too, had come. The two men had been estranged ever since Cosima [Pl. 130], the daughter of Liszt and the Countess d'Agoult, had left her husband, the eminent musician and enthusiastic Wagnerite, Hans von Bülow, that she might follow Wagner. Liszt knew how deeply Bülow had been wounded and found it hard to forgive. But then he went to Bayreuth after all. Wagner and Cosima, married and blissfully happy, hardly noticed him among so many illustrious visitors.

Wagner had been at work on his *Ring des Nibelungen* for almost thirty years. The monumental work is divided into a "Preliminary Evening,'" *Das Rheingold*, and three "Evenings," *Die Walküre, Siegfried*, and *Götterdämmerung*. It represents a gathering together of his life work, the mirror of his development, and the artistic expression of his philosophy of life.

The symbolism of the work is obscure and has led to many interpretative attempts. Its evolutionary history is symptomatic of Wagner's emotional transformations. At first, the figure of Siegfried kindled his imagination. He saw in him the expression of sublime purity and brilliant heroism, an ideal embodiment of what mankind might some day come to be, a man full of love, free from fear, and ready to take up the fight against the hereditary evil of gold. When Wagner was thus planning the work, his head was full of socialist ideas. He had not as yet conceived the thought of a tetralogy, but was thinking of a single drama. When he had finally finished with it, it had grown into an enormously ramified gigantic tragedy of gods, men, giants, and dwarfs. It must therefore not be assumed that Wagner began the great work by sketching the "Preliminary Evening" or even the entire drama. He was at first mainly concerned with its last part, *Götterdämmerung*, in which Siegfried's death occurs, The ensuing downfall of Walhalla, symbolizing the Twilight of the Gods, may still have been a reflection of Wagner's dream of 1848, in which he envisioned the end of a decaying world in a sea of fire and the victorious emergence of the New, the Great.

Slowly, however, another figure of the drama had come to occupy the place of prominence in Wagner's imagination. It was Wotan, the chief god. Siegfried's unproblematic luminous figure gave way in importance to the tragic god who sees his power wane, a slave to his own laws even where their injustice has become manifest to him. In the depths of his heart he wishes for but one thing: the end, and thus the release from compulsion. Wagner's way led from Nietzsche's Superman to Schopenhauer's abysmal pessimism, but he clothed everything in a symbolism and an ideology of his own.

Every detail in this work is profoundly symbolic: the rape of the Rheingold, the dwarf's curse of love, the giants' quarrel over the treasure. Equally symbolic is the act of Wotan who had fathered Sigmund and Sieglinde and then permitted them to commit the double crime of incest and adultery; symbolic, too, the long controversy between Wotan and his wife Fricka, the guardian of matrimony, and the god's final decision reached after grave pondering that Siegmund must die, even though the Valkyrie Brünnhilde for the first time tries to disobey his explicit command. There is symbolism, too, in all that follows.

This drama furnished food for unlimited thought. What had happened to the simple Nibelungen tale of the Middle Ages? Hardly more than a few of its figures found their way into the Wagner version; in fact, no more than their names. Everything else was Wagner's very own creation, a monumental edifice whose building stones were made of Philosophy and mysticism. Was it not the custom in cultural epochs of long, long ago to place in the grave of a prominent person his most cherished possessions: his weapons, his wife, his horse? Does not Brünnhilde's death have its motivation in that distant source? And were there not ancient cultural epochs in which he of highest rank was permited to marry but one woman, his own sister, because no other could be his equal? May not this legendary usage be responsible for the union of Siegmund and Sieglinde, from which sprang the type of the ideal man?

In his last stage work, Wagner probed the depths of religious mysticism. *Parsifal*, too, is based upon an age-old legend, sung in great epics by the French troubadours and, later, by Wolfram von Eschenbach. There is a hint of the Parsifal idea in *Lohengrin* and its Holy Grail. And yet, *Parsifal* deals with problems which are entirely different and much more profound than those of his youthful work: the eternal feminine, embodied here in the strange figure of Kundry, partly a satanic seductress, partly a deeply repentant woman; the redemption from an evil by the very weapon that had caused it, the nobility of naive man who,

230 .

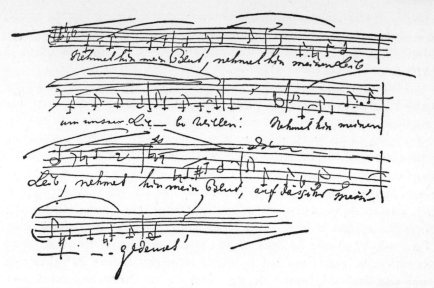

118. Wagner's manuscript of the "Words of Institution" from the Lord's Supper, occurring in "Parsifal."

ignorant of human laws—another Siegfried—must himself find the way to purification that he may be worthy of his sacred mission.

This mystical drama of *Parsifal*, for which Wagner wrote the most sublime music of his life, was meant to be the exclusive property of the Bayreuth Festival Playhouse, in which it sounded for the first time, in 1882. But man, who so often puts to naught the dreams of artists and idealists, disregarded Wagner's provisions. Bayreuth soon had to be changed into a business enterprise where, as in any other theater, everybody had to pay to be admitted. And when the lawful copyright period expired, all the prominent theaters of the world swooped upon *Parsifal* which, according to its creator's will should have been performed in Bayreuth only. Copyrights are not the same in every country. In the United States, the law permitted a performance as early as 1904. The announcement of a New York performance was greeted with a general outcry of indignation. But when the management of the Metropolitan Opera offered to relinquish the performance provided the work would not be staged by any of the European opera houses, the latter refused to subscribe to that condition. And so, since the copyright laws of most countries provide for a protective period of thirty years, *Parsifal*, since 1913 has become a repertory opera like all other Wagner works. Strange to say, however, all theatres adopted the Bayreuth law—unwritten, so far as I know—which prohibits applause. People listen to *Parsifal* with profound emotion and without noisy demonstrations of approval, as if it were indeed a religious work.

There was one man missing in Bayreuth. He hated *Parsifal* and even hated Wagner as ardently as he had formerly loved him. The man was Friedrich Nietzsche. He had seen in Wagner the renovator of all art, had worshiped his work and his ideas, had seen in Siegfried the artistic embodiment of his Superman, and had been an enthusiastic Bayreuth prophet. Then he reversed himself entirely and began to sense in Wagner all he reproached him for in his treatise *The Case of Wagner*: hypocrisy, insincerity, weakness, and a "collapse before the Cross." And finally Nietzsche applied a cruel word to his entire era, the word decadence. "I am like Wagner a product of this time, meaning: a decadent. With the difference that I realized it, that I struggled against it." Was that true? Can anybody dare to decide? Was not the entire nineteenth century already in a state of decadence? But did it not, like every epoch drawing to its close, produce wonderful works of art? There was the art of a Beethoven, of a Wagner, to which one is regretfully tempted again and again to apply Thomas Mann's sentence: "The word is able only to praise sensuous beauty, not to reproduce it." It will be for a far distant future to decide what decadence was and when it began.

At the end of the summer of 1882, at the last performance of *Parsifal* during that Festival Play season, Wagner descended into the orchestra pit before the final scene, seized the baton, and himself conducted the blissful passages that bring the opera to its close. None in the audience knew it, for the invisibility of the Bayreuth orchestra is complete. Could Wagner have foreseen that it was to be his own finale? A leave-taking from his Festival Playhouse on its green hill, from his work, from his life?

Winter came, and the aging Wagner felt drawn toward the South. Venice had become his favorite place. Long years had passed since he fled from the arms of Mathilde Wesendonck to the city of lagoons, to finish his *Tristan* there. Now Cosima was with him, and they were happy, for she forgave him everything, both past and present. The couple spent the winter of 1882-1883 at the Palazzo Vendramin on the Canal Grande. In that old palace, beneath the clear skies of Italy, Wagner died, on February 13, 1883. Future musicologists may incline toward the opinion that Wagner's death was at the same time the end of an entire cultural epoch.

In the shady park of his Bayreuth villa, named *Haus Wahnfried* in true Wagnerian style—"where my vain imaginings found peace"—stands his simple grave. In keeping with Wagner's' supreme theatrical instinct, it shows neither cross nor inscription.

23

Verdi: or The Singer of His People

THE fight over Wagner was waged in every corner of the musical world. When he died, he had conquered. The earth resounded with his glory, and enthusiastic youth was carrying aloft his banner. Nobody could be compared to him.

Nobody? While Wagner, as none before him, kept the world in a kind of hypnotic enthrallment, another genius, less ostentatious and less noticed outside of his own homeland, was mounting to the highest pinnacle of dramatic art. He was Giuseppe Verdi [Pl. 140]. Verdi was the embodiment of centuries-old Italian opera in its greatest splendor and unimpaired vitality; opera with its undeniable weak points, but also with its elevating, enrapturing, immortal melodies.

Those were the days when a man had to choose sides: for Wagner, who hated opera and wanted to deal it a death blow with the establishment of the musical drama; or for Verdi, who had the sensuous magic of melodies and belcanto bloom richly once more and who, by long and arduous work, managed to establish a mature form of Italian opera. Today, the swords that were brandished in a fight lasting half a century have lost their keen edge. Today, we may look at both great men with the same degree of admiration, may let the purity of their intentions, the strength of their creative power, and the enthusiasm of their hearts speak to us with equal eloquence. Wagner here—Brahms there! a forgotten battlecry; Wagner here—Verdi there!—a discarded contraposition.

True, even today, Wagner and Verdi have a different effect; for two more antithetic creative minds could hardly be imagined. Perhaps Wagner represents the spirit, philosophy, reason—the man Schiller called a sentimental artist; while Verdi, represents the originality, the simplicity, and the healthiness and fertility of his native soil. "I am, and I shall always be, the peasant of Roncole ..." But Wagner, too, had moments when he "sang his fill" and melody ruled supreme, while Verdi, more than once, came very close to the musical drama.

The two geniuses of dramatic art were born in the same year. One, a townsman and member of a circle with intellectual inclinations, the other, born on October 10, 1813, a native of Roncole, a village of the wide Lombardic plain, near Busseto, and not far from Parma. What could have been in that tiny village with its steepled church and its wheezy organ to inspire the peasant child to become a musician? Wagner referred to his genius as a demon. Verdi did not like high-sounding phrases, but what he felt was similar: that irresistible force which brought to light melody upon melody and compelled him—as it compels all those in its thrall—to serve art and regard it as the supreme essence of his life.

When Verdi was nineteen, he wanted to enter the Milan Conservatory, but was rejected. Well, he would acquire the necessary musical equipment in another way. Were there any better teachers than the scores of Rossini, Bellini, and Donizetti, those unsurpassed masters of belcanto? Verdi, with the peasant's heavy blood in his veins, decided in favor of the serious, the tragic, opera. A youthful work, *Un giorno de regno*, forgotten today, was his one feeble attempt in the realm of comic opera, until the "Miracle of Verdi" occurred and he wrote his *Falstaff*. But more about that later.

Verdi knew little of dramatic laws when he began to write operas. As for music, he knew as much about it as any Italian operatic composer who, in the course of more than two hundred years, had espoused that profession. Long and thorny was the road he had to travel until he reached maturity. He was especially attracted by Shakespeare with his weighty and frequently bloodthirsty dramatics, and by Manzoni, the poet of his fatherland, to whom he later erected so beautiful a monument in his *Requiem*.

Verdi wrote a total of twenty-eight operas, or to be exact, twenty-nine, but he burned his *King Lear* before anybody had seen or heard it. His early operas are almost entirely forgotten today, but in one of them, *Nabucco*, there is a passage that has found a place in the hearts of the people. It is the gripping chorus of the Hebrew slaves, *Va, pensiero, sull' ale dorate*. Somehow, that melody expressed the yearning of the Italians of those days, and when Verdi later touched upon national themes in other works, especially in *I Lombardi*, the people recognized in him their prophet, the composer of the great national unification, whose music called the masses to battle for a new and united Italy. The five letters of his name seemed to lend added weight to this recognition when they

119. Manuscript by Verdi: "Rigoletto," quartet in final act.

were given this curious interpretation: V (itteorio) E (manuele) R (e) D'I (talia), the battlecry of the generation. Verdi, Italy's symbol by virtue of his name as well as his music, even had to be made a member of parliament—a strange honor for the country's most taciturn man.

His first four operas, performed in Milan, between 1839 and 1843, aroused considerable interest. The success of *Ernani*, performed in Venice, in 1844, was undisputed, though *I due Foscari* did not fare so well in Rome. In the course of the following six years, Verdi wrote ten operas, none of which was more than passably successful. Being a severe critic of his own works, Verdi did not deceive himself about their weak points. Looking at those scores today, we are able to recognize in some of the details the future titan of Italian opera. But what impossible libretti! Verdi who, like Mozart and Weber, was a born dramatist, was at the mercy, as they had been, of the text writers who, with an unbelievable lack of responsibility, used even Schiller and Shakespeare in the "manufacture" of scenes which bordered upon the ridiculous.

Luisa Miller, an opera which was well received in Naples, in 1849, reveals pronounced progress in many details. But it was on the eleventh of March, 1851, that Verdi's immortality was definitely assured. On that day, his *Rigoletto* scored a tremendous success in Venice. It was followed two years later by *Il Trovatore* and *La Traviata*, in Rome. Verdi's victory was complete. In the latter work, he found a new, intimate tone language for a modern society drama. Here, too, is revealed, more strikingly than ever before, Verdi's ability to express himself musically in a manner that created wonderful points of rest in the dramatic construction of the works. This very ability was to become increasingly pronounced until it reached its culminating point in *Aida* and *Otello*.

Rigoletto, *La Traviata*, and *Il Trovatore* suddenly raised Verdi above his Italian contemporaries. Rossini, living in Paris, had been silent for a quarter of a century. Bellini and Donizetti were dead. There was only Verdi to uphold the tradition. His heart overflowed with melodies, but now he knew how to suit them to every dramatic situation and how to impart vitality to every phrase. He still was rather lax in the choice of his libretti, as shown by his *Trovatore*, but his unique mastery in giving musical shape to great and compact dramatic scenes, in supplying the singing voices with widely arching melodies, and in imparting electrifying rhythms to mass scenes silenced all criticisms. He had become a true stage dramatist, aided by an unerring instinct, so that even banal melodies like the Duke's *La donna è mobile* in *Rigoletto* and Manrico's stretta in *Trovatore* were so perfectly adapted to the respective situations that their dramatic effect could not possibly have been surpassed.

His next work was intended for a famous theater beyond the borders of his fatherland, the Grande Opéra in Paris. It was *The Sicilian Vespers*, an opera which, after a fair initial success, could not maintain its place on the reportoire. There followed, in brief intervals, six works of unequal value: *Simone Boccanegra* (1857), *Aroldo* (1857), *Un Ballo in Maschera* (1859) [Pl. 143], Verdi's most vigorous drama since *Traviata*, *La Forza del Destino* (1862), with a wealth of beautiful music but a very weak text, a new version of *Macbeth* (1865) [Pl. 142], and *Don Carlos* (1867), full of brilliant arias in the noblest Italian style.

120. "Celeste Aida," tenor aria in Act I of "Aida," Manuscript of Verdi's score.

Verdi was now fifty-six years old. His popularity knew no bounds in Italy, but Wagnerian tendencies intruded even there, and heated discussion concerning the German master were an everyday occurrence. "Why still write operas?" Verdi asked bitterly and furnished the reply by adding: "So that I might be told I know less of dramatic art than that man Wagner, or worse yet, that I imitated him."

The year 1869 came and with it a strange offer. The Khedive of Egypt wished Verdi to write a festival opera for the occasion of the opening of the Suez Canal. Verdi refused. Was he to leave the peace of his Sant' Agata estate and once more enter the arena of operatic premières? Was he again to submit to the bickerings of the stage folk, to all manner of devices by which conductors, primadonnas, and impresarios were to be convinced, persuaded, and pacified? No, never! But Fate took a hand and changed his decision. One day, the mail brought him the dramatic sketch of an Egyptian opera, rich in magnificent scenes and full of glowing passion. Verdi hesitated no longer. The theater, his beloved theater, had won him back.

And so *Aida* came into being, based on the sketch by Mariette Bey, an Egyptologist. It was the most splendid opera Italy had thus far come to know. What a wealth of excitingly agitated mass scenes, of impassioned arias and duets! And all of it crowned by a heavenly beautiful melody, *O terra, addio*, comparable only to a scene by "that man Wagner," the love death of Tristan and Isolde. This, too, was the height of dematerialization. Two angelic voices, accompanied by a violin which guided them on their way to Paradise.

It was on Christmas Eve of the 1871 that *Aida* was first performed at the New Opera of Cairo before a distinguished audience from all countries, gathered to witness the historic event of the Canal's opening. For the first time, a Verdi première was played in the presence of representatives of the international press. The fanfares of the triumphal march were excuted by colored musicians, and more than three hundred Arabs took part in the procession. On that evening, the Italian operatic art of the nineteenth century scored its supreme international triumph. The composer alone was conspicuous by his absence. Sea voyages were not to his taste.

But a few weeks later, on February 8, 1872, he attended the Italian première at the Scala of Milan and experienced the greatest satisfaction of his life: an ecstatic audience, brought to its feet, waving scarves, throwing flowers, and demonstrating their genuine love and gratitude by endless salvos of applause and enthusiastic shouts of approval. Verdi was deeply moved. He felt that he had in truth become the singer of his people. But he also felt that it would be difficult, if not impossible, once more to write a successful opera after *Aida*.

Fifteen years passed. Famous, but far from the theater, Verdi lived in the midst of his beloved fields. Nobody seriously thought that the septuagenarian would ever write another work. His last public appearance had been at St. Mark's of Venice, when he conducted his *Requiem*, in 1874. After that performance, the work, dedicated to the memory of Manzoni on the anniversary of his death, was taken over by the Scala and was as enthusiastically received there as if it had been an opera and not a religious composition. Was Verdi religious? The question is not easily answered. I believe he was—with that pure instinct that is the property of all soil-bound people; with the profound faith instilled into all simple souls by Nature. That was why his God could be worshipped with all the means at his command, with the beating of drums and sounding of trumpets, with mass effects, and operatic tone pictures. And that was why his truly magnificent *Requiem* was no less profoundly and religiously conceived than any other religious work. True, what a wide difference, both in the means and in the artistic idea, between Verdi's work and the Heaven-inspired *Lacrimosa* sung by Mozart!

Once more, Verdi fell silent. It was the decisive decade in the life of Wagner, the realization of Bayreuth. And Verdi, as old as Wagner, was no less vigorous and healthy than the German master. Anxiously did those of his friends who were admitted to Sant' Agata watch him. Giulio Ricordi, his publisher, expressed what they all felt: "How sad to see a man, whom nobody would take to be even sixty, who never has as much as a headache, who has the appetite of a youth, and who for three or four hours every day tends his fields under a burning sun—to have such a man refuse to write even a single note!"

One evening at Sant' Agata, the conversation turned once more to Shakespeare; likewise, to Arrigo Boito, an Italian poet and musician of the younger generation whom Verdi did not know personally, but whose *Mefistofele* had strongly impressed him. Shortly thereafter, Boito called at Sant' Agata and, forsaking his activity as a composer, became the only one of Verdi's librettists worthy of his music. He completed the scenic sketch of Othello in three days. Verdi was not as yet ready to reveal his newly awakened interest. He was still undecided as late as 1884. In the meantime, Boito improved the libretto of *Simone Boccanegra* for a revival at the Scala. But on November 1, 1886, he received the joyous message from Verdi: *"Otello è finito."* Verdi was then more than seventy-three years old.

For the first time in his long career, it pained Verdi to be separated from his work. For the first time, he seemed to feel that a composer lost his work by giving it to the world. But it had to be. On February 5, 1887, a reverently listening and astounded audience at the Scala of Milan came

121. Note by Verdi after having finished "Falstaff." "The last notes of Falstaff—Everything is finished. Go, go, old John! On your way, as far as you can. . . . Amusing type of a rascal; eternally true, under various guises, at every time, in every place!! Go, go—forward—Addio!!!"

to know a new, a different, an immeasurably matured Verdi. *Otello* was something new, absolutely new. A continuous dramatic breath permeated every one of the four long acts. The singing voice was of course still dominant. In that respect, Verdi, the Italian, could never change without doing violence to himself. But the orchestra had gained new importance. The musical characterization of the three fundamental types —Othello, Desdemona, Iago—is so clear that we may use the term "musical drama" in its truest sense and without for a moment suggesting that Verdi, as has frequently been asserted, consciously or unconsciously had copied Wagner. No, *Otello* was merely a milestone on the road of Verdi's natural development. It was but a matter of his reaching that advanced point. How unspeakably beautiful the love duet of the first act: Othello and Desdemona, lost to the world in the Venetian night, on the shore of the softly murmuring sea.... And the fourth act—a masterpiece in itself, with its gloomy foreboding of death, its sad folk song of the willow tree, and the world-removed *Ave Maria*. The old melodic power was still alive in Verdi, but it had been transported to a higher and more spiritual plane.

Had Verdi's creative power been exhausted now? No! The greatest

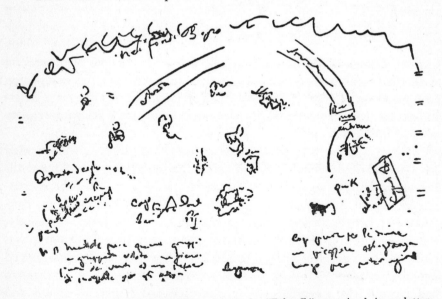

122. Verdi's sketch of the garden scenery in "Falstaff," contained in a letter dated Sept. 18, 1892. The accompanying remark: "What is needed is a large real garden with paths and masses of shrubs and plants, making it possible for people to hide, to appear, and to disappear."

miracle of all was yet to come. Once, decades before, Rossini had said of the young Verdi: "He is a musician with a serious character; he'll never be able to write a gay opera. . . ." It seemed that Rossini had been right—until Verdi, at eighty, proved him wrong. And how wrong! His imagination had always inclined toward melancholy. Passion seemed to have been the driving force in his works. Age had now dispersed all sultriness and fog. Life had become serene and clear, the world sunny. Through many a silent struggle, Verdi had attained to the ultimate philosophy of the smile.

Boito had written another splendid libretto, once more after Shakespeare. Somehow, the world heard of it. Whispered comments ran through all the musical circles of Europe: What could the eighty-year-old maestro still produce? What he did produce was the gayest of comedies, a manifestation of the clearest and most sparkling humor, and proof of the ultimate stage of mastery: *Falstaff* [Ill. 121]. The first performance took place at the Scala, on February 9, 1893. The audience went wild with enthusiasm and joy.

Little has been said here of Verdi's life. The life of the "peasant of Roncole" was as simple as it could be. He was quite young when he married the daughter of his first benefactor, Antonio Barezzi, who aided him in the pursuit of his musical studies. Death soon took from him both his wife and the two children she had borne him. This was the one tragic blow in the life of Verdi. He finished his days at the side of his second wife, the famous singer Giuseppina Strepponi, who was a real companion to him. From his fine country seat, he traveled—reluctantly, as a rule— to attend the first performance of one of his operas or to Milan, to confer with his publisher.

Verdi was able to greet the new century. He made his will on May 14, 1900, leaving the major part of his fortune to a home for old and ailing musicians. On January 27, 1901, death finally conquered the incredible vitality of the eighty-eight-year-old man. The funeral was an overwhelming demonstration of a nation's love and gratitude. Somebody, somewhere, started singing and the melody, slowly and solemnly, was taken up by one after another until it swelled into a thousand-voiced choral: *Va, pensiero, sull' ale dorate . . .*" It was the melody their maestro had written half a century before, as artless and simple, as honest and straightforward, as everything he had done and written in his life. For had not his motto been: In art and in love, one must above all be sincere?

24

The Last Romanticists

OPERA'S DAYS OF MATURITY

DURING the latter half of the nineteenth century, the history of musi-co-dramatic art was centered upon the two colossal figures of Wagner and Verdi. Consciously or unconsciously, they were bound to out-shine all other stage composers. Musical composition for the theater had reached its maturity in them. With Verdi, it had been the opera; with Wagner, the musical drama. This shining maturity cast its light upon all dramatic composers of Europe, during the lifetime of the two great ones, and far beyond it.

In Germany, Wagner's influence was so despotic that almost all his contemporaries who devoted themselves to opera tried to imitate his style. Like all imitators and eclectics, they are forgotten today. There were two composers, however, who deserve being mentioned: Peter Cornelius (1824-1874), because of his fine and poetic comic opera *The Barber of Bagdad*, a work relatively free from Wagnerian influence; and Hermann Goetz (1840-1876), who wrote a delightful opera based on Shakespeare's *Taming of the Shrew*. Cornelius also composed a number of finely conceived songs, but he was one of those quiet men with a good deal of talent but little luck.

Still less is to be reported of Italy. The land of the melody was to be practically silent until the advent of *verismo*, a worthy successor to the art of Verdi.

On the other hand, operatic history of that period has to record highly interesting facts from other countries. Moussorgsky, Rimsky-Korsakov, and Smetana have already been discussed. A number of other names must be added here. There was Stanislav Moniuszko, (1820-1872), whose Polish national opera *Halka* was first performed in Warsaw, in 1848. A little later, Karl Goldmark, a Hungarian, wrote some successful operatic works, one of which, *The Queen of Sheba*, even became inter-nationally known.

France, at the time, was highly productive in the field of opera. Not only had an entirely new and remarkably ingenious school of musical thought been established there, whose works are still being played everywhere, but there had also emerged a masterpiece able to maintain a place of equality at the side of the works of Wagner and Verdi. It was *Carmen*, the colorful opera by George Bizet (1838-1875). The unhappy composer died in the prime of his life. Although Bizet had never left French soil, the Spanish milieu of his chief opera was masterfully portrayed. It is a work full of genuine passion and based upon an exceptionally good libretto. There is in it not a single weak measure, no dramatic gap, no lukewarm melody [Pl. 146].

Bizet [Pl. 144] had on several occasions furnished proof of his great talent, but fate had not been kind to him. There were in his operas *La jolie fille de Perth*, *Djamileh*, and, above all, *Les pêcheurs de perles*, as well as in his music to Daudet's drama *L'Arlésienne* enough beautiful melodies and brilliantly conceived combinations of sound to assure the fame of a more fortunate composer. Bizet was well known, esteemed— but that was all. And now he had with his heart's blood written the work that had its first performance in Paris, on March 3, 1875. His very life depended on the fate of *Carmen*. The inconceivable thing, the cruel thing, happened: the audience remained cool and indifferent, and the

123. From Bizet's manuscript of the "Carmen" score.

opera, the greatest ever written by a Frenchman, was a failure. Bizet did not survive this blow. He died the same year, at the age of thirty-seven.

We have a rather revealing letter from Bizet, expressing his attitude toward Wagner, the source of the problems that agitated the minds of musicians the world over. Bizet declared himself an enthusiastic Wagnerite, although he fully realized the man's human frailties. He called Wagner the incarnation of the German spirit and his music the most perfect expression of love, tenderness, and sensuousness. "Wagner's position is unassailable," he said in conclusion, "for he stands high above all the living. Beside him, I consider Verdi and Gounod the most talented. . . ."

Bizet considered Charles Gounod (1818-1893) [Pl. 148] the most highly gifted among his French contemporaries, and history bore out his judgment—if we except Bizet himself. Gounod's *Faust* (known as *Marguerite* in many countries) is a truly beautiful opera, although Goethe's spirit is hardly alive in it. It contains fine scenes, sweet melodies, and cleverly captures the romantic atmosphere of the love drama. Gounod's success was incomparably more pronounced than that of Bizet, though the latter was a genius of a higher order. Gounod's *Romeo and Juliet* was for many decades one of the most popular repertory operas and is still heard occasionally.

Goethe was the innocent instigator of many another opera, as, for instance, of *Mignon*, which has saved its composer, Ambroise Thomas (1811-1896), from oblivion. Effective vocal numbers reveal the hand of a good musician and an imaginative melodist.

Camille Saint-Saëns (1834-1921) [Pl. 145] also belongs in this group. He was one of the best French musicians of the romantic century. Together with Bizet and Edouard Lalo (1823-1892), the gifted composer of the *Symphonie espagnole,* he founded in Paris the *Société Nationale de Musique,* in 1871, which was the means of giving a strong impetus to French symphonic art. At this time, Saint-Saëns had some reputation as a piano and organ virtuoso, and had already written a symphony; but the musical world was slow to welcome him as a composer. Beginning in 1872, however, he produced a half-dozen symphonic poems which helped strengthen interest in French orchestral music; and about the same period he appeared as soloist, and occasionally conductor, of his five piano concertos. Soon, Saint-Saëns had triumphed in every musical field except the theater. *Le Timbre d'Argent,* which he had written in 1864-65 was at length produced in 1877. Its success secured a performance that same year for *Samson et Dalila*, which had been completed 1875. This biblical opera marked more by musical beauty than dramatic vigor, has a brilliant presentation of orientalism; it is an unusual repertory piece in that it affords the mezzo-soprano an opportunity to rise from her usual secondary level to indulge in some most effective singing and acting. Saint-Saëns' *Third Symphony in C Minor* is a masterpiece of the French symphonic form. In its cyclic form—one reappearing theme unifying the music—it resembles *The Second Concerto, in G Minor*, for piano and orchestra, which was written in seventeen days. Of the composer's other music, there are pieces for the piano, somewhat overshadowed by pieces for two pianos, such as the *Variations on a Theme of Beethoven;* and chamber music for many combinations of instruments.

Léo Delibes (1836-1891) was a graceful and technically skilled composer. His opera *Lakmé* contains effective bravura arias for a coloratura soprano, and his *Coppélia* is a charming ballet. Some of his songs, too, such as *Les filles de Cadix*, may still be heard today.

A great success was scored by Gustave Charpentier (1860) with his opera *Louise* which, in 1900, had in a certain sense the significance of a national reaction against German influences, and especially against Wagner. At the same time, however, it was an enthusiastic hymn to Paris. The musical beauty of this work is unmatched by any of Charpentier's other compositions.

Jules Massenet (1842-1912) [Pl. 147], although he was considerably more modern in the means he used, must still be numbered among the last romanticists. An exceptional orchestral technician, he also had the gift of genuine melodic conception and that certain ability, essential for one writing for the stage, to move people. Two of his works still maintain themselves on the repertory: *Manon*, which, in many countries, has succeeded in crowding out Puccini's *Manon Lescaut*, and *Werther*, based on Goethe's tragical youthful work. His melodious and heart-warming *Le Jongleur de Notre Dame* had quite a vogue for a number of years. The same may be said of his opera *Thäis*, although its American popularity was in a large measure due to a superlative presentation of the title part. Excerpts from the latter opera and from Massenet's *Le Cid* are still heard occasionally on the radio. His picturesque opera *Don Quixote* was written for the great basso Chaliapin, after whose death it sank into oblivion.

TWO OF GOD'S MUSICIANS:

CESAR FRANCK AND ANTON BRUCKNER

Like beings from another time, another world, there appear in the midst of an era of mechanization, of haste, and of materialism, two musicians of different nationalities and without personal contact with each other. But they are brothers in spirit and members of that higher community to which, in another epoch, belonged Bach and Palestrina. One of Bruckner's biographers once called him "God's musician." It seems but just to apply the term also to Franck. Being God's musicians, Bruckner and Franck lived the major part of their lives almost unnoticed by the world, finding security in the Almighty and devoting themselves quietly and indefatigably to their work, with no regard for sensational success.

César Franck (1822-1890) [Pl. 156] was born in the Belgian town of Liège, but spent most of his life in Paris. There he earned a poor living as a teacher. Two hours every day, however, from five to seven in the morning, belonged to his work. During these brief creative moments, adhered to religiously, great compositions came into being, the products of arduous work and critical conscientiousness. In those lonely hours between night and morning were born a beautiful symphony, profoundly and nobly conceived oratorios—*Rédemption, Les Béatitudes, Ruth*—and numerous pieces of organ, piano, and chamber music. Let us mention but one work, whose imperishable beauty has hardly its equal: his sonata for violin and piano. Ysaye, the famous violinist, carried it round the world, but no reflection of the triumphs he reaped reached the poverty-stricken composer or lighted up his obscure existence as an organist. Quietly and modestly he attended to that occupation at St. Loreto's, and later at St. Clotilde's, by no means focal points of the brilliant life of Paris. There were but few who recognized the exaltation of his playing and the purity and greatness of his music. Liszt once heard him play some of his own works and felt moved to the depths of his soul. He remained silent for some time and then said: "I thought I heard Johann Sebastian Bach." No greater tribute could have been paid a musician.

It seemed that Providence did not want to see his work and his person fall into oblivion. Pupils began to gather round the venerable man, a circle of prominent musicians, of whom especially Vincent d'Indy (1851-1931) [Ill. 124] and Gabriel Pierné (1863-1937) faithfully followed in his footsteps. There was also his Argentine pupil, Alberto Williams, through whom Franck exerted considerable influence on more than one generation of South American composers.

The life of Anton Bruckner has many points of similarity with that of César Franck. They had in common their pious inclination, the fact that the world was slow to recognize their worth, their predilection for the organ, their activity as teachers, and the slow and organic development of their creative forces.

To Bruckner's childlike and pure soul, God was not the Great Omnipotent, the stern Master of the Day of Judgment visualized by the soul of many another artist. No, Bruckner spoke to Him throughout his life as one speaks to an elder brother, to a kindly counselor, to an ideal comrade. Bruckner's symphonies are like sounding cathedrals or gorgeous baroque monuments, imperishable mementos of security, tranquility, infinity, plentitude, and unworldliness. His leitmotifs were expressed in an upward soaring of the soul, in a peaceful overcoming of mundane things, and in a constant glorification of the divine. If he ever experienced the inward agony and the terrible and torturing doubts of Beethoven, the crushing melancholy of Schubert, the tormenting and never-satisfied search for the supreme ideal and ultimate truth of his pupil, Gustav Mahler, if he ever went through the cruel labor pains accompanying the birth of so many masterpieces, he had succeeded in overcoming it all without letting the world know about it.

124. Vincent d'Indy (1851-1931).

Anton Bruckner [Pl. 158] was born in the year 1824, the son of a poor schoolmaster in Upper Austria. When his parents died, the boy was taken to the Seminary of St. Florian, which became to him a real home, a place of rest for his body and soul. Just as the vision of Mecca lives in the heart of every Mohammedan, so the picture of his sanctum, the great organ of St. Florian, never faded from Bruckner's mind. There he went whenever his heart felt in need of a sanctuary or whenever through its majestic chords he wished to commune with his God.

Bruckner's outward circumstances of life were miserable. A schoolmaster's apprentice in paltry out-of-the-way places of his native province, he studied music by himself and under great difficulties. Far from the cities, far from musical life, he acquired all he knew of harmony and

125. Bruckner's first sketch of the scherzo in his First Symphony, 1865. He later replaced it by another scherzo. Nationalbiblothek, Vienna.

counterpoint, of composition and instrumentation. Finally, in 1855, he scored a brilliant victory when applying for the post of cathedral organist in Linz. There, his first works of major importance came into being, though they failed to gain general recognition. The main point was that Bruckner was now able to go to Vienna occasionally and receive personal tuition from Sechter, whose books had served to guide his studies before. Vienna was a place of strife and controversy at that time. We shall have more to say about that when discussing the life of Brahms. When Bruckner was summoned to Vienna to assume the duties of a Court-Chapel organist and to act as professor of organ-playing, counterpoint, and harmony at the conservatory, the rustic, naive, and kind-hearted musician happened into a strange and contrary world, from which he was

to suffer a great deal. In the following year—he was forty-four years
old then—one of his symphonies was performed for the first time—in
Linz. Vienna was not to give him a hearing for another few years. Fame
came to him late, very late. He was almost sixty when Europe began to
realize his worth. And this in spite of the fact that some of the most eminent musicians of his time fought valiantly on his behalf: Levi (the great
Bayreuth conductor), Hans Richter, Wilhelm Jahn, Franz Schalk, and
Gustav Mahler. Opposed to him were Hanslick and every anti-Wagner-
ite. But Hanslick was more than a run-of-the-mill musical critic. The
keenness of his mind was undeniable, even though his vision may have
been obscured. His criticisms of Bruckner were at least in the form of
concrete objections. To quote him: ". . . Wagnerian orchestra effects,
like the tremolo of the divided violins in the topmost range, harp arpeg-
gios over hollow trombone chords, and added to it all the latest acquisi-
tion, the Siegfried Tuba . . . a sudden juxtaposition of dry contrapuntal
schoolroom technique and extravagant exaltation. . . ." That Bruckner,
like so many of his day, was under the spell of Wagner, was frankly admitted by himself. But it would be a gross misjudgment of his spirit were
one to call him an imitator of Wagner, just because he had adopted the
master's art of instrumentation. Above everything else, Bruckner's world
of ideas and forms was entirely different from that of Wagner, as different as were the original sources of his creative work. Bruckner's monumental style was the subject of many commentaries and controversies.
It was averred that he was essentially lacking in form, but it was long
unknown that his symphonies were not performed in their original version but with considerable retouchings, whose deeply affecting changes
were eliminated only in our century.

Bruckner is the creator of grand works. Few composers have devoted themselves so exclusively to grandiose forms. He wrote three
masses and nine symphonies. But as if Fate had wished to prevent the
existence of another Ninth after the brilliant achievement of Beethoven,
Bruckner died before he was able to complete the work. His Seventh
was the first one to find its way into the world outside of Vienna. Leipzig witnessed its performance by Nikisch, in 1884. Best-known of all is
his Fourth, which was given the name "Romantic," a title which, as far
as fundamental structure and detail work are concerned, is suitable to all
of Bruckner's music. His work is still gaining in appreciation. New coun-

tries are opening their doors to it, even those to whose spirit its gorgeous baroque style is essentially alien.

Bruckner had grown old and ill. Ever more rarely was he able to make his pilgrimage to the beloved organ of St. Florian, and ever greater became his longing for it. After he had died in Vienna, in 1896, he was at last granted the brief yearned-for journey. He found a final resting place at the foot of his organ.

JOHANNES BRAHMS

For decades, pure symphonic form had failed to produce works worthy to be compared to those of Beethoven. Only now, at the decline of romanticism, this form of art blossomed anew, introducing a final brief period of splendor in several countries.

Bruckner, the Austrian, and Franck, the Belgian, have already been discussed. Active at the same time were Brahms, the German, who had made Vienna his second home, Tchaikovsky, the Russian, who formed a bridge between his country and the rest of the world, and Dvořák, the Czech, who made contact with American music and took over some of its motifs into his work. We are beginning to realize that the borderlines established by musical nationalism were losing their distinctness. Melodies of one people mixed with the technique of another, ideas of one with the forms of expression of another. There began the great process of unification which culminated in our century.

Schumann, shortly before he attempted to take his own life in a fit of insanity, had, with the noble enthusiasm characteristic of him, taken up the cause of a young musician in whom he felt the stirring of genius. The young man was Johannes Brahms. Schumann, who regarded music as a great brotherhood, predicated for the newly initiated brother a high rank, many a wound, and many a success. He was proved right, although the laurels were late in coming and had to cover many an injury sustained during the interim.

Johannes Brahms [Pl. 150] was a son of northern Germany, born in Hamburg, in the year 1833. But in him, as in so many others, there dwelt the longing for the South. He went to Italy, wrote waltzes in praise of Vienna, and composed his famous Hungarian Dances, captivated by the exotic charm of that country's folklore. He finally settled in Vienna and continued to live in the gay metropolis on the Danube to the end of his days. But he spent many holidays in Switzerland whose natural beauty attracted him powerfully. Quite a number of his works came into being in Ruschlikon near Zurich [Pl. 152] and in Thun, and his *German Requiem* was first published in Winterthur. His love of Vienna was not the only point he had in common with Beethoven. His character, too, revealed many surprising parallels with the master of Bonn. Brahms, serious and heavy in body as well as in soul, had a soft and kind heart, a profound love of humanity and nature. Long walks took him over the paths trod by Beethoven, and his life, too, was heavily weighed down by loneliness.

Thus, the form of his music can not come to us as a surprise. It is neither amiable, nor elegant, nor easily accessible. Profoundly serious, it yet contains the highest ethical and musical values and, more than that, a wealth of love and tenderness. And though it frequently seems gloomy at the first hearing, it reveals at times even a refreshing sense of humor.

The character of the composer and of his work manifests itself most plainly in his songs. In them is mirrored his life and his heart, lighting up even the most secret corners. Many of them tell of loneliness, of tragic love, of a longing for death, Here, Brahms travels the paths of his great lyric predecessors, especially Schubert and Schumann. A clever contemporary, referring to the melancholy of his melodies, said: "When Brahms is in a gay mood he composes 'The Grave is my Joy.'" Let us, from a larger number, pick at random some of the most beautiful songs whose fundamental mood is one of smoldering sorrow and profound sadness: *O wüsst' ich doch den Weg zurück* (If I but knew the way's return—Klaus Groth), *Der Tod das ist die kühle Nacht* (Death truly is the cool of Night—Heine), *Immer leiser wird mein Schlummer* (Ever lighter grows my slumber—Herman Ling), *Mainacht* (May Night—Ludwig Holty), *An die Nachtigall* (To the nightingale—Ludwig Holty), *Sapphiche Ode* (Sapphic Ode—Hans Schmidt). The irresistible power of love is depicted in the following: *Von ewiger Liebe* (Of e'erlasting love—based on a popular Slav text), and *Liebestreu* (True Love—Robert Reinick). Let us recall the wonderfully impressive sound of nature, the tranquility, and sense of world oblivion in his *Feldeinsamkeit* (Field Loneliness—Karl Lemcke) and the striking example, become world-famous, of a most tender mood in his *Wiegenlied* (Cradle Song—Carl Simrock). And as for examples of a fine sense of humor, there are *Der Jäger* (The Huntsman—Friedrich Halm) and *Vergebliches Ständchen* (Futile Serenade—based on a popular Rhenish text). To know Brahm's songs is to know the man, not only because of the music but also because of his choice of texts. The names of the lyricists are indicated. Many of them may be forgotten today, but the fact that they inspired this immortal music assures them a measure of reflected glory.

To find the way to Brahm's purely instrumental works is a much more difficult task. There are four symphonies, masterful in every detail.

126. A Brahms manuscript. Score of the "Variations for Orchestra on a Theme by Hadyn," op. 56, 1873. Nationalbibliothek, Vienna.

Brahms was a contemporary of Bruckner—but what a difference! They walked the streets of the same city, but when they wrote music they were immeasurably far from each other. It would seem even more difficult to get to the core of his concertos: the two grandly conceived piano concertos which make so high a demand of the soloist but can afford also so high a degree of satisfaction; the violin concerto, which like Beetroven's is Brahms' only one and is also written in D major; and the double concerto for violin and cello.

His *German Requiem* [Pl. 153] deserves to be called a truly extra-

254 .

ordinary work. It is remarkable for the fact that it has a German text instead of the usual Latin one. Here, too, as in the *Four Serious Songs*, his swan song, the profundity of the composer is strikingly revealed, as is that melancholy which, though touchingly restrained at times, is present in all his creations, even when he seems to have triumphed over it.

The chamber music of Brahms presents a group of compositions which are almost without exception masterpieces. The characteristics of Brahms' music, economy and concentration, structure organism, and thematic imagination, made this form of composition a perfect vehicle for his genius. Examples of his mastery in his field may be selected at random: the *Horn Trio, Opus 40;* the *Clarinet Quintet, Opus 115;* the *D Minor Violin Sonata, Opus 108;* the three quartets for piano and strings.

127. Brahms on his way to the "Red Hedgehog" inn. Caricature silhouette by Otto Bohler.

Besides the Concertos, Brahms wrote much for the piano, both solo and duet. His solo *Sonata No. 2, F-Sharp Minor, Sonata No. 3, F Minor,* and *Variations on a Theme by Schumann* (his life-long friend) are outstanding. The graceful waltzes and Hungarian dances already mentioned are included among the duets.

In the course of time, Brahms became a highly popular personage in Vienna. His short and stout figure with its large head and its long beard and hair was frequently seen in the coffee-houses which, as in hardly any other city, were the meeting points for artists and literary men. Few of his intimate friends knew that he, who had remained a bachelor and had never had a real home, entertained a romantic and never-admitted love in the deep recesses of his heart. Its object was Clara Schumann, the widow of the great musician. Ever since her husband's death, her only aim in life had been the propagation of his work. It seems that for almost half a century Brahms had loved Clara without ever telling her or even hinting at it. When, in 1898, he stood at her grave he felt that his life, too, was nearing its end. The struggle for or against Wagner which had for years agitated the musical atmosphere of Vienna was slowly calming down. Brahms had been drawn into it against his will. Hanslick had proclaimed him the anti-Wagnerian counter-pope (which, like whatever Hanslick did, was not without sense) making him the very antipode of all musicians who had espoused the cause of Wagner, chief among whom were Bruckner and Wolf. Well, the fight was abating. There were neither victors nor vanquished, which is as it should be when men of genius confront each other. Outwardly, to be sure, the spirit of Bayreuth was triumphant. But the work of Brahms, too, stood unshakable. Brahms outlived Bruckner and Clara by but a single year. He died on April 3, 1897.

THE FLOWER OF ROMANTICISM: THE LIED

The Lied is perhaps the most genuine flower of romantic music. Many composers since the days of Schubert cultivated it. From the cosy intimacy of the home, from the friendly atmosphere of the early-nineteenth-century drawing-room the Lied had stepped into the glaring light of the concert halls. Only true masterpieces could maintain themselves in places where everything seemed to be in league against the expression of an intimate mood. After all, the Lied is the counterpole of opera. That may be the reason why only in the rarest instances was a musician able to accomplish great things in both.

In the eras of Haydn, Mozart, and Beethoven, the Lied had not as yet acquired its distinguishing marks. Schubert, Schumann, Mendelssohn, and Wolf were its first great representatives, and not one of them played a prominent part in the history of opera. Conversely, Wagner wrote but five songs (to words by Mathilde Wesendonck) and they were merely preliminary studies for one of his dramas. Verdi did not write a single song. But there is no rule without exceptions, and the exceptions seem to be represented here by a number of Slav composers, like Moussorgsky, Rimsky-Korsakov, and Tchaikovsky, and, among the musicians of the twentieth century, especially Richard Strauss.

It was mentioned that there existed about 42,000 actually performed operatic works. Understandably, the number of songs is ten times, twenty times, perhaps even a hundred times as large. And yet, how few of them deserve to be called a Meisterlied, to use a Wagnerian term. At first, the art song was a purely German product. In the epoch of musical nationalism, every country tried to adapt it to its own individual conditions. The latter half of the romantic century witnessed its nation-wide cultivation.

Peter Cornelius has already been mentioned. His exquisite *Brautlieder* (Bridal Songs) were greatly in vogue at one time. Mention must

128. Hugo Wolf's manuscript of the song "The Ghosts on Mummel Lake," to words by Mörike. Stadtbiblithek, Vienna.

be made here of the highly gifted Robert Franz (1815-1892) whose style was rather similar to that of Schumann. There was also Karl Loewe, the spectacularly successful composer of forceful ballads, every one of which represents a miniature musical drama. His *Die Uhr* (The Watch), *Archibald Douglas*, *Prinz Eugen* (Prince Eugene), *Nächtliche Heerschau* (Nocturnal Army Review), and *Tom der Reimer* (Tom, the Rhymer), are occasionally heard even today.

The songs of Brahms have already been accorded the place of honor due them. We shall now speak of one of the greatest geniuses in the realm of the Lied, a man who was at the same time one of the most tragic figures in the history of music: Hugo Wolf.

Just as Chopin's specialty was the piano, Paganini's the violin, so Wolf centered all of his creative power on the Lied. He was born in Windischgräz, in the Austrian province of Styria, in 1860. From his very childhood, he revealed a melancholy trend.

Wolf was active in Vienna as a music critic. Being an ardent Wagnerite, he soon came into conflict with the "official" musical circles. It was made practically impossible for him to gain a performance of his compositions, eruptively born in the lonely hours of the night amid the squalor of his quarters. His songs were entirely novel and revolutionary. They went far beyond anything written before. The declamation—in the spirit of Wagner—was dramatically tensed to the utmost. Every word, every thought, had a tonal inflection of its own. The piano accompaniment, already quite independent of the singing voice, depicted moods, at times merely furnished hints, in a manner later adopted by impressionists. Of Wolf's hundreds of songs but a few can be mentioned here, although all of them deserve to be counted among the most beautiful in the world. There are the *Eichendorff Lieder*, the *Mörike Lieder*, and the songs based on texts by Goethe and Michaelangelo. His *Italian* and *Spanish Book of Songs* reveal an incredible adaptability to the spirit of those countries, which his poor mortal eyes had never really beheld.

Wolf, a "genius of suffering," did not live to taste the fruits of his success. His songs, to say nothing of his beautiful opera *Der Corregidor*, failed to arouse the interest of his contemporaries. Only a very few friends held the key to his unsociable and difficult character. When, on February 22, 1903, news of his death came from out the dark walls of the Vienna Lunatic Asylum, it made hardly a stir.

As in opera, so in the Lied, too, a notable French school came into existence. Having had its source in late-romanticism, it imperceptibly found its way to impressionism.

Among the chief representatives of that school was Henri Duparc (1848-1933) who, while still quite young, was overtaken by the tragic fate of Schumann and Wolf. After a brilliant beginning, his mental derangement condemned him to inactivity. Among his beautiful songs, there was one especially that became known the world over: his *Chanson triste*. There were furthermore Ernest Chausson (1855-1899) and Gabriel Fauré (1845-1924). The latter's *Après un rêve* and *Les Berceaux* are fine examples of the well developed sense of sound and the melodic treatment of the voice of these French masters. Reynaldo Hahn (1874-1947) also must be numbered among these French musicians, although he was born in Caracas, Venezuela. He was a pupil of Massenet and also wrote for the theater and the ballet. Among his most beautiful songs, many of which are based on the glorious verses of Verlaine, are: *Chansons grises*, *Fêtes galantes*, *Chanson d'automne*, *Offrande*, *D'une prison*, and *La Lune blanche*. His work, like that of his colleagues, must be placed between late-romanticism and the impressionism of Debussy. It represents a flight from workaday things, music that is far from every reality, very delicately conceived, melancholy, and just a bit tired.

Among the "new" peoples, the folklore element played an important part in the creation of songs. That was but natural with composers who, observing the trend of romanticism, delved into the soul of their people, thereby gaining strength and individuality. Thus we find typically Czech melodic turns and many a pleasant polka among the songs of Dvorák. How splendid are his *Gypsy Songs*, how deeply felt his *Biblical Songs;* Zdenek Fibich (1850-1900) and Viteslav Novak (1870-   ) also composed beautiful airs. Russia produced a huge quantity of impressive songs. Those of the "Five" were discussed before. True, the most familiar ones by Tchaikovsky (*None but the Lonely Heart* and *During the Ball*) reveal a western orientation. On the other hand, in the rich store of songs by Alexander Grechaninov (1864) there may be found many genuinely Russian turns (*Home of Mine*, *Lullaby*, *Over the Mountains*, and perhaps the most beautiful of all, *Before me the Steppe*). The melodies by the famous pianist Sergei Rachmaninoff (1873-1943), delicately inspired, also reveal occasional national traits (*The Soldier's Wife*, *The Lilies*, *Morning*, *Dusk*).

In Grieg's songs, too, a folklike turn often appears, as in *Solvejg's*

Song and *On the Lake*, while the famous *I Love Thee* and *A Swan* are more internationally conceived. Hungary has its songs, and so has Poland. Spain and England will be discussed in greater detail later. And in the young American music, the song represents one of the earliest forms of composition.

Thus, the Lied has come to be a true expression of international romanticism. What Schubert had begun within the narrow confines of his life had turned, before his century had come to its end, into a form of art in which the whole world could give expression to its feelings.

TWO GREAT SLAV ROMANTICISTS: TSCHAIKOVSKY AND DVORAK

The Slav soil, so rich in musical substance, continued to produce creative artists. Anton Rubinstein (1830-1894), who during his lifetime was one of the most celebrated pianists and musical personalities, continues to lose caste as a composer in the judgment of history. His most successful opera, *The Demon*, as well as his symphonies and oratorios, all of them technically perfect, are more or less forgotten today. A snatch of a melody here and there is all that reminds us of the man who served the musical life of Russia so eminently well. Among other things, he was responsible for the foundation of the Petersburg Conservatory, which has managed to retain its reputation as one of the finest institutions of its kind.

The opposite is true of Piotr Ilyitch Tchaikovsky (1840-1893) [Pl. 154]. He is gaining new admirers every day, and many of his works, such as his ballets and the last three of his symphonies, are among the most popular musical pieces of today. Tchaikovsky, who spent many years outside of Russia, combines Russian thematics with an international technique. His works form a bridge between the oriental soul and occidental civilization.

Tchaikovsky was born in an out-of-the-way corner of the Ural Mountains. He went to St. Petersburg to take up the career of a civil servant. But with one of those genuinely Russian gestures—remember Moussorgsky?—he suddenly gave up everything and plunged into music. There followed hard times, a desperate struggle for existence, days of violent moral crises. But, as in a fairy tale, he finally received his reward. A female admirer of his art settled a considerable life annuity on him, that he might devote himself entirely to composition. She made but one condition, and it was scrupulously observed by both parties: they were never to meet.

Tchaikovsky was now free from pressing care. He undertook long journeys, settling wherever he liked and creating work upon work. He went home from time to time to present his compositions to the public. Was his benefactress seated anywhere within the vast hall? He had no idea how near to him she often was, that Madame von Meck, who was also to play a part—albeit a less important one—in the life of Debussy. Neither had he any idea how deeply she, who was heroically enduring an unhappy existence, was affected by his music.

The year 1885 witnessed his permanent return to Russia. There he worked on his Sixth Symphony. He gave it, contrary to all rules, a mournful final movement, a deeply stirring lament of weeping violins. It was like a farewell to life. The people failed to understand it; a few weeks later he was dead.

Mention has already been made of his strongly impressive last three symphonies. The Fourth contains a quite unique second movement, played only by the strings, pizzicato throughout. In the Fifth, there are pronouncedly Russian themes in the first and last movements, a widely arched and powerfully climactic second movement in which a melancholy horn solo carries the principal melody, and a third movement in the form of a graceful waltz, which had always strangely attracted Tchaikovsky. The Sixth has a gloomy first movement whose melodic line rises slowly, as if from the bowels of the earth, a pleasant second movement in an unusual five-eight measure, a third-movement march of amazingly skillful construction and electrifying effectiveness, followed by the already mentioned finale which breaks with all established symphonic rules and represents a great musician's moving leave-taking of life.

Sure in its effect, and therefore frequently played, is Tchaikovsky's First Piano Concerto in B-flat minor with its mightily onrushing introductory theme. Nobler, perhaps, is his violin concerto. And there are his many overtures. That of *Romeo and Juliet* contains beautiful and softly singing melodies, while *1812* is a magnificent depiction of the Napoleonic wars. The Corsican's Russian campaign is portrayed with amazing plasticity, the Marseillaise characterizing the French and a Russian folksong the defenders of Moscow. The end, when to the victorious tolling of the Moscow bells the Marseillaise is drowned out by the thunder of cannon, represents—in spite of many objections to this piece—both enormously effective and truly inspired music. Among his works for string orchestra there is a charming Serenade. The best-known of his ballets are *Swan Lake* [Ill. 129], *The Nutcracker*, and *Sleeping Beauty*. Tchaikovsky was also a gifted operatic composer, his principal works in this field being *Eugene Onegin* and *Pique Dame*.

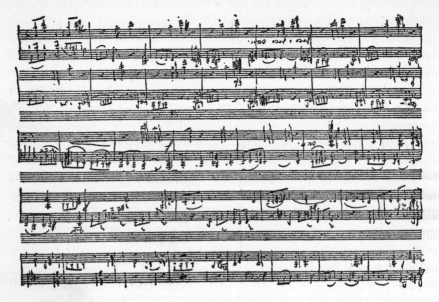

129. Tchaikovsky's manuscript of the piano score of the introduction to the "Swan Lake" ballet.

Anatol Liadov (1855-1914), Sergei Liapounov (1859-1924), and Alexander Glazounov (1865-1936) are other important names of that Russian musical epoch which was somehow connected with European romanticism.

Liadov was a remarkably fine tone painter, his *Eight Russian Folk Airs* being little masterpieces. Glazounov, whose beginnings were influenced by the young-Russian school, become a vigorous symphonist who frequently combined the use of Russian themes with European technique. Among other things, he composed eight symphonies, several symphonic poems (*Stenka Razin* among them), a fine violin concerto, and interesting pieces of chamber music.

Czech music, whose star rose so brilliantly in the person of Smetana, now found a no less gifted representative in Antonin Dvorák (1841-1904) [Pl. 157]. A peasant's son, he was born in Kralup and early learned to play the violin. Like a genuine Bohemian musician, he started to fiddle at weddings and balls. He earned his living that way when he moved to Prague to study music. Great personal sacrifices and an iron energy enabled him to acquire an amazing amount of knowledge and ability. Smetana gave him a violinist's job at the National Opera and soon also recognized the young man's talent for composition. Beyond the border, it was Liszt once more who scented a genius in the making.

A hymn composed by Dvořák in 1873 was highly successful, and from that point on things moved forward at a rapid pace. He received honorary doctor's degrees in Prague, Oxford, and Cambridge, and was active as a professor at the conservatory when in 1891 he was invited to head the National Conservatory of New York. Thus he became the first prominent European composer to come in direct contact with American music, and it is noteworthy that the influence of the New World is quite evident in his work. The wonderfully heartfelt theme in the second movement of his Fifth Symphony, for instance, which he significantly called *From the New World*, is in the manner of a genuine Negro melody with all its thousand-year-old sadness. The singing of the Negro folk can be heard in this heart-rending melody, played softly and mellowly by an English horn and accompanied by the strings whose vibrating harmonies sound like the rustling of the trees in Bohemia's woods. Mississippi and Moldau at the same time, and behold, when they sing together the nations understand each other; when they sing they are all one. . . .

Dvořák returned to his home in 1895. His European fame was still growing. Now that Liszt was dead, Brahms was the man who appreciated him most in Germany. His work embraced all fields. He composed eight operas which, to be sure, gained no more than local popularity, the famous *Slavonic Dances*, symphonic and religious works, including a beautiful *Stabat Mater*, and the already mentioned splendid songs. In 1904, the City of Prague honored its three great musicians, Smetana, Fibich, and Dvořák, by arranging a cyclical performance of their works. This was the last gratifying experience in the life of Dvořák who had risen from a poor village boy to one of his era's leading musicians. A few days later, he closed his eyes forever.

THE RE-AWAKENING OF SPAIN

For quite some time now, we have made no mention of Spanish music which, toward the end of the Middle Ages, was one of the most brilliant in Europe. It may be that the creative musical power of the Iberian peninsula had declined, a development that would be parallel to that in other branches of art which had likewise passed their golden era, or it may be that the waning political importance of Spain had relegated the country to a place in the background—at any rate, there had not thus far been a Spaniard among the great masters of classic or romantic music.

It would nevertheless be wrong to assume that the Spanish people's love of music had declined. As a matter of fact, there is hardly a country in Europe, with the exception of Russia, to match Spain's genuine and vital folk music, whose mixture of Latin and Arabian elements has been productive of highly characteristic and typical melodies and rhythms. Among the accomplished Spanish musicians of the eighteenth century were Mateo Albéniz and Antonio Soler, although their works did not penetrate beyond the Pyrenees.

Only when the nineteenth century began to wane, in the days of late-romanticism, did musical creators of world importance arise in the Iberian peninsula. They were Isaac Albéniz (1860-1909) and Enrique Granados (1867-1916).

Catalans by birth, they received their musical education from a great master, Felipe Pedrell (1841-1922), a true prophet of the new Spanish music. Both men were eminent pianists and so dedicated the best part of their creative work to that instrument. Both died at the age of forty-eight. Albéniz had an adventurous spirit. He gave his first piano concert at the age of four. Later, he ran away from home and crossed the Peninsula back and forth, supporting himself by giving concerts. When the police finally caught up with him and wanted to send him home, he eluded them once more and stowed away on an America-bound steamer. That was the first of a number of similar escapades. In that manner, he came to see many parts of Latin America. He gave concerts from Cuba to Buenos Aires, made a good deal of money, spent it again, and never was able to settle in any one place. He had already begun to play his own compositions, but they were short and insignificant drawing-room pieces.

The great change in his life occurred in 1883. The beneficial influence of a young woman made him give up his roving life. He began to study harmony seriously and listened to the teachings of Pedrell. It was the latter who introduced him to romanticism and to the first stirrings of French impressionism. This was to prove of great importance to Albéniz whose genuinely Spanish temperament enabled him to combine both romanticism and impressionism with the melodies and dances of his homeland.

Albéniz' comic opera, *Pepita Jiménez,* must be considered a valuable contribution to Spanish opera, while his piano concerto on Sevillian motifs is, together with da Falla's *Nights in the Gardens of Spain,* the most important Spanish work of its kind. His genius was most aptly manifested, however, in his depictions of his native landscape, the music-saturated brilliant nights of Granada and Sevilla, the colorful festivals of hot-blooded Andalusia, and the strange dances of the gypsy quarters. He called the collection of these marvelous miniatures *Iberia,* every one of which had a different glitter, melancholy and passionate at the same time. The world received this work as a great promise for the future. Debussy said that never before had music succeeded in capturing so great a variety of colorful impressions. But the body of Albéniz, weakened by the extravagant deeds of his youth, succumbed before his spirit was able to continue the work in which he had shown to the world a piece of the soul of Spain.

Enrique Granados, born in Lérida, in 1867, was a man of an entirely different temperament. Traveling held no attraction for him, and as for sea voyages, he loathed them. After having studied in Paris, he settled in Barcelona. By that time, he had already acquired a reputation as a good pianist and composer of typically Spanish melodies and dances. Granados was a stylist who, beyond the Pyrenees, would have been called a romantic. He lived somewhat outside of his time, going back in his dreams to the brilliant epoch of Goya. His compositions tried to recapture the magic of those long-ago Madrid days and their typical figures and dances. That was how the cycle *Goyescas* came into existence, soon thereafter changed by Granados into an opera.

It was during the days of the First World War that the Metropolitan Opera of New York put on his opera for the first time anywhere. Not only did this mark the first Spanish-language performance at that famous theater, but also the first premiere in the United States of a work with a Spanish milieu. For once, Granados overcame his horror of sea voyages. Especially acclaimed was the *Intermezzo,* a brief and effective orchestral interlude, composed by Granados only a few days before the premiere, because the stage manager had pleaded for a little additional time in which to change the scenery. A few weeks later, Granados and his wife started on their homeward voyage. They had reached European waters when their ship was struck by a German torpedo and sunk. To those who believed in symbols, this catastrophe had a hidden meaning: the disaster spreading over Europe to the accompaniment of wars and revolutions, hunger and hatred, had been responsible for the death of the last romanticist. Two epochs had clashed at that moment.

SECOND INTERMEZZO

The summit lies behind us. The two golden centuries are over. The second stop on our journey occurs at a critical moment: the advent of the twentieth century, weighted down by difficult problems, shaken by feverish crises. The skies seem still clear and serene, but to those with a keen power of observation, alarming symptoms can be noticed here and there, the rumbling of subterranean thunder, the flare of distant lightning.

Cultural epochs, too, may grow tired. Just as a fertile soil may become exhausted by a succession of rich harvests, so a cultural soil, too, may lose its vigor after having produced a succession of creative generations. Masters, great masters even, still grew from Europe's cultural soil. Works of imperishable value were born. But they were not the blossoms of a new spring. They were the last fruits of a rich, proud harvest. Autumn was about to descend on European civilization, autumn with its storms and tempests. And one day, everything would be covered by the snows of winter.

Accounts of storms and tempests form a large part of the Third Book, at whose threshold we have arrived. It will tell of an ebbing-away, of a descent, of a way into the unknown. No longer may we listen to tales of tranquil and logical developments, of imperceptible transitions, of creative activities by those who hopefully and trustingly looked to the future. Europe, the brilliant center of an almost two-thousand-year-old culture, seems to feel that her fateful hour is about to strike. The Continent and the century, having brought forth the most highly developed civilization within the knowledge of man, are about to drown their works in streams of anguish, blood, and tears. Let us never forget this when contemplating modern art. Never can an ailing epoch produce a healthy art. And yet, you will say, there were ailing epochs in the history of the world which gave birth to wonderful art. The works that conclude an era are different, quite different, from those that usher it in. But they may be equally beautiful.

Culture cannot die as long as there is a single person ready to save it. And the cultural will, the yearning for art, is strong in our day. Technical progress has made the surface of the earth into one cultural realm. Social development will make all mankind into one cultural mass. Today, streams of thought flow with incredible swiftness from their source to the farthest corners of the world. And the seed of European culture and art, borne by favorable winds, has found lodgment in the strong virgin soil of America.

It may be recalled that we compared our book to a journey. We have passed the summit. There it lies behind us, still brilliantly lighted by the last red rays of the sun. Slowly, out of the valley, the shadows come to meet us. The skies are still clear, bright in the reflection of a long and overripe day. The wanderers may still rejoice in their glowing colors. But when they gaze down at the way spreading before them, their eyes seem to be dazzled by all the light they have just admired, and so the darkness ahead of them appears yet darker, more impenetrable. They are seized with unrest. They see lights flare up, dull flames, here and there. Are they will-o'-the-wisps? Are they torches? Confusion sets in. Each one follows one of the lights, each one thinks his is the right one, the one that will guide him through the night, and to another summit. They fight one another in the name of their will-o'-the-wisp, they lose one another in the swampy abyss. They also try to destroy the other's light, their increasing loneliness makes them shout louder and louder, and they preach words that are ever more hollow. Suddenly they realize that they can no longer hear or understand one another. A new babel has set in, in which everybody speaks his own language, the language of his egoism. There may be some few in that night who, enlightened by the reflection of a true ideal in their own breast, are able to stride through the darkness on a narrow path and to whom it may be vouchsafed to see the rise of another dawn.

Whenever in one realm of our planet the sun sets, there comes in another, a distant, realm the rise of a new day.

BOOK THREE

The Way Into Uncertainty

Beloved earth is clad anew in robes of spring,
and from afar eternal shine the Heavens . . .
Eternal . . . Eternal. . . .

> (*Version of an Old-Chinese poem by Mong Kao
> Yen and Wang Wai, used by Gustav Mahler in
> "Das Lied von der Erde.*")

25

The New Century

THE world greeted the new century with shouts of joy. Optimism, prosperity, peace—everywhere! How far away seemed all the disquieting problems! Middle-class culture had reached its zenith. The only note of alarm was sounded by the arts. From the stage and in books, the Dostoyevskys, Zolas and Hauptmanns, the Strindbergs and Ibsens of all countries hurled their *J'accuse* into the face of society. On the painter's canvas appeared new figures, strange lights, alarming perspectives. And music was seized with a deep unrest, with a nervous urge to search. . . .

Wagner's death had been the great milestone on the road of music. He had consciously removed art from the commonplace atmosphere of the day and had guided music into the realm of fantasy. His genius had been able to captivate all minds by his tales of legendary beings and mystic figures, of gods, heroes, giants, dwarfs, magic potions, and symbolic events. What road were his successors to take? Adopt the pattern fashioned by him who had gathered together all romanticism? Many tried to follow in his footsteps. Among them were Wagner's own son, Siegfried (1869-1930) [Pl. 31], and a few others, whom we shall meet later. But the feet of most of them were too narrow to fit the prints left by Wagner—they were but pale imitators.

So, away from Wagner! Against him! That became the battlecry of many, even of some of those who had unconsciously absorbed much of his spirit. Against Wagner! That might mean any number of things. In opera, for instance, it led to the Italian *verismo*, which soon assumed international proportions. It matched the naturalism in other arts and represented an abrupt return to reality, an attempt to mirror everyday life—unvarnished, naked, cruel. From a purely musical standpoint, the anti-Wagnerian tendency meant a turning away from his yearning chromatics, from his leitmotifs, from his infinite melodies, from his turbulent orchestra, and from his musical symbolism. In a word, it meant the way to many of the tendencies encountered in our century, such as neoclassicism, or expressionism. We chose the example of the musical stage

130. Mannerism Chart for Conductors. Drawing by Schliessmann, from "Lustige Blätter," 1906.

work because it seemed to show our point with particular clearness. But the very same development took place also in symphonic music, in the Lied, and in chamber music. It embraced the technique as well as the choice of themes. It will be shown how the search for realistic subjects led to the introduction of physical projects into music, to the musical glorification of factories, machines, technical works, and other symbols of modern life.

Away from Wagner! That was one way. The other, although those who pursued it were unaware of it, led even beyond him. It represented the striving for the ultimate romantic ideal by the abjuration of every rough reality, and so it led to the final development of symbolism. It was the way of so-called impressionism. In the art of painting, it fused perspective, drawing, and contour into a blurred totality of great homogeneousness. In literature, it paid exclusive heed to coloring, sensation, and mood, as in the writings of Baudelaire or of that strange bohemian of Montmartre, Verlaine. And in music, the search for new ideals led to the progressive disintegration of the main elements of melody, harmony, and rhythm, dissolving them like the basic pictorial elements in the paintings of a Cézanne, a Renoir, or a Monet. Everything became unreal, dreamlike, nebulously distant, vague—like the feeble glow of the wintry sun on a pond covered with faded blossoms. Snatches of melodies soared in melancholy sequences over dreamily soft harmonic combinations which, in spite of all dissonances, never became strident. If we closed our eyes, we felt our senses enveloped as in the sweet fragrance of distant gardens.

It was Claude Debussy [Pl. 161] who represented musical impressionism in its purest form. He was born in St. Germain-en-Laye, in France, in the year 1862, and, when he was but twenty-two, won the coveted *Prix de Rome* of the Paris Conservatory. For a moment, public attention was focused on this new and officially proclaimed musical hope of France and accompanied him on his journey to the Eternal City. But the overture which he wrote there and which he submitted to the Paris jury, as was the custom, startled the learned men by its highly individual musical language. Debussy was trying to find a way beyond Wagner by the use of new sound combinations which in their boldness outdid even those of *Tristan*. And that at a time when the work of Wagner had not as yet fully penetrated French understanding! Contrary to every usage, Debussy's overture was not performed, and the young musician's name was shunted aside. Debussy removed himself more and more from the world. For a long time, this picturesque and exceptionally interesting artist lived the life of a recluse, listening to his inward voices and building up a world of tones which was his exclusively. He spent the years from 1892 to 1902 on a single creation, the greatest of his life, the musical drama *Pelléas et Mélisande*, inspired by the lyrics of Maurice Maeterlinck. This work cannot be compared to any other opera. It occupies a unique place in musico-dramatic literature. Perhaps it is the only entirely successful attempt to unite two conflicting worlds: impressionism and the theater. Not even Debussy himself made another such attempt. The other work he wrote for the stage was a sort of medieval mystery play, *The Martyrdom of St. Sebastian*, based on a text by Gabriele d'Annunzio, in which all dramatic action is supplanted by intoxicating and never-before-heard harmonies.

There is a striking similarity between Debussy's art and the ideological world of his impressionistic colleagues of the brush. Their subjects are frequently the same: delicate landscapes—lost as in a fog, clouds, and above all, and over and over again, the water to which Debussy felt mystically attracted. It returns in hundreds of forms in his music, from the spring representing the eternal leitmotif in *Pelléas et Mélisande*, the *Reflets dans l'eau*, and the *Jardins sous la pluie*, to the *Nuages*, the *Sirènes*, the age-old Breton legend of the *Cathedrale engloutie*, and finally to the superb symphonic poem *La Mer*. Again and again, Debussy finds his way back to the water, inventing new tones and shadings for the mysterious element, which once had so powerfully stirred Schubert.

Symphonic art, with the constantly expanding sound possibilities of the modern orchestra, offered to Debussy's impressionism an inexhaustible field of activity. In every one of the following works, a definite picture rises before our eyes: *L'après-midi d'un faune*, written for the famous Russian dancer Nijinsky; the three Nocturnes—*Nuages*, *Fêtes*, *Sirènes*—in the last of which the composer added the mysterious effect of an inarticulate humming female chorus; *Iberia*, full of genuine Spanish life, although the composer had never set foot on that country's soil—neither had Bizet when he wrote *Carmen*, nor the highly gifted Alexis Chabrier (1841-1894) when he composed the fiery tone poem *España*—and finally *La Mer*, the culminating point of Debussy's orchestral art, with its subdivisions: *The Sea from Sunrise to Noon*, *Play of the Waves*, and *Discourse between Wind and Sea*.

But also in the much more limited realm of the piano, Debussy succeeded in producing entirely new, magical sound effects, as in the *Suite Bergamesque* which contains the wonderful *Clair de Lune*, the *Arabesques*, the scintillating *Préludes*, and finally the enchanting *Children's Corner* with its rhythmically agitated climactic *Golliwog's Cake-Walk*, in which elements of jazz are already discernible.

The application of the impressionistic style to the Lied form has been accompanied understandably by happy results. Wherever the seemingly floating melody is supported by the verses of a congenial poet, the expression of the most mature and ultimate beauty, of the most delicate coloring, and of the profoundest wisdom of life has been achieved. The new style had been conceived in the art of Duparc, Fauré, and Hahn.

Debussy carried it to its ultimate conclusion in *Fêtes galantes* and *Ariettes oubliées*—cycles based on the melancholy verses of Verlaine—*Five Poems by Baudelaire,* and the *Ballads of François Villon.*

In the course of his lonely creative life, Debussy went through many stages of inward development. It seemed as if his soul were forever roaming. It finally found a resting place in a far-off cultural milieu—that of Malay and Indonesia. Not that he ever traveled there in the flesh; but Javanese and other Far-Eastern groups of musicians could be heard in Paris from time to time.

The First World War filled the hearts of all artists with horror. Debussy retired to a quiet villa at the seashore near the Spanish frontier. For days on end, he would let his gaze rest on the waters. Then again, he would start to write feverishly day and night. He, the laborious producer, was tortured by the thought that many, many works were as yet unwritten and that he would not be able to complete them. For he realized that his body was wasting away from day to day. He died in Paris, in March, 1918, while the Germans were bombarding the city.

One of the significant symptoms of modern art is that increasingly it loses its national characteristics. Just as the great cities of our century resemble each other because of a uniformly adopted style of building, so the musical styles of our era, too, quickly adapt themselves to one another. Modern technique with its railways, planes, and radio is largely responsible for that. The outer confines of musical tendencies no longer coincide with national borderlines, as was the case in the romantic century, when a clear distinction could be made between German, Italian, Polish, and Scandinavian music. The line of demarcation separating the various musical styles of the twentieth century runs between individual groups of the same country, so that, for instance, a French impressionist feels much more akin to impressionists in England, Spain, Italy, or Russia than, say, to the verists, expressionists, and neo-classicists of his own country. This development is also influenced by the fact that national characteristics, which to the romanticists were often all-important, are being eliminated by a great many composers as bases of artistic music. It will be shown, however, that these characteristics are once more essentially important in the development of budding American music.

Although it would not do to assert that Debussy had established a school, in the strict sense of the word, since he was too much of an individualist and kept too much to himself, impressionism nevertheless spread all over the world, as if it were the answer to an era s deep yearning.

Russia's contribution to impressionism was largely due to the interesting figure of Alexander Scriabin (1873-1915), but this Slav genius at the same time expanded the idea to the very limits of music itself. His inexhaustibly imaginative spirit, in which mysticism and fanaticism dwelt side by side with the characteristic melancholy and dreaminess of impressionism, was responsible for rather strange productions. *Prometheus* is generally considered his most characteristic work. In it, man is symbolized by the piano, while the orchestra represents the cosmos and a mixed chorus supplies utterances from the primordial depths of humanity. But sound effects alone did not satisfy the composer. His imagination suggested to him a blending of acoustic and visual effects.

He had a "Light and Color Piano" constructed, an instrument which, according to the tones produced, projected light and color effects on a screen. This strange instrument, widely discussed at the time, but never used again except in similar experiments made by Schönberg, plays a part in some of Scriabin's works, which are thus lifted from the realm of pure sound.

Another interesting work by Scriabin is significantly entitled *Poem of Ecstasy*. Here the composer tries to express by all the means at his command and a veritably all-consuming ecstasy that which lies slumbering in the primordial depths of existence, of the earth, and of mankind. Scriabin's piano compositions also reveal his flaming temperament. There are ten sonatas which fill the old form with an entirely new and revolutionary content, as indicated by the very titles of two of them: *The Black Mass* and *The White Mass*. For the first time, secret sciences, occultism, and magic are transposed into tone language. Of his etudes, the *Pathetic* was the one to become most widely known. Today, his works are almost forgotten, neither is there any trace of the considerable influence exerted by him on a following musical generation; on the young Stravinsky, for instance.

Let us return to France where, in the person of Maurice Ravel (1875-1937) [Pl. 160], we come face to face with not only the most remarkable of Debussy's successors but also with one of the greatest geniuses among the composers of our century. He felt drawn especially to the artistic dance, to the ballet. In partnership with the Russian choreographer, Sergei Diaghilev (1872-1929), he created a number of highly important dance poems. This renewal of a close contact between the two sister arts proved beneficial to both. It may have saved musical impressionism from the danger of ever increasing abstraction and inanimateness by supplying new impulses originating in the realm of rhythm. On the other hand, it induced the dancer to adhere more strictly to certain rules common to both arts and to discard some of the arbitrariness he had displayed for decades, if not longer, toward music, which he had come to regard as a necessary evil.

Thus came into being the enchanting ballet operas *Ma mère l'oye* and *Daphnis et Chloë*. But many others of Ravel's works were also inspired by dance rhythms, such as *La valse*, his portrait of the city of Johann Strauss [Pl. 159], and the world-famous *Bolero* in which a simple theme, taken from Spanish folk music, is by the most ingenious use of the art of instrumentation carried from a delicate melody, in a continuous and most exciting crescendo, to a thundering climax. It is characteristic of all modern composers, children of a technical age, that they are masters in the use of the modern orchestra. Ravel was no exception, as proved by the previously mentioned instrumentation of Moussorgsky's *Pictures from an Exhibition*. A wealth of attractive sound effects is revealed in his opera *L'heure espagnole*, while in his many piano compositions, such as *Pavane pour une infante défunte*, *Valses nobles et sentimentales*, *Tombeau de Couperin* (an homage to the great clavecinist of the French seventeenth and eighteenth centuries,) as well as in his beautiful string quartet and in his songs he continued to walk in the paths of Debussy's impressionism, although he never failed to sound a personal note of his own.

Some French composers plainly belong, at least in certain periods of their creative activity, to the impressionist school. In this group were Erik Satie (1866-1925), a man who somehow presents a connecting link with Stravinsky, and Albert Roussel (1869-1937), a pupil of Vincent d'Indy, who left to the world a number of important works: symphonies, a notable sinfonietta, chamber music, and a great many other compositions. Not least of all, there was Paul Dukas (1865-1935) who, like Debussy, wrote an opera to a text by Maeterlinck, *Ariane et Barbe-Bleu*, and, with his brilliant *Sorcerer's Apprentice*, created a truly inspired musical interpretation of Goethe's ballad as well as one of the most effective modern orchestral works.

Very close to the world of Debussy is an Englishman, Cyril Scott (1879-   ), whose finely conceived *Poems* for piano are comparable to some of his British contemporaries' aquarelles, with their exquisite coloring and their slightly foggy atmosphere. England! We have not spoken of music since Handel, and that is a matter of a century and a half. Mention should have been made of John Field (1782-1837), whose Nocturnes inspired Chopin to write his own. There are in fact some which are almost undistinguishable from those of the great Pole. But although, thanks to the orchestras, the excellent choruses, and the population's general love of music, England's part in the world's musical life never sank to the level of insignificance— proved by the fact that almost all the prominent composers of the romantic century maintained a personal contact with the British Isles—the country did not rejoin the circle of musically creative nations until the turn of the new century. Then came Edward Elgar (1857-1934) and Frederick Delius (1863-1934).

131. Knight Bluebeard. Pen-and-ink drawing by H. Holm.

Elgar centered his attention on the large orchestra and the oratorio. For the former he wrote symphonies, symphonic poems (one of which, *Falstaff*, makes one think of Richard Strauss), and above all, the *Enigma Variations*, which has become an established item in the repertory of not only all English but also many North American orchestras. His oratorio, *The Dream of Gerontius*, a form of composition of great interest to the English ever since the days of Handel, is a fine specimen of this category.

Delius was one of the finest impressionists and one of the loneliest creators, lonelier than Debussy or Moussorgsky. To the text of Nietzsche's *Zarathustra* he composed his *Mass of Life*. Among his six operas, *A Village Romeo and Juliet* stands out especially, based on Gottfried Keller's profound novel. But he probably achieved his greatest stature in the idyllic, tender orchestral pieces inspired by nature, called *On Hearing the First Cuckoo in Spring* and *Song before Sunrise*. *Appalachia*, a series of variations on a North American Negro song, and *Brigg Fair* must also be mentioned. Delius' life is shadowed in tragedy: he was crippled and he became blind. Despite this, the spring of melody always flowed inside him. *A Song of Summer* was written as a hymn to the sun, to light and life. How spiritually poor are men who believe that the artist must actually see and experience whatever he is to portray. The artist's world lies within himself. Self-sufficient, Delius never sought recognition from the outside world. It came to him only shortly before he died.

Elgar and Delius were not solitary figures in England's musical renaissance. They were merely outstanding composers, among a great many others of the period, from today's standpoint. There were, in the years at the turn of the century, such composers as the Irish Charles Villiers Stanford who wrote the *Irish Symphony, Irish Rhapsody* and several operas; the Scotchman Alexander Mackenzie, who is closest to the late German romantic period and whose *Scottish Pianoforte Concerto*, sponsored by Paderewski, had a great success; the symphonies of Hubert Parry and the successful composer Ethel Smyth who produced two operas. To write an opera in the England of those years took a large measure of courage since the chances of its being performed were negligible. That situation soon changed, however, and when we return to a consideration of English music we shall find that England has become one of the first countries in the world in musical performance.

The homeland of Chopin gave us the impressionist Karol Szymanowski (1883-1937), whose work again bears out our contention that the music of our century has lost its national characteristics. While Chopin's music still drew its strength from his native soil, that of his successor was wholly international in its character. Like Chopin, Szymanowski spent the major part of his life outside his country. Most of his works came into being on the idyllic shores of Lake Geneva. Among them are three symphonies (one of them has a tenor solo and chorus), *Song of the Night*, a song cycle with orchestra accompaniment, (the individual parts are entitled *The Siren Island, Calypso*, and *Nausikaa*), a string quartet, a great deal of chamber music, and many songs.

Ottorino Respighi (1879-1936) was the first symphonist from the

land of opera. While his beautiful symphonic poems unmistakably bear
the imprint of Debussy's influence, his melodies are just as unmistakably
Italian. His most prominent, and at the time most impressionistic, works
are *The Pines of Rome* and *The Fountains of Rome*, veritable sound
paintings depicting in all their glory and splendor the trees and fountains
of the Eternal City, the brilliance of the rising sun, and the magic of the
deep blue night. The voice of a bird is heard in Respighi's pines. The
sweet melody rising above the soft rustle of the trees is so overwhelmingly beautiful that the listener uneasily holds his breath. No man-made instrument this, no human voice. . . . It is—every hearing makes us marvel
anew at the simplicity and ingenuity of the idea—a recording of the
actual voice of a nightingale.

Respighi's operas will be discussed in a later chapter. To be mentioned here are his beautiful chamber music and his magnificent songs
(like *Nebbie*, *La notte*, and many others).   ....

Manuel de Falla may well be called the greatest genius in the more
recent musical history of Spain. True, he had absorbed many traits of
Debussy and Ravel, but the essence of his style is nevertheless wholly
his own. And strong though the influence of national folklore may be
in his work, he has succeeded in imparting to Spanish music a fully artistic form and in raising it to an international level. In all the nervous
confusion of our time and its countless stylistic experiments, Falla is a
creative genius whose feet were firmly planted on the ground—the ground
of his native land.

Manuel de Falla y Matheu [Pl. 167] was born in Cadiz, on November 22, 1876. His first musical impression was of a strange kind. In an
old church of his home town, on every Good Friday, there was a performance of a Haydn string quartet which the Vienna master had dedicated to that house of worship for its exclusive use and to which he had
given the title "The Redeemer's Seven Words on the Cross." The wonderful symmetry of the classic work, in which there was "not a single
note too many, not one too few," as Falla himself expressed it, made a
profound impression on him and instilled into him, subconsciously, that
sense of symmetry and artistic economy which today is the possession
of but a few. Of decisive importance for his artistic growth were Pedrell's instructions and the seven years of study in Paris. There he became friendly with Debussy, Dukas, Ravel, and Stravinsky and wrote his
Seven Spanish Songs. The sketch of his piano concerto, *Nights in the*

Gardens of Spain, was also completed when the outbreak of hostilities made him return to his native land. Only very slowly did he gain recognition there. The brilliant work of his youth, the ballet *La vida breve*,

132. Manuel de Falla's manuscript of "El retablo de Maese Pedro."

has not been performed in his fatherland to this day. His way of composing was exceedingly slow, and he gave full attention to even the minutest detail. He was one of those who do an enormous amount of correcting and polishing before considering a work worthy of being released. In this manner he wrote *El amor brujo*, a ballet with vocal music, whose orgiastic-ritual *Fire Dance* is a well-known piece in today's concert music; *The Three-Cornered Hat*, based on the Corregidor theme, which the hapless Hugo Wolf had treated before him; the extraordinarily strange operatic work *El retablo de Maese Pedro*, a Don Quixote episode, in which living singers as well as marionettes are used; instrumental compositions, like the *Fantasia Baetica* or the *Cembello Concerto*, the first performance of which was given by Falla in the Pleyel Salon in Paris, a few days before that celebrated hall was turned over to a wrecking crew.

In 1939, Falla, whose sensitive artist's soul was profoundly affected by the happenings in Europe, sought peace in the New Continent and settled in the Cordoban Mountains of Argentina. But his health was so weakened that he was able to work but a few hours a day. That was not enough to finish the monumental oratorio *Atlantida*, intended as a hymn to that legendary submerged continent. A few days before he would have reached the age of seventy, Falla died in Alta Gracia, in the Argentine province of Cordoba, on November 15, 1946.

From the opposite end of Europe there rose a mighty voice. Like that of de Falla, it had drawn its strength from home soil. It was a voice both full-bodied and tranquil, serene in the assurance that it would outlive its own time. Jan Sibelius [Pl. 168], born in 1865, is the singer of Finland. In his music there is the breath of the Nordic landscape, of snow-covered woods and gloomy swamps, of long winters in the pale light of the midnight sun, and of brief joyous summer days during which an old and strong people celebrates its soil-related festivals.

Sibelius is one of the last symphonists in the classic and romantic sense, even thought much of his music is programmatic. Let us mention here *Finlandia*, *Karelia*, *Kullervo*, *En Saga*, and the four *Legends*, the best-known of which is the deeply moving *Swan of Tuonela*. It sings of a black swan which guides the souls of the dead across a dark lake to the beyond. The swan is characterized by a never-to-be-forgotten passage of the English horn. Sibelius scored a pronounced success with his *Valse Triste*, which is part of the stage music for a drama by the Finnish poet Arvid Järnefelt, entitled *Kuolema* (Death). The music is descriptive of a ghostly scene in which the soul of a woman who had died an early death tries to make itself known to her friends.

Sibelius, who spent long years of his life traveling and who frequently conducted his own works in the musical centers of the world, including America, where he was hailed enthusiastically, had to live through the horrors of two wars. Though well advanced in years, he still (1949) leads a creatively active life in his homeland. He and the late Richard Strauss are the last giants of Europe's glorious musical past.

And now we have come to the musical developments in Central Europe after the death of Wagner. The epoch is given its imprint by two eminent composers, widely differing in temperament, but both of gigantic artistic stature: Gustav Mahler and Richard Strauss.

Mahler [Pl. 162] was born in Kalischt, a small Moravian village, in

1860. The simple heartfelt airs of the people and the trumpet calls of the nearby garrison were his first musical impressions. They were never to fade from his soul. When he was still a young man, he went to Vienna, which was then at the zenith of its glory. The magnificence of the city

133. From Mahler's manuscript score of his Fourth Symphony, composed 1901.
Society of Friends of Music, Vienna.

also found its way into the work of the highly impressionable man. The loneliness of the Moravian fields and the splendor of Vienna were fundamentally represented in his music. There was a perpetual yearning in Mahler's soul. He was a mere youth when he said in a letter: "My whole life is one great homsesickness"; or, to express it in the words he used in connection with his Second Symphony: "I have come from God and want to return to Him. . . ." To seek, was the motto of this ardent life.

His activity as a conductor carried him with incredible swiftness to the top. From Hamburg, Budapest, and a number of way stations, he reached the Vienna Court Opera at a comparatively early age. His coming marked the beginning of the most brilliant epoch in the history of that venerable institute. Mahler was a fanatic in everything that concerned art. Routine performances were anathema to him, bureaucratic obstacles to the presentation of new works were swept away, budgetary difficulties connected with the unheard-of number of rehearsals demanded by the new director for the achievement of ultimate perfection were overcome. Mahler remained at the head of the Court Opera for ten years and for some seasons also led the Vienna Philharmonic Orchestra. At that time, Vienna really deserved to be called the world's leading musical city, thanks mainly to his indefatigable work. The circumstances accompanying his leaving Vienna, however, were far from pleasant. The intrigues spun against him and the wave of resentment caused by his dictatorial manner, though it was all in the service of art, had risen to such proportions that his resignation from the position to which he had given his very heart's blood was unavoidable.

During the ten years of Mahler's activity in Vienna, he devoted nine months of each year exclusively to the operatic institute. That left only three brief summer months for his creative work. Leading a more or less secluded life at one of the picturesque Austrian lakes, he wrote his mighty symphonic creations. In them, he often chose new and revolutionary paths, fantastically enlarging the orchestral apparatus and increasing the number of movements, which had hardly ever been changed from four since the days of Haydn and Mozart. And what in Beethoven's Ninth had been a single exception, became almost the rule in Mahler's symphonies.

The First Symphony was purely orchestral, but in it, too, were mirrored all the contradictions raging in Mahler's struggling and searching soul: profound pain, tormenting loneliness, and a sense of humor which not infrequently turned into irony. In the Second Symphony, he introduced large choruses and an alto voice singing a simple folklike air. The Third is a super-dimensional pastoral symphony: there is the sound of celestial and earthly voices, of children's voices and large choruses, and Nature is made to reveal musically some of its secrets and beauties. The Fourth Symphony is basically serene in its mood. The final movement includes a charming soprano solo sung to the cheerful and contented words of a medieval German text. Highly problematical, on the other hand, are his next three symphonies. They express inward struggles and deep sorrow, a yearning for peace and deliverance. This brings us to the Eighth Symphony, which holds a unique position in musical literature. Not without reason has it been called the "Symphony of a Thousand." Everything is enlarged to gigantic proportions: a giant orchestra and giant choruses. Of course, there are solo voices, too. The words used were taken partly from a Latin hymn, partly from Goethe. The effects achieved are grandiose. Symphonic music has here reached its last and utmost extreme which, as always, already bears within it the seed of decay. In a letter to the conductor Mengelberg, Mahler had this to say: "The universe begins to sound and to sing. No longer human voices, but planets and suns. . ."

Mahler stood in almost religious awe of Beethoven and his Ninth. As he himself once said, no mortal man should every try again to write a ninth symphony. And so, after he had completed eight symphonies, and since his heart was still full of melodies, he wrote *Das Lied von der Erde*, a composition midway between a song cycle and a symphony. As it happened, *Das Lied von der Erde* became his greatest, his purest, his most exalted composition. Two human voices, alto and tenor, alternate in singing these songs based on the profound poetry of Old Chinese lyrics. In the last song, *Der Abschied* (Farewell), he reached heights which only very few are permitted to scale.

After leaving the Vienna Court Opera, Mahler set out on concert tours. Enthusiastically acclaimed, he conducted the New York Philharmonic Orchestra, but when he felt that death was not far away, an irresistible urge made him turn back to Vienna. In the city of his greatest triumphs and of his bitterest disappointments he died, in the year 1911.

Only now do his symphonies slowly begin to take their place in the concert programs of the world. His beautiful songs made quicker progress, both his deeply moving *Kindertotenlieder* (Children's Death Songs) and the melancholy *Lieder eines fahrenden Gesellen* (Songs of a Wayfarer), as well as the frequently cheerful ones which he took from the old treasure chest of *Des Knaben Wunderhorn* (The Youth's Magic Horn).

How wholly different are the character and the work of Richard Strauss! He represents a rather rare type of genius: one who is methodically exact, incredibly disciplined, and thoroughly organized. In the course of strictly allotted hours, maintained as if he were a scrupulous banker, he created a many-hued magical world, a world so wholly different from his seemingly meticulous habits. His creative vein became accustomed to this methodical rhythm of work, to a mode of production that know none of the volcanic eruptions, nervous crises, attacks of rage, or crying fits which so often accompany a genius's work. Let us mention at the very outset that Strauss is one of those extremely rare musical geniuses who could with equal mastery write operas, symphonic poems, and songs.

The dramatic work of Richard Strauss owed much of its perfection to the ideal collaboration of a poetic genius, Hugo von Hofmannstahl. Only *Feuersnot, Guntram,* and *Salome,* whose spiritual father was Oscar Wilde, antedated the great collaboration. It started with *Electra* and led to *Rosenkavalier, Ariadne auf Naxos, Frau ohne Schatten, Aegyptische Helena,* and *Arabella,* a period of more than twenty years of joint creation. Let us leave a discussion of these works to the following chapter, dedicated to modern opera, and confine ourselves here to a contemplation of Strauss's symphonic creations which have become an integral part of the repertory of all large orchestras. The technical perfection with which this man masters a gigantic sound apparatus is as astounding as the inventive melodic power distinguishing his every work. Most of these works date back to the master's early creative period, before his operas, and reveal in many details the influence of Wagner. Again, as we emphasized in the case of other composers, there can be no question of imitations. Strauss traveled new and individual paths. He merely availed himself of his time's technique of sound in its most perfectly elaborated form, the one created by Wagner. Strauss's symphonic poems are program music in the finest sense of the word. They are not merely depictions of extra-musical thoughts and events, but the masterfully treated fusion of a picturesque fundamental idea and a pure musical form. *Don Juan* may be considered the first of these works wholly characteristic of the composer. And Strauss—born in 1864, the son of a Munich musician —was only twenty-five years old when he first conducted it in Weimar. A musical theme describes this brilliant and tragic hero, the subject of countless poems, dramas, novels, comedies, and operas, and does it so perfectly within the brief space of twenty seconds, so clearly and with so throbbing a vitality, that a hundred printed pages could not have furnished a more plastic picturization of a personage, masterly, knightly, grandiose, proud, compelling.

So, too in his electrifying *Till Eulenspiegel,* which was first performed in Cologne six years later (1895). The few jolly themes characterizing the medieval rascal make us feel as if we saw him before our very eyes, skipping boldly over the country, committing his pranks, and finally being condemned to death by a pathetically solemn town council. Unspeakably delicious, how the orchestra sparkles, glitters, giggles, struts, questions and answers, cannot contain itself for joy, expresses the most light-hearted frivolity, and quakes in fear of death! Hardly ever since the days of Haydn has a humorous subject been so plastically set to music. As if Strauss meant to convey to us: a little story, a fairy tale, that's all. . . .

Strauss completed the tone poem *Thus Spake Zarathustra* within the space of six months of the year 1896. In the same year, he conducted its first performance in Frankfort. It was, in a very broad sense, inspired by Nietzsche, the unhappy philosopher (he was a musician besides) to whom we have had occasion to refer several times. Had Strauss succeeded here in capturing a philosophy in sound, if that were at all possible? Or had he, the arch musician, merely been set afire by the hymn-like exuberance revealed in the philosopher's profound writing? The second alternative seems the more plausible. How singular a work composed here by Strauss, how brilliant and vibrating, but also how difficult to understand if we inquire into its meaning! *Of Back-World Men, Of Great Yearnings, Of Joys and Passions, Grave Song, Of Science*—these are some of the composer's captions. In the finale, mysteriously ending between C major and B major, Richard Specht, the eminent Strauss biographer, saw the "unbridgeable contrast between nature and the spirit."

In the same epoch belongs *Macbeth, Death and Transfiguration,* and *Don Quixote.* In the latter work, the musician's imagination once more invades the realm of great Spanish literature, although his *Don Juan* was based on Lenau's German version and not on the Spanish original. The "Knight of the Woeful Countenance," Cervantes' immortal prototype of the idealist ridiculed by the world, inspired Strauss to a brilliant work of variations, the main part of which calls for a virtuoso performance of the strings. *Death and Transfiguration* follows a simple basic idea expressed in a poem quoted as the work's motto:

> There resounds the final blow
> Of grim Death's unflinching hammer,
> Bursting worldly realms in twain,
> Cov'ring eyes with mortal darkness.
> Mighty, though, there comes the sound
> Soaring from the far-flung Heavens,
> Bringing balm to searching hearts:
> After death—transfiguration!

A Hero's Life is the name of the symphonic poem conducted by Strauss for the first time in 1899, once more in Frankfort (shortly after the thirty-five-year-old musician had been summoned as conductor to the Prussian Court Opera in Berlin). Had Strauss here an autobiographical work, and was he himself the "hero" of this music? Some details would make it seem so, but the question in itself is idle in the face of the purely musical values of the score.

Strauss, who is a technical wizard in the treatment of orchestral masses, is at the same time one of the great Lieder composers, having to his credit a large number of highly expressive musical miniatures and mood paintings. By far the major portion of his songs belongs to Strauss's early creative period. Only his operas, of which we shall speak presently, cover the entire long span of his life.

These main groups of Strauss's creative work frequently make us overlook his other compositions, among which we may find many a gem of the purest water. The French horn, a hereditary instrument in his family, has long held his affectionate regard. His Opus 11 is a horn concerto, first performed in Meiningen by Hans von Bülow. A second horn concerto bears the date 1943. Various periods in his life witnessed the writing of some chamber music, the *Burleske* for piano and orchestra, and an oboe concerto. At the age of eight-one, he proved his mastery of the strict chamber music style. The year 1945 is the birth-date of a sonatina for sixteen winds and of a "Study for Twenty-Three Solo Strings," entitled *Metamorphoses*, a piece of serious and solemn structure in which Beethoven's Funeral March from the *Eroica* is cited.

Richard Strauss's life was spent in Bavaria, where he was born and in which, for decades every summer, he devoted his time to creative work at his villa in Garmisch-Partenkirchen; in Vienna, where he lived quite a number of years, some of them as director of the State Opera; and finally in Switzerland, to which he turned after the collapse of Germany in 1945 and where he lived peacefully in Baden, a pleasant place near Zurich. Finally he returned to Bavaria where he died September 8, 1949. He outlived many a "modern" tendency in the course of his long life. Like so many others, he undoubtedly had his beginnings in the influence of Wagner, but he early found the way into the open. A late-romanticist at heart, with a strongly developed and frequently classicist feeling for form, he was not deterred from the most striking dissonances as long as they were in the end (at times, at the very end) resolved. He

134. From Reger's manuscript of the piano quartet, op. 133. Reger Archiv.

is reported to have said to a young musician: "Look here, why do you insist on writing atonal music? You've got talent, you know!"

We must mention here three other musicians. One of them, Max Bruch (1830-1920) ought to be counted among the romanticists, although his life did not end until after the first World War. He was an exceptionally prolific composer, and many of his violin concertos can still be heard today. Less may be said of his symphonic creations. The other two were considerably more "modern." They were Max Reger (1873-1916) [Pl. 163] and Ferruccio Busoni (1866-1924). Both still had their roots in the late-romanticism, which kept flourishing in Germany at a time when impressionism and *verismo* were matters of course in other countries. Reger was the successor of Brahms in the strict maintenance of classic lines and, like Brahms, showed a particular liking for variations. While he was quite progressive in his harmonics, he really longed for a return of the pre-classic forms. He wrote for the small orchestra, when all those about him tried still to enlarge and develop the modern sound apparatus. True, this tendency of his merely represented a slight anticipation of a future development. We shall soon hear of the reaction which turned some of our contemporaries into neoclassicists. Reger's predilection for the organ, on which he was an improvisor of real genius, moved him into the line represented by Bach, Bruckner, and Franck, while it also explains to us his inclination toward the variation form, which is a direct outgrowth of improvisation. The themes of his principal works of variations were taken from old classic masters like Bach, Telemann, Mozart, and Beethoven. Reger, a Bavarian like Richard Strauss, died an early death in the dark days of World War I.

Busoni (1866-1924) occupied a place between nations and styles. Born in Florence, Italy, the son of an Italian father and a German mother, he spent the major part of his life north of the Alps. He was in favor of a "return to the melody" and to a "new classicism," which he rather vaguely described as the "supreme rule and cultivation of all experiences gained from the past and their use on behalf of beautiful and healthy forms." How to return to classic art, when the time took giant strides in the development of diametrically opposed tendencies?

Busoni upheld the cause of melody in an unfettered era which tabooed and despised everything that was melodious. He found an ally in Schreker, of whom we shall hear more in the chapter on opera. Busoni, who achieved world fame as one of the most fascinating pianists, was the creator of exceptionally interesting works, among which were his operas *Turandot* and *Doctor Faust*, an *Indian Fantasy*, and a *Symphonic Nocturne*.

Still another musican must be mentioned here, whose illustrious figure stood at the turning point of the eras. He was Felix Weingartner (1863-1942). The long span of his life led from a personal friendship with Wagner and Liszt into the days of the Second World War. An Aus-

129. Richard Wagner (1813-1884). [*Photo Grosz*]

130. Cosima Wagner 1837-1930. [*Photo Albert*]

131. Siegfried Wagner, Richard's son, with his 3 children. [*Photo Ramme*]

132. The Bayreuth Festival Playhouse, opened 1876.

133. Wagner at home. At the window, Franz Liszt; facing him, Cosima Wagner.
[*Painting by W. Beckmann, 1880*]

134. Final scene from *Tannhäuser*, at Bayreuth, 1931.

135. Final scene from *The Flying Dutchman*, at the Leipzig State Opera.

136. Gunnar Graarud, Norwegian tenor, as Parsifal, Bayreuth. [*Photo Tillmann*]

137.   Max Lorenz, as Siegfried, Bayreuth. [*Photo Weirich*]

138. Nanny Larsén-Todson, as Isolde, Bayreuth.

139. Kirsten Flagstad, as Brünnhilde, Metropolitan Opera, New York.

140. Giuseppe Verdi (1813-
1901. [*Photo Nadar*]

141. Verdi's *Otello*, Act
III, at the Milan Scala.

142. The Witches' Forest in Verdi's *Macbeth*. Charlottenburg Opera, Berlin.
Stage setting by Caspar Neher. [*Photo Schmidt*]

143. Verdi's *A Masked Ball*, Act III, at the Berlin State Opera. Baroque stage
setting by Caspar Neher. [*Photo Schmidt*]

144. Georges Bizet (1838-1875). [*Portrait by Giacometti*]

145. Charles Camille Saint-Saëns (1835-1922). [*Photo Nadar*]

146. Sketch of a stage design for Bizet's *Carmen*, by Karl Walser.

147. Jules F. Massenet (1842-1912). 148. Charles Gounod (1818-1893). [Draw-
   [Photo Nadar]   ing by Ingres, Rome, 1840]

149. Walpurgis Night Ballet from Gounod's *Faust*. Zurich Stadttheater.

150. Brahms, in 1895.   151. Johannes Brahms (1833-1897). [*Photograph, abt. 1876*]

152. The *Alte Niedelbad*, in Rüschlikon, near Zurich, where Brahms spent the summer of 1874. [*Painting by Fritz Widmann*]

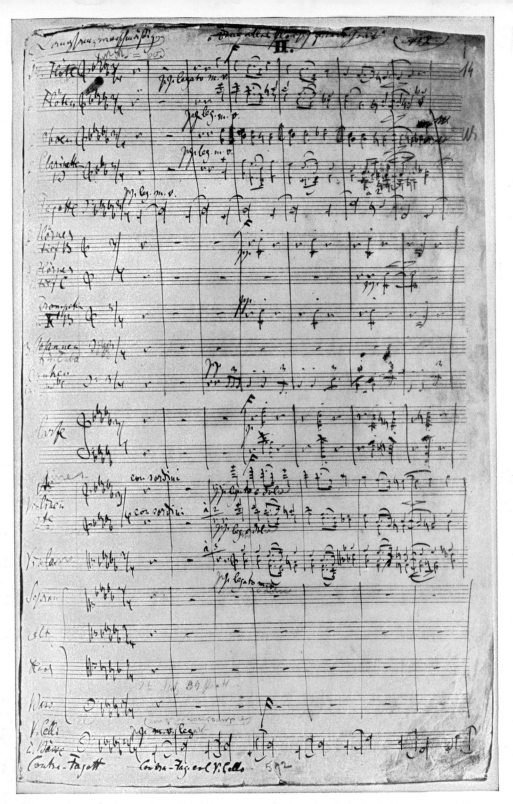

153. Brahm's manuscript of the *German Requiem*. [*Gesellschaft der Musik-freunde, Vienna*]

154. Piotr Ilyrich Tchaikovsky (1840-1893). [*Portrait by Nicolay Kusnezov, Moscow, 1893*]

155. Mozart's *Marriage of Figaro*, Act I, at the Metropolitan, with Alessio de Paolis as Don Basilio, Jarmila Novotna as Cherubino, John Brownlee as Count, and Bidú Sayao as Susanna. [*Photo Louis Melançon*]

156. César Franck (1822-1890). [*Painting by J. Rongier*]

157. (lower left) Antonin Dvorák (1841-1904. [*Lithograph by Svabinski*]

158. (lower right) Anton Bruckner (1823-1896. [*Photogr. by Ges., Berlin*]

159. *La valse*, by Ravel, at the Zurich Stadttheater. [*Photo Zimmerman*]

160. Maurice Ravel (1875-1937). [*Photo Lipnitzki*]

161. Claude Debussy (1862-1918).

162. Gustav Mahler (1860-1911). [*Photo, 1894*]

163. Max Reger (1873-1916).

164. Richard Strauss, conducting one of his operas. [*Photo Salomon*]

165. Richard Strauss (1864-1949).

166. Richard Strauss and the soprano Elisabeth Rethberg after the first performance, in Dresden, of the *Egyptian Helena*. [*Photo Salomon*]

167. Manuel de Falla (1876-1946).   168. Jan Sibelius (born 1865).

169. Wilhelm Furtwängler (born 1886) conducting at London's Queen's Hall.
[*Photo Salomon*]

trian by birth, he conquered with his baton the whole world and finally found peace and quiet for his declining years in Switzerland. His rich life was a creative one to the last moment. Weingartner's noble character made him follow the example of Liszt in that he never tried to enforce recognition of a work, although there were times when he had at his command ample opportunity for doing just that. If the work had merit, its time was bound to come.

In addition to operas, which will be discussed later, Weingartner wrote symphonic music, chamber music, piano pieces, and Lieder, of which only *Liebsfeier* has become widely known. He was one of the most prominent musical figures in the days of the great crisis, a searcher for beauty, a true believer in art.

135. Caruso and Sembrich in "Bohème."

· 26 ·

The Modern Opera

LET us turn a new leaf, the last one, in the richly colored book of the opera. Wagner and Verdi had inscribed many of its pages, and their works still form the firm foundation of the repertoire. In former times, this repertoire consisted mainly of contemporary works. Today, this condition has changed. We hear mainly works of the past. The same is true of concert activities. The so-called "modern" opera leads a miserable existence in present-day musical life. If we were asked to enumerate the contemporary operas maintaining a regular place in the repertoire of the world's opera houses, we would feel greatly embarrassed. Of course, we might try to get out of our difficulty by including Strauss and Puccini. But—how time does rush on!—from *Bohème* and *Tosca*, from *Salome* and *Rosenkavalier* we are already separated by many decades. And it was in the course of these very decades that the great change in style took place. Well, then, which of the truly "modern" operas (in the sense of a contemporary style) are alive today? The charming *Schwanda*, the memorable *Wozzeck*, the masterful *Mathis*. Are they really alive? Do they not rather represent exceptional phenomena in operatic activities? *Dreigroschenoper? Jonny?* Ephemeral successes, owing the stir they made mainly to extra-artistic circumstances. Pfitzner? Ah yes, his *Palestrina!* But that opera, too, was born in the days of the First World War, and it is magnificent romantic opera. Schreker? Where are his zestful operas performed today? And Italy? Many a world première there; but none of the operas finds its way into the standard repertoire. Are modern operas, then, so difficult to perform? Or are there other and more weighty reasons for existing conditions?

There are probably more reasons than one. To begin with, there is the disinclination of the public to be bothered with stylistic struggles and experiments when it expects to revel in music. Understandably, people prefer to listen for the hundredth time to *Traviata* or to be stirred to their depths by *Tristan*, rather than to have to follow for the first time a hard-to-grasp "melody-less" opera. Another reason lies in the difficulties connected with musical and technical preparations. Only a subsidized theater can afford to spend months on the rehearsing of a new work which in all likelihood will never be a box-office success. Above all, however, it seems likely that a musical species as wholly dependent on sensuous beauty and harmony as opera is fundamentally unsuited to the many stylistic experiments which have emerged in the course of our century. It is for this reason that Oscar Bie, in his clever monograph on the lyric art, calls the subject of this chapter the "Chaos of the Opera," although he is of course quite ready to accord full recognition to outstanding accomplishments. We live in an age of mighty social upheavals. New audiences, new social strata, find their way into the theaters and concert halls. It would be a mistake to assume that the new classes are more likely to embrace modern art because they are not bound by traditions. It seems that every individual wishing to understand and partake of cultural delights must go through a course of development similar to that of the embryo on its journey through the whole scale of human evolution.

Within the past fifty years, operatic styles have been changing with the rapidity of film flashes. What was "modern" yesterday becomes obsolete before you know it. Never since its course became chartable has art lived in such a state of nervous haste. There are nevertheless a number of valuable works, the products of intensive concentration, which emerge like beacons from the sea of fleeting phenomena. Let us try to observe them more closely.

At the turn of the century, after Wagner's and Verdi's deaths, composers were feverishly looking for some way that had not been barred by the two Titans; a way on which it would be possible to progress without running the risk of getting into a dead-end road. Which ways were open? First, there was the one leading beyond Wagner. Many tried to travel it, tried to outdo the master of Bayreuth, but they all fell by the wayside. To keep Wagner's romanticism alive, one had to be a Wagner. Another group tried to carry Wagner's tendencies of dissolution to their ultimate conclusion. Their efforts are exemplified by Debussy's *Pellèas et Mélisande*, that sublime work standing on a lonely summit, close to the brink of the abyss. That road led no farther.

Wagner was dead, but people kept fighting his spirit. The slogan "Away from Wagner!" for a time united the most heterogeneous elements and ideas: *verismo*, as musical naturalism was called; a return to the "number opera" and the old chamber opera; a fusion of opera and oratorio, of opera and ballet; the didactic opera; the song opera. They all represented reactionary tendencies against Wagner, but they were so different among one another that to speak of a uniform tendency was out of the question. The dissolution of a firm regimen—in all human realms— always leads at first to a confused raging of various individual forces.

There were preeminently two great musicians who succeeded, thanks to their powerful personalities, in finding an organic continuation and in opening ways along which a further logical development of opera was possible. As if the old order were trying to maintain itself, they were a German and an Italian: Richard Strauss and Giacomo Puccini. Their creations must be discussed in detail.

Richard Strauss began in the footsteps of Wagner. His *Guntram* had not as yet any features of its own, and *Feuersnot*, too, although much more mature, would not have sufficed to secure for its creator a place among the great. But then, as if a dam had burst, there came *Salome*, based on Oscar Wilde's magnificent play. Rarely before had a more relentless tension, a more breath-taking dramatic action, been achieved.

Within a bare ninety minutes, in a single act, a tragedy full of sultry passion is unfolded.

Strauss had succeeded here in outdoing the sensuality of *Tristan* and the passion of *Carmen*, while adding a never-before-heard demonic element that makes the listener's blood run cold. Here, in musical language, spiritual abysses are illumined which, about that time, were probed also by the young science of psychoanalysis. *Salome* unleashed an unparalleled storm of conflicting emotions and opinions, but nobody could deny that the opera's creator was a man of exceptional talent. At any rate, it was clear to many that here at last a way had been opened, though a dangerous one, on which Wagner's successors would be able to proceed.

The potentialities of this exceptionally gifted composer were still more plainly revealed in his following opera *Electra* [Pl. 170]. Once more we have a one-act concentration of a drama and a cruelly bloodthirsty action.

This grandiose drama marked the beginning of the ideal collaboration between a great composer and an equally great poet, Hugo von Hofmannsthal. What Wagner had achieved by himself was accomplished now by two artists perfectly complementing each other—a collaboration almost as rare as the combination of these gifts in one man. The music of *Electra*, first performed in 1909, is extraordinarily daring. Another step, and Strauss would have left the firm ground of tonality, for the opera's dissonances are of exceptional stridency. All the more wonderful is the contrast here when Strauss starts to develop one of his magnificent melodic embroideries.

Strauss did not take the step which would have carried him into the realm of "atonality." On the contrary, in his next operatic work he once more gave full recognition to the supremacy of the melody and the blissful reveling in harmonious sound. Hofmannsthal had submitted to him an Old Vienna comedy, *Der Rosenkavalier*, drenched in an atmosphere of waltzes, replete with finely contrived situations, and alive with highly effective figures of a day gone by, but yet not too far removed to have lost its grip. And, true poet that he was, Hofmannsthal had succeeded in introducing into an air of seeming frivolity, superficiality, and boisterous gaiety, a profound drama, more deeply moving in its tranquil course than many of a blood-curdling tragedy. It is the drama of the aging woman who, still young at heart, loses her lover to one of fewer years

. 295

and who, with a gesture revealing the utmost nobility of heart, is reconciled to her fate.

This work, first performed in 1911 with sensational success, was followed during the war by the chamber opera, *Ariadne auf Naxos*, whose action served to explain an epoch of earlier operatic history. Strauss, who hardly had his equal in the treatment of the grand orchestra, here confined himself to an almost Mozartesque chamber ensemble. This reflects a trend to which we referred when speaking of Busoni. Even composers of an entirely different caliber, such as Schönberg and Stravinsky, were unable to escape it. *Ariadne auf Naxos* is, however, not only an example demonstrating opera's course of development and the orchestra's reduction to chamber-music proportions during a certain phase of the twentieth century, but it also strikingly proves that two lofty spirits —librettist and composer—are able to "have their fun" even while probing the utmost depths of art.

The most profound and difficult of all the dramas created by Hofmannsthal and Strauss followed in 1919. It was *Die Frau ohne Schatten*. In this mystic-symbolic play of the turning of a figure from the spirit realm into a mundane woman through the eternal miracle of giving birth, the "throwing of a shadow," in this action which is so world-removed from every reality and which touches so directly upon primordial problems, Hofmannsthal succeeded in creating his most soul-stirring drama. Strauss poured over it a lavish stream of his most brilliantly glowing and grandiose music. And yet, even the genius of both could not keep the work alive as a stage drama.

The year 1925 marked the beginning of another, a new, epoch in Strauss's creative activity. There may be justification in calling it the retrospective period. While new ideas still emerged and other epochs and milieus beckoned, he did not take a single musical step forward into unexplored territory, content to let his masterfully produced gems of harmony sparkle again and again.

Strauss was his own librettist in *Intermezzo*, an opera with a middleclass, perhaps an all-too-middle class, setting, dealing with the comic matrimonial woes of Kapellmeister Storch. Behind it all was a rather tame episode in his own life. Hofmannsthal and Strauss joined forces again in the production of *Die ägyptische Helena* (1928), a mythological subject. In *Arabella* (1933) they found their way back into an atmosphere which was distinctly related to that of *Rosenkavalier*. It was the last collabora-

136. "Electrocution." Caricature by Jüttner, referring to Richard Strauss's "Electra," 1909.

tion of these two men, for Hugo von Hofmannsthal died in 1929, before *Arabella* was ready for production. His place was taken, for a single work, by Stefan Zweig, another great literary light of Vienna. The product of their collaboration was *Die schweigsame Frau* (1935), an old-style buffo opera full of charming ideas and sparkling music.

There followed a number of other works by the man who had already passed the three-score-and-ten-mark. *Der Friedenstag* (1938) and *Daphne* were combined into a twin bill. The former was based upon a sketch by Zweig, and dealt with problems of war and peace which, less than a year later, were to become horribly real, while the latter was a bucolic play full of natural beauty, and with a tragic ending. Joseph Gregor, another Austrian poet, was the librettist of both operas, as he was of *Die Liebe der Danae* (1940), a "gay mythology," based upon an idea by Hofmannsthal. Finally, in 1942, there appeared a sort of genteel musical comedy, entitled *Capriccio*, whose sparklingly clever text was written by Clemens Krauss, the conductor. The musically expressed thoughts about tonal art and poetry, their interrelations and laws, as well as many another idea set forth in this work formed a kind of profession of faith on the part of the aging master. His mastery had achieved its supreme maturity, but perhaps he, like many another who had reached the pinnacle, had already begun to live outside his time. Never again did he return to the eruptive magnificence of *Salome* and *Electra* or to the deeply human qualities of *Rosenkavalier*.

Engelbert Humperdinck (1854-1921) was another composer who began by following in the footsteps of Wagner, but a fortunate choice of subjects saved him from being considered a mere imitator. He gained well-deserved lasting popularity with his charming fairy-tale opera *Hänsel und Gretel*. His *Königskinder*, though successful, was not able to match the high mark set by the former work.

Humperdinck had managed to blend guilelessly simple and heartfelt melodics with the witchcraft of the Bayreuth orchestra. Other composers succeeded in forming combinations which at first sight seemed equally difficult. There was Wilhelm Kienzl (1857-1941), an Austrian, who, in his *Evangelimann*, created a genuine folk opera to a text written by himself after an actual occurrence. In spite of this, it unmistakably bore the imprint of Wagner's influence. Still more striking, perhaps, was his revolutionary drama, *Der Kuhreigen*, in which the old Swiss song *Ranz des vaches* appears as a leitmotif. Kienzl's opera *Don Quixote*, performed at the Vienna State Opera under Felix Weingartner, in 1936, was not particularly successful. Julius Bittner (1874-1934), likewise an Austrian, transposed Kienzl into a peasant key. His *Höllische Gold* and *Die rote Gret* are powerful musical dramas with a rural milieu and soil-bound figures drawn by the composer's own pen. And there was still a third Austrian, Franz Schmidt (1874-1939) who also was a spiritual descendant of late romanticism. He composed the remarkable and magnificently sounding opera *Notre Dame*, after Victor Hugo, which did not receive nearly the attention it merited.

Hans Pfitzner (1889-1949) was one of the most robust representatives of modern opera. His first two operas, *Die Rose vom Liebesgarten* and *Der arme Heinrich*, were replete with Wagnerian symbols and written in Wagner's musical language. But in both works there dwelt so genuinely felt a romantic spirit and so profound a faith in art that they made the listener prick up his ears. What followed was a truly inspired and magnificent work: *Palestrina*, expressed in the composer's personal masterly style. This vigorous work takes us back to the colorful epoch of the Tridentine Council, mentioned in an early chapter. It places the great Roman musician and the legendary creation of his *Missa Papae Marcelli* in the center of events (how wonderful the scene in which the angels sing the melodies of the work to the sleeping musician!) and very effectively contrasts the modest artist's lonely study with the lavish and brilliant atmosphere of the great ecclesiastical gathering. His next works of importance were *Das Herz* and the oratorios *Von deutscher Seele* and *Das dunkle Reich*, based on texts by Michelangelo, Goethe, Dehmel, and Conrad Ferdinand Meyer. In these works Pfitzner returned to romantic symbolism, another master to flee the confused present and seek sanctuary in the sober past. A great admirer of Wagner, Schumann, Schopenhauer, and Eichendorff, Pfitzner more than once in his writings expressed an emphatic dislike for modern musical tendencies. He died in a Munich Home for the Aged, a penniless ward of the Vienna Philharmonic Orchestra.

The majority of the late romanticists clothed their works in modern raiment, the word "raiment" being used here not merely in a scenic sense. Their harmonics were daring, they were by no means afraid of even the most extreme dissonances, but they still remained on the firm ground of tonality. Dissonance to them was still an idea—that is the essential point. They used it where and when it was necessary, when it was needed to underscore something or give it particular pregnancy, and when a subsequent return to consonance meant relaxation and a happy resolution.

The number of late romanticists in opera is much larger than we might be led to expect. Let us continue their list. There is Erich Wolfgang Korngold (1897-   ) who attracted attention to himself when, still a boy, he composed the pantomime *Der Schneemann*. This was followed by *Der Ring des Poycrates* and the fiery *Violanta* and finally by his most successful opera, *Die tote Stadt*. Less appealing was *Das Wunder der Heliane*. Shortly thereafter, he went to Hollywood, where he is still engaged in writing interesting film music. To be mentioned here are the following artists and their works: the talented Viennese Hans Gál (1890-   ) and his *Heilige Ente, Lied von der Nacht,* and *Rattenfänger von Hameln;* Max von Schilling (1868-1933) and his *Mona Lisa;* E. M. Reznicek (1865-1945) and his *Donna Diana* (the Schilling and Reznicek works were among the most successful operas of our century) and Leo Blech (1871-   ) and his delightful comedy *Versiegelt.*

This is the place, too, to mention Felix Weingartner's operas: *Die Dorfschule, Dame Kobold, Orest, Kain und Abel,* and *Sakuntala.* Walter Braunfels (1882-   ) set to music ancient themes, such as *Die Vögel,* based on Aristophanes, and *Don Gil von den grünen Hosen,* a frequently used Spanish subject. Spiritually somehow related to him, another German, Paul Graener (1872-   ), wrote many valuable operatic works, such as *Don Juan's letztes Abenteuer, Hanneles Himmelfahrt,* and *Friedemann Bach.* To be sure, they were lacking in the one essential prerequisite of opera: public appeal.

An entirely different place in our chapter on modern opera must be accorded Franz Schreker (1878-1934). An Austrian by birth, he soon realized that his rather conservative fatherland did not understand his music. He moved to Berlin which, in the early post-war period, had become the rallying point for all modern stylistic experimenters and the center of a bewilderingly variegated musical life. Schreker was a genuine musical dramatist, equally gifted as a poet and a composer, and hardly less so as a conductor and teacher. He was a fanatic of sound who never ceased conjuring up from the modern orchestra new mixtures, effects, and colorings. Much of what Schreker wrote is truly beautiful, and everything is impelled by genuine passion. At any rate, the unbridled sensuality permeating all his works was a symbol of his time, whose yawning abysses, intricate problems, and vague hopes were portrayed in almost all of his dramas with a skill hardly matched by any other composer. His works included *Der ferne Klang, Das Spielwerk und die Prinzessin, Die Gezeichneten, Der Schatzgräber, Irrelohe, Der Schmied von Gent,* and the unfinished *Memnon.*

The twentieth century has witnessed the advance of one country into the forefront of operatic activities, a place never before occupied by any of its representatives. That country is Switzerland. Honegger's works will be discussed elsewhere. Let us speak here of three musicians from that country's German-language area, men who, to a greater or lesser degree, still had their roots in romanticism: Othmar Schoeck (1886-   ) [Pl. 172], Hans Haug (1900-   ) and Heinrich Sutermeister (1910-   ). Foremost is Schoeck, the composer of exquisite

137. "The marked Ones," by Schrecker, at the Berlin State Opera. Scenic sketch of the Isle of Elysium, by Pankok.

songs, whose lyrically sensuous emotionalism and delicate depiction of moods did not preclude their creator's penetration into the wholly different world of the operatic theater. Two Singspiel-like works—*Erwin und Elmire*, after Goethe, and *Don Ranudo*—were followed by a striking creation: *Venus* (1922). Then came *Penthesilea* (after Kleist), the fairy-tale opera *Vom Fischer und syner Fru*, *Massimila Doni* [Pl. 173] (after Balzac), and *Schloss Durande* (after Eichendorff). These works show the composer pursuing ever new paths, a seeker after beauty on the road of a late, but still blooming and fruit-bearing, romanticism.

Heinrich Sutermeister (1910-   ) is a musician of a different stature, a man well versed in matters theatrical, whose *Romeo und Julia* made quite a stir. Hans Haug, a composer with a good deal of sympathetic appeal, is equally versed in opera and operetta, since his melodies are saturated with a genuine warm folk atmosphere and he is at the same time a master of modern orchestral technique, imbuing his music with a striking brilliance of sound. Perhaps his best achievement is *Don Juan in*

der Fremde, but his *Tartuffe,* too, and—Molière once more!—*Der einge-
bildete Kranke* (*Le malade imaginaire*) deserve to be mentioned.

Among the large number of other Swiss operatic composers there is
Walter Furrer, whose opera *Der Faun* reveals considerable talent, and
Pierre Wissmer, a gifted native of Geneva, who wrote *Marion.*

These musicians, although they were animated by a modern spirit,
were not really revolutionaries. It was different with another group of
actual "new-sounders." Perhaps they should not be called a group, for
there were as many tendencies as there were composers. The most they
had in common was that they considered necessary and aimed at a fundamental reform of both the laws of tonality and the forms of opera. The
result was a number of works which were interesting in themselves, although the public did not react favorably to them. We do not wish to
touch here again upon the fundamental problem of contemporary art—
the growing gulf between the creative artists and the public—but rather
will try to let the most important works representative of that tendency
pass in review before us.

The leader of the most radical school of thought, Arnold Schönberg,
of whom we shall have more to say in the following chapter, tried his
hand at two stage works. Understandably, they were not operas in the
traditional sense. Just as his theories implied the total dissolution of all
heretofore valid harmonic laws, so he attempted here a thorough disrup-
tion of the old operatic form. There remained not a trace of singing.
The concise text was recited at a certain pitch and constantly accompanied and supported not only by a complicated orchestral apparatus but
also by light and color effects. The action was restricted to a kind of
pantomime. The two works, *Die glückliche Hand* and *Erwartung,* were
considered experimental by Schönberg himself and presented only to a
small circle. But they are characteristic and important in the panorama
of our time.

Schönberg's pupil, Alban Berg (1885-1935), was far from considering a mere experiment his opera *Wozzeck,* based on a vigorous drama by
Büchner. He succeeded in putting on the stage a highly effective work.
Berg, too, walked along entirely new paths. His harmonics and melodics
were quite in conformity with his teacher's twelve-tone theory. Interspersed in the work, we find forms of "absolute" music, such as fugues,
canons, and variations which, in an operatic work, might easily be considered too abstract and theoretical. But Berg's formative power was so

great that the listener felt compelled to enter into the spirit of the fiery score. For his second opera, Berg, who died an unimely death, again chose for his sources two literary works that were psychologically interesting and dipped deep into the subconscious: Wedekind's *Erdgeist* and *Die Büchse der Pandora,* which he fused into his *Lulu.*

Let us mention another pupil of Schönberg: Egon Wellesz (1885-   ). In addition to writing a number of interesting works, he attempted to adapt ultra-modern music to a mythological trilogy in the Old Greek style.

Ernst Krenek (1900-   ) also started with the Greeks when he wrote his *Das Leben des Orest.* What made him suddenly famous, however, was *Jonny spielt auf* (Johnny strikes up the band), which provoked one of the biggest scandals in the history of European opera. There were those who—rather unjustly—considered the colorful spectacle a glorification of jazz and an attempt to demonstrate America's musical superiority to Europe. The conservatives were indignant about a work (the libretto was written by Krenek himself) which introduced to the stage a locomotive [Pl. 181], a railway accident, a hotel theft, a saxophone-blowing Negro, and a singing glacier. Oh yes, there was some music, too; but what with all the novelties and the storms of indignation, it was hardly noticed. It was quite cleverly fashioned, even beautiful in spots, but frequently banal; and it hardly justified all the great to-do. When, later, Krenek wrote the thoroughly worth-while *Orestes,* without saxophones and almost without jazz, but with profound psychological problems striving for modern musical expression, there was hardly anyone willing to listen. And his deeply serious *Karl V* (Prague, 1938) became wholly submerged in the pre-War confusion.

Speaking of theatrical scandals brings to mind the resurrection of the *Beggar's Opera,* of 1728, which, two centuries later, had an amazing effect upon the churning and unstable Europe of the post-War I days. The highly gifted authors of the remodeled work, the poet Bert Brecht and the composer Kurt Weill, called it *Die Dreigroschenoper* (The Three-Penny Opera) not with any idea of expressing its value, but to indicate its tawdry milieu of beggars, robbers, and prostitutes. An opera so wholly unsuited to the ears of the under-aged was a novelty, and since moreover the songs, offered in cabaret style rather than in an operatic manner, were tuneful and stirring, the work's tremendous success was understandable. It expressed itself in countless performances in any number of cities, in scandals and interdictions, in the proverb-like quotation of certain lines (especially lines that were critical of politics and society), in the popularity of many of the melodies, in the advent of a film version, and—most unfailing proof of a great success—in the production of a great many imitations.

None of the imitations was able to match the success of the original, not even the same collaborators' *Mahagonny* and *Die Bürgschaft*. Highly interesting was the attempt by Brecht and Weill, repeated also by other poets and musicians, to establish a new artistic form in the so-called *Lehrstück* (didactic piece). Perhaps the most successful specimen of this category was *Der Jasager* (The Yes-Man) which, to be sure, aligned itself politically with radical Marxism; but then, the *Dreigroschenoper*, too, had come rather close to such an alignment. Once more the theater was used to mirror the spirit of the time and the prevailing political tendencies, just as there had been pieces in the days of the French Revolution singing the praises of the middle classes and glorifying their triumph over the aristocracy. Whether the "topical operas" of our era will have a greater vitality than those of the French, cannot be predicted at this time.

Paul Hindemith (1895-   ) [Pl. 185] who was also rather in favor of the "topical theater," and was forever bubbling over with new and sparkling ideas, went through a considerably broader period of development than those mentioned before. After a problematic work, *Cardillac*, in which "atonal" music seems to have been placed in contrast to the Hoffmannesque figure of a medieval goldsmith, he arrived at the satyrical comedy *Neues vom Tage*, musicianly and ingenious like everything he has written. But all he had thus far conceived was discarded and forgotten when he succeeded in purifying his style to an extent vouchsafed only to a very few of the heavenly gifted. Hindemith succeeded in his *Mathis der Maler* in creating a truly inspired work, a masterpiece [Pl. 179]. Musically, it meant that he had found his way back to the mighty polyphony of the Middle Ages, to a time long before Bach, when musical art knew nothing as yet of theaters and concert halls but, under the lofty arches of cathedrals, addressed itself to the hearts of a congregation of believers.

Of the immense number of operatic works which had their first performance on German-language stages during the time between the two world wars, another few may be cited here. Werner Egk wrote, *Colum-*

bus, Bericht und Darstellung, a piece in the manner of the Lehrstück. Was it still an opera, or an oratorio, or neither? It was frequently difficult, what with the countless experiments dealing with stage technique and style, to draw a dividing line. In others of his works, like *Die Zaubergeige, Peer Gynt,* and the fairy opera *Circe,* Egk remained on the firm ground of opera, though he had nothing to say that was essentially new. In some dance dramas, on the other hand (*Joan de Jarissa, Abraxas*), he seemed to advance into virgin territory. Carl Orff was the creator of another strange work, *Carmina Burana,* whose style lay midway between a renewal of the Greek tragedy and an agitated oratorio. His *Bernauerin,* first performed in 1947, once more represents an intermediary form (actors, chorus, vocal soloists, and orchestra) closely approaching the mystery play. A notable, though rather ephemeral, success was scored by Rudolf Wagner-Regeny's operas *Der Günstling, Die Bürger von Calais,* and *Johanna Balk,* and by Max Brand's *Machinist Hopkins.*

During recent years, since the end of World War II, quite a number of new figures have emerged. There is, to begin with, Boris Blacher, whose operas have been frequently performed. *Die Flut* (1946) was originally intended for the radio and therefore conceived with more consideration for the ear than the eye. It is an epic-dramatic combination, approaching the oratorio. There is also his music to Gerhart Hauptmann's *Agamemnon's Tod,* his *Fürstin Terakanova,* and his comedy opera *Amor verliebt sich,* first performed in 1947. The operas of Leo Justinus Kauffmann, an Alsatian killed by a bomb in the last year of the war, (*Geschichte vom schönen Annerl, Das Perlenhemd*) reveal the hand of a sensitive musician.

While, after World War I, opera was subjected to the most uninhibited naturalistic experiments, the incomparably worse collapse following in the wake of the last war produced unsurveyable tendencies in the opposite direction: a turning away from reality, from the present. The titles of numerous operatic works would prove this assertion. Some of them were mentioned in the preceding paragraph. It may be stated that Walter Braunfels, one of Germany's leading composers, brought back from his exile works like *Mariä Verkündigung* (after Claudel), *Der Traum ein Leben* (after Grillparzer), and *Die heilige Johanna.* The following world premières took place in post-war Germany: *Die Hochzeit des Job* by Josepeh Haas, *Das verzauberte Ich* by Otmar Gerster (who had previously come forward with the folk opera *Enoch Arden*), Dramatic Music to Aristophanes' *Lysistrata* by Wolfgang Fortner, the epic operas *Odysseus* and *Dr. Johannes Faust* by Hermann Reutter, *Corean Fairy Tale* by Waldemar Wendland, and the lyric melodrama *Das steigende Jahr* by Siegfried Borries.

Before passing on to Italian operatic composers, whose problems are considerably less weighty than those of their German colleagues (somehow, they still seem to have had in their blood Rossini's motto requiring of opera but three things: Voice, voice, and, once more, voice!) let us consider some border cases, composers who stood between the North and the South, either because of their birthplace, their tendencies, or simply because of their style. In this category belongs Ermanno Wolf-Ferrari (1876-1948) who, of mixed German and Italian parentage, is a synthesis of both countries also in his music. He was quite successful with his *Secret of Suzanne*, *The Jewels of the Madonna*, and *The Curious Women*. The interesting artistic personality of Ferruccio Busoni and his fine operas *Arlecchino*, *Doctor Faust*, and *Turandot* have already been discussed. The most vigorous composer in this group may well have been Eugene d'Albert (1864-1932), a man of German origin but born in Scotland, who had always had a yearning in his heart for Italy and its opera. He was able to score a well-deserved universal success with his realistic tone drama *Tiefland*, whose Spanish milieu was aptly characterized by a number of well-rounded and beautiful melodies. Rather less successful was his *Die toten Augen*, and still less *Die schwarze Orchidee*. D'Albert was one of the greatest piano virtuosos in the history of music. In striking contrast to his stirring life is the impressively lonely grave he chose for himself in idyllic Morcote, on the Lake of Lugano.

And now for Italy herself. After Verdi's death, problems arose which were not dissimilar to those confronting the German composers after Wagner's passing. But none of the Italian operatic composers, not even the most fervid supporters of *verismo*, would have dreamed of attacking the supremacy of the melody. *Verismo*, which was the exact counterpart of contemporaneous naturalism and realism in other arts, succeeded, above all, in changing the operatic scenes of action. No more Middle Ages, no more palaces, but real, contemporary life, everyday figures, everyday problems, love among common people, everyday passions and tragedies. That, approximately, was the program, although, like all programs, it could not be carried through with entire faithfulness. It was obvious, however, that the change of milieu would principally have to affect the libretti. But there was nothing to prevent a little seamstress in a Montmartre garret from singing melodies as sweet as those uttered by a princess in flowing robes, even if the one had to die of consumption and the other in a much more heroic manner. And the strolling comedian was permitted to sing of his breaking heart as melodiously as any knightly hero in a belcanto opera.

Perhaps one of the first Italian "veristic" composers was Amilcare Ponchielli (1834-1886), whose *Gioconda* is still included in modern repertoires [Pl. 180].

Umberto Giordano (1867-1948) scored a genuine success with his striking revolutionary drama *Andrea Chenier*. *Fedora* was less fortunate, and *Siberia* soon fell into oblivion. The same fate was shared by the works of Alberto Franchetti (1860-   ), although they were rather frequently performed for a short time. Their titles were *Germania* and *Cristoforo Colombo*, the latter commissioned by the City of Genoa for the quatro-centenary of the discovery of America. The operas of the gifted Alfredo Catalani (1854-1893), *Loreley* and *La Wally*, also appear only occasionally in their country of origin. From *Adriana Lecouvreur*, by Francesco Cilea (1866-   ), an excerpt may still be heard now and then, just as the *Lamento* from his opera *L'Arlesiana* is still a favorite with many tenors. None of the foregoing operas may be called examples of true *verismo*. They were transition operas, many of them still strongly influenced by the style of Verdi.

Then, about 1890, the new style emerged in its full glory. It was represented particularly by two highly successful operas which, although they were the outcome of a prize contest, were truly meritorious. We are of course referring to the perennial favorites *Cavalleria Rusticana* by Pietro Mascagni (1863-1946) and *Pagliacci* by Ruggiero Leoncavallo (1858-1919). Both operas are strikingly effective on the stage. The contrast between the solemn Easter mood and the passionate drama enacted by four persons in Mascagni's work; the ever closer linking together of play and reality in the Leoncavallo opus, until Canio's knife spills Nedda's blood at the very feet of the peasants—these are among the most gripping experiences on the operatic stage.

Neither of these two composers was able to repeat his initial success. Leoncavallo's *Bohème* was put in the shade by Puccini's masterpiece, and Mascagni was only able to score transitory or partial successes with his many later operas, such as *Amico Fritz, Iris* (with the beautiful hymn to the sun), and *Nerone*. Internationally, the two prize-winning youthful works remained the only lasting successes of their creators.

At the turn of the century, musical naturalism was in full bloom. By far its most popular representative and, at the same time, one of the most eminent operatic composers of Italy—and of the whole world—was Giacomo Puccini (1858-1924). He proved himself the possessor of realistic tendencies as well as a romantic soul, and—how happy a combination!— an exceptional gift for melodics and orchestration. His first important work was *Manon Lescaut*, successful in Italy, but pushed into the background elsewhere by Massenet's more fortunate opera on the same subject. The year 1896, however, marked the beginning of Puccini's great world triumphs. His *Bohème* proved him a genius of the first rank. Few operas, if any, have ever succeeded in including so masterful a portrayal of the most heterogeneous moods: everyday life and tender poetic sentiment, the stir and bustle of Montmartre and a quiet love idyl, humor and tragedy—and all that fused into a flawlessly uniform whole. Never for a moment is the melodic arch broken. The culminating points, represented by Rodolfo's and Mimi's accounts of their life in the first act, the inimitably beautiful quartet in the third act, and Mimi's death scene in the final act, thrill the listener at every new hearing [Ill. 138]. The death of the ailing seamstress—Traviata's proletarian twin—in the wretched cold garret in which she had dreamt her first and only dream of true love has moved, and will continue to move, millions of people to tears, more so even than Puccini's next and more tragic opera, *Madame Butterfly*, remarkable for its dramatic texture and replete with musical gems (think of the wonderful love duet at the end of the first act!) and still more so than his blood-curdling *Tosca* [Pl. 177], whose cruel libretto is made bearable only by the composer's glorious music. Puccini succeeded in writing a brilliant *opera buffa*—the most difficult of all operatic forms, as we have learned—in his *Gianni Schicchi*, which is frequently joined to his serious one-act operas *Suor Angelica* and *Il tabarro*, to make up a tryptich of full-evening proportions. Puccini's *Girl of the Golden West*, although it contains some beautiful passages and was performed by eminent casts in all the principal opera houses of the world, never was able to achieve the popularity of his other great operas. At the very end of his life, Puccini rose once more to his full height. Combining his inexhaustible melodic flow with his unmatched flair for stage dramatics and his brilliant orchestra virtuosity, he wrote *Turandot*. Death wrenched the pen from

138. From Puccini's manuscript score of "Bohème": Mimi's death.

his hand before he was able to complete it, but his friend and pupil, Franco Alfano (1876-   ), himself a noteworthy composer, finished it by using the master's sketches. The subject, dealing with the proud Chinese princess, outwitted at first and then conquered by love, offered to Puccini's inventiveness a wealth of the most varied possibilities. In order to remain true to the milieu, he made effective use of the five-tone scale. The great riddle scene in which the Strange Prince emerges victorious from the test is among the most impressive scenes of the world's operatic literature.

How quickly naturalism in music came to the end of its line! Frequently its own representatives were the ones who passed beyond it: Puccini in Italy, Strauss in Germany. We might say the same of Mascagni, of d'Albert, and of some others whose work is not so well known. This did not, of course, mean that naturalism was dead. Almost like romanticism, it has become one of the ever-present styles. It merely ceased to be the only leading tendency; it stepped somewhat into the background. The rapid succession of the most divergent styles, frequently even directly opposed to one another, the malady of our century's art, had set in.

It was mentioned in the preceding chapter that Italy's greatest symphonist, Ottorino Respighi, also made his contribution to operatic history. Both *The Flame* and *The Sunken Bell* (based on Gerhart Hauptmann's fairy tale) were noble tone paintings whose style proved their creator's close allegiance to impressionism. Respighi was thus already far removed from *verismo*.

Finally, modernism, too, had its representatives in Italy's operatic activities. It was not so advanced as that of its contemporary Central European and French confrères, but the searching for a new way, for new forms of expression, made itself plainly felt also in the fatherland of opera.

G. Francesco Malipiero's operatic work includes three trilogies. *L'Orfeide* is comprised of *Seven Songs*, an unconventional music drama in which each scene has its song, mood, and dramatic action; *Orpheus, or the Seventh Song;* and *The Death of the Masks.* To well-known libretti, Malipiero composed *Three Comedies after Goldoni: The Coffee Shop, Sir Todero Brontolon,* and *The Quarrels of Chiogga.* These pieces are given sometimes independently, sometimes on one evening's program. *The Mystery of Venice,* a portrayal of the decadence of that city, includes *The Eagles of Aquileia, The False Harlequin,* and *The Ravens of St. Mark,* a dance drama. Malipiero wrote two Shakespeare operas, *Giulio Cesare,* and *Antonio e Cleopatra;* and *The Fable of the Changed Son,* to a Pirandello cycle which he did not live to complete.

Mario Castelnuovo-Tedesco wrote *La Mandragola*, musically interesting for its novel chord structure, which is of great variety.

Besides these two, the following composers and their works may be mentioned: Ildebrando Pizzetti (1880-   ) and his *Fedra, The Stranger*, and a few other operas written to texts by d'Annunzio; Alfredo Casella (1883-1947) and his *La donna serpente* (based on Gozzi's book which had also inspired Wagner's youthful work *Die Feen*) and *Il deserto tentato;* Riccardo Zandonai (1883-1944) and his *Francesca da Rimini;* Italo Montemezzi (1875-   ) and his *L'amore dei tre re;* Ludovico Rocca (1895-   ) and his *Dybbuk;* Victor de Sabata (1892-   ), and a considerable number of young lyric writers whose creative talent searched for a way out of the confusion of the years during and after the war.

Before passing on to a discussion of contemporary French operas, another "border case" ought to be interpolated, that of Arthur Honegger (1892-   ). The scion of an old Zurich family, his culture and the style of his music are wholly western. He did not write operas in the traditional style. Almost all of his works performed on the stage could as well, and even to better advantage, be presented on the concert platform. This is especially true of the two main pillars of his creative work,

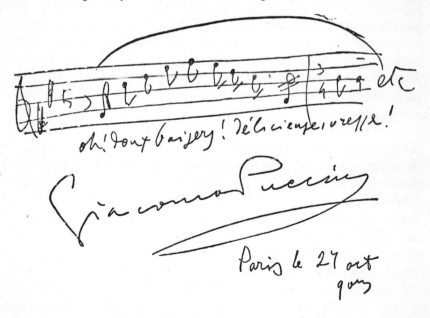

139. Puccini autograph: a "Tosca" quotation from French text.

Le roi David and *Jeanne d'Arc au bûcher* [Pl. 188]. The former contributed largely, and deservedly, to Honegger's fame and placed him at once in the forefront of the musical European post-War-I generation. René Morax, the poet, who jointly with his brother Jean, the painter, had founded the open-air theater Mézières near Lausanne, in 1903, invited Honegger, in 1921, to write the music to his drama *Le roi David*, after a number of other musicians had refused to tackle the difficult undertaking. It took Honegger two months to do the job. He later revised the work, originally intended for the small open-air theater, and there came into being the larger, symphonic, or, if you will, oratorial version. Honegger's *Judith*, now an opera, also owes its birth to the Mézières theater, where it was used as stage music to a Biblical drama. His *Antigone*, too, is incidental stage music. Opera in its traditional sense, with its trivialities-spouting singing actors, is far removed from Honegger's artistic activity. He is most impressive in his masterly choruses which he actually succeeded in raising to the status of a fully equal partner of the modern magically sounding orchestra.

In his *Jeanne d'Arc au bûcher* Honegger scaled prodigious heights. He formed one of the most interesting syntheses ever attempted by making this work a combination of opera, oratorio, terpsichorean motion, and deeply penetrating psychology. And strange, indeed: this most modern achievement of contemporary stagecraft—accompanied by Paul Claudel's wonderfully mystical text—takes us back to the point at which the modern development of the theater began: to the medieval mystery play. Just as in the case of Hindemith and his *Mathis*, the Middle Ages provided Honegger with his most striking, profound, and vital inspirations. The work of the magnificent choruses greatly surpasses anything so far achieved. Gregorian turns, French street songs, and simple children's airs are treated with equal mastery. But these, and other, ingredients do not emerge individually. They interlock and at times are even made to sound at once in perfect contrapuntal union. There arises before our eyes the vision of an era, with its faith and superstitions, courtly activities and church bells, fabulous beings and supernatural apparitions. In the center stands the figure of Joan at the stake, her fettered hands folded, unmoving during the entire play, which evolves rather within her than about her, speaking, singing, and listening to her inward voices. Claudel made this vision come orally and pictorially true. Ida Rubinstein, who had been the moving spirit behind the *Martyrdom of St. Se-*

bastian in which the mastery of d'Annunzio and Debussy were united, again furnished the necessary impetus. She wanted the work performed at the portals of a church, as if it were a medieval mystery play. The first performance took place in Switzerland, whence the work spread rapidly, furnishing an inexhaustible source of inspiration to stage designers, choreographers, regisseurs, and, not least of all, to musicians who found in the score an overflowing wealth of new ideas. It may be mentioned here that—perhaps for the first time in an important work—Honegger made use in this composition of the "martenot," an electrical instrument producing a veritable "music of the spheres" and, in spite of its sensationally new sounds, fitting ideally into the symphonic orchestra.

Modern French opera presents a motley picture of widely different tendencies. Massenet, Saint-Saëns, and Chapentier have already been discussed. Henri Rabaud (1873-   ) wrote his amusing *Marouf* in a cleverly orientalized style. The chief representative of modernism, in the strict sense of the word, is Darius Milhaud who, like Honegger, was born in 1892. He wrote, among other things, short operas in an almost cabaret-like style. Some of these thumb-nail sketches took only a few minutes to perform, for instance *Le boeuf sur le toit*. That was pioneer work, a smashing of barriers, a mockery of the past. Later, in 1930, he concentrated upon a work of considerable scope. It was his *Christophe Colomb,* a magnificent vision of the discovery of America, one of the finest musical representations, among many others, of that historical event. Paul Claudel's libretto calls for a multiple division of the stage, so that different scenes may take place at the same time—a musically highly interesting and thankful task. At the same time, the cooperation of the film is also required. Since hardly any of our present-day theaters is able to cope with the magnitude of the required apparatus, there have been but very few performances of this work. Milhaud, who has been living in America for years, feels strongly attracted to subjects connected with the New Continent. This inclination was given expression in the operas *Maximilian* and *Bolivar.*

A new breath of life has invaded England's operatic stages of our time. Ralph Vaughan Williams (1872-   ) [Ill. 143], whose role as a pioneer of modern English music will presently be given due recognition, wrote in addition to a large number of other compositions, several operas which, to be sure, have not as yet started on their way into the world. On the other hand, there is young Benjamin Britten (1913-   ),

. 313

whose *Peter Grimes* has been successfully performed in all parts of the world. His *Rape of Lucretia* bears further testimony to the exceptional gifts of this highly promising composer.

The foundations of operatic activities, expanded in the course of the last century through the admission of several new nations, have again been broadened in our century. Some of the principal newcomers have already been duly referred to; so has Manuel de Falla's valuable contribution to Spanish music. Slavs, Hungarians, and Scandinavians remain to be discussed. And, for the first time in connection with musical stage productions, American composers have to be taken into account, in North America as well as in the Latin part of the New World. But let us take everything in its proper sequence.

A few important data concerning Czech opera may be recorded. After the death of Dvorák, a strange personality appeared on the operatic horizon. His name was Leo Janacék (1854-1928). He was a self-taught man and already advanced in years when he was first heard from. His unquestionably remarkable *Jenufa* drew attention to him. It was followed later by the horribly gloomy *Pictures from a Death House*, after Dostoyevsky, the hardly less tragical *Katia Kabanova*, based on Ostrovsky's drama, *The Storm*, and a number of less-known works.

One of the most striking modern operatic successes, *Schwanda, der Dudelsackpfeifer*, by Jaromir Weinberger (1896-   ), is grown from Czech soil and based partly on genuine Czech folk tales. A work so cleverly fashioned, with so entertaining a libretto and such charming music is indeed a great rarity in the literature of *opéra comique*, especially in the literature of our day. How the swaggering Schwanda gets himself into the most awkward situations and always manages to slip out again, how he engages the devil himself in a game of cards, how he visits the castle of the Ice Queen, how he profits by the generous spirit of a notorious robber, how he plays the bagpipe which makes everybody around him gaily dance polkas and galops, how he finally returns to the little farm where the faithful Dorothea waits and the geese cackle—all this results in a most delightful opera in which there are neither experiments nor problems, only joy.

Bohuslav Martinu, to whom recognition came at an early age, wrote seven operas during ten years, and six ballets; of the latter, *Spalicec* employs a chorus.

Igor Stravinsky (1882-   ) is one of the chief exponents of modern

Slav music. Since he achieved entirely new forms of the musical stage drama, his course of development is of particular interest. He started with a very harmonious opera, *Le rossignol* (The Nightingale), which goes back to his youthful days when *L'oiseau de feu* (Fire Bird), *Petrouchka*, and *Le sacre du printemps* (Rites of Spring) created such a stir. Then he proceeded to combine the ballet with singing voices in *Les Noces* (Peasant Wedding). In 1917, he took the step which so decisively influenced his further development. Turning his back upon the *grand ensemble*, he took up the cause of the chamber orchestra. It meant a change from exuberance to asceticism, from tonal intoxication to spiritual clarity, from the heritage of the nineteenth century to expressionistic or neoclassicistic music. His desire for an "epic" musical theater in place of an opera somehow inescapably linked to romanticism carried him farther and farther. His next stage was marked by *L'histoire du soldat* (The Soldier's Story) (1918). Does so strange a piece still belong in a chapter of opera? The interesting experiment, based on a gloomy Russian legend, required the services of merely one speaker, one female dancer, two actors, and seven instrumentalists. After a brief interlude, marked by the birth of the grotesque opera *Mavra* (1922)—a far cry from comedy opera in its accepted sense—Stravinsky continued to pursue his way toward realism and a strongly anti-Wagnerian musical objectivity. His next way station was *Oedipus Rex* (1927). It had an exceptionally striking effect upon international musical life. There was a Speaker, explaining and linking up the various scenes which gave the impression of inanimate pictures rather than operatic acts. The prominently used chorus was made to sing in Latin and in almost Gregorian musical turns. This consciously changed it from an acting into a contemplative element and, together with the pronounced rigidity of the scenic picture, evoked thoughts of the oratorio. There followed, in 1934, an ideologically similar work based on a mystical text by André Gide. Its name was *Persephone*. Again there was a Speaker, although this time he was given a few melodic phrases, and a chorus resembling that of the Old Greek tragedies, whose absolute lack of motion virtually placed it outside the action and the stage. Most of the action was expressed by pantomime and dancing, and only at the culminating points of the work was there occasional articulation and singing.

The species "opera" had been sharply defined in the nineteenth century. Even before, there had been a clear-cut division between it and all other musical forms, with the exception, perhaps, of the works of Handel which frequently were operas as well as oratorios. And now, every conceivable combination: opera and drama, opera and pantomime, opera plus drama and pantomime, drama and ballet, opera and film, opera and operetta. And all this to save opera, to save a patient who perhaps was not sick at all!

Sergei Prokofiev (1891-   ) is another highly gifted Russian composer. He was compelled to live outside his native land. But, after decades of banishment, he returned to Russia in the middle Thirties. He scored a considerable international success with his fairy-tale opera *The Love for Three Oranges*, from which excerpts, such as a sparkling march and other highly effective pieces, are still frequently heard.

Of the current modern Russian musical theater very little is known outside the country's frontiers. That is a pity, for it would be highly fascinating and instructive to study the connections between social and artistic activities. How does an anti-bourgeois regime view the most bourgeois of all musical forms, the opera? Perhaps the much maligned opera isn't bourgeois at all, but merely universally human. All we know is that it is being as intensively cultivated in Soviet Russia as all art. The only work that penetrated beyond the country's frontiers was Shostakovitch's *Lady Macbeth of Mzensk*, a strange mixture of superlative skill and banality, of revolutionary and traditional elements. In this opera, a suggestive empty-stage musical interlude during a love story caused an attack so severe that Shostakovitch's career was almost cut short. His earlier operatic satire, *The Nose*, from Gogol's amusing short story, employed the most modern musical idioms, such as atonality, and was also attacked so bitterly in Russia that it lasted only a few performances.

Poland's national opera *Halka* has already been mentioned. Karol Szymanowski and Ignace Paderewski, perhaps the two most important of Chopin's successors, made contributions to Poland's operatic production, although their works were able to score no more than a local success.

Yugoslav opera, too, has been unable so far to penetrate beyond its own native frontiers. Two typical examples are *Ero, the Rascal*, by Jakob Gotovacs, and *The Devil in the Village*, by Fran Kotka.

Of greater importance are the Hungarians of our century. Both Béla Bartók and Zoltán Kodály created important works in the realm of opera. Bartók's *Duke Bluebeard's Castle* is a one-act opera with an unusual score in which the speaking parts are accompanied by music which impersonates the human voice. *The Wooden Prince* is a seven-dance ballet linked by dramatic interludes. *The Miraculous Mandarin,* a macabre mime-play, is somewhat weakened by a poor libretto. Kodály's *Háry János* is a humorous opera of a good-natured, boastful soldier who is the Hungarian folklore companion to such characters as Falstaff and Till Eulenspiegel. *The Spinning Room,* a light opera set in Transylvania, presents a sequence of jolly scenes and songs, another lyric treatment of folk material. The highly-gifted Eugene Zador wrote a very effective *Columbus.*

In Scandinavia, the cultivation of opera has become greatly intensified in our century. Although hardly anything has found its way into the world, it must be stated that Sweden and Finland especially have given birth to interesting native operas.

American music will be discussed in a chapter of its own. But let us say here that both the United States and South America have brought forth quite a number of operas, some of which are as impressive as they are characteristic. There is, first of all, George Gershwin's *Porgy and Bess,* whose action is laid in the Negro quarter of an American metropolis. It is one of the few American operas which succeeded in crossing the Atlantic. Gershwin, who died at the age of thirty-nine, first became famous through his brilliant *Rhapsody in Blue. Porgy and Bess* is true jazz, a real folk opera, the first one to come out of the United States.

Douglas Moore, who also inclines toward folk opera, is the composer of *The Devil and Daniel Webster.* Deems Taylor's two operas, *The King's Henchman* and *Peter Ibbetson,* Howard Hanson's *Merrymount,* Victor Herbert's *Natoma,* and Reginald de Koven's *Robin Hood,* while successful in varying degrees in their own country, are still unknown to the rest of the world. A similar condition prevails in the Latin part of the New Continent. There is a good deal of production, but none of the frequently highly interesting works has gone beyond its native land, with the exception of the Brazilian opera *Il Guarany,* by Carlos Gomes, which, in the last century, was loudly acclaimed at the Scala of Milan and was subsequently performed at a large number of theaters in different parts of the world. Other operas succeeded only in isolated instances in making an international appearance, such as *El Matrero,* the Argentine national opera by Felipe Boero, *The Southern Cross* by the Uruguayan, Alfonso Brocqua, and some of the works of the well-known conductor Ettore Panizza, a citizen of Argentina, but of so pronounced an Italian orientation that he ought rather to be counted among the lyric artists of his native country.

It may be said that today almost all the civilized nations of the world have a national operatic production of their own, although in most instances the works have not gained more than local importance. But even the more weighty works were only rarely able to cross their native borders, in spite of radio, phonograph records, and a constant interchange of musicians. This is due principally to the fact that operatic theaters everywhere stick either to the sure-fire successes of the "great" classic repertory or give their support to promising local products.

THE MODERN OPERETTA

We were present, in Paris and in Vienna, at the birth of the operetta, the graceful little sister of the opera. Rapidly it conquered the world, more rapidly almost than its more serious relative. At times it even tried to imitate the older member of the family with so much success that the two might have been taken for twins. The operetta would deserve a book of its own; it would even require it, were one to enumerate and do justice to all its creative geniuses, their scintillating products, and their rousing international successes.

In France, Offenbach was so overshadowing a figure that the branch of art in which he excelled was bound to slip from its high level after his death. The more pretentious of his successors allied themselves with the *opéra comique*, while lesser lights found their way into vaudeville. Still, there are names that should be mentioned, as, for instance, Charles Lecocq (1832-1918) who wrote the charming operettas *Madame Angot* and *Giroflé Giroflà*, Robert Planquette (1848-1903), the composer of the successful *Cloches de Corneville*, Florimond Hervé (1825-1892), and André Messager (1853-1929).

England may proudly call her own two exceptionally successful composers in the realm of the lighter Muse. There was above all Sir Arthur S. Sullivan (1842-1900), a genius who, in collaboration with the equally brilliant poet Sir William S. Gilbert, wrote such universally admired masterpieces as *The Mikado, Patience*, and *The Pirates of Penzance*, and whose works, if properly staged and cast, still play to packed houses in the English-speaking realms of the world. And there was Sidney Jones (1869-1914), whose *Geisha* was heard and acclaimed in all parts of the globe.

More and more plainly, however, did Vienna become the center of the operetta. So much so, that to say "Vienna" was tantamount to saying "operetta." Even in the days of Johann Strauss, there lived in that city other highly gifted musicians, such as Franz von Suppé (1819-1895), the composer of the spirited *Boccaccio, Fatinitza, Pensionat*, and *Leichte Kavallerie* (Light Cavalry), whose overture is still a most popular orchestral piece; Karl Millöcker (1843-1899), whose *Bettelstudent* was immensely and deservedly successful; and Karl Zeller (1842-1898), the composer of the equally popular *Vogelhändler*.

The beginning of the new century witnessed the emergence of new lights in the realm of the Vienna operetta, after the old ones, within a short time of each other, had been snuffed out. Leo Fall (1873-1925) was one of the cleverest and most ingenious composers ever heard in this branch of art. His *Die Dollarprinzessin, Rose von Stambul, Brüderlein fein, Der fidele Bauer*, and, above all, *Madame Pompadour* were brilliant examples of his skill and inventiveness. And there was Franz Lehar (1870-1948) [Pl. 183], who became the acknowledged master of widely swinging, frequently sentimental, but always gripping melodies. *Die lustige Witwe* (The Merry Widow) shattered all existing records and was heard hundreds of times in every country of the world and in every tongue. It was followed by an uninterrupted series of popular works, such as *Der Graf von Luxemburg, Frasquita, Eva, Paganini, Das Land des Lächelns* [Pl. 184], and *Friederike*. The latter, a musical version of an episode in Goethe's life, represented the composer's approach to the *Singspiel* with an operatic touch. This inclination toward a larger form became even more evident in his *Giuditta*, performed on the hallowed boards of the Vienna State Opera, which had previously opened its doors only twice to works of a lighter genre: to Johann Strauss's two principal works, *The Bat* and *Gypsy Baron*. Perhaps to save appearances, they had been called "comic operas," although their every measure, their every melody, and their every stirring rhythm was Vienna operetta of the purest stamp.

In spite of his Hungarian descent, Emmerich Kalman (1882-   ) must also be numbered among the great masters of the Vienna operetta. He combined an exceptionally developed melodic gift with an ability to make clever use of his native folk music. Having a fine sense for the dramatic, he knew how to make even the simplest tunes sound impressive. Among his tremendously popular works are *Die Czardasfürstin, Herbstmanöver, Die Bajadere, Gräfin Maritza*, and *Die Zirkusprinzessin*.

Oscar Straus (1870-   ) may, in spite of his differently-spelled name, be considered a rightful member of the waltz dynasty. This affinity is indicated by the very titles of his most successful operettas: *Ein Walzertraum, Der letzte Walzer*, and *Drei Walzer*. *The Chocolate Soldier*, based on George Bernard Shaw's *Arms and the Man*, was an outstanding success.

Oskar Granichstädten made a hit with his *Orloff*, and Edmund Eysler with a series of folk-like pieces, among them *Die goldene Meisterin*.

Robert Stolz (1882-   ) is one of our day's most gifted composers of light music, and Ralph Benatzky (1887-   ), too, has succeeded in gaining world fame, not least of all through his *Das weisse Rössl* (The White-Horse Inn) whose genuine Austrian atmosphere captured the hearts of all continents.

In the days between the two world wars, a new star began to shine. Paul Abraham (1898-   ) was a Hungarian by birth, and his music reveals the first influence of jazz. Some of his operettas, such as *Viktoria und ihr Husar, Die Blume von Hawaii,* and *Ein Ball im Savoy* were triumphantly successful in Vienna as well as in other cities of the world.

The Czechs scored with *Polenblut* by Oskar Nedbal (1874-1930) and the Germans with quite a number of operettas by Paul Linke (1886-   ), Walter Kollo (1883-   ), Eduard Künnecke (1885-   ), and, last but not least, Jean Gilbert (1878-1943), whose *Keusche Susanna* had quite a vogue. Poland gave us the greatly gifted Joseph Beer, whose *Polnische Hochzeit* atracted a good deal of attention and whose *Stradella in Venedig* is a comic opera of exceptional merit.

In Switzerland, Paul Burkhard (1911-   ) was quite successful with a number of pleasant operettas, such as *Hopsa, 3 x Georges, Tic-Tac, Casanova in der Schweiz,* and with the *entr'acte* music for Goldoni's *Kaffeehaus.*

In the realm of the operetta, too, America is beginning to be a serious threat to European tradition and leadership. The tremendous success of the music of Victor Herbert (1859-1924) has not failed to arouse an international echo, and that of Rudolf Friml (1881-   ), the enchanting *Rose Marie, The Vagabond King,* and many other works, have met with enthusiastic approval.

*   *   *

This concludes our account of the history of opera, begun with Count Bardi's experiments in the old cultural center of Florence. We followed it through its principal stages, witnessed its problems and triumphs, and observed how it was frequently declared dead, or at least moribund, but always managed to emerge more vital than ever. Today, opera is faced by only one threat: a lack of new additions to the repertory. The repertory cannot be normally expanded because of a lack of new creations with a sufficiently durable general appeal. The countless stylistic experiments of our century have failed to bring about a clarification. Let us not forget the guiding principle of all contemplation of art: art is a reflection of life, is deeply rooted in life, and indissolubly connected with it. A new style of music can only follow a new style of life, never precede it. True, an artist may become a prophet—ideologically. But never will he be able to establish a style while his era is still groping to find a style of its own.

As for the public, opera has nothing to fear from that quarter, in spite of many assertions to the contrary. There has always been a public, a large public, an enthusiastic public, to support opera. For three hundred years and more, whenever the magic world of the opera has unfolded, there have been those whose eager hearts were uplifted by it and who found in it that for which they were yearning: illusion, inspiration, enjoyment, enchantment.

The Age of Dissonance

THE world had passed through the terrors of the First Great War. Empires and ideas had been shattered. The classes which, but yesterday, had been the supports of civilization had either been swept away or were engaged in a hard fight for existence.

Millions of men, on their return from the trenches, were looking in despair for a world which might make up to them for what they had gone through. Not only had they lost battles but also their belief in traditional values.

Technical science was their ally. It built for them what their imaginations had but dared to dream of: towering skyscrapers, speeding automobiles, airplanes that brought countries and continents within hours of one another, radios, and sound films. What had been a source of gaping wonderment yesterday had come to be a matter of course. Everything was in a state of flux. Every minute gave birth to something new, and people rushed to see it.

Art is a reflection of life. So we said in a much earlier chapter, when dealing with an age when timeless monks were standing before dimly lit altars, singing hymns to their timeless God, and a thousand nights and days were but as one day. Now each day had to be newer, more sensational, and more exciting than the preceding one; for that which did not excite had forfeited its right to live. If the tension relaxed, one had to die; and to live, to live, was the password after so much dying.

The arts were drawn into the mad whirl, wildly searching for new themes. No matter what, they had to be different. The painter's canvas showed us distorted figures, and we did not realize that they were portraits of ourselves. Literature stammered, reveled in contractions and distortions—it was our language. Music heaped dissonance on dissonance, shattered forms, warped sounds.

And nobody can understand the art of our age who has not carefully considered this. Beethoven and Haydn described storms in their music, but they were hardly ever accompanied by any dissonances. When the romanticist sang in their music of death, or of war, they did it harmoniously. But to a modern composer, even a sunset suggests dissonance. It all depends upon the point of view.

All this does not mean that our age must do without melody, harmony, or consonance. Humanity is not a uniform army marching in but one direction. Epochs overlap, not only because there are still some romanticists in an age whose youth has become anti-romantic, but also because every individual bears within him a different picture of the world, entertains different ideals, different conceptions of beauty. That is why an epoch as disturbed as ours, when old ties are shattered before new ones can be established, must reveal a motley of every imaginable artistic tendency.

Remarkable is the yawning gulf existing today between so-called modern art and the public. Is the voice of the people truly the voice of God? Was Hans Sachs right when he suggested that the common people, at least once a year, be allowed to judge, lest the guardians of art lose themselves in the abstract? The audience of our age has pronounced its judgment quite clearly. It is against modern art. And music, the most emotional of all arts, may have its roots in any place but the one in which our century is trying to plant them: in reason. That is why 90 per cent of our theatrical and concert programs are composed of products of the past. The people, hungry for art as never before, take refuge in the past, since the present cannot satisfy them. They take refuge in the cinema because it offers them what they cannot find in modern art: illusion.

But the problem of modern music is also a problem of our sense of hearing. This is what one of our leading young musicians, Rodolfo Halffter, has to say about it: "The historical development of harmony reveals a continuous adoption of ever more acute dissonances. The explanation is quite simple. No sooner has the ear become accustomed to a certain dissonance—a question merely of time and schooling—than the tingling sensation of that dissonance has vanished, and with it the restful feeling brought about by its resolution. No doubt, that dissonance has become worn out, has lost its potency. It is necessary to find a new and more potent power. And so our sense of hearing gets ready to absorb and conquer ever more acute dissonances." This explanation is clear and logical. But while in past centuries this development proceeded with hardly noticeable slowness, it tumbles all over itself in our time. There must come an end of dissonances, too. And then what?

While we have to deal here with a dissolution of a centuries-old principle of harmonics, it is a fact that every musical—and extra-musical—art form is faced with similar problems today. Let us pick out one more example, one that is especially interesting: the relation of "absolute" music to "program" or "descriptive" music. Each represented one of the culminating points of absolute music, music that wanted to be nothing but music, music for its own sake, to be evaluated only by purely musical standards. Soon thereafter, program music began to appear on the scene with increasing frequency. Haydn and Beethoven entertained thoughts of it, although the general musical orientation of their day still tended toward absolute music. People were still able to listen to a piece of music and to admire it without the need of an interpretation or an extra-musical description. And yet, the way led ever more plainly toward such an interpretation, toward a "program." Almost all of the music of romanticism was descriptive. This development may have reached its culminating point in Wagner, whose minutest musical particle —the leitmotif—represented a program. For several decades after Wagner's death, program music held full sway, with the exception of some isolated cases. Then the reaction set in. It was marked by tendencies which, in our century, we considered a musical revolution. A parallel phenomenon was noticeable in pictorial art. A flowerpot no longer was a flowerpot, for that would have been all too descriptive; a seated woman by Picasso was neither a woman nor did she sit. We have here a search for the absolute, a turning away from the descriptive. The public did not understand that, at first, and muttered about mannerism and perversity. Many years will have to pass before "absolute" thinking can become the norm, just as it took generations before absolute music was ready to cede its hegemony to "interpretative" art.

The pendulum theory manifesting itself in this development is extremely interesting. It is identical with the frequently advanced "Theory of Generations" which, in connection with musical history, has led to startling conclusions, though this does by no means signify that it has been scientifically proven. This thesis, supported mainly by Alfred Ottokar Lorenz, assumed that occidental musical history is a curve oscillating according to definite laws between two opposite principles: the polyphonic (including counterpoint, musical absolutism, and rational

. 325

understanding) and the homophonic (including subjectivism, consciousness of feeling, melodics on a harmonic basis, and program music). It seems that a period of three hundred years is required to form a cycle, from St. Ambrose, at the beginning of the fifth century, to the "atonality" of the twentieth century. The last period of polyphony reached from 1300 to 1600, so that Bach would appear to have been a late offshoot, or, let us say, a last and all-encompassing summit, while his own time was already striving toward another goal. The years between 1600 and 1900 represent the breaking through of the harmonic feeling, which no doubt is true; and so we have reached a unique explanation of why our time is taking the "way back," and why the composers of our day are returning to counterpoint and flying from harmony.

But let us be done now with theories and contemplations and try to envision the colorful panorama offered by modern music, though we are still unable to evaluate it. For that, as always, must be left to time.

It is an interesting tendency of many musicians to transpose pictures of the time, themes of the day, into music. Arthur Honegger, in his *Pacific 231*, sings of the ponderous drive of a giant transcontinental locomotive and, in another work, called *Rugby*, tries to express in tones the enthusiasm of a sport-minded crowd. Alexander Mossolov, in his *Iron Foundry*, paints a most realistic tone picture of a modern factory, trying to make a symphonic orchestra imitate the pounding, screeching, hammering, and grinding of gigantic machines. Eugene Zador wrote a *Technical Symphony* in which he sang the praises of humanity's new accomplishments. In his *Bridges of New York*, H. E. Heller tried to express in music the atmosphere of a city of skyscrapers. Milhaud even went so far as to compose a *Catalogue of Agricultural Machinery*. One wonders whether he wrote that with tongue in cheek or meant it as an "objective" lesson. Kurt Weill made the flight of Lindbergh into a cantata, and Edmund Nick described in a song oratorio, *Life in Our Time*, the social and moral condition of Central Europe in the epoch between the two great wars, giving voice to the misery, the unemployment, the disappointment, and the spiritual loneliness in populated cities. One of its songs—the words are by Erich Kästner, who knows how to paint our time in verses as bitter as they are authentic—expresses the emotional mood of a whole generation: "We'd have to be sixteen again and clean forget what since befell . . ."

Most of what was composed in the years between the two World

Wars has fallen into oblivion with startling rapidity. Slogans were coined, were defended vigorously, only to disappear without leaving a trace. These slogans were of a thoroughly international character. Modern composers in Berlin and New York, in London and in Rome, wrote in exactly the same style, once they had adopted the same slogan. How easy it would be again to draw a parallel between political and social development on the one hand, and artistic development on the other!

I have long hesitated to use the word "modern" in connection with music. It means nothing at all in itself, for almost every music was modern at some moment or other. But there is no other word descriptive of all the different and frequently conflicting tendencies of our time. Let us begin our discussion of this modern music with Igor Stravinsky (1882-   ) [Pl. 189, Ill. 140], a Russian by birth, who began by following in the footsteps of Rimsky-Korsakov and Scriabin and then, after he had settled in the United States, became a true musical cosmopolite. His artistic development was strange and followed many a winding turn. His personality is a mixture of elemental inspiration and mathematical calculation. He himself said that he constructed a musical work as an engineer built a bridge. From his very youth, he was a sworn enemy of romanticism. None of Wagner's adversaries was more violent than he. Even in his earliest productive period, he fought against romantic influence without, however, being able to rid himself of it completely, Creatively, it was his most potent period. He outdid in elementary force and energetic fury anything ever written before. In his *Sacre du printemps* primordial worlds rage, the earth is cleaved by volcanoes, primitive men perform bloodily-sacrificial ritual dances. The work is distinguished by rhythms of shattering force, by daring harmonics which are fascinating and breath-taking. Though he no longer used Russian melodies, as he had in his preceding ballet *Petrouchka*, the work's mystical kinship to earth and nature still places it in the Slav sphere of production. The same period—it com-

140. Igor Stravinsky. Drawing by Picasso, Kunstblatt.

prised the years before and during the First World War—was responsible for the colorful and brilliant ballet *L'oiseau de feu*. To understand the three works mentioned so far one has to link them to motion, to elements of dynamics and the dance.

Stravinsky's second period comprised the years 1917 and 1918. He was searching for new land in another direction, as was pointed out in the chapter dealing with opera. He wrote *Les Noces* and *L'histoire du soldat*, which seemed to contradict everything he had written before. The inward bonds that tied him to his fatherland still existed. However, they were revealed by polished arguments rather than by musical turns. Stravinsky, who from his early days had felt at home in the great western metropolises—first in Paris, and then in New York—became increasingly emancipated from Russia, humanly as well as artistically. His music grew more and more cosmopolitan, and at the same time his retrospective striving became more pronounced. He wished to reanimate musical forms of the past, forms which had not been tainted by the poison of romanticism. He published a *Symphony for Wind Instruments* (1920), an *Octet* for the same orchestral choir (1923), a *Piano Concerto* (1924), and a *Violin Concerto* (1931). Every one of these pieces represented "absolute'" music and was emphatically anti-programatic. And that was ten years or more after his immensely picturesque and descriptive ballet compositions! Then followed an important work, *Symphony of Psalms*, which, in a certain sense, meant a turning back. And in 1933, he once more wrote a ballet with chorus and narration, *Persephone*, and a pure ballet.

Stravinsky's powerful influence on contemporary music is undeniable. He also published a number of essays revealing interesting viewpoints. And most of them were directed against Wagner, half a century after his death!

Arnold Schönberg (1874-   ) is another pioneer of contemporary music. A Viennese by birth, he started out as a convinced Wagnerite. Among his earliest compositions were *Verklärte Nacht* (Transfigured Night), a nobly-sounding work for string orchestra based on an inspired poem by Richard Dehmel, and *Pelleas und Melisande*, written at about the same time as the *Pelléas* of Debussy, and yet so wholly different from it. There followed the gigantic edifice of his *Gurrelieder* for solo voices, chorus, and orchestra, a work of mighty dimensions, profound thought, and daring harmonics, although it was still "tonal." Written in 1911 and spiritually somehow related to Mahler's monumental compositions, it would seem to be the last port touched by Schönberg before he set out on the shoreless sea of tonal revolutions. To furnish a practical foundation for his new-style compositions, he wrote an interesting book on harmony, which became the gospel of his disciples. A new "Twelve-Tone Theory," based on a chromatic scale of equidistant semitones, replaced the former laws of composition. It was an outright denial of the diatonic—key—system, and led him to abolish also our general systems of harmonics and melodics. Schönberg's system may have its points as a mathematical formula, but musically it has rarely been able to produce anything but purely intellectual creations. This music is frequently called "atonal," a term as familiar today as it is misleading. Schönberg himself repudiated it, preferring the word "pantonality." Although the influence exerted by Stravinsky was exceptionally strong, he was not the founder of a "school." Schönberg certainly was. The number of his pupils is large, and their importance considerable. Schönberg's didactic activity, in the New World, for the past years, as well as in the Old, has always occupied a prominent place in his highly intellectual existence. That it did not make him neglect his compositions is proved by a number of works, among which is the moving tone poem, written in 1947, *A Survivor from Warsaw*, for a narrator, male chorus, and chamber orchestra.

The musical reformers of our time were not satisfied to stop at Schönberg's revolutionary teachings, fundamental though they were. They even dared to put their finger on our system of the half-tone and of the tempered pitch. Alois Haba (1893-   ), a Czech, attempted to introduce quarter-tones. He constructed a piano on which the new tone progression could be demonstrated. He succeeded, at any rate, in being made the center of animated discussions for a number of years [Pl. 192]. A Mexican, Julian Carillo, went even farther. He set out to eliminate all the impurities of the tempered system by still further subdivisions. It may be remarked in passing that these impurities actually exist, but that they have become so familiar to the normal occidental ear that any change is considered "false" though it may in fact be a rectification. Carillo declared in his writings that all harmonic and melodic possibilities had been exhausted within the existing musical systems, so that he was justified in introducing quarter-, eighth-, sixteenth-, thirty-second-, sixty-fourth-, and one-hundred-and-twenty-eighth-tones. Today, his is but a voice in the wilderness. In decades or centuries to come, he and his kind may, for

all we know, be called the first heralds of the then prevailing musical
laws. For, after all, our tempered musical system of the twelve equal
half-tones, too, was at one time definitely established by Bach and will
likely come to its end at some future time.

A third leading spirit in contemporary music—a man of a caliber entirely different from that of Stravinsky and Schönberg—is the German
Paul Hindemith (1895-   ) [Pl. 185]. Although his early efforts were
dominated by Brahms and Reger, he, too, felt the imperative need
for fundamental innovations. His restless spirit went exploring in every
conceivable direction. He was not a theorist like Schönberg, not a con-
structor like the Stravinsky of later years, but a man who might best be
described as a "maker of music." So it need not surprise us to learn that
Hindemith, at least temporarily, espoused the cause of "community
music" and of "sing-movements," endeavors having for their object a revival of folk singing and of lay music. In Germany, Austria, England,
and Switzerland, vigorous efforts are being made to bring music back to
the people. Let us, in this connection, and before touching upon Hindemith's much more ambitious works, mention his seemingly "insignificant"
children's play, *We are Building a City*, which cleverly points the way
to modern musical education.

Hindemith is the typical representative of contemporary music's
"storm and stress" period. He mocks at rules, ridicules tradition, and
shakes off the fetters of convention whenever he wants to pursue a new
way. He is attracted by the most contrasting subjects. At one time it
is everday life, the noise and bustle of the metropolis, haste and restlessness, at another mysterious romanticism, and at a third the loftiness of
the Gothic style, unworldly and striving heavenward. To give an idea
of the interesting scope of his versatility, here are some of his compositions: the sketch *There and Back*, in whose second part the music is
simply reversed, proceeding from the end to the beginning, like a film
rewound; the operatic persiflage, *News of the Day;* the expressionist
opera, *Murder, Woman's Hope*, to a text by the poet and painter Oskar
Kokoschka; the puppet ballet, *The Nush-Nushy;* the instrumental piece
For Directional Use; Plon's Day of Music, which belongs in the above-
mentioned category of community music; the mature and beautiful oratorio *The Unceasing* (1931) to a text by Gottfried Benn; the turbulent early piano pieces prefaced by the introductory remark that it is im-
material whether a certain note be struck by the fourth or sixth finger; the

viola sonata whose last movement is superscribed: "Raging tempo. Impetuous. Beauty of tone a secondary consideration." But there is also *The Life of Mary*, to Rilke's wonderful verses, and again beauty of sound is very much the main point. Hindemith is one of the most fascinating personalities of the twentieth century, although he may be quite a headache to future historians.

Hindemith's most mature work, *Mathis, der Maler*, was discussed before. It seems incredible that it was written by the same man who had gone through so many experimental and contrasting stages. And yet, if we listen carefully to this magnificent work we will find, masterfully molded into one great idea, the most varied experiences of a musician's stormy life.

In Paris of the post-War days, a group of musicians united to form "The Six," an allusion to the "Five" of Russian music. In this instance, there were five Frenchmen and one Swiss: Darius Milhaud (1892-   ), Louis Durey (1888-   ), Georges Auric (1899-   ), François Poulenc (1899-   ), Germaine Tailleferre (1892-   ), and Arthur Honegger (1892-   ). The pillars of the group were the first and the last of these. Milhaud, whose operas were mentioned before, lived for several years in Brazil whose colorfulness and exotic music fascinated him. Brazilian themes appear in some of his works, and one of them, *Saudades do Brasil* (meaning "Homesickness for Brazil,") is built entirely on the interesting folklore of that country.

Among the younger generation of French composers are the clever Jacques Ibert and the considerably more profound Olivier Messiaen.

A discussion of Honegger naturally leads to Switzerland's musical activities. Here we are faced with a many-sided and exceedingly vivid panorama, influenced not only by the country's triple linguism—which actually means a triple temperament—but also, and even more so, by the leading political role played by this small and centrally located federation, left spiritually and materially untouched by world catastrophes. Swiss musical activity, which in the last century produced such robust musical figures as Hans Georg Nägeli (1773-1836), Hans Huber, and Karl Attenhofer, all of whom, to be sure, were able to attain no more than local fame, has since flourished considerably and is today among the most important in Europe.

Arthur Honegger and Othmar Schoeck are the country's most prominent musical representatives. Honegger [Pl. 186] was born in Le

Havre, in 1892, of Swiss parents. Turning his gaze westward at an early age, he studied with Vincent d'Indy and finally settled in Paris. Among his works already discussed are *Le roi David*, which started his meteoric rise to world fame, his equally important stage work, *Jeanne d'Arc au bûcher* [Pl. 188], his symphonic poem *Pacific 231*, and his unique *Rugby*. He is one of the most versatile of the modern composers. The works so far enumerated would suffice to prove that: from football to the Maid of Orleans! But Honegger's inward conviction enabled him to shape forcefully and convincingly everything he wrote. He composed incidental music to a most startling variety of subjects, ballets and operettas, puppet shows, operas, oratorios, festival plays, and what not. Not everything was of equal value, but never was his competence in doubt. In addition, he wrote songs, choral works (a prominent example: *Cris du Monde*), orchestral music, chamber and piano pieces, and compositions for the organ. And if all that were not enough, he also composed a good deal of radio and film music, opening a new field of musical endeavor to his generation.

Othmar Schoeck [Pl. 172] was cast in an entirely different mold. Born in Brunnen, in 1886, he was the faithful guardian and true representative of romantic traditions, expressing himself most forcefully and clearly where he joined his music to the wonderful poetic writings of Eichendorff, Heine, Lenau, Michelangelo, Dante, Goethe, and his great compatriot Gottfried Keller, and made it soar into heights where the two sister arts were once more as one. This enumeration of great authors reminds us of all great romantic Lieder composers, from Schubert to Schumann to Brahms to Wolf. In this realm Schoeck was most at home, and here he succeeded in creating imperishable works.

Another of the large number of gifted contemporary Swiss composers is Willy Burkhard (1900-   ). His musical manner is strangely harsh and austere, suggesting at times an attempt to form a bridge between medieval polyphony and the mechanical rhythms of our day. *The Face of Isaiah* is the name of one of his important oratorios revealing this style, while in *The Year*—a modern counterpart to Haydn's *Seasons*—he showed that he could strike softer tones, too, as, for instance, in the hauntingly beautiful *Summerday* movement. His compositions already comprise a large number of pieces for orchestra, chorus, and chamber music.

There are Paul Muller, who harks back to the grandiose loftiness of

Palestrina; Walter Geiser, who has his beginnings in Busoni and Reger; Conrad Beck, a strict contrapuntist; Robert Oboussier, a modern symphonist with a feeling for the classic form; Robert Blum, whose exceptional versatility takes in the entire gamut from the symphony to the film, from opera to the mystery play, from ballet to chamber music. In addition, there are the gifted Franz Tischenhauser and the more mature Fritz Brun, who follows in the footsteps of Brahms; Volkmar Andreae, whose works are remarkable for the Straussesque luxuriance of their sound; Emil Frey, who mainly devotes his gifts to masterfully treated piano pieces; and Karl Henrich David, remarkable for the seriousness of his style.

French Switzerland has also produced a considerable number of gifted composers. Frank Martin (1890-   ) may be said to top the list. He goes his own way in the choice of subjects and in style, as shown in *Le Vin Herbé*, after the old legend of Tristan and Isolde, written for twelve solo voices, seven string instruments, and piano. Not to be omitted is the name of Emile Jaques-Dalcroze (1865-   ) [Ill. 141], the originator of a widely known rhythmic-gymnastic method. Countless schools have adopted his idea. Mindful of the Old Hellenic ideal, Dalcroze aims at the fusion of music and physical grace and at the use of rhythm, that primordial secret of life, for the attainment of a high spiritual level. Let us mention also Otto Barblan, Gustav Doret, the profound Roger Vuataz (his *Abraham* is especially

141. Jaques-Dalcroze.
Caricature by Salzmann.

interesting), André François Morescotti, whose beautiful Savoyard melodies and other compositions give evidence of exceptional talent, and Pierre Wissmer, the composer of an opera, of ballets, several concertos, and orchestral works.

Also of Swiss descent is Ernest Bloch (1880-   ), who is today considered the representative composer of Jewish national music. Religious melodies which for thousands of years had lain dormant in the people's consciousness have been lifted by him to the rank of works of art. *Schelomo, Israel, Baal Shem*, and others of his compositions indicate the fact that the Jews, as a people, have joined the concert of nations. Bloch has also dedicated one beautiful work to the land of his origin, *Helvetia*, and another to the land of his adoption, *American Symphony*.

Let us try in the following to continue our review of contemporary European musical activities. It is no easy undertaking. Just or unjustly, history has already passed judgment on the past. All a modern observer can do now and then, and usually without success, is to try to influence established opinion. Only time will be able either to confirm or overthrow present evaluations. *Which of the contemporary musicians, from a truly bewildering number, are to be mentioned?* What considerations are to guide the choice? Let us assume for a moment that this book had appeared in the year 1825. If it contained but the names of "recognized" composers, or of those who had drawn attention to themselves by works of some magnitude, one name would surely be missing: that of Schubert. And at that, he had already written almost everything that today places him among the greatest of them all. Or let us assume that the book had appeared in 1875. It is most probable that the name of Anton Bruckner would not appear. For although he was then past fifty, he was not, as viewed by his contemporaries, among the day's leading musicians. It would contain the names of many composers who are completely forgotten today. These considerations make it understandable why in this chapter, and in others dealing with contemporary music, so many names have been mentioned. Many of those mentioned will sink into oblivion. But if we have succeeded in drawing forth one who by future recorders of musical happenings will be considered important in the confused panorama of the twentieth century, we shall be satisfied.

There are other problems, too, confronting the writer of a chapter on modern music. How should such a chapter be arranged? According to countries? The work of some present-day composers would surely justify the adoption of such a system. Men like Bartók, Falla, and Vaughan Williams, to mention but three of the most important, are strongly influenced by folk music and by the atmosphere of their home country. Others, again, ought rather to be grouped according to style—if that were feasible. That would make it necessary to use a great many descriptive terms, such as cubism, surrealism, linear music, and expressionism. How to explain them clearly when their lines of demarcation are so vague? So it may be best, after all, to adhere to a country-wise discussion, though one important reservation ought to be noted: never in the world's history has the number of artists living as emigrants or in exile been so large as in our century. And the "Away-from-Europe!" trend is becoming more pronounced all the time, due to the unsettled conditions in the Old Continent. Artists need freedom, the chance for unfoldment, hope in the future. A list of those living in voluntary or involuntary banishment would reveal the fact that it included a large percentage of all contemporary artists. Stravinsky, Grechaninov, Milhaud, Schönberg, Hindemith, and Krenek share, at least temporarily, a fate which, even if accompanied by success, is always somehow tragic. Rachmaninoff, Bartók, and Manuel de Falla died on foreign soil. And these are but ten names out of hundreds, or thousands.

But now, after all these digressions, let us begin.

Twentieth-Century Hungary ranks high in musical creation. Let us name first three of the great: Béla Bartók (1881-1945) [Ill. 142], Zoltan Kodály (1882-   ) and Ernst von Dohnányi (1887-   ). Bartók started as a late-romanticist, as shown by his symphonic poem *Kossuth*, a patriotic composition which was a great success. At the same time, he and Kodály were revitalizing Hungarian folk music, which had lost its vigor by a conventional imitation of ornate gipsy style. Bartók is the author of the definitive book on the subject. His *Fourteen Bagatelles* (1908) for piano marked a turning point in his development, and he became the leading personage in Hungarian music with the theater works already discussed. Bartók's works, marked by a rhythmic vigor, include three piano concertos, one violin concerto, *Music for Stringed Instruments, Timpani, and Celesta*, a dance suite for orchestra, a sonata for two pianos and percussion instruments, and several quartets. In 1943, after he had taken up residence in the United States, he published a concerto for orchestra. His work remains a strange mixture of national and international musical trends, often described as the "leftist" branch of Hungarian music, as contrasted with that of Dohnányi. (It is interesting to note that Hans Koessler, a German musician, was the teacher of all three of these leading Hungarian masters.)

Kodály, after working mostly at chamber music, began to collaborate with Bartók on his revision of Hungarian folk music. His orchestral work *Summer Evening*, and sonata for cello and piano, comprised all his well-known pre-war output. By 1924, two further string quartets had made Kodály famous, and he was commissioned to write, for the 50th anniversary of the twin city of Budapest, the *Psalmus Hungaricus*. This choral work instantly made its mark in the musical world. There followed *Háry János* and *The Spinning Room*, mentioned previously; a *Ballet Suite;* and orchestral compositions.

Ernst von Dohnányi, first known throughout Europe as a piano virtuoso, became director of the Budapest Conservatory and of the Hungarian radio. As a composer, he is famous for piano works, such as the four *Rhapsodies;* chamber music; two symphonies including his prize *Symphony in F;* concertos for the piano and the violin; and *The Tower of Voivod*, an opera with a strong nationalistic spirit.

Jenö Hubay (1858-1937) is noted both for his pedagogical and creative accomplishments. Eugene Zador and Tibor Harsanyi are perhaps the most prominent of the younger generation of composers.

Further contemporary Hungarian composers: Laszlo Laytha (1891-   ), Paul Kadosa (1903-   ), Janos Viski (1906-   ), Sandor Veress (1907-   ), Paul Jardanyi (1920-   ), Georg Kosa (1897-   ), and Andreas Szervanszky (1911-   ).

Modern Spanish music, whose grand master, Manuel de Falla, we have met, has a large number of important representatives who, since the civil war, have been living dispersed over many countries. Foremost mention is due the brothers Halffter, Ernesto (1905-   ) and Rodolfo (1900-   ), both pupils of de Falla, and Joaquín Turina, the composer of a number of striking works, who died in 1949.

Further contemporary Spanish composers: Joaquín Nin (1883-   ), Jaime Pahissa (1880-   ), Adolfo Salazar (1890-   ), who must be considered the most eminent Spanish-language musicologist, Salvador Bacarisse (1898-   ), Federico Mompou (1893-   ), Roberto Gerhard (1896-   ), Enrique Fernández Arbós, for many years the highly esteemed leader of the symphonic orchestra of Madrid, Julián Bautista, Conrado del Campo, Oscar Esplá, Jesús Guridi, Juan Manen, Fernando J. Obradors, Bartolomé Perez Casas, conductor of the Madrid Philharmonic Orchestra, Gustavo Pittaluga, Joaquín Rodrigo, José Maria Usandizago, Rogelio Villar, and Federico Longas.

The majority of the contemporary Italian operatic composers were mentioned in the chapter on opera, a medium to which they felt attracted by tradition. Two other outstanding composers are G. Francesco Malipiero (1882-   ) and Mario Castelnuovo-Tedesco (1895-   ). Malipiero, during the early years of the century destroyed his first works—two operas, as well as several symphonies and concertos—and began to compose in virtually every form, using a new type of music which he has made his own. There are four symphonies and many large works for full orchestra including three sets of *Impressions*, which are outstanding instrumental tone poems. Composition for solo music and orchestra include: *Concerti*, a series of short movements which give the various symphonic instruments full play, in turn; and concertos for the Violin, the Violoncello, and the Piano; chamber music; string quartets; and five choral works. Of these latter, *Princess Eulalia* is a tissue of charming old Italian songs; a Requiem Mass for the late Gabriele d'Annunzio; and three religious oratorios. Several sets of songs, and an immense edition of Monteverdi round out the musical compositions (except for the operas), but Malipiero is known as well for books of music.

Castelnuovo-Tedesco is an exponent of neo-romantic program music, particularly in its shorter forms. He has produced other varieties of composition (including opera), however. Among these are: the *Italian Concerto* for violin and orchestra; a *Concerto* for piano and orchestra; the *Variazioni sinfoniche* for violin and orchestra; sonatas for violin and piano, and for cello; and a *Concertino* for harp and seven instruments. There are several "Shakespeare" overtures, also.

Ildebrando Pizzetti has written a *Concerto dell'estate* and a cello concerto. Alfredo Casella is the composer of several symphonies, the rhapsody *Italia, May Night*, concertos, and chamber music, to which must be added his latest work, the grandly conceived *Missa Solemnis Pro Pace*.

Further contemporary Italian composers: Alceo Toni, Riccardo Pick-Mangiagalli, Leone Sinigaglia, Victor de Sabata, Francesco Santoliquido, Domenico Alaleona, Giorgio Federico Ghedini, Vittorio Rieti, Renzo Biancho, Go"redo Petrassi (*Don Quijote*), Antonio Pedrotti (*La collina*, a dramatic madrigal), and Lorenzo Perosi, the author of fine ecclesiastical compositions and oratorios.

As we have already noted, the music of England attained new and magnificent heights in the twentieth century. The sources of musical vitality have always been complex and diversified, and one may rarely predict what new impulse will give rise to new musical life. Certainly those who regard the English people as a "cold" audience are in great error regarding their musical tastes. An institution like the Promenade Concerts, the famous "Proms," would hardly be possible in another country. They were established in 1895 by Sir Henry Wood, a man to whom England's music owes a great deal. He conducted these concerts for half a century, broadened musical culture in England and discovered much new talent. Shortly before his death in his fiftieth season, the hall in which his triumphs had been celebrated before many thousands of people, was demolished. Queen's Hall was a victim of a German bomb. But the institution did not die, and in Royal Albert Hall the "Proms" were performed before larger audiences than ever.

The dark days of the second World War will rank among England's greatest in more ways than one: for music achieved glorious heights even in the midst of the "blood, sweat and tears" of the conflict. Everywhere in England, despite prodigious difficulties, music flourished. Concerts and rehearsals had to be interrupted when the sirens sounded. The thunder of destruction tried desperately to drown out the voice of music—but with no result. In one of the most impressive concerts of the war period, held in London's National Gallery under the auspices of Myra Hess, a German bomb fell and did not explode. The quartet on the stage did not hesitate for a second or interrupt a single measure. The audience did not stir from its seats.

Up and down the land music sounded bravely. In Manchester the famous Hallé Orchestra gave no fewer than 260 concerts in 1944, despite the fact that its Free Trade Hall suffered the same fate as London's Queen's Hall. The Liverpool Philharmonic, the Scottish Orchestra of Glasgow, the Birmingham Orchestra, to name only the greatest, offered music to the provincial cities. In London itself there were the London Philharmonic Orchestra, the London Symphony Orchestra and the National Symphony Orchestra as well as the Orchestra of the British Broadcasting Corporation.

Today in England there is not a child who does not know the meaning of the three letters, BBC, for the British Broadcasting Corporation is a great deal more than a radio station. It has realized the full value of the radio, its cultural mission and its educational duty, and the role of the BBC in the life of English music cannot be overemphasized. It has an effect as well beyond the borders of its own country.

In a moral sense the Music Department of the British Council has served equally with the BBC in spreading English music over the entire world. More than that, not a few of the musical works which we shall discuss as characteristic of the spirit of the new England originated as a result of inspiration or commissions by the British Council.

Those who travel in the English countryside and discover the people's love of music in the most remote sections, and the number of choirs there are everywhere, can understand the classic calibre of the people's choirs. School music and the playing of music by the young is given precedence in the broadest sense. How these young girls and boys sing in four and more parts from sight, both old and new music! With what understanding do they solve the problems of harmony and counterpoint because they have been taught to feel music, not merely to learn it!

Even the Opera, for a long time the step-child of English music, is having a rebirth today. The noble tradition of Covent Garden, an international opera house with guest stars, has been sustained. That institution naturally has done little exploring in experimental territory. But Sadler's Wells, a national Opera which presents performances in English and in part with young English actors, has become the forerunner of many operatic and experimental theaters throughout the country.

Finally we come to the creators of music in present-day England. Nineteen-thirty-four was a tragic year for English music. In that year the British lost not only Elgar and Delius, but the seventy-year-old Gustav Holst (1874-1934), one of the most gifted composers of his time. Most eminent of his great symphonic works is *Die Planeten* (The Planets), his oratorio *Hymn to Jesus* and *St. Paul's Suite*, originally written for a school orchestra.

The guiding spirit in English music is still Ralph Vaughan Williams (1872-   ), whose work is redolent with folk flavor. Up to now he has produced six symphonies, four operas, two ballets. He also composed a concerto for oboes, chamber music, film music and the *Thanksgiving for Victory* for speaking voice, choir and orchestra, written on May 8, 1945, the day of victory in Europe.

John Ireland (1879-   ) too belongs to the older generation. He composes beautiful chamber music and piano works. Well-known are his piano concertos and his choral work, *These Things Shall Be*. At the outbreak of the war Ireland was living in the Channel Islands and he narrowly escaped living under German occupation. In London he then finished his piano work *Sarnia, an Island Sequence*. (Sarnia was the old Roman name for Guernsey, "his" islands.)

Arnold Bax, born in 1883, still plays an important role. His seven symphonies, his tone poems, chorales, concertos and chamber music are performed often. During the war he composed a work on the heroic de-

142. Cubistic portrait of Béla Bartók.

fense of the island of Malta and an *Ode to Russia*. 1891 is the birth year of Arthur Bliss, who wrote two ballets, a march, *The Phoenix*, to honor France, chamber and film music, *Seven American Poems*, in honor of the United States, where he lived until 1941. In 1883 came Eugene Goossens, who is not only an internationally famous conductor but also a distinguished composer.

An unusually interesting generation was born around the turn of the century. To it belong a group of England's best composers, among them Benjamin Britten (1913-) and William Walton (1902-), both of international stature. Britten was first known for his *Quartet for Oboe and Strings* which was performed at the Florence session of the International Society for Contemporary Music. He was then 21 years old. Then fol-

143. Ralph Vaughan Williams.

lowed *Variations on a Theme of Frank Bridge*, who was his teacher, and since then a great variety of work. His greatest success, however, was the opera *Peter Grimes* about which we have had occasion to speak elsewhere.

Walton's most important works are his viola concerto and his violin concerto, which Jascha Heifetz played for the first time in 1939; a symphony; the suite *Façade;* the overture *Portsmouth Point* and *Scapino;* film music, music for children; the profound oratorio *Belshazzar's Feast* and *The First of the Few*, which was inspired by the war.

Edmund Rubbra (1901-) has already finished four symphonies, a *Sinfonie Concertante*, a great Mass for Canterbury Cathedral, a work entitled *Soliloquy* for solo cello and small orchestra, and lovely chamber music. E. J. Moeran, born in 1894, has published a violin concerto, a rhapsody for piano and orchestra, a cello concerto and other interesting compositions.

Without question the most gifted British composer is Michael Tippett (1905-), if only for his cantata *A Child of our Time*, which deals with the murder of a member of the Germany Embassy in Paris by a

340.

young Jewish emigrant. Tippett is especially powerful portraying the terror in concentration camps and synagogues. That composition will live at least as a document of our times.

In the same year as Tippett, Alan Rawsthorne was born. He won recognition with *Theme and Variations* for two violins, and with his *Symphonic Studies* for orchestra. He proved himself a remarkable composer with his piano concerto and violin concerto, the original manuscript of which was destroyed by German bombs. Constant Lambert was also born in 1905, a fanciful composer and the author of a brilliant book on modern music, *Music Ho!* Lennox Berkeley (1903-) belongs in the first rank of the new generation; he has written an oratorio, stage music, music for films, and chamber music. Patrick Hadley's (1899-) most important work is *The Hills* for chorus, orchestra and eight soloists. Among women composers—and women were known earlier as English composers—the names of Elisabeth Lutyens and Elizabeth Maconchy stand out with a great range of work. Many others should be mentioned as contributors to England's wealth of creative music. We will limit ourselves to the names of Howard Ferguson, Anthony Hopkins, Gerald Finzi, Gordon Jacob, Alan Bush and Roger Quilter.

Scandinavian music, whose great men, Grieg and Sibelius, were accorded places of honor in this book, is represented today by quite a number of composers: Kurt Atterberg (1887-), Hugo Alfven, Bror Beckman, Natanael Berg, Ture Rangström (died 1947), Oscar Lindberg, Edwin Kallstenius, Hilding Rosenberg, Gösta Nystroem (symphonic overture *1945*)—of Sweden; Hjalmer Bergström, Johan Halvorsen, Monrad Johannsen, Sverre Jordan, Gerhard Schjelderup—of Norway; Carl Nielsen (1865-1931), Paul Klenau (1883-1947), August Enna, Asger Hamerik—of Denmark; Armas Launis, (opera *Kullervo*) and Oskar Merikanto—of Finland.

Polish contemporary music has a worthy representative in the well-known figure of the great pianist and patriot Ignace Paderewski (1860-1941), whose *Minuet* has become tremendously popular. To Paderewski fell the honor of being made the first head of the new Polish state after World War I. He died in America while his fatherland was again invaded and occupied.

Among the modern composers of Slav and Balkan countries are the following: Mieczyslav Karlovicz, Joseph Brzezinski (a late-romanticist of fine stamp), Gregor Fitelberg, Paul Kletzki, and Karol Rathaus—of Poland; Jossip Slavenski—of Yugoslavia; Georges Enesco—of Rumania; Pantscho Vladigeroff, the composer of striking piano concertos—of Bulgaria.

Czechoslovakia produced—before and after the war—a large number of composers. Among the pre-War ones were Karel B. Jirak, the efficient head of the Prague Broadcasting Station, Joseph Suk, and Bohuslav Martinu (1890-). Martinu, besides his operas and ballets, wrote chamber music for strings and piano; concertos for the violin and the piano; and the *Field Mass* for male voices, wind instruments, and percussion. Among the composers of recent years are Eugene Suchon (*Psalm of the Lower Carpathian Land*), the aging Viteslav Novak (choral *Autumn Symphony*), and Rudolf Karel, whose fairy-tale opera *The Three Hairs of the All-Knowing Grandfather* was written under particularly tragic circumstances, while he was a prisoner in the concentration camp of Theresienstadt. He died there, but not until he had been able to smuggle out the score of his work, scribbled on pieces of paper Another work closely connected with political events was Vycpalek's *Czech Requiem.*

Holland and Belgium, rather sterile in musical production for centuries, may now point to a number of fine modern musicians: Jan Brandts-Buys, Johan Wagenaar, Daniel Runemann, Henk Bading, Michel Brusselmans, Guillaume Lekeu, Hans Osiek (concerto for piano and orchestra), Edgar Tinel (*Ouverture pour une Sainte Catherine*), Norbert Rosso (*Suite Agreste*), Raymond Chevreuille (four symphonies).

Portugal, too, fell into a long eclipse after the flowery days of the troubadours. Among the country's leading contemporary composers are Freitas Branco (1890-   ), the head of the Symphonic Orchestra of Lisbon, Vianna da Motta, and Oscar da Silva.

Very little is known about Russian music during the first twenty-five years of the Soviet regime. This is all the more regrettable since it would be of the greatest interest to be able to judge whether the political and social changes have already been productive of the inevitable change in style, and what this changed style represents. At any rate, from what we know, musical life in present-day Russia is quite brisk and the support given by the state to all artistic endeavors generous.

Stravinsky was discussed in detail before. He is today a cosmopolite rather than a Russian. Next to him, the most gifted man of the generation that grew up before the great change came seems to be Sergei Prokofiev (1891). It was pointed outthat he scored a great operatic success with his *Love of the Three Oranges.* After having lived in North America and in France, he returned to Russia in the middle Thirties and there wrote an *Overture on Russian Themes*, the music for a *Pique Dame* film, based on Pushkin's tale, and that most enchanting juvenile piece, *Peter and the Wolf.* He also wrote *Songs of our Time* (op. 77), the cantatas *Alexander Nevsky* (for an Eisenstein film) and *Salute to Stalin*, the operas *Simeon Kotko* and *War and Peace* (after Tolstoy), *Romeo and Juliet*, and a violin concerto in G minor. Among his important works written while he still lived in exile are five most brilliantly conceived piano concertos, two violin concertos, a cello concerto, and four symphonies, the best known of the latter being the *Classical Symphony.*

Less known outside of their own country are the works of Nikolai Tcherepnin (1873-   ), Nikolai Medtner (1879-   ), and Nikolai Miaskovsky (1881-   ), the latter having written more than twenty-five symphonies. Of Sergei Taneyev's work, too, (1865-1915) little has been preserved. Alexander Mossolov (1900-   ) is already part of the New Russia. In addition to the realistic study, *Iron Foundry*, mentioned before, and other similar pieces, such as *Dnieprostroi*, he is known to have written the music for a number of sound films. Among the younger generation of Soviet Russian composers one particularly has become internationally known: Dmitri Shostakovitch (1906-   ). His many compositions include, above all, symphonies, and one of them, the seventh, has been played all over the world. It is known by the name *Leningrad Symphony* because it was written during the heroic defense of the besieged city. It is a glorious profession of faith in Russia and its final victory is musically interesting, gripping in places, beautiful in others, although it has nothing new to say and can therefore not be considered representative of a change in style. Besides his two abortive operas, discussed earlier, Shostakovitch wrote two ballets, *The Age of Gold* and *Bolt*, satirical in style, but nationalistic in content. He has produced much piano work, chamber music, and several scores for Soviet films. Finally, in most recent times, an Armenian has attracted attention to himself. He is Aram Khatchaturian (1903-   ), a creative musician of striking individuality, whose ballet suite *Gayne* and piano concerto reveal him to be a radical composer representing a strange synthesis of linear and savagely earthy idioms. He also wrote a symphony, a *Poem for Stalin*, violin and piano concertos, and ballets.

The following are the names and the principal works of some of the more prominent modern Russian composers. Leo Knipper: *Revolutionary Episodes, Northwind, Lyric Suite, Towns and Years,* symphonies, of which one is entitled *The Far East,* another *Song of the Komsomolzes,* and an opera, called *The Rising Sun.* Vissarion Shebalin: *Moscow,* a cantata celebrating the 800th anniversary of that city; symphonies, of which one is entitled *Lenin.* Dimitri Kabalevsky: *The Master of Clamecy,* an opera based on Romain Rolland's *Colas Breugnon; Battle Song* for chorus and orchestra; children's songs; *Requiem for Lenin;* symphonies; film music; ballets. Ivan Dcerzhinsky: the opera *On the Quiet Don* and several other operas.

The music of Central Europe—of Germany and Austria, from the First World War to the cataclysmic collapse of the year 1945, is symptomatic of the era's spirit of restlessness and discord.

There were the composers "of the day." The term is not meant to suggest that their influence was ephemeral. It rather indicates that they stood in the midst of the day's events, wanted to stand there or had to stand there, because they must capture the sounds of a fermenting and surging time. There was Weill, the writer of catchy songs to words of brutal timeliness, the man who made the workman, the shopgirl, the criminal, and the prostitute sing, each according to his or her individuality, and who fashioned these songs into stage plays. Perhaps he, too, fulfilled some artistic mission by thus holding up a mirror to the world. There was Hans Eissler, who compressed the thudding steps of columns of revolutionary workmen into stirring scraps of melodies and irresistible rhythms. And there was Krenek, who wrote an opera which raised a storm of controversies: jazz versus "old music," America versus Europe.

The growing restlessness of the time—soon the drift toward a still more horrible war and collapse was to become apparent!—caused ideas upon ideas to be cast into the witches' cauldron of an unchained artistic life, but none of these ideas could reach fruition. Young men of talent were unable to unfold. They were plunged into doubt, bitterness, temptation, theoretical experimentation, and into struggles from which even the victors did not emerge with any sense of direction. Material want increased, political chaos grew, while moral and ethical values became more illusory from day to day. Future historians will most likely consider highly tragic the artist's position during this period of the twentieth century.

Despite this, musical life in Central Europe in the time between the two World Wars was extremely active. Perhaps more music was produced than ever before. Germany proved remarkably receptive to international influences, and Berlin became temporarily the world center of the most radically modern music, the city of world premieres, the meeting point of the most interesting representatives of modern art. Vienna, on the other hand, was content to play a more conservative part, still clinging to romanticism and impressionism. Her "atonal" musicians, if they wanted to get a hearing, had to go to Berlin. But even there, they were actually heard only by the comparatively small group of their partisans, by that group of modern musicians who, without noticing it, were increasingly losing contact with the public. And each one of them would have let himself be drawn and quartered rather than subscribe to the view of Busoni, who once had declared with a sigh that he would be most happy if but a single one of his melodies were played by a street organ.

Expressionism, impressionism, naturalism, twelve-tone music, late-romanticism, neoclassicism, community music, music as a political tool, l'art pour l'art, overrefined and world-removed would-be-esthetic art, trashy melodies of the utmost banality, brain music, paper counterpoint—all this, and all at the same time—represents the music of Germany during the decades here discussed.

Whom should we mention from among the German composers? Their name is legion. They formed associations, arranged music festivals, and gave concerts. More intensively than ever before did the century foster its contemporary artists. But no amount of nurturing could bridge the gulf that separated them from the people. Let us pick out but a few of those who seemed to continue a line of development. They represented almost exclusively a moderate modern orientation, and, more than once, their compositions, or parts of them, were borne up by genuine sentiment and made a direct appeal to the heart.

Walter Braunfels (1882-   ), composer of the operas *Die Vögel* and *Don Gil von den grünen Hosen;* Paul Graener (1872-1944), who wrote *Don Juans Letztes Abenteuer* and *Hanneles Himmelfahrt;* Heinrich Kaminski (1886-   ), whose profound sense of polyphonics expressed itself in ecclesiastical works, especially in psalms; Armin Knab, who wrote expressive songs and instrumental music; Philipp Jarnach (1892-   ), who completed Busoni's *Dr. Faust* and himself wrote fine piano pieces; Werner Egk (1901-   ), the operatic composer whose *Columbus* reveals a certin affinity with Stravinsky; Carl Orff, also of the opera, whose *Carmina Burana* seems to be searching a stage style all its own; Josef Haas (1897-   ), who wrote the highly competent *Tobias Wunderlich;* Hermann Reutter (1900-   ), who displayed a remarkable gift for oratorio writing; Erwin Dressel, who made an addition to the Columbus literature by his strange work *Armer Columbus!;* Rudolf Stephan, who would today likely stand in the forefront of contemporary German musicians had not the war snuffed out his life at the age of twenty-eight (1887-1915)

Other contemporary German composers: Heinrich Tiessen, Kurt Wolfurt, Rudolf Wagner-Regény, Max Brand, Robert Heger, Bernhard Sekles, Ernst Pepping, Gerhard Maasz, Wolfgang Fortner, Harald Genzmer, Max Trapp.

Understandably, the German production during the Second World War and the following years is still difficult to survey. It seems that, especially after the catastrophe, a tendency toward contemplativeness was revealed. This is proved by the appearance of a large number of cantatas with profoundly poetic, and frequently philosophic, texts. To mention but a few: Boris Blacher's *Cantata of the German War, Romeo and Juliet,* and *Grand Inquisitor;* four cantatas by Braunfels, written while in exile; Paul Hoeffer's *Eichendorff Cantata;* Heinrich Kaminski's last work (he died in 1946), *To the Memory of a Wounded Soldier;* Otto Miehler's *Claudius Cantata;* Wolfgang Fortner's *Fragment Maria;* Hermann Reutter's *Matthias Claudius Cantata;* and Werner Egk's *Love-Nature-Death* (after Hölty) and *Temptation of St. Anthony.*

A similar tendency was manifested by other nations. Again, only a few examples are cited: Britten's *Sinfonia da Requiem,* Mario Peragallo's oratorios, Alfredo Casella's last work, *Missa Solemnis Pro Pace,* Karl Schiske's (Austria) beautiful *Of Death,* Willy Burkhard's (Switzerland) *Autumn Cantata* (after Morgenstern) and *Eternal Crashing* (after Hamsun). How intense this search for abstract music has become in recent years will be further proved by American examples.

And now for Austria. Late-romanticism still produced many fine artists. Wilhelm Kienzl (1857-1941) was one of them, and so was Max von Oberleithner, the composer of harmonious stage works, such as *Der eiserne Heiland.* The romantic tendency was noticeable especially in the realm of the Lied (Carl Lafite, Karl Prohaska, Egon Kornauth, Otto Siegl, Rudolph Kattnig, and the youthfully deceased Fritz Egon Pamer).

Vienna's most potent musical representatives since Bruckner and Mahler were Franz Schmidt (1874-1939) and Joseph Marx (1882). Schmidt was pre-eminently a symphonist. Constantly warring against ultra-modern tendencies, he created a style of his own, linked somehow to tradition and culminating in his Fourth Symphony. Let us mention once more his opera *Notre Dame* and add his *Variations on a Hussar Song*, the profound oratorio *The Book with Seven Seals*, and some excellent chamber music. Marx has his roots in impressionism. Debussy, and perhaps the early Reger, may have first influenced him. Above all and always, however, he is an Austrian thoroughbred musician, which means that he loves to indulge in beautiful sound and sensuousness. Among his scintillating and exuberant orchestral works are *A Spring Music* and *Autumn Festivals*. He also wrote a piano concerto entitled *Castelli Romani*. In the realm of chamber music, too, he knew how to express himself eloquently, especially in his string quartets, *In modo classico* and *In modo antico*. He is most convincing, perhaps, in his Lieder, some of which are beautifully expressive (*Hat dich die Liebe berührt, Marienlied, Japanisches Regenlied, Waldseligkeit, Selige Nacht, Und gestern hat er mir Rosen gebracht*).

Gustav Mahler had a loyal disciple in Alexander von Zemlinsky (1872-1942), while the Schönberg school is represented by Alban Berg and Anton von Webern. Here it may be seen how the same idea entertained by men of different temperamental qualities is apt to lead to entirely different results. Berg's eminently expressive music never fails to make a vital impression (*Wozzek, Lulu*, and the violin concerto, *To the Memory of an Angel*, dedicated to his youthfully deceased friend, Manon Gropius, and representing his swan-song), while Webern's ultra-compressed form—pieces of but a few seconds' duration—overstepped the bounds of music. Ernest Krenek may have had his roots in Schreker, but other influences, too, are alive in him, the emphasis being on the word "alive," for he is not a theorist but a musician. He has proved this most aptly in his grandiosely conceived *Travel Diary from the Austrian Alps*.

A number of new and noteworthy musicians have emerged in Austria during the past few years. There is Franz Salmhofer, the composer of the operas *Dream Lady, Ivan Tarrassenko*, and *Recruiting Song* and of a powerful *Hymn of Liberation* which, written in several parts, is descriptive of the fighting around Vienna, in 1945. Alfred Uhl tried his fine sense of sound on a number of cultural films before turning to the composition of highly impressive chamber and orchestral music.

Further contemporary Austrian composers: Karl Weigl (massive symphonies, the oratorio *World Celebration*), Hans Gál (his choral work *De Profundis*, composed in England, is exceptionally fine), Egon Lustgarten, Hans Ewald Heller, Ernst Kanitz, Walter Bricht, Frank Mittler (who wrote the gem *Folk Air* to Rilke's spirited verses), Friedrich Bloch, Erich Zeisl (a skilful manipulator of the orchestra), Ernst Ludwig Uray,

Georg Pirkmeyer, Karl Senn, Franz Burkhart, Reinhold Schmid, Egon Wellesz, Rudolf Reti, Hans Erich Apostel, Alexander von Spitzmüller, Hans Jelinek, Matthias Hauer (who arrived at a twelve-tone technique by ways different from those of Schönberg), Paul A. Pisk, Felix Petyrek, Walter Gmeindl, Wilhelm Grosz, Ernst Toch (a musician midway between Schönberg and Krenek, if such a classification be at all permissible), Theodor Berger, Friedrich Wilgans, Gottfried von Einem (whose opera *Danton's Death* was mentioned before), Alexander Jemnitz (a Hungarian by birth, but more closely linked to Austrian cultural circles), Anton Heiller (who, together with Berger, Uhl, and von Einem, is among the youngest of the younger generation). The following composers devote themselves particularly to church music, a species always highly cultivated in Austria: Johann Nepomuk David, Raimund Weissensteiner, Josef Lechthaler, Hans Daubrawa. Erich Wolfgang Korngold was discussed in detail in the chapter on opera.

Were we justified in calling this chapter *The Age of Dissonance?* Probably we were, although dissonance does not mean the same thing to all the composers here mentioned. It may even be the essential point that to many it still does mean something, while to others it has ceased to mean anything. Twelve-tone music, "linear" music, and "atonal" music, as it sometimes is called without actual justification, no longer recognize the traditional differences between consonance and dissonance, making the latter term seem out of place. Strange things are apt to happen in this "new" music. A simple C-major triad occurring in one of the "ultra-linear" works, may, for instance, suddenly be felt by the public as a disturbing discord. None of the present-day styles is without its dissonances. They are prominently used as a means of expression, or as the product of of strictly polyphonic melodics. Had not dissonance always been present? In the music of Mozart, for instance? Certainly; but it was a means, rarely used, for producing tension. However, just as events tumble over each other these days, dissonances, too, seem to be engaged in a helter-skelter race. The rhythm of their appearance, of their growth, and of their diminishing effect on the human ear and feeling is getting faster and faster, more and more frantic, as if it were rushing to some final outpost.

Let us leave aside the famous question concerning the "music of the future." It is more unanswerable today than it was in any past epoch. Two things seem obvious. First, music must turn back to the people. There must be a half-way meeting. There must be an earnest effort to lead people to an intelligent appreciation of art and music, while art and music must find themes and forms that will prove to be man's solace, support, and hope; will give him joy and faith. Art must once more be made a matter of all the people, if humanity is to progress.

Second, music which does not come from the heart of its creator, but from his brain, even if it were the cleverest brain in the world, will never be able to reach the listener's heart. In all rationalistic eras, a vast amount of art has had its source in reason. Bülow drastically expressed this thought when he said: "What ideas people get when they haven't any!" In our century, a great deal of music has been dictated by the brain. Such music may be interesting, perhaps even fruitful as a theoretical experiment, pointing the way into the future. But it cannot reach the heart, it is not music in the only true sense of the word.

·28·

America

CULTURAL epochs arise and vanish. They are born, grow, flourish, and decay. Some leave traces behind them, others mere memories, still others, perhaps, nothing at all. There arises the fearful question: Can a cultural epoch indeed disappear without a sign? Can human accomplishment be obliterated? The very posing of the question indicates that the questioner himself does not think so; that he assumes the existence of a *Weltgeist*—an eternal world spirit—which humanity is unconsciously developing all the time and in which nothing of any value can ever become lost. There may be a but barely noticeable trickle that finds its way down into succeeding cultures, or there may be a dramatic reawakening or rebirth of a cultural influence, as if what had apparently been forgotten were merely lying dormant in some unknown region.

When the Orient ceded its political hegemony to Europe, many revealing marks of its spirit crept into the new culture. This was mentioned before. Europe became the heart and center of a cultural epoch. We saw it come into being, grow, and flourish. And we, the children of the twentieth century, are seeing its decay. So potent was the splendor of European culture that it put everything else in the shade. But that "everything else" existed and pursued its course. What we call history is always but a segment, or a distortion of proportions, depending on the observer's point of view.

Europe's spirit flowed out in every direction. Its essence nourished new soil; its blood, pure or mixed, pulsed also under other skies. Europe hardly noticed this, so centrally vigorous was she, with a super-abundance of forces to bestow. She lived the life of a beautiful woman who tries to ignore the fact that her daughter is coming of age.

America is the daughter. She begins to lead a life of her own, no matter whether her mother approves or not. Twenty-five years ago, no European gave consideration to the New World when writing a history of music. Today, such a book would be woefully incomplete without a thorough discussion of America. Not that a musical history of the New World can yet be written. That would be like writing a musical history of Europe and stopping with the coming of the troubadours.

During the first century of the new continent's settlement, nobody gave a thought to the establishment of an American culture. The principal aim of those who might have been the means of bringing about such such a prospering was to maintain contact with the fatherlands beyond the sea. In their minds, they continued to live in Europe, animated by the desire to keep abreast of things against the day—which they hoped would dawn soon—when, laden with American wealth, they would return to the civilized capitols of the Old World. In the meantime, music —usually the successful kind—and musicians—invariably the unsuccessful ones—kept pouring into the new country in a broad stream.

It was not long before traveling virtuosos discovered that America was the land of extremely lucrative concert tours. But at first this, too, led to no fruitful contact between Europe and what was the first faint stirring of an independent American musical life. Later, European musicians of some repute occasionally went to America for a temporary stay, to teach and to found institutes. On the other hand, scholarships sent increasing numbers of talented young musicians to Europe that they might study there and later be able to pass on to their own country what they had acquired.

America took everything Europe had to offer. At first, what it received was frequently but the outer shell, the form; for the content, which had been hundreds of years in growing and was the result of innumerable influences, was not so readily transplantable. At any rate, America eagerly imitated what it could imitate, at times with startling results. It sometimes happened that the imitation outshone in brilliance the original. And then the decisive change occurred. It was as if America came to realize that the forms it received were inadequate and would have to be filled with a new content. In short, America realized that it was about ready to give birth to a culture of its own, that it must cease to be tied to Europe's traditions. With the coming of the twentieth-century upheaval which shook Europe to its very foundations the young American culture received a powerful stimulus. Unprecedented numbers of European artists and scientists found their way to the shores of the New World. It was now their turn to adapt themselves, for American culture had come of age.

INDIAN TIMES

Ancient Indian sculpture shows us figures with musical instruments, usually of the wind group, a rare drum beater, never a stringed instrument [Pl. 193]. Almost all ancient Indian cultural epochs of which remains are extant have given us such figures: the high cultures between the Pacific Ocean and the chain of the Cordilleras and occasionally others, like that of Chaco-Santiago which had its home in the north of Argentina and in the stretches covered by primeval forests in the heart of the South American continent. Most frequently, we find an instrument shaped like a beaked flute, which to this day represents the favorite instrument of a great many Indians and is called by them quena (kena). Its sounds are usually accompanied by the dull beats of a large primitive drum. It may be fashioned from any number of materials: from reeds or clay, from silver or human bones. An ancient Indian legend tells of a youth who fashioned a quena from the shinbone of his deceased bride and kept playing sweet songs for the departed, whose spirit thus listened to him.

The Indians also had an early knowledge of the combination of several reeds of various lengths for the formation of a polytonal instrument which is found in many cultures and is at times called syrinx or Pan's pipes [Pl. 194].

What may music have sounded like in those far-off days? It has become lost as wholly as that of the old Asiatic civilizations. Does the music sung and played by Indian tribes today possibly represent remnants of it? We must keep in mind that America's physical proportions are immense; that the continent could never have formed a uniform cultural realm; and that at all times local differences were as great as they are today. The fact that the music of contemporary Indians is primitive and knows but few tones and practically no harmony does not permit us to conclude that the Chimu, the Incas, the Mayas, the Aztecs, and the Toltecs had none but the most primitive music. That would be as if a historian of the year 5,000 presumed to judge European culture of today on the basis of discoveries in a mountainous valley of Montenegro.

The musicality of the Indians is strongly developed even today. To be sure, the Indians' most primitive music, or what of it is still extant, is ruled by laws entirely different from ours. Music to the Indians is what it used to be to those Asiatic races of nebulous ancient times: a part of life, the sister of religion, a mystical primordial element able to conjure up rain and heal the sick.

Wherever the remnants of Indian music were subjected to scientific investigation, wide regional differences were revealed. Vast areas had a music so primitive that it was devoid even of phrasing, that first musical achievement. In those cases it was mostly tri-tonal, which to our ears is equivalent to extreme monotony, especially in the absence of every rhythmic and harmonic element. More frequently met was five-tone music, based on the penatonic scale, whose world-wide existence raises interesting questions. Greenland and Africa, Polynesia and Eastern Asia, had five-tone music without half-tone intervals, and now we meet it again in the most diverse regions of North and South America! Could this be proof of a common primordial cradle of humanity? How wonderful, if musical science were able to contribute to the solution of such a question, but unfortunately this cannot be. A Paraguayan professor recently pointed out that the Indian Guaraní language, which to this day is greatly in use in his country, showed a remarkable similarity with that of the Egyptians. Music might have come to the aid of linguistic research; but lost is Egypt's music of pre-Christian times, and lost the Guaraní music of the pre-Columbian epoch.

When the Europeans arrived, they found splendid and superlatively organized cities side by side with cannibalistic dwellers in primeval forests. Music, which always mirrors life, very likely was expressive of both aspects and was as different in itself as a Beethoven symphony of the year 1810 was different from the song of a contemporary Arabian camel driver.

After more than four hundred years of American music, from the conquest to our days, the Indian ingredient has disappeared from it almost entirely. As a matter of fact, genuine American music ceased to exist with the invasion of the Europeans. Only in our time, did America grow strong and independent, become conscious of its origins. Attempts were made to form some kind of connection between the growing young culture and that of ancient times. We shall soon have occasion to refer to the "Indianistic" cultural epoch which quite plainly put its imprint upon the American arts of our century.

COLONIAL TIMES

Adventurers, warriors, and priests formed the vanguard of Europe at the time when, at the end of the fifteenth century, that continent, rapidly approaching the zenith of its power and bloom, discovered America. Spaniards and Portuguese, foremost, embarked upon the daring voyages which were to impart new and undreamt-of proportions to the lineaments of the world. Although only in exceptional cases did they represent the more cultured strata of their country, they were all nevertheless somehow glorified by the reflected splendor of the brilliant spiritual and artistic life which at that time radiated from Europe's cities and universities. The Indian music they encountered on the new continent seemed to them mostly primitive, alien, and ugly. The music with which Pizarro and Cortez were received at the courts of Mexico and Peru was surely quite different from that of the uncivilized Indian races. But there was no musician among the early arrivals to record for us the interesting details. A few of the first voyagers to the shores of the new country did refer to Indian music, as for instance Jean de Léry in his book *Histoire d'un voyage faict en la terre du Brésil,* published in 1556. He described the Indians' festivals and dramatic performances, mentioned their responsive chants, and spoke of choruses and instruments.

With incredible swiftness, everything that was Indian disappeared from the visible life of Spanish America. It retreated into far-away virgin forests, into inaccessible mountain valleys, and into other places where white men would not set foot for many centuries to come. Hardly a trace was left of the former culture. The race sank into a state of lethargy, and the constant struggle for survival against the indomitable powers of nature made the Indians drop to a primitive level. The Spanish warriors had but one goal: to subdue the continent and exploit it. The priests' goal was to do away with heathenism and to win new souls for the Christian God.

Among the first victims was music which in peoples living close to nature always represents a strong cementing force. Realizing this, the Europeans destroyed it in order to crush a national symbol. And since music also forms a bridge to the deities, the priests decried it in their effort to do away with every memory of the old system of worship. Only a few decades had passed, and practically nothing was left of the Indians' history and culture. The new towns of the white men were imitations of European towns. Symbols of the victor, they rose up at times from the very ruins of Indian towns. A new kind of music sounded within their walls, wholly alien to that other music which, but a few years before, had filled the streets.

As in Europe a thousand years earlier, music had once more become a weapon in America. Often, the priests converted the Indians more by music than by the word. We know of one, San Francisco Solano, who, defying the dangers of the primeval forest and the giant Parana and Paraguay rivers, paddled his boat upstream and by the sound of his fiddle lured to the banks the Indians who had been hiding in the underbrush and now let themselves be baptized in droves. The white god's music was more beautiful.

The musical life of the new cities on American soil began as if they had been European centers. As early as 1524, a school of music was founded in the Mexican city of Texcoco. It was conducted by a Franciscan priest who had studied at the Flemish university of Louvain. Other settlements followed suit. Thus, European musical learning, polyphony, and counterpoint made an early appearance in America. However, they were not taught to the natives. Only sons of Europeans were students at those schools of music.

The earliest churches were equipped with organs. The wonderful Cathedral of Mexico, consecrated by Cortez in 1525, and representing one of the most perfect colonial edifices in America, received a large organ which, even by European standards, was a valuable instrument. In the monasteries, Gregorian chorales and religious polyphony were cultivated. The great majority of the monks were Europeans, and rarely only did a converted Indian gain admission and tuition.

When the human stream from Europe began to flow more strongly, increasing numbers of musicians found their way to the new country. Most of them had been rather unsuccessful at home and thought that a new field of activity was now beckoning. At first, in the sixteenth century, they were occasionally representatives of Flemish polyphony. In addition, the Spaniards began to pay attention to the cultivation of the short musical plays which they called *tonadillas* and which had become so popular in their native land.

The new colonials' interest in music was exceedingly keen, a fact easily explained by the desire to keep well informed against the longed-for day of their return. On the other hand, it must be considered that

170. Richard Strauss's *Electra*, at the Salzburg Festival Playhouse.

171. Richard Strauss's *Rosenkavalier*, Act II, Vienna State Opera. [*Photo Pittner*]

172. Othmar Schoeck (1886).

173. Schoeck's *Massimilla Doni*, at the Zurich Stadttheater.

174. Donizetti's *Lucia di Lammermoor*, at the Metropolitan, with Lily Pons and Jan Peerce.

175. Bizet's *Carmen*, Act IV, at the Metropolitan, with Risë Stevens. [*Photo Melançon*]

176: Puccini's *La Bohème*, Act III, at the Metropolitan, with Frances Greer as Musetta, at the Cafe Momus.

177. Puccini's *Tosca*, Act I, at the Milan Scala, 1938.

178. Benjamin Britten's *Peter Grimes*, Act II, Scene I, at the Metropolitan, with Regina Resnik. [*Photo Melançon*]

179. Paul Hindemith's *Mathis, the Painter*, Act I, at the Zurich Stadttheater.

180. Ponchielli's *Gioconda*, Act III, Dance of the Hours, at the Milan Scala.

181. Krenek's *Johnny Strikes Up the Band*, at the Vienna State Opera.

182. The Ballet Theater's celebrated children's ballet, *Peter and the Wolf*, with music by Prokofiev.

183. Franz Lehar, right, (1870-1948) with Jarmila Novotna and Richard Tauber.
184. Lehar's *Land of Smiles*. Dancers, gilt from top to toe, present a Cambodian
dance.

185. Paul Hindemith (born 1895). [*Photo Dräyer*]

186. Arthur Honegger (born 1892).

187. Monte Carlo Ballet Russe's *The Nutcracker Suite*, with music by Tchaikovski. Frederic Franklin and Alexandra Danilova star. [*Photo Fred Fehl*]

188. Arthur Honegger's *Joan of Arc at the Stake*, showing Maria Becker and Heinrich Gretler, at the Zurich Stadttheater, on June 13, 1942. [*Photo Guggenbühl*]

189. Igor Stravinsky (born 1882).

190. The Ballet Theater's ballet by Agnes de Mille, *Fall River Legend*, with music by Morton Gould. [*Photo Melançon*]

191. Prokofiev's and Jakulov's ballet *Le pas d'acier*. Model of stage setting for the first Paris performance by the Diaghilev Ballet, 1927.

192. Alois Haba playing his quarter-tone piano, constructed by August Förster.

193. Old Indian representations of music on Peruvian earthen vessels (Chimu art).
(a) Tambourine player above a death-dance relief; (b) Pitcher in the shape of a
flute player; (c) Corpse with Pandean Pipe; (d) Mythical musical scene. [*From
Leicht's Indian Art and Culture*]

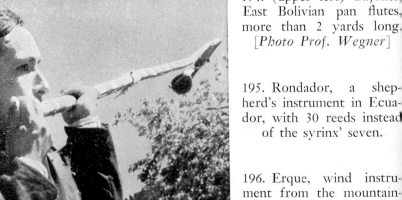

194. (upper left) Bajones, East Bolivian pan flutes, more than 2 yards long. [*Photo Prof. Wegner*]

195. Rondador, a shepherd's instrument in Ecuador, with 30 reeds instead of the syrinx' seven.

196. Erque, wind instrument from the mountainous districts of north-western Argentina. Similar to the alp horn.

197. George Gershwin (1898-1937).
[*Photo N. Haz.*]

198. *Catfish Row*, in Gershwin's *Porgy and Bess*, at the Alvin Theater, New York, with Todd Duncan and Anne Brown. [*Photo Vandamm*]

199. Arturo Toscanini (1867-   ) with the New York Symphony Orchestra.

200. Toscanini conducting at the International Music Festival at Lucerne.
[*Photo ATP*]

life in Lima, in Quito and Bogotá, in Mexico and Santiago, in Asunción and Buenos Aires, offered but little variety, in spite of a viceroy and of court activities in some of these cities. After all, they were little more than overgrown villages with primitive houses and unpaved streets. The arrival of the European mail was still the chief event, and not infrequently, the bags brought over by the ships contained sheets of music. There are still in existence bills of lading which list a great deal of musical literature. Eight years after the works of the great Spanish composer, Antonio de Cabezón, had first been performed in his native land, they were already sung in the Spanish American colony. And the Cathedral of Mexico owns the original of a mass of Tomás Luis de Victoria, the famous Spanish colleague of Palestrina.

The printing of music, too, was introduced in America at an early date. A short half-century after its invention (about 1500), the first locally printed missals with music made their appearance in Mexico and in the country called Colombia today. Naturally, all the music printed, sung, played, or taught, was European. Even if occasionally a piece first saw the light of day on American soil, its author was nearly always a European. While in the plastic arts more than one work has been preserved —like the Indian Madonna of Copacabana on Lake Titicaca—in which a native artist succeeded in producing a happy combination of Indian perception and European symbols, nothing of the kind is extant in music. It is true that much remains to be sifted and examined in old American archives, in colonial churches, and, above all, in missionary monasteries. It may be that some day a musical counterpart of the pictures of the Virgin and the Saints painted by Indian hands, will be found.

The careful observer of the development of American cultural history will surely not have failed to notice that during the first centuries after the discovery, the Latin South was far ahead of the North. True, the North not only managed to catch up but eventually assumed the unquestioned spiritual leadership. Musically, the very same process may be recorded. The principal Spanish colonial cities, whose names were given before, led a musical life of their own at a time when North America had hardly got beyond the beginnings of cultural cooperation. But South America remained within the European sphere of influence long after the North had refused to cling further to Old-World ideas.

The first American theaters were opened in the cities of Latin America. Occasionally, in old paintings, we come upon a placard on a house wall with an invitation to attend a performance. And not infrequently, in genre pictures of that time, we see scenes connected with theatrical life, say, a family of modish Spaniards on the way to the theater, preceded by a little negro slave carrying a lantern through the still unlit street; or a caricature ridiculing the high society ladies of those days because of their gigantic combs which deprived the cavaliers sitting behind them of any sight of the stage. We know of musical performances at the court of the viceroy in Lima, during the latter half of the seventeenth century, the music for which was written in Peru, while previously the works in their entirety had been imported from Spain. Theatrical history on the banks of the La Plata had its beginnings only much later. The first playhouse of Buenos Aires was erected in the year 1778.

The flourishing colonial city of Caracas is deserving of special mention. Her university, founded in 1725, made music an important part of its curriculum. When, in the following century, the Emperor of Austria sent a present to the young Venezuelan republic, it was significantly made up of manuscripts by Haydn, Mozart, and Beethoven.

There were still no orchestras in the Latin American colonial cities. It was not until the turn of the nineteenth century that town bands came into existence, an approximate counterpart of the pipers of medieval European cities. They were among the viceroy's followers on public occasions, played dance music on festival days, and assisted at ecclesiastical processions, but were of course still a long way from being real orchestras. And yet, there actually were orchestras in South America at that time. Far from the cities, in the primeval forest districts of the continent's interior, the strange phenomenon of the Jesuit missions existed. They represent one of the most interesting, and least known, chapters in the history of mankind. On the soil of what is today Paraguay and the north-eastern provinces of Argentina Jesuit priests had established a "Kingdom of God on Earth," where Indians lived in peace and cultivated the ground, and where no money, no social distinctions, and no wars were known. It was there, under the guidance of the priests, that the first orchestras came into being, made up of Indians, most of whom played home-made instruments. There was, for instance, the orchestra of the Apostoles settlement, in the present Argentine territory called Missiones. It numbered eight violins, three harps, one bassoon, two lyres, two trumpets, and four contrabasses. In its vault reposed the scores of fifty-three sonatas and other works by European masters. That was in the year 1767.

EARLY MUSIC IN THE UNITED STATES

By that time, the Anglo-Saxon North had already made rapid musical strides forward. It had caught up with and overtaken the South. Its first printed music made its appearance in 1698. As in South America, it was of a religious nature, the *Bay Psalm Book*, whose earlier editions had been without music. As a matter of course, early United States music was wholly dependent on Europe. While in the South it had first been Spain and later Italy whose influence predominated, most of the early music of the United States came from England. When concert life came into existence, the programs were more or less exact replicas of the prevailing English ones. Handel, and somewhat later Haydn, considered Englishmen in the United States, were the most-played composers. One of the prominent musical societies of that time even carried the names of both these men in its title.

Of English origin, too, was the popularity of the so-called Ballad Operas. There is a record of one such performance (*Flora, or Hob-in-the-Well*) Charleston, S. C., as early as 1735. In the year 1750, a little more than twenty years after the London premiere, New York witnessed performances of the *Beggar's Opera*, the operatic satire on society. A strange whim of fate, indeed, that brought to the New World first a parody and only much later opera in its true form.

A few prominent events of those early concert days may be recorded here. There were musical performances in Boston, in the years 1731 and 1732. New York, in 1736, witnessed the appearance of the son of the great German composer Pachelbel. In the same city, Handel's *Messiah* was performed on January 4, 1770, under the direction of William Tuckey, an English immigrant. That was only eleven years after the master's death and two years before the work was heard in Germany, proof of the fact that efficient orchestras and choruses must have existed in that part of the New World at that time. As a matter of fact, the records tell of the early formation of musical associations, whose highly beneficial effect upon the country's growing musical culture should not be underestimated. In the above-mentioned city of Charleston, South Carolina, such an association was formed in the year 1762 and continued its activity for exactly a century and a half. Its first concert with vocal soloists was given in 1773, the program consisting of English and Scotch songs. One of the most important musical societies in the United States was formed in Stoughton, in 1776. But perhaps the shining example was that of the Colony of Bethlehem, founded in 1741 by Bohemian immigrants, and actively in existence to this day. It was responsible, among other things, for the first performance of Haydn's *Creation* and *Seasons* and for the launching of a number of composers of serious music, such as John Antes, David Moritz Michael, and John Frederick Peter. These men should nevertheless not be considered American composers, both because of their origin and their style, which faithfully copied the Central European forms then in use.

There are even records of musical festivals in the eighteenth century. Festival performances of works by Gluck and "Dr." Haydn—the Oxford degree had been conferred on him a short time before—took place in 1796. Let us judge the importance of these events from a European viewpoint: Beethoven had gone to Vienna four years before, Mozart had been dead five years, Schubert had not yet been born, and musical life was generally confined to the palaces of the aristocracy. Indeed, the United States had lost no time in catching up! However, love and understanding of music which led to the foundation of serious musical associations must not tempt us wrongly to evaluate the country's cultural level. As in any other young community, that level, as far as musical questions were concerned, was low for a long time to come.

New York's first musical society was formed in 1774. At first, there were choruses, small orchestras, and chamber music ensembles. Even open-air concerts were soon introduced, their performances taking place in a public garden, called *Vauxhall* after its London model.

As always, this expanding musical life was accompanied by the appearance of the first musical creations. Perhaps the earliest United States composers were a certain Conrad Beissel, who lived at the beginning of the eighteenth century, but of whom but very little data is available; James Lyon (1735-1794), to whom we are indebted for a collection of psalm tunes, anthems, and hymns; William Billings (1746-1800), whose musical activity included the formation of the above-mentioned Stoughton society and the publication of a great deal of printed music, among which was a volume entitled *The Continental Harmony*, and, finally, perhaps the best known of these early composers, Francis Hopkinson (1737-1791), who wrote the first American songs (*My Days Have Been So Wondrous Free*), an allegorical opera, *The Temple of Minerva*, and a number of other compositions. An ardent supporter of Independence, he was a friend of George Washington, to whom some of his works are dedicated.

A young country's earliest "national" music is likely to be represented by its National Hymn. So it was in the United States whose hymn was born in 1814 on the battlefield. Francis Scott Key, a young lawyer, happened to be on board a ship entering the port of Baltimore for an exchange of prisoners. There he witnessed the garrison's heroic resistance to the mighty English fleet. Under those conditions, the words of *The Star-Spangled Banner* were written. Ironically enough, for lack of a suitable original melody, they were sung to the tune of an old English song.

At the turn of the nineteenth century, quite a number of musicians of some stature were active in the United States. It would be impossible to enumerate them all. The following are mentioned because they were true pioneers fighting under difficult circumstances on behalf of a budding musical culture. Hans Gram, in 1791, produced an orchestral suite—it may have been the first one originating in the New World—and called it *The Death-Song of an Indian Chief.* Peter Albrecht van Hagen not only composed program music—quite bombastic, as his time demanded it—(*Columbus, or The Discovery of America* and *Zorinski, or Freedom of the Slaves*) but seems also to have been somewhat original as a teacher, since he taught more than ten instruments in addition to voice. Among the first writers on musical matters was the clever Andrew Law, who died in 1821.

A rather important part in North America's early music was played by the Hewitt family. Its most prominent representative was James Hewitt (1770-1827), whose vital data are remarkably similar to those of Beethoven. Arriving from England in 1792, he was active in America in various musical capacities: organist, conductor of orchestras and bands, and even publisher. The year 1794 witnessed the production of his opera *Tammany*, which was followed by *Columbus, Robin Hood,* and *Pizarro.* In one of his concerts he presented a work entitled *The Battle of Trenton,* consisting of nine parts, each one of which had a programmatic title. The same program included the work of a colleague entitled *A Voyage from England to America,* in which not only arrival and departure were musically described but also the sea and the major and minor incidents of the crossing. Although these works were of no lasting importance, they give an idea of the taste of those days.

Other English immigrants, too, played a part in the musical life of the United States. Raynor Taylor came over in the same year as Hewitt, and was also active as conductor and composer. Of greater importance was Johann Gottlieb Graupner, who died in 1836. He had been a member of Haydn's London orchestra, a fact which contributed greatly to the esteem in which he was held. He founded a regular Philharmonic Society in Boston, in 1810. Five years later, the same city witnessed the birth of the Handel and Haydn Society, which had the benefit of Graupner's German and English choral experiences. The Society appealed to Beethoven, asking that he write an oratorio for it. Unfortunately, we do not know whether this appeal ever reached the master. If it had, we might conceivably be able to record an American world premiere of a work by Beethoven. In 1842, New York's great permanent orchestra, the Philharmonic, was formed. It has developed into one of the world's leading orchestras.

One of the most important musicians of that epoch may have been Lowell Mason (1792-1872). Unaided at first, and then supported by a number of enthusiastic cooperators, Mason began, in 1829, to use Pestalozzi's system of musical education and to lay the foundation for a truly progressive tuition. The United States is largely indebted to these endeavors for the magnificently high level of musical culture it has since attained. To Mason was awarded the first "Doctor of Music" degree in the United States.

Three years later, another musician was similarly honored. He was Thomas Hastings, the writer of about six hundred texts and more than one thousand melodies. Active along similar lines were other song composers, among them some members of the Hewitt family. But they were all put in the shade by a genius: Stephen Collins Foster (1826-1864). Born on July 4th, the same day that Thomas Jefferson and John Adams died, he wrote his first song at the age of seventeen. It was followed in the course of time by about 150 melodies in which Foster may be said to have succeeded in creating the genuine American song. So genuine were his tunes that the people as a whole adopted them as their own. Although he was born in the North near Pittsburgh, Pa., he had a fine ear for the Negro melodies of the South. Foster became the singer not only of the South but of the entire nation. Who does not know his catchy, and yet frequently melancholy airs, like *My Old Kentucky Home, Old Folks at Home, Old Black Joe, De Camptown Races, Oh Susanna,* and many others? Quite recently, his *Jeanie with the Light Brown Hair* swept the country via radio when the networks were madly searching for popular songs in the public domain.

In addition to Foster, there was another musician who did more than the early operatic and symphonic composers in carrying the sounds of North America into the world. His name was John Philip Sousa (1854–1932). His long and successful life contrasted sharply with the brief, and in a sense tragic, existence of Foster, an existence which reminds us forcibly of the strangely characteristic fate of lyricists all over the world. Sousa was the son of a Spanish father and a German mother. As an American, he had to go to war against both these countries and permit the electrifying effect of his marches to put added zest into the efforts of the American troops. When he wrote his first march—it was for a celebration of the newspaper *Washington Post*, in 1889—he had no idea that his music was a typical expression of the America of those days, as typical as at one time the Vienna minuet was of the court life of that city, and the waltz of its middle-class activities. Once, when fame had already caught up with him, Sousa said: "I have written ten operas in my life, and hundreds of other things: cantatas, symphonic poems, suites, songs. The American people did not want to hear them. They insisted on my being a composer of marches expressing the will and vigor of the nation."

In the course of the nineteenth century, the relation between European music and its American counterpart had gradually become closer. While at first the latter had been little more than an exact replica of the former, points of contact occurred with increasing frequency, and it even happened quite often that Europe was the beneficiary.

The American tour had come to be a matter of course in the life of the prominent virtuosos, while toward the middle of the century it had still smacked somewhat of adventure. In 1850, Jenny Lind, the Swedish Nightingale, traveled to North America. Reports of her success sounded so fantastic that the Europeans were reluctant to believe them. There appeared a series of caricatures in a widely read theatrical magazine of Vienna, dealing with Jenny Lind's tour: a rich farmer followed by slaves carrying bags of gold with which he hoped to be able to buy a concert ticket; the American who sold his house at auction in order to obtain the price of admission; the public in the hall listening to the great singer, not sitting or standing, but devoutly kneeling; members of the Senate drawing Jenny's carriage. . . .

That, approximately, represented Europe's idea of America: a land given to exaggeration, fantastic, and not to be taken quite seriously, not even in her musical life. But the virtuosos returned and not only told of the steadily growing number of new theaters and concert halls shooting up practically overnight, of the unbelievable enthusiasm displayed by a receptive and unsophisticated public, and of the honorable receptions accorded them by the democratic authorities—they also brought home a good deal of money. The stream broadened. Improved travel facilities made possible the inclusion in tours of more cities in the United States and, subsequently, in South America, too. Whole opera companies often spent months in the New World. Symphony orchestras, large choirs, ballet groups, and chamber music ensembles—they all found their way to the land of promise and fulfillment.

Once in a while, some virtuoso also traveled in the opposite direction. Let us mention one of them, perhaps the first American musician to attract world-wide attention. His name was Louis Moreau Gottschalk. He was a pianistic child prodigy, became the pupil of Berlioz in Paris, and was called by Chopin "the future king of pianists." He was triumphantly successful both in Europe and on his own continent. Gottschalk seems to have been a true musician, in spite of certain almost circus-like mannerisms then in vogue, like the wearing and nonchalant discarding of white kid gloves when appearing on a concert platform, the improvising on popular themes desired and called out by the public, fits of hysterics and swoonings of ladies of all ages among the audience, and other goings on of that kind. Gottschalk died in Rio de Janeiro at the age of forty-four, in 1869, while on a South American tour, and in spite of the absence of any tangible evidence, rumors of his having been assassinated have never completely died down.

America was learning with burning zeal, quickly and well. She sent her talented young men and women to Paris, Berlin, Vienna, and the cities of Italy, that they might return to teach, and to organize conservatories, opera houses, orchestras, and whatever else there was on the old continent. The young republic was generous in granting scholarships enabling the budding native musicians to study in Europe. A new and undreamt-of world was opened to them. Their American experiences had acquainted them with hardly more than Italian opera and the classic and early-romantic part of orchestral literature. Traveling virtuosos and singers rarely deviated from the tried-and-true standard repertoire. Now the

Americans came to know other styles, late-romanticism and the beginnings of impressionism. They were brought in touch with national musical tendencies—Russian, Scandinavian, Spanish—and began to reflect upon a serious problem: the possibility of creating a national music in America, an individual musical language, which had its roots in folk music, clung to the native soil, and yet would be able to bridge the gap between America and the rest of the world. They realized that music of a purely American stamp, of Indian or Negro origin, could never become amalgamated with the style of Italian opera, with classic symphonic art, or with romantic drawing-room compositions. Impressionism, however, the tonal coloring of the modern orchestra, and the examples set by other "young" peoples, opened up new vistas and possibilities. Groping at first, and then with ever greater assurance and determination, these young Americans began to make the best of their opportunities.

At the time when American music began to assume individual features, there arose in the United States a composer of genius: Edward MacDowell (1861-1908). He had been Debussy's fellow student in Paris, and something of this Frenchman's influence seems to cling to many of his works. His *Indian Suite* however contains traditional folk motifs. In some of his other compositions, especially in symphonic poems, piano pieces, and songs, he created a personal style, somewhere between romanticism and impressionism, and succeeded in producing unique emotional effects. He had hardly passed the fourth decade of his life when the sad fate of Schumann and Wolf befell him: mental derangement.

MacDowell was one of the members of what is generally called the "New England" group of composers. Within this group, the most prominent were George W. Chadwick (1854-1931), who composed many works for orchestra, the opera *Judith*, and many songs; Horatio Parker, whose oratorio *Hora Novissima* is performed to this day and whose opera *Mona* won him a $10,000 prize and a performance at the Metropolitan Opera House; Arthur Foote and Mrs. H. H. A. Beach whose *Ah, Love, but a Day* and *The Year's at the Spring* still have a place on many vocal programs. Mrs. Beach also composed piano concertos, a *Gaelic Symphony*, chamber and religious music.

The New England school of composers was definitely influenced by European, particularly German, models, and naturally so, since most of these composers went to Germany to study and returned to imitate their masters. Their resulting works were largely permeated with the sentimentality of German romanticism and lacked as yet a true American base.

Two well-known composers, Rubin Goldmark (1872-1936) and Henry Kimball Hadley, though not of the New England school, were developed under the German influence. Even Goldmark's *Negro Rhapsody*, which used American Negro folk themes was, in essence, academically European and the same may be said of his *Requiem*, based on Lincoln's Gettysburg Address. On the other hand, as a teacher, Goldmark was responsible for a new crop of more indigenous American composers, notably Aaron Copland and George Gershwin. Henry Hadley (1871-1937) has to his credit five pronouncedly programmatic symphonies and symphonic poems, the operas *Azora, Daughter of Montezuma* and *Cleopatra's Night*. As a conductor, he crusaded for performances of the works of new American composers.

Musical life developed fast in the United States in those years. This is the place to mention a great man who played a decisive part in this development: Theodore Thomas. He was born in Germany in 1835, came to the United States at the age of ten, and died in Chicago in 1905. He was the true organizer, the moving spirit, and one of the foremost conductors in the States. It was due to his efforts that the American orchestra reached the artistic level of those in Europe. He was responsible for orchestral tours all over the country, carrying symphonic music to distant places which thus far had hardly even heard of its existence. American composers found in him a vigorous advocate of their art. Many of them were able to gain recognition, thanks to his forceful and incredibly successful personality. His importance and influence were rivaled by another conductor, Leopold Damrosch (1832-1885). He, too, had come from Germany and also became thoroughly Americanized. A fighter in the cause of Richard Wagner, he had a worthy successor in his son, Walter Damrosch.

What a rise from the days of the first orchestra concerts to those of Thomas and Damrosch! The year 1821 marked the first performance of a Beethoven symphony (the *First*) on United States soil. Not so tardy a date, if we consider that a great many rather important European cities did not register this event until later. Some of the present-day musicologists are inclined to find fault with the fact that, at that performance, vocal numbers were interpolated between the symphony's four movements. But why criticize America for something that was an everyday occurrence in Vienna, the place where Beethoven's symphonies were first performed and where the master lived? No, in speaking of a rise we refer rather to the elimination of grotesque conditions which were prevalent in America until far into the nineteenth century—in America, and elsewhere, too. There were, for instance, the bombastic circumstances accompanying certain concerts and making of them almost a circus performance. Everything had to be sensational, spectacular, colossal. "Stage effects" in addition to purely acoustic sensations were greatly in vogue for a long time. Accounts of early American musical life include descriptions of what would be today highly amusing incidents and details. In a certain sense, the famous 1872 Boston Monster Concert of Johann Strauss, the Waltz King, comes under this classification: 20,000 singers, 10,000 musicians, 100 assistant conductors, more than 100,000 persons in the audience, a cannon shot to make the giant body of executants start at the same moment—it was "so infernal a racket that I'll not forget it to the end of my days," Strauss himself related. And all this for the sake of one of the most poetic blossoms of the Vienna Waltz: *The Blue Danube*. . . .

The year 1883 marked the opening of the Metropolitan Opera in New York. The date was October 22, the opera *Faust*. There ensued a bitter rivalry between the new house and The Academy of Music, a previously established opera house whose main attraction was the great Adelina Patti. American operatic history is hardly less fantastic than that of Italy or of Italianesque Europe in the art's early centuries. The central point of many a violent struggle was Richard Wagner, staunchly upheld by Damrosch. A century before, in Paris, Gluck had opposed the Italians. Now, in New York, it was Wagner versus Italy. But musical life progressed undaunted by outward circumstances and events. The yearning of the people for music, for its intrinsic worth, grew, and all else was dross.

Artur Nikisch, one of Europe's most famous conductors, came to Boston, in 1889, and was active in that city for four years. Carnegie Hall was built in 1891. Ten years later, there were 90,000 people in the United States whose profession was music. A century-and-a-half had passed since the Moravians in Bethlehem, Pa., had introduced regular "sing hours," community music called by a properly medieval name: *Collegium Musicum*. And now, at the start of the twentieth century, this idealism began to be the common property of a whole nation which grew and became stronger from day to day. In New York, at the beginning of this century, there were quite a number of simultaneously active orchestras: the Philharmonic, Symphony, Russian, People's Symphony. Similar conditions prevailed in Boston and Chicago. Philadelphia's orchestra, which has since become so famous, was organized in 1901. Minneapolis followed in 1903, St. Paul in 1905, New Orleans in 1906, Seattle in 1908, San Francisco in 1909. Music was conquering the country as the pioneers had conquered it before: westward! In 1907, America summoned Gustav Mahler, the most brilliant conductor of his day, who, embittered, had just turned his back upon Vienna. For four years, he toured the States, baton in hand. He did not always meet with ready understanding; perhaps, too, he had grown more than a bit tired.

But not only was professional musicianship triumphant. Concerts multiplied, the audiences grew and became more enthusiastic all the time. Music took hold of the country's youth. Lowell Mason's dreams began to materialize. In the year 1930, there were in the United States the unbelievable number of 30,000 pupils' orchestras. Could anything more strikingly refute the oft-repeated allegation of a "purely materialistic" nation and culture?

PRESENT-DAY MUSIC IN THE UNITED STATES

The First World War may be said to mark the beginning of the American present in the realm of art. During the Second, it reached a plainly visible culminating point. American poets had emerged who could talk to the whole world, American prose writings were translated into every language of the globe and read avidly everywhere, and American painters and sculptors revealed to their contemporaries everywhere that they had become at least their equals. American music, too, had taken the decisive step: it had ceased to be a copy—it had turned into an original. How had that happened?

From all parts of the world people had come to America. Every one of them, even if he had nothing else, brought with him the melodies of his homeland. They became mixed a hundredfold with the melodies of all the others: with ancient Indian chants which at times reached the large cities from far-away districts, suddenly to gain the distinction of being the continent's original music; with Negro rhythms and melodies which, after hundreds of years of existence, had finally come into their own; with music from any number of Old-World countries. Dances, fashionable in Europe a great many years before, furnished ingredients that found their way by strangely intricate paths from European palaces to American villages. National dances of all peoples ceded this or that characteristic detail, amounting at times to no more than a tiny turn or a dotted note. Slowly, an American music came into being, just as, plainly visible before our eyes, an American race was growing up. Today, the expert is still able to analyze American music; its original sources are clearly discernible. It is the same with people: they pass us in the streets, they speak to us, and the keenly observing eye and ear will have little difficulty in placing their origin. A hundred years or more from now, these distinguishing marks will have become blurred.

The American music of the twentieth century, exactly like that of many European peoples in the nineteenth century, is built largely on folk music, offering to the scholar delving into folklore an inexhaustible reservoir filled with the most interesting material. Music lovers all over the world who in years to come will surely hear an ever increasing amount of American music will no doubt be able to detect here and there some racial detail, some primordial element, be it the lofty and melancholy high-plains mood of the Indian, the wildly sensual and bewitching rhythms of the Negro, or a faint reminder of some gavot, minuet, or saraband, which they have long forgotten, but which lives on in America, hidden among other forms and oblivious of its noble origin.

To survey and discuss contemporary musical life in the United States, especially within the narrow scope of this book, is an exceedingly difficult undertaking. Let us keep in mind the enormous dimensions of the country, the existence of thousands of localities in which orchestras, choral associations, concert artists, and university teachers pay the most intensive attention to the cultivation of music, the fact that everywhere composers are at work, that radio stations and artists strive to have a most bewildering variety of musical products brought before the public, that the phonograph record has achieved undreamt-of importance both in the home and in the schools, and that the sound film and television are forever seeking new means of musical expression. In so tremendously active a field it is most difficult, too, to differentiate between what has real value and what has merely been prompted by reasons of momentary expediency, between seriously striving composers and musical opportunists—a class which has never flourished so abundantly as it does today.

In North America, the musical influence of folklore is considerably weaker than in Latin America. Our Indian music is practically non-exist-ent, and Negro music has mingled but very little with white music. Again we see how truly music mirrors social and political life and happenings. At one point only has the black element succeeded in effecting a decisive musical breach—in jazz. But that is a subject which requires careful thought and discussion.

JAZZ

What is jazz? Where does it come from? Does it bear fruitful seed for the further development of music, or is it a danger to it? Let us attempt an objective analysis. There is no gainsaying the fact that jazz is doing its share in softening the rhythmic rigidity of contemporary, and especially of occidental, music. It has supplied new sound effects, not through the introduction of new instruments, but through the shifting of sound proportions within the ensemble and through the novel use of old instruments. To mention but three of the innumerable effects: the contrabass as a rhythmic percussion instrument, the muting of the trumpet, and the glissando of the trombone. Inquiring into the origin of jazz we must keep in mind that what is today usually presented to the world as jazz, principally as dance music, has really little more than a nodding acquaintance with the real, the "hot" jazz. It is a watered-down and commercialized edition, greatly misunderstood by its white listeners. The real jazz is of black origin. It was born in the Negro quarters of North American cities: New Orleans, St. Louis, Memphis, Chicago, New York. To them the Negro brought their old melodies which contained a mixture of distant and greatly blurred memories, yearning, sadness, religiosity, and a great many other emotional characteristics. So had they sung at cotton picking, at the cradle of the child entrusted to their care, and at the religious services, first in the southern states where they were slaves, and then in the rather squalid quarters inhabited by them in the large cities, where they were free but even more looked down upon than before. A large variety of types had come into existence in their songs. "Spirituals" was the name given to choral songs of a religious character, "Blues" that of sad, but worldly solo songs, and to these were added rhythmically agitated dance songs, work songs, and heartfelt lullabies. Melancholy and yearning are the chief ingredients of most of them. The naive texts are frequently of a touchingly poetic beauty. They are the true expression of the soul of a race. For a long time, the Americans showed no interest whatever in the music of the Negoes in their country.

And yet, when Foster created the "genuinely" American song, he introduced into it many a black element. It was in the year 1871 that the choir of a Negro university (Fisk, in Nashville) made its first tour and created a sensation by the rendition of airs which were practically unknown. Slowly, contacts became closer. Today, Negro artists, like Marian Anderson, Paul Robeson, and Dorothy Maynor, draw capacity audiences and are enthusiastically acclaimed.

But even they, and a number of others, would have remained exceptional phenomena, had not the days of the First World War been instrumental in furnishing the psychological moment for the pouring forth of Negro music from its restricted quarters, and for its firm installation as an internationally accepted dance music. What is the origin of the word jazz? No uncontested explanation has ever been furnished.

Negro singing is inseparably connected with, and accompanied by, dancing, and vice versa. None of the movements corresponds to generally accepted rhythms because, in the first place, there is much flexibility in selection of accented or unaccented parts of a measure. Any note may be accepted, according to the momentary inspiration of the singer or the dancer. In the accompaniment to song and dance, percussion instruments predominate. Here, too, the word instrument is not to be interpreted in the generally accepted sense. Everything capable of producing a noise or a tone may become an instrument. From the very beginning, the meaning of a piece of music became entirely secondary to its rendition. The Negro is not so much concerned with the "what" as with the "how." In the New York Negro quarter of Harlem, for instance, a classic cradle song melody might be turned into an agitated dance piece, a street song into a fervid religious chorale. The Negro interpreted not only his own music but, as was just mentioned, any music he heard and absorbed. He embellished it with a rich garland of improvisations, a custom which was considered not only the right but the duty of every musician. The same symptom may be observed in connection with all primitive peoples, or those who lived close to nature, for written music was foreign to their musicians and every piece may have appeared to them new and different.

The enumerated style elements of Negro music plainly demonstrate that they fully contain the fundamentals of jazz music: the arbitrary rhythms which strikingly deviate from all generally accepted norms, the preponderance of percussion instruments, the virtuoso-like improvising ability of the executants, and the adoption of any melody whatever. In connection with masterpieces, this last symptom may appear to us like sacrilege, but it should not be so considered because of the Negro's lack of any ulterior motive.

Several times before, American-made musical elements had found their way across the ocean. The cakewalk, with its characteristic syncopations, had even furnished inspiration to great composers, like Debussy in his *Golliwog's Cakewalk* in the *Children's' Corner Suite*. Of greater importance had been the intrusion of the tango which, composed of Spanish and Cuban (Habanera) ingredients, had seen the light of day in Buenos Aires and from there found its way into the dance music of all countries.

But what happened to jazz music during the First World War was something else again, something that went much deeper. In the days when the American soldiers were to be sent across the sea, the land was seized with a reckless desire to enjoy life, perhaps in an effort to gloss over oppressed feelings. People wanted to dance, to be as gay and boisterous as never before. Because of this tendency, Negro bands were fetched from their quarters that they might regale listeners with their novel and "crazy" airs and with the strange irresistible rythms that made one feel young and vigorous. America's youth brought the jazz along with them to Europe and so infected the entire Old Continent. A frenzied will to live was the consequence of so much blood and misery. Jazz became the expression of an unfettered epoch, always looking for new sensations, for sensuous stimulations, and for means of stupefaction. Jazz spread like wildfire. From Paris to Shanghai, from San Francisco to Rio de Janeiro it dominated dancing and musical entertainment. The vital expression of a naive, childlike race had become a gigantic international business. In that metamorphosis, jazz lost many of its original symptoms, but, to make up for that, the whites stamped it with some of their own characteristics, and so, to future observers it will be bound to appear as an expression of the time, like all artistic manifestations, indissolubly connected with the epoch of its birth.

Originally, jazz was played only by small ensembles. Rarely were there more than six or seven musicians. They were divided into two groups: the "rhythmic," composed of the percussion set, piano (!) and contrabass (!), and the "melodic," comprising banjo, clarinet, trumpet, trombone, and, later, saxophone. But the number of executing musicians kept growing when the whites took hold of jazz. Naturally, the larger the orchestra became, the more the characteristic improvisions disappeared until they became quite unmanageable in the symphonic jazz orchestra. There was a time when such orchestras were hotly discussed. Some people even predicted the end of the old symphony orchestra. On the contrary, symphonic jazz beat a full retreat, but not before it had produced a number of interesting works, chief of which is the *Rhapsody in Blue* by the highly gifted George Gershwin.

More weighty, on the other hand, was the influence jazz exerted upon the contemporary technique of composition in general. Many rhythmic relaxations and novel ideas of instrumentation, adopted by any number of modern composers, may have had their origin in jazz.

CONTEMPORARY UNITED STATES COMPOSERS

It is a matter of course that a discussion of contemporary American composers, within the scope of this book, cannot possibly represent an exhaustive survey. It was pointed out before that musical activities throughout the United States had assumed enormous proportions. New composers are coming to the fore all the time, new works are being presented, new effects introduced in every realm of musical endeavor. After all, any history—and a history of music is no exception—can go only to a certain point. We must therefore confine ourselves to talking of some of the leading contemporary composers in the United States and leave it to some future historian to continue where we had to stop.

The name of George Gershwin was mentioned before. Among the many gifted creative musicians the country has produced he may claim the distinction of being the most original. In addition to the *Rhapsody in Blue* which still enjoys great popularity, there is his Negro opera *Porgy and Bess*, his overture *An American in Paris*, and a piano concerto. The first performance of the Rhapsody took place in 1924. Paul Whiteman played it with his symphonic jazz orchestra. Gershwin, born in 1898, died at the early age of thirty-nine.

Along with Gershwin, four names stand out in the field of American popular composition which had its roots in jazz. These are Irving Berlin (1888-   ), Jerome Kern (1885-1945), Richard Rodgers (1902-   ), and Cole Porter (1892-   ). Berlin is practically a history of popular music in the twentieth century all by himself, having written countless popular songs in and out of musical comedies and revues. Berlin has assigned the royalty proceeds from one of his most famous songs, the patriotic *God Bless America*, to the Boy Scouts and Girl Scouts of America. Kern's *Showboat*, one among many of his musical shows, has become an American classic, its tunes, *Old Man River* especially, having reached practically folksong status. Following in Kern's footsteps and yet developing a personality of his own, Richard Rodgers has become one of the outstanding popular composers of our day. His *Oklahoma, Carousel*, and the new *South Pacific* form a connecting link between musical comedy and opera. Cole Porter is a musical interpreter of the sophisticated social set of which he is himself a member. His piquant scores have enlivened such famous musicals as *The Gay Divorcée* and *Anything Goes*, and his suave melodies such as *Night and Day* are now semi-classics.

Bridging the gap between the purely nineteenth-century musicians and the contemporary composers are men like Deems Taylor (1885-   ), one of the most widely known American composers whose operas *The King's Henchman* and *Peter Ibbetson* have had performances at the Metropolitan Opera House and whose *Through the Looking Glass* has been played by practically all of America's larger symphony orchestras. He is perhaps equally known for his lectures and radio broadcasts.

John Alden Carpenter (1876-   ), the Chicago businessman-composer, is best known for his orchestral suite *Adventures in a Perambulator* and his ballets *Krazy Kat*, in which he made a bow in the direction of jazz, and *Skyscrapers*, in which considerable dissonance portrays modern pulsating American life. He also wrote *Sea Drift*, after Whitman, a subject which has inspired a number of other composers.

Charles Wakefield Cadman (1881-1946), the composer of operas and songs based on Indian motifs (*Shanewis, The Sunset Trail*) and Ethelbert Nevin (1862-1901), whose popularity rests mainly on a few songs sung all over the country (*At Dawning, The Rosary*) and a piano piece, *Narcissus*, are also part of this period.

The music of the American Indians began to be studied and used by such composers as Arthur Farwell (1872-), Charles Skilton (1868-1941), and Cadman. In such turn-of-the-century composers as Martin Loeffler (1861-1935) the French influence begins to be felt. It finds its flower in Charles Griffes (1884-1920), who is an exponent of French impressionism or, more aptly, an American impressionist. He died early, so that one cannot know what directions his music might have taken. His *Pleasure Dome of Kubla Khan* and his songs have a Debussy flavor, yet possess a beauty in their own right. His four *Roman Sketches*, particularly the *White Peacock* and *The Fountain of the Acquo Paolo*, appear frequently on American programs.

Two composers who have worked without benefit of European influence and training are Carl Ruggles (1876-   ) and Charles Ives (1874-   ). They are both experimenters. Ives came upon dissonances and impressionism by himself. Though using neither Indian nor Negro material, he is utterly American, employing the village band, the square-dance fiddler, and the wheezes of the old-fashioned reed harmonium as background for his original music. His *Concord Sonata* is New England in spirit as well as in its title, and its movements are named after Emerson, Hawthorne, the Alcotts, and Thoreau. He also wrote *New England Scenes,* cantatas, overtures, and chamber music.

The best known of the truly twentieth-century American composers, those who consciously have sloughed off the nineteenth century and European influences are Aaron Copland, Roy Harris, Roger Sessions, Howard Hanson, Virgil Thomson, Marc Blitzstein, and those two *enfants terribles* of the dissonant and the mechanical, Henry Cowell and George Antheil.

Aaron Copland (1900-   ) is not only one of the most important of American composers but also has been the foremost champion of other American musical works. With Roger Sessions he founded the Copland-Sessions concerts of contemporary music. His musical style has been molded by his Russian-Jewish heritage, his contact with French music of the Twenties, jazz, and the American folksong. His concerto for piano and orchestra uses the jazz medium brilliantly. In his three ballets, *Rodeo, Billy the Kid,* and *Appalachian Spring* the American folk idiom is used in a masterful way, and the frequently played *El Salon Mexico* is another example of his beautiful blending of popular songs into a well integrated composition. He has written several film scores and an opera for high schools, *The Second Hurricane.*

Virgil Thomson (1896-   ) is equally known as a penetrating writer and critic and as a composer. Though he lived in Paris for a number of years and is a propagandist for modern French music, his style is simple and straightforward. In his two operas, *Four Saints in Three Acts* and *The Mother of Us All,* both of which show traces of Protestant hymnology, there is an almost homespun quality which is most attractive and most American. Probably his most successful pieces are his scores for documentary films like *The River, The Plough that Broke the Plains,* and his Pulitzer Prize winning score for *Louisiana Story*, which has a most haunting quality.

Perhaps one of the most earthy present-day American composers is Roy Harris (1898-   ). Though he studied with Arthur Farwell and Nadia Boulanger, he has consciously developed his own style—austere, stark, polytonal, and polychordal. His best-known works are his *Piano Sonata*, his *Third Symphony*, and his *Chorale for String Sextet*. Among his many recorded works one of the most popular is the piece based on the song *When Johnny Comes Marching Home*. He also wrote six symphonies and choruses based on Whitman verses.

As mentioned before, Roger Sessions (1896-   ) was instrumental with Copland in bringing out new American music. In late years, he has been known primarily for his teaching at Princeton University and the University of California. He is also regarded as a serious, gifted composer, having written two symphonies, a string quartet, a violin concerto, as well as miscellaneous works, all masterly examples of form and counterpoint.

As director of the Eastman School of Music for many years, Howard Hanson (1896-   ) has been responsible for furthering many of the younger composers of whom mention will be made later. Hanson's four symphonies, five symphonic poems, the *Lament for Beowulf* for chorus and orchestra, have often found a place on American programs, and his opera *Merrymount* was staged at the Metropolitan Opera House.

Marc Blitzstein (1905-   ) has contributed mainly in the field of the theater, his outstanding musical plays being the smart jazzy *Triple Sec*, *No for an Answer*, and particularly *The Cradle Will Rock*. His symphony *The Airborne* is also as much of a theatrical work as a purely musical one.

Two composers who at the start shocked their audiences with their dissonances and innovations are Henry Cowell (1897-   ) and George Antheil (1900-   ). Cowell with his piano chord clusters achieved through elbows and forearms striking the keyboard of the piano and his plucked piano strings has now settled down to a more conventional style, much of his work being based on the study of early American composers, such as Billings and his fugueing tunes and of Irish folk material. Antheil in his *Ballet Mécanique* experimented with rhythmic noises from all kinds of odd instruments, musical and otherwise. He has in later years been composing for Hollywood pictures and occasionally emerging with a new symphonic work .

No less important among this group, each contributing in his own way to American music development, are Walter Piston (1894-   ) with his *Incredible Flutist, Piano Concertino*, and two excellent books on harmony and counterpoint; Douglas Moore (1893-   ) with his opera *The Devil and Daniel Webster;* Louis Gruenberg (1884-   ) with his *Emperor Jones*, the symphonic poem *Hills of Dreams*, and numerous pieces in a jazz idiom, such as *The Daniel Jazz* for voice and eight instruments, and *Jazz Suite;* Randall Thompson (1899-   ) with excellent choral and symphonic works; Wallingford Riegger (1885-   ) with compositions in many styles, including the twelve-tone system; and Frederick Jacobi (1891-   ) who has written considerable liturgical music.

These fully established composers have been followed by a new group who are today making America's musical history. William Schuman (1910-   ), a student of Roy Harris, has to his credit six symphonies, a ballet *Undertow*, and numerous choral works. He is also president of the Juillard School of Music in New York which, with the Curtis Institute in Philadelphia, ranks as one of the best music schools in the United States. From Curtis Institute have emerged Samuel Barber, Gian-Carlo Menotti, Leonard Bernstein, and Lukas Foss, four of the most successful and most diverse of the younger generation of composers. Barber (1910-   ), who is played in Europe more than in his native country, is somewhat conservative in style, polished and aristocratic. His *Adagio for Strings* and *Essays for Orchestra* are rather romantic, though his later works, the sonata and concerto for cello, are more stern. He has been successful with songs.

Gian-Carlo Menotti (1911-   ) has found enormous success in the operatic field. He is in a sense a latter-day Puccini, the Italian melodic fertility being very strong in his make-up. His own librettist, he has written four well-received operas, *Amelia Goes to the Ball, The Old Maid and the Thief* (originally a radio opera), *The Medium*, and *The Telephone*.

Successful in almost everything he has undertaken, Bernstein (1918-   ), has turned to practically every musical field. As a conductor and pianist he has achieved a vast popularity both in the United States and abroad. His compositions, though few, have covered a large territory. *Fancy Free* and *Facsimile* are ballets, *On the Town* is a musical comedy, and *Jeremiah* a symphony. They have won critical and public acclaim, and the latter work received the New York Music Critics Circle's prize, in 1944. His latest work is a symphony based on W. H. Auden's *The Age of Anxiety.*

The youngest of this group, Lukas Foss (1922-   ), though foreign born, has tried to adopt the American idiom in his larger works, notably *The Prairie,* a cantata-setting of Sandburg's poem. Foss studied with Hindemith and shows his influence at many points in his work.

From the Eastman School in Rochester by way of Roger Sessions, Nadia Boulanger, and other teachers has come David Diamond (1915-   ), one of the most striking present-day American composers. His *Rounds* for orchestra, his theater music for *The Tempest,* and his *Romeo and Juliet* suite are arresting scores. He is prolific, having written several symphonies, chamber music, and beautiful songs. One might round out this group with Morton Gould (1913-   ), the most performed of younger composers (his *Foster Gallery* celebrates many of Foster's tunes); Norman Dello Joio, whose *Ricercare* was performed abroad; Henry Brant, whose music has a satiric, humorous slant; Paul Bowles (1911-   ), whose travels in Latin America and Europe have greatly influenced his works.

There was a time when the American composer found great difficulty in having his works performed. This disheartening situation is little by little being rectified, and the composer of talent can usually achieve production through one channel or another. Such organizations as the Koussevitzky Foundation, the Alice M. Ditson Fund, and the League of Composers, to mention but a few, not only commission works but see to their production. The radio and the phonograph have spread American as well as European music, new and old, throughout the country.

At this juncture, it is interesting to notice the reversal in the American-European art relation. During the nineteenth and early part of the twentieth centuries the developing American composers went to Europe to study. For political as well as economic reasons the tide has now turned. The European masters have come to America and have given of their art to the young American composer, so that he has been able to imbibe modern European trends without being deprived of his American base. Schönberg, Hindemith, Stravinsky, Toch, Krenek, Milhaud—all of them living in the United States—have played a great rôle in fashioning the young composer's style. A long list of creative artists from all parts of the Old World could be appended.

The following is a list of further noted American composers and their chief accomplishments:

Henry F. Gilbert (1868-1928): *Negro Rhapsody, Dance in Place Congo,* which was originally an orchestral piece and received choreographic additions later.

Charles Sanford Skilton (1868-1941): *Indian Dances* and the operas *Kalopin* and *The Sun Bride,* the former based on native Indian motifs.

Daniel Gregory Mason (1873-   ): *Lincoln Symphony.*

Walter Damrosch (1862-   ): *Dunkirk* (1943). *Cyrano de Bergerac* (1913) and *The Man Without a Country* (1937); commissioned Gershwin's piano concerto.

Frederick Shepherd Converse (1871-1940): specialized in musical depictions of United States scenes: *Flivver Ten Million* (a Ford satire), *California, American Sketches,* etc.

Arthur Nevin (1871-1942): the opera *Poia,* inspired by a visit to an Indian reservation, and the one-act opera *Twilight.*

John Powell (1882-   ): *Rhapsodie Nègre* for piano and orchestra.

Arthur Shepherd (1880-   ): Symphonies; *Triptych* for soprano and string quartet.

Lazare Saminsky (1882-   ): symphonic music, ballet operas, choral works.

R. Nathanael Dett (1882-1943): one of the foremost representatives of Negro music. *Juba Dance* for piano. Arrangements of spirituals.

Richard Hageman (1882-   ): Active as an operatic conductor in New York, Chicago, and Los Angeles. His opera *Caponsacchi* was performed not only at the Metropolitan but also in various cities of Europe, but with rather indifferent success. He wrote quite a number of charming songs, some of which are still included in many singers' programs.

William Grant Still (1895-   ): Symphonic works *Darker America, Afro-American Symphony, Kaintuck, Lenox Avenue, In Memoriam,* written for the fallen Negro soldiers, and *Troubled Island.*

Naturally, our all-too-brief record included only the names of composers. It was merely our intention to demonstrate the wealth of contemporary musical production and the powerful infusion of European blood during the time between the two wars. One thing, however, we wish to emphasize: when the newcomers came in contact with American music, they realized that it had ceased to be a vaguely defined amorphous mass. Twentieth-century music in the United States has become a fact, with laws of its own, and an organic growth of its own. It vividly reflects the evolvement of a new culture.

MUSIC IN LATIN AMERICA

Latin America's struggle for independence had been directed principally against Spain, and Spain had long ceased to be the musically predominating power in her colonies. There, Italian music had gained a firm footing which it was not to relinquish for more than a hundred years. (Artistic and musical independence of Europe was something to which nobody gave even a passing thought.)

Among the victims of the struggle for political independence were quite a number of musicians. Some fell in battle, others were imprisoned or put to death. Many had to pay with their lives for the fact that they had participated in the revolt against the mother country, others merely because they had musically glorified the new freedom.

It was said before that in any new republic the first musical emanation with a nationalist tinge was likely to be its national anthem. The republics forming the South American continent were no exception in that respect. But the only "national" ingredients in those anthems were their enthusiasm and their text. The music moved along wholly conventional European lines. Anything else would have been impossible. Where was a new "South American" style to come from? Many of these hymns are impressive and finely wrought. That of Argentina hails back to the year 1813, when it was solemnly chosen by the constitutional National Assembly. Its thrice repeated call of *Libertad, Libertad, Libertad!* became a symbol. The fact that the use of European tunes for their national anthems was not objectionable to the young republics becomes understandable when it is considered that no hatred existed between the colonies and the mother country, but solely the will to freedom on the part of the colonials. Though they were no less Spaniards than those living across the ocean, they longed for liberation from an absolutist regime. To cite one more example, the Peruvian hymn was personally selected by that champion of liberty, San Martín, from the works of a Spanish musician living in Lima.

Independence and steamship transportation were two great factors in South America's cultural rise. Musical life multiplied. While, in the colonial epoch, Lima had been the spiritual center of the continent, Buenos Aires soon irresistibly forged to the fore. Its inhabitants still called it *la gran aldea*, the great village, referring not only to its architecture but also to its spirit. The first concert orchestra was heard there in 1813, and twelve years later, when the population had grown to 56,000, the first complete opera was given: Rossini's *Barber of Seville*. As chance would have it, New York's operatic activity started in the same year and with the same work. It is a noteworthy coincidence that the two American operatic centers which, even in our day, may be counted among the most brilliant in the world, thus had an almost identical beginning.

At that time, opera represented by far the most important and successful musical form in all Latin countries, and the Latin part of America was no exception. Just as the Europe of those days had her drawing-rooms in which high-minded people met for the purpose of literary and musical enjoyment, so America, too, could boast of similar institutions.

Let us enumerate some of Latin America's early operas, although all of them have long since been relegated to the limbo of forgotten things. In Mexico, Manuel Covarrubias composed *The Peruvian Priestess*, and Aniceto Ortega *Guatimotzin*; a Peruvian, Carlos E. Pasta, wrote *Atahualpa*, and his fellow countryman, José María Valle, *Ollantay*; as early as 1846, *Telesfora*, an opera by Aquiles Ried, was printed in Chile. The very titles of these operas reveal an interesting fact. The American artists were beginning to look for their subjects in the history of their continent, and mostly at the point where it was most dramatic, at the clashing of the Indian culture with that of the whites.

This theme, by the way, also served to furnish some European musicians with inspiration. Frederick the Great's director of the Royal Orchestra, *Hofkapellmeister* Graun, may have been the first of them. He wrote the opera *Montezuma* whose costumes and scenery are still in existence. Spontini composed *Fernand Cortez*, which was successful and had the enthusiastic approval of Napoleon—true, more because of its anti-Spanish tendency than because of its music. Finally, Verdi, too, touched upon Peruvian history in his early opera *Alzira*. The scene of his *Masked Ball*, on the other hand, was rather arbitrarily transferred to America simply because the Italian censor would not have a monarch assassinated in a European state. In the end, the discoverer of the New World also became an operatic figure. Mention was already made in Franchetti's work which was written for the quatro-centenary of the famous voyage. There was also Milhaud's grandiose modern opera dealing with the same subject. In addition, Columbus is the central figure of operas written by the Germans Egk and Dressel and the Hungarian Zador. Who knows how many more there are?

From the steadily growing number of American operatic works, one stands out prominently, the only one that was able to gain international fame in the last century. It is *Il Guarany*, by the Brazilian Carlos Gomes (1836-1896). The first performance of this musical drama, which also had for its theme the clashing of the victorious invaders—Portuguese, this time—with the Indian natives of Brazil, the Guaranís, took place at the

Scala of Milan, in the year 1870. The music is of the purest Italian school even in places where Indian tonal sequences are used. A little later, the work was performed in Rio de Janeiro, on the occasion of the Brazilian Emperor Pedro II's birthday. It was proclaimed the National Opera, and Gomes the National Composer, although he composed exclusively in the Italian style. Gomes traveled the same paths when he wrote his opera *The Slave*, upon which, too, the honor of National Opera was conferred. His last work, which in a symphonic-choral form dealt with the previously mentioned Columbus theme, was a failure.

Among the many musical drawing-rooms of Latin America, one deserves to be mentioned specially. In the house of Amancio Alcorta, in Buenos Aires, people with artistic inclinations gathered to listen to new poetry and music. At that time, European romanticism was greatly in vogue in America. Nocturnes were composed, "album leaves," waltzes, and ballads. In addition to Alcorta, men like Salustiano Zavalia, Juan Pedro Esnaola, and Juan Bautista Alberdi may be counted among the pioneers of South American orchestral and chamber music. All of them held prominent public positions, none was a professional musician. Nevertheless, they managed to produce many a pretty piece. Moreover, the influence of these four friends on the musical culture of their city was by no means negligible. Of the Argentine musicians of that time, outstanding are the two brothers Berutti. Pablo (1866-1914) won the Leipzig Mozart Prize, a feat accomplished by but one other foreigner—Saint Saëns—while Arturo (1862-1938) glorified episodes from the history of his continent in his operas, such as the memorable Andes campaign of San Martín (*The Heroes*) and an Inca theme (*Yupanqui*). The latter opera had the distinction of having Caruso in the cast at its first performance.

Orchestral concerts were introduced in Buenos Aires in the Twenties of the last century. President Rivadavia encouraged the influx of European musicians, provided they did not come from Spain, a country for which he had little sympathy. Orchestras, choruses, and the opera had long been under the guidance of Italians. On April 25, 1857, the old Colón Theater was inaugurated as an operatic house with a performance of *La Traviata*. Before it closed its doors, in 1888, it had achieved the distinction of being among the world's most brilliant temples dedicated to opera. Exactly twenty years later, on the National Holiday (May 25), the new theater of the same name was opened. There was a time when Buenos Aires had three opera houses. In addition to the Colón Theater (the name is the Spanish version of Columbus), there was the Coliseum and the Opera Theater. None of the great artists of the lyrical art failed to appear in the increasingly flourishing city at the mouth of the La Plata.

Mexico gradually became the other musical center in Spanish-speaking America. The population, with its strongly Indian admixture, had been fond of music from the very beginning, while the proximity of the United States, whose musical life was expanding all the time, served as an added stimulus. The first Mexican Philharmonic Society was founded in 1825. To be sure, another forty-five years had to elapse before a Beethoven symphony had its first performance. The man who shared the program with Beethoven on that occasion was a Mexican by the name of Melesio Morales. The following is an excerpt from a newspaper criticism of the latter's work: ". . . after a few orchestral chords, we hear the bell-jingle of the mules drawing the cars from the center of the city to the station where the locomotive is waiting. We hear its whistle, the hiss of the escaping steam, the clanking of the wheels while the train is in motion—and all this is accompanied by the most unique harmonies, sounding like a hymn to the civilization of the nineteenth century. . . ." In 1870, mind you! The composition of this railway lyric may have stamped Morales as one of the first musical realists, a distant precursor of Honegger and his *Pacific 231*.

It goes without saying that what is today considered Latin American music had its roots in folk music. It developed in different directions, influenced mainly by the predominating color of the various republics' inhabitants. While Argentina, Uruguay, and Chile are practically pure white and have received all their music from Europe, there are other realms with strong Indian characteristics (Peru, Bolivia, Mexico, Central America) and still others in which the Negro element predominates (Brazil, Cuba, Haiti). And so, country by country, music is different, and yet possesses something in common. To express it in figures and percentages: Argentina's music may be called 90% European and 10% Indian; that of Brazil 50% Negroid, 30% white, and 20% Indian, that of Peru 50% Indian, 45% white, and 5% Asiatic and African. But while this would show that there exists some kind of common denominator, it is really no more than an idle playing with figures, for the Indian element no longer exists in its pure form and neither does the black, and as for the white, many an influence, like that of Russia, Hungary, and Spain has been at work.

An account of Latin American music of recent time could be rendered by enumerating the countries' composers according to the prominence they have achieved in the world's musical affairs. We might, for instance, start with Villa-Lobos, the Brazilian, whose vigorous and highly individualistic personality has aroused world-wide interest. But the better procedure would seem to be to pass quickly through the various South American republics and record their musical life and their composers. Let us begin in the South.

In Argentina, we meet the patriarchal figure of Alberto Williams (1862-   ). He was a pupil of César Franck in Paris and returned to Buenos Aires, perhaps the first thoroughly coached South American musician. He taught, conducted, kept in constant touch with modern European tendencies, composed nine symphonies and many songs that have attained popularity. His style is late-romantic, classicistic at times, and thoroughly European in its orientation, with a French and German inflection. Quite a number of the country's composers are adherents of the Italian school, even though some of them are championing the cause of Argentine national music, like Felipe Boero (1884-   ), whose *El Matrero* has become the most popular of the many great operas the country has produced. This is the place, too, to mention Argentina's two finest lyric composers, Julián Aguirre (1868-1924), who succeeded in producing many a beautiful melody with a national coloring, and Carlos López Buchardo (1881-   ), whose compositions are few but who knew how to capture in some songs and brief orchestral pieces the magic of the far-flung Argentine pampas. Today, Juan José Castro (1895-   ) is undoubtedly one of the most important Argentine musicians. As a conductor, he is held in high esteem in all parts of the continent. Among his works, written in a thoroughly modern idiom, are three symphonies: the *Argentine*, the *Biblical*, and the *Symphony of the Fields*, expressive of far distances and loneliness, elements which the Argentine pampas have suggested to a great many poets, painters, and musicians. His friendship with Manuel de Falla was the source of a deeply moving mourning song on the occasion of the latter's death. Mention must be made of Luis Gianneo (1897-   ), a master of instrumentation, whose works are pictures in sound of Old Indian legends or natural scenery. Gilardo Gilardi (1889-   ), like Gianneo and many other Argentine musicians of Italian origin, wrote a beautiful opera, *The Legend of Urutaú*, a primeval forest bird, whose song is made to play a part in the tragic clash between

Indians and whites. In his *Cradle Song of an Indian Mother* he succeeded in creating a colorful chamber piece. Another gifted Argentine composer is Alberto Ginastera (1916-   ), who also chose for his subjects far-flung scenery and Old Indian legends. Carlos Guastavino (1914-   ) has written songs of remarkably effective national coloring.

To render as complete a picture as possible of Argentina's contemporary creative musical activity, we are again adding a list of composers, the caliber of whose work entitles them to mention These men represent a great diversity of schools, from romanticism to neoclassicism to twelve-tone music: José André, José Gil, Hector Iglesias Villoud, Arturo Luzzatti, Juan Bautista Massa, Roberto García Morillo, Athos Palma, Hetore Panizza, Juan Carlos Paz, Celestino Piaggio, Pascual de Rogatis (composer of highly interesting operas), Alfredo Schiuma, Celia Torra, Floro M. Ugarte (who wrote the beautiful orchestral suite *From My Fatherland*). Among the country's prominent musicologists are Ernesto de la Guardia, the translator of Wagner's works into Spanish, and Carlos Vega, whose writings on folklore are a notable achievement.

Chile is another South American country whose musical ascent during the past twenty years has been remarkable. Her music is perhaps the "whitest" of all, with no Negro influence and hardly any traces of Indian elements. Humberto Allende (1885-   ) is the champion of Chilean music. Foremost among his compositions are his *Rural Chilean Scenes* and his strange symphonic poem *Voices of the Street*, in which he gives orchestral expression to the melodious cries of the street vendors. Allende's music found its way to Europe on a number of occasions and made a deep impression on artists like Pedrell, Florent Schmitt, and Debussy. There is also Domingo Santa Cruz (1899-   ), to whose organizing skill Chilean musical life is greatly indebted and who is also prominent as a modernly schooled composer revealing influences of neoclassicism, linear counterpoint, and folk music. He set to music some of the poems of his great compatriot, Gabriela Mistral, who was honored with the Nobel Prize, in 1946. Carlos Isamitt (1885-   ) is equally gifted as a painter and a musician, and Enrique Soro (1884-   ) is a most prolific composer, the number of his works nearing the thousand-mark.

Other Chilean composers: Adolfo Allende, René Amengual, Próspero Bisquett, Armando Carvajal, Acario Cotapos, Pablo Garrido, Carlos Lavin, Alfonso Leng, Alfonso Letellier, Carmela Mackenna, Héctor Meolo Gorigotía, Samuel Negrete, Pedro Nuñez Navarrete, Jorge Urrutia (a pupil of Dukas and Hindemith).

The center of Chile's musical life is Santiago, which has a well-equipped opera, an excellent national symphony orchestra, and a number of chamber music associations. It is the scene of numerous concerts. The University has a large share in communicating musical understanding to the broad masses. The South of the country manifests a great popular affection for choral singing, a tendency which has been productive of fine results.

Uruguay is also a "white" country. Most of its compositions were inspired by its scenery. First mention is due Eduardo Fabini (1883), an internationally prominent figure. His large symphonic poems—the *Isle of the Ceibos, Campo, Mburucuyá,*[1] and *Symphony of the Cultivated Soil*—are written in a national style approaching impressionism.

Uruguayan composers: Vicente Ascone (composer of the opera *Paraná Guazü*)[2] Luis Cluzeau Mortet, Carlos Estrada, Luis Pedro Mondino, Carlos Pedrell, Ramón Rodríguez, Guido Santórsola, Héctor Tosar Errecart. The leading figure among the country's musicologists is Francisco Curt Lange, Head of an Inter-American Institute, which has done much to foster a feeling of solidarity among Latin-American composers. The *Boletín* published by him prints a great deal of little-known material from all epochs of South American music.

Montevideo, the capital of Uruguay, leads an active musical life, whose center is a state institute. It has a fine orchestra, a well-trained chorus, chamber music groups, and a corps de ballet, in addition to a young and gifted operatic ensemble. Furthermore, the institute is the possessor of one of the largest South American collections of phonograph records which it makes available to the public by regularly occurring concerts and radio broadcasts.

Musically less prominent are South America's only two inland republics, Paraguay and Bolivia. Both countries are pronouncedly Indian in the make-up of their population and are far removed from the continent's cultural centers. On the other hand, both have interesting autochtonous music, use Indian instruments, and are fond of Indian dances.

Paraguayan composers: José Asunción Flores (1904-), the creator of a musical form called *Guarania* (from Guaraní, the name of the country's Indian inhabitants), in which native rhythms and melodies are raised to the level of artistic music; Remberto Giménez, Juan Carlos Moreno. It may be worth mentioning that Paraguay is the only country on the South American continent still making general use of an Indian tongue (Guaraní), with the result that most of the vocal compositions of the Paraguayan musicians (and naturally almost all of the country's folk music) are based upon it.

Bolivian composers: Bolivia is composed of two large Indian territories, that of the Quechuas and that of the Aymarás, whose melodies have been frequently used by the country's composers. The tunes represent typical pentatonic musical systems. Eduardo Caba (1890-) stylized this music in a highly interesting manner. Working along the same lines are Antonio González Bravo and José Maria Velasco Maidana, whose ballet *Amerindia* (symbolic name for Indian America) was produced in Berlin. Teófilo Vargas collected Bolivian melodies in many volumes, and Humberto Viscarra Monjé composed colorful *Impressions of the Bolivian Highland.* Bolivia's largest city, La Paz, has a national orchestra. In addition, music is being taught at the Universities (La Paz, Sucre, Oruro, Potosí). Opera and vocal concerts meet with great difficulties at an altitude of more than 12,000 feet above sea level.

The music of Peru bears a striking similarity to that of Bolivia. The country's topography is much like that of the neighboring country. The high cordillera with its lonely valleys, inhabited by what is left of ancient Indian tribes, forms the land's main characteristic. No wonder that in Peru's folk and artistic music, too, the Indian element predominates. To

---

1 Ceibo and Mburucuyá are flowers typical of Uruguay
2 Paraná Guazú is the Indian name of the Great Paraná River

what extent it has remained unchanged since the glorious days of the Old Indian rule is of course unknown. Peru's most interesting composer in our century was an Indian, Teodoro Valcárcel (1900-1942). He was born on the shore of Lake Titicaca, sacred to the people since time immemorial and woven round with lengendary lore. Among other compositions, he left behind an Indian concerto for violin and orchestra, a suite of native dances, *Suray-Surita,* and the symphonic poem *Among the Ruins of the Sun Temple.*

Peruvian composers: Policarpo Caballero, Roberto Carpio Valdés, Pablo Chávez Aguilar, Alfonso de Silva (who died at the age of thirty-three), Rodolfo Holzmann, André Sas (composer of a *Peruvian Rhapsody,* an *Indian Poem,* and a great deal of other typically Peruvian music based on Indian elements), and Raoul de Verneuil (who wrote a noteworthy *Inca Legend* and a *Peruvian Dance* for orchestra).

Today Lima has an adequate national orchestra and other musical institutions. Besides, thanks to modern plane connections, it is frequently visited by virtuosos traveling between North and South America.

And now we come to Brazil which by many is considered the most interesting musical country of Latin America. Its racial mixture is more pronounced than that of any of the so-far-mentioned countries. The Negroid element, with its innate and vital musicality, is strongly in evidence. In Heitor Villa-Lobos (1881-   ) Brazil has an eminent musical personality. He succeeded in giving voice in his works to his country's every basic element, to the Indian, the Negro, and the white man. He knew how to amalgamate all styles (in his *Bachianas Brasileiras* he wrote Negro music in strict Bach style!) and to produce an immensely vital tone picture of his beautiful homeland. His inexhaustible wealth of ideas and his unbelievable capacity for work (he has written more than a thousand compositions, many of them of the highest caliber) stamp him as one of the internationally prominent creative men of our day. He was asked once about his country's folklore. His answer was: "Folklore—that's me!" in the manner of the king who said: *"L'Etat, c'est moi!"* And there is a measure of truth in Villa-Lobos' words. It is he who has done most toward making the multiform music of his country into a homogeneous entity. He is familar with Brazil's every feature: the roaring modern metropolis of Rio de Janeiro (he states proudly that it is the most beautiful in the world), the impenetrable virgin forest at the Amazon, and the Negro huts nestling in a crazy pattern against a mountain slope. Above all, he is familiar with the carnival in his city, a festival to which should be devoted a whole book instead of merely a line or two. For days on end, all normal life ceases, to be replaced by ecstasy and an orgy of color and sound. Without let-up, the dull drum-beats of the Negroes drill themselves into the ear with their mysterious ritual rhythms; and each year the people sing new songs, hatched in the fertile womb of the country. Villa-Lobos has put all this into his music, into symphonies, symphonic poems, concertos, chamber music, sonatas, songs, operas, oratorios. He is always original, always surprising, always revolutionary, and always self-willed. He has written works of all styles. Polyphony and the utmost realism—there is the choral work portraying the noises of a steel mill,—romanticism and impressionism, dwell side by side in a most fascinating mixture.

It would be unjust to let Villa-Lobos make us forget two other Brazilian composers of prominence. One is Oscar Lorenzo Fernandez (1897-   ) who has given to the world a number of highly interesting works, also inspired by the sounds of his country. We have his Indian legend *Imbapara, Batuque*,[1] several symphonies, the opera *Malazarte* (which, in 1941, had to be sung in Italian because adequate native singers were not available), and the *Suburban Waltz* for piano, which is included in the repertoire of all American pianists. The other is Francisco Mignone (1897-   ), whose best-known works are the orchestral pieces *In the Country*, *Dionysian Festival*, *Old Legend*, *On Quiet Paths*, *Lyrical Intermezzo*, and the Negro dance *Congada*, remarkable for its fiery rhythm.

Brazilian composers: Mario de Andrade (one of the most prominent collectors of folk music), Francisco Braga (1868-   ), who as a creative musician and conductor did much for his country's music, Ernani Braga, José Vieira, Walter Burle Marx, Eleazar de Carvalho, Luiz Cosme, Joao Itiberé da Cunha, Radames Gnatalli, Camargo Guarnieri (the guiding spirit among the young modernists), Brasilio Itiberé, Souza Lima, Leopoldo Miguez, Arturo Napoleao, Ernesto Nazareth, Alberto Nepumoceno, Barrozo Netto, Joao Octaviano, Henrique Oswald (of Swiss origin), Assis Republicano, Claudio Santoro, Hekel Tavares, Fructuoso Vianna.

Rio's musical life has become greatly intensified during the past years. There are a good National Theater, in which, occasionally, talented young natives are given a chance; two symphony orchestras; conservatories; musical periodicals, and a large number of concerts. But there are other cities, too, on the wide soil of Brazil where musical life flourishes, although it will take another few years to have it fully organized. This is true of Sao Paulo, a city of a million, of Porto Allegre, and the populated Negro towns of the North. One of the most surprising impressions for the musician of today is the virgin-forest city of Manaos, thousands of miles in the wholly trackless interior of the country, in which, thanks to the airplane, a wealth of concerts may be attended and a rather adequate local orchestra be heard. A similar case is that of the city of Belo Horizonte, although the character of this place is an entirely different one. It was built a few years ago in accordance with set plans in which, with equal precision, the musical equipment was included—a rare case in Latin America.

―――――――

[1] *Batuque* is one of the most characteristic Negro dances of Brazil.

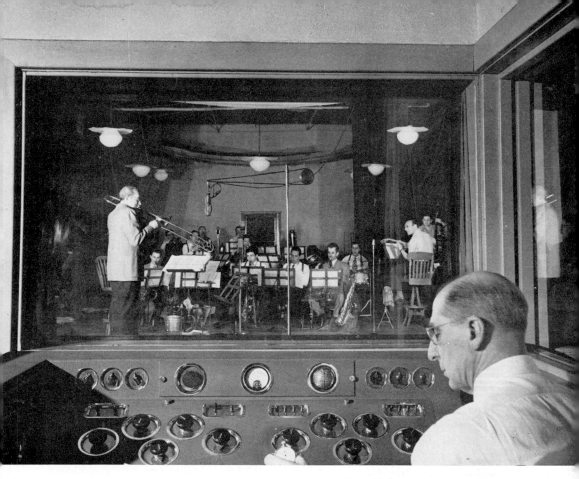

201. Popular band making a recording, while the engineer notes his stop watch. [*Photo RCA Victor*]

202. Re-recording the original lacquer disc onto wax. [*Photo RCA Victor*]

203. The original Dixieland Five at Reisenweber's' Columbus Circle in 1915.
[*Photo Apeda*]

204. Benny Goodman's orchestra in Chicago, 1935.
205. The famous Duke Ellington and his musical combination.

206. August 6, 1947. The first recording ever made in the music shed at Tanglewood, Massachusetts, was the recording of Beethoven's Ninth Symphony, made by the Boston Symphony Orchestra directed by Dr. Serge Koussevitsky, chorus and soloists directed by Robert Shaw. [*Photo RCA Victor*]

207. The recording of a side completed, Dr. Koussevitsky (left) listens to a playback, following the score closely. Sometimes five or six "takes" are necessary before one perfect master record is secured that is satisfactory to conductor and recording director. [*RCA Victor photo by Babbitt*]

208. A modern broadcasting studio at NBC. [*Photo NBC*]

209. Great music for American audiences: Arturo Toscanini conducts the NBC Symphony, and the performance is enjoyed by studio listeners, radio and television fans—and also recorded.

[*Photo NBC*]

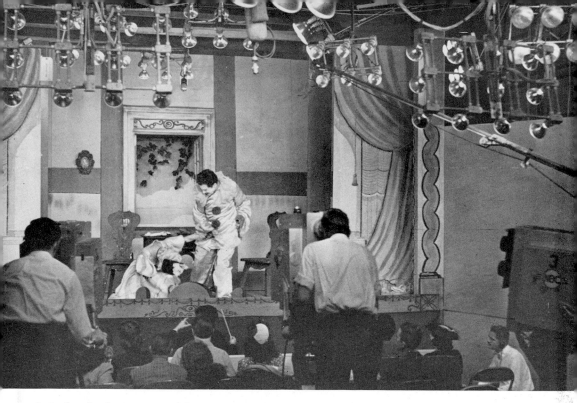

210. In the last scene of Leonconvallo's *Pagliacci*, Canio (William Horne) stabs Nedda (Majorie Hess)—and the drama goes by television into millions of American homes. [*Photo NBC*]

211. In the television control room, an engineer closely watches images, during the progress of a program. [*Photo NBC*]

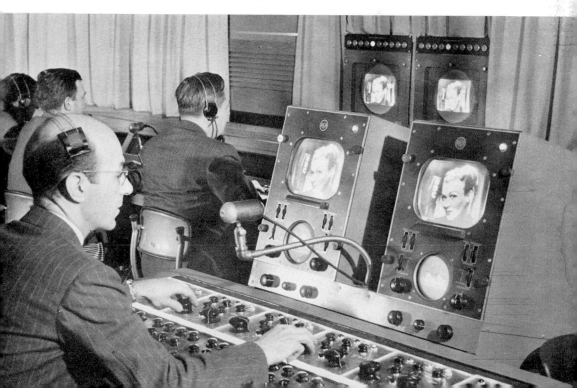

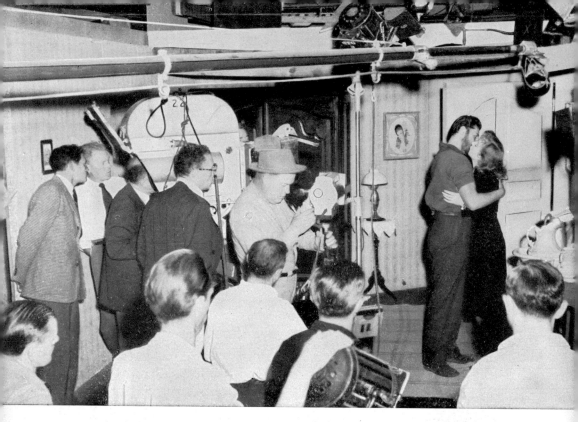

212. A studio "take" of Greer Garson and Robert Mitchum. [*Photo MGM*]

213. Donna Reed has "just been saved" from drowning. [*Photo MGM*]

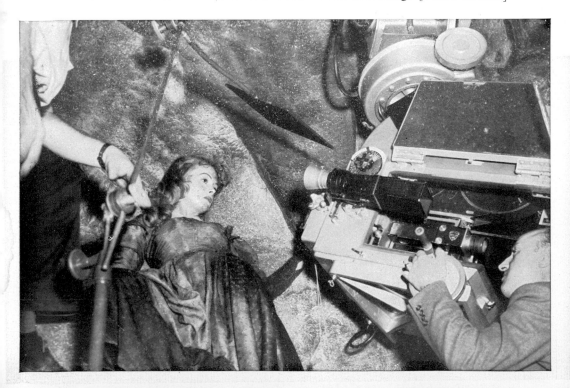

214. Open-air performance at the Hollywood Bowl, Los Angeles, attended by an audience of 20,000.

215. Open-air performance of Verdi's *Aida* by a touring company, in Civita-vecchia, Italy.

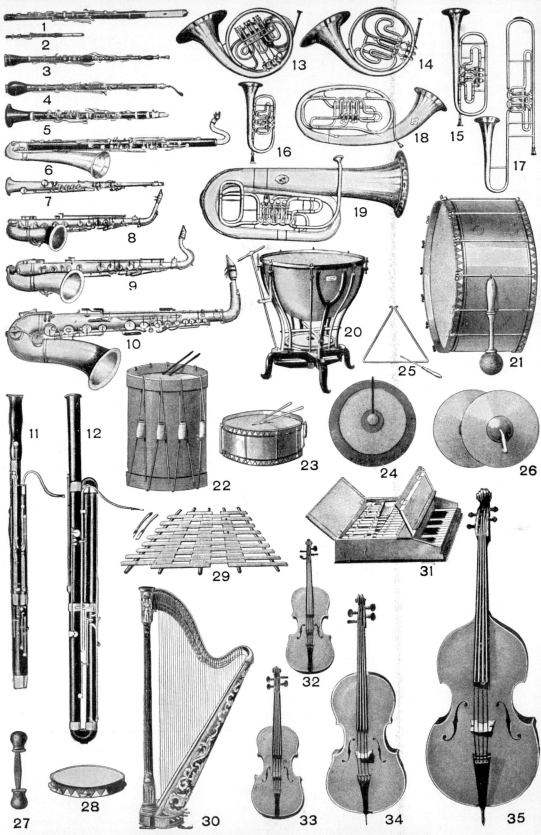

216. The instruments of the modern orchestra.

Colombia which until recently did not play a noteworthy part in musical life, has, like all her sister republics, taken rapid strides forward in our century. Here again, we come to appreciate the blessings of modern air connections, the only ones by which Bogotá, the country's capital can be comfortably reached; and the no less fruitful occupation of the musicians with their homeland's folklore which, in Colombia, is mainly Indian and, in many a far-off region, still wholly unexplored. The same may be said of the small Republic of Ecuador, in which the major part of the Indian population lives with hardly any contact with the whites and the state. Colombia, on the other hand, has a number of important cities in which musical life has gratifyingly progressed. Some have their own orchestras, none has a permanent opera house, but all of them (fortunate twentieth century!) have powerful radio stations which are deserving of high commendation for the part they play in the musical enlightenment of the people.

Composers from Colombia: Jesús Bermúdez Silva, Guillermo Espinosa, Adolfo Mejía, Emilio Murillo, Carlos Posada Amador, José Rozo Contreras, Guillermo Uribe Holguin. The latter, born in 1880, is the most important musician of his country, composer of several symphonies and concertos in late-impressionistic style.

Composers from Ecuador: Segundo Luis Moreno, Luis H. Salgado (composer of the symphonic suite *Atahualpa, or The Downfall of a Country*), and Pedro Traversari.

Venezuela has for centuries produced good music in her churches. The country has therefore the right to cherish a certain choral tradition. Its development runs parallel to that of the other Latin American republics. It is now reaching back to the *musical* language of its aboriginal inhabitants in an effort to create a national music.

Composers from Venezuela: María Luisa Escobar, Juan Lecuna, Moisés Moleiro, Juan Bautista Plaza, Vicente Emilio Sojo. And let us mention that two internationally known names are connected with Venezuela's musical history: Terresa Careño, the great pianist, whose grandfather had been choirmaster and organist of the Cathedral of Caracas, and Reynoldo Hahn, the fine impressionist of the French school. Both were born in Caracas.

As for Central America, there is not much to be said as yet. Culturally and musically, her small republics are not fully developed, although Costa Rica and Guatemala are farther advanced. Quite recently, a number of them such as San Salvador, Santo Domingo, and Haiti, have called into being State Symphony Orchestras, and all of them are trying hard to guide some of the stream of artists constantly flowing between North and South America into their parts. There are not a few interesting musical personalities from these countries. Nicaragua, for instance, the home of the great poet Rubén Darío, gave us an Indian composer,

Juan de la Cruz Mena, who, when he fell victim to leprosy, wrote his own requiem. Costa Rica is perhaps the most progressive of this group of small countries, a fact clearly reflected in her active musical life.

Composers from Panama: Herbert de Castro, Ricardo Fábrega, Narciso Garay, Alfredo de Saint-Malo. From Costa Rica: Ismaél Cárdona, Julio Fonseca (born 1885, composer of a *Tropical Suite* and a *Cantata to Music*), Julio Mata, Alejandro Monestel, César Nieto. From Honduras: Francisco Diaz Zelaya, Ramón Ruíz, Ignacio Villanueva Galeano. From Nicaragua: Luis A. Delgadillo, Juan de la Cruz Mena. From Santo Domingo: Clodomiro Arredondo Miura, Enrique Casal Chapi (the grandson of the highly successful Spanish zarzuela composer), Juan Francisco García, Enrique de Marchena, Esteban Peña Morell, José de Jesús Ravelo (composer of the oratorio *The Death of Jesus*), Luis Rivera, Augusto Vega.

Composers from El Salvador: Jesús Alas, María de Baratta, Alejandro Muñoz, Domingo Santos. From Guatemala: Felipe Arias (murdered in his youth), José Castañeda, Jesús Castillo, Ricardo Castillo, José Molina Pinillo, Julián Paniagua Martínez.

Composers from Haiti: Justin Elie, Ludovic Lamothe, a pianist of the Paris school, who, because of his many piano pieces of a romantic character is at times called "The black Chopin."

On our musical journey through the wide realms of America we have now come to Mexico, which must be numbered among the most interesting countries by far. First, because there the Indian element has been most vitally preserved, and second, because the country's more prominent composers have known how to blend successfully elements of a European, North American, and Indian character. Mexico, revolutionary soil from time immemorial, is revolutionary also in its music. First place among its musicians may be accorded to Manuel M. Ponce (1886-   ), whose work actually marks the beginning of national Mexican music. His first symphonic composition of some importance (after his studies with Dukas in Paris) was *Chapultepec*.[1] But he also composed music of the European kind, like his *Suite in the Old Style*, *Prelude, Canon, Pavan, and Fugue*, and some duo-sonatas. He dedicated to Andrés Segovia, the famous Spanish guitarist, a unique *Concerto of the South* with chamber orchestra accompaniment. His Mexican song *Estrellita* became internationally known. Mention should also be made of the picturesquely tragic figure of Silvestre Revueltas who, in 1940, at the age of forty, died in true Montmartre style after an adventurous life and on the eve of the first performance of one of his ballets. Julián Carillo (1875-   ) also deserves mention. Among all of the modern revolutionaries in music he is perhaps the most advanced. In 1895, prior to all his European colleagues, he split our smallest musical unit, the half-

---

[1] Chapultepec is the name of a quarter in Mexico City

tone, into an infinite number of smaller parts, into quarters, eighths sixteenths, and so on, until he had reached a one-hundred-and-twenty-eighth part of a tone. He called his discovery *Revolution of the Sound Thirteen,* because with the discovery of the thirteenth tone he had breached the centuries-old system of our twelve notes. He constructed instruments to demonstrate his discovery, wrote compositions based on it, propagated a new way of writing music and a great many other things, but his success was as negative as had been that of the European quarter-toners. (Nevertheless, his train of thought in itself was correct and thoroughly logical.) And finally, it is but fair to make special mention of Carlos Chávez (1899-   ), the outstanding representative and champion of "Indianistic" art. In his endeavor, he is aided by many a poet and by painters of such importance as his compatriots Diego Rivera and Orozco. Among his numerous works are the *Indian Symphony,* the ballet *HP* (horse power) and the unpronounceable and almost equally unperformable symphonic poem *Xochipili-Macuilxochitl,* so named after the Mexican god of music and for whose performance, in addition to the standard symphonic instruments, a number of Indian instruments are required. Chávez was organizer and conductor of the Symphony Orchestra of Mexico, and director of the National Conservatory of Music in Mexico. He is also the author of a book on music and electricity.

Mexican composers: Daniel Ayala, Gerónimo Baqueiro Foster (who is also the publisher of a good musical periodical), Miguel Bernal (who in his work *Tata Vasco* erected to a popular bishop of his home province a sounding memorial in which Gregorian chorales and Indian pentatonics appear in a strange mixture), Gustavo Campa, Salvador Contreras, Blas Galindo, Candelario Huizar (born in 1888, of Indian origin, and composer of several vigorous symphonies and symphonic poems), Carlos Jiménez Mabarak, Juan León Mariscal, Vicente T. Mendoza, Arnulfo Miramontes, José Rolón (composer of the symphonic poems *Zapotlan, Cuauhtemoc, The Feast of the Dwarfs, Dance from Michoacán,* and others), Luis Sandi, Rafael Tello, and José Vásquez.

Musical life in Mexico is exceptionally. Special attention is given to symphonic music. In addition, there are concerts by soloists and choral associations, and lately regular operatic performances have also been given. After Buenos Aires, it is the most important publishing point for Latin American music and other musical output. Ever since the Spanish civil war, there live in Mexico a number of important Spanish composers and the most prominent Spanish musicologist, Adolfo Salazar.

The last of the Latin American countries to be visited is Cuba. Here, to a locally smaller degree, the Brazilian experience is repeated: the black element preponderates, giving its unmistakable imprint to Cuban music. Habanera, rumba, and conga have their home on the beautiful island of the Antilles which today occupies one of the important places in Latin American musical life. In Havana, the Pro Arte Society has a concert hall that accommodates 2,500 people, while a good symphony orchestra communicates to its listeners the entire international and the interesting national repertoire. The island's most gifted composer, Alejandor García Caturla (1906-1940), a man of pure Spanish origin, died a tragic death. A judge in his daily profession, he was shot by a defendant. His entire work was inspired by that folk music which is significantly called "Afro-Cuban." Another of Cuba's gifted composers, a mulatto, was Amadeo Roldán (1900-1839) who also died a premature death. Among his works are an *Overture on Cuban Themes*, *Negro Festival*, and the ballet *Rebambaramba*, in which ritual Negro music is reproduced by the use of a bewildering number of percussion instruments.

Cuban composers: Juan Antonio Cámara, Harald Gramatges, Ernesto Lecuona (composer of a Negro rhapsody for piano and orchestra), Gonzalo Roig, Eduardo Sánchez de Fuentes (who was both a composer and the most intensive explorer of Cuban music).

* * * *

And so we have reached the end of our extensive chapter dealing with the Americas. Today, the New World represents an important cultural factor and, beyond that, a cultural will. It combines the old, which it tries to draw forth from oblivion, with the new, the present. It has saturated itself with the knowledge and ability which Europe had been able to communicate to it. Stefan Zweig, who clung with all his heart to European culture, addressed the following words to American intellectuals and artists assembled in Buenos Aires on the occasion of the Pen Club Congress, in 1939:

"In battle, it is the soldier's supreme duty, even in the event of defeat, to prevent the flag from falling into the hands of the enemy. When a standard bearer sinks to the ground, another fighter rushes up to save the banner and carry it farther forward. For a long time, Europe was the standard bearer of ideas and ideals; but during the present catastrophe the flag has slipped from her hands. Who knows but what it may be forever! And that is why I say to you: Save the flag! Since we are wounded and exhausted, you must pridefully carry the spiritual ideals of mankind farther forward. In this hour, you are our foremost, nay, our only, hope for the salvation of our culture, of western civilization."

Mechanical Music

THERE are in musical history any number of highly important dates which have no direct bearing on the lives of the great composers. Such a date undoubtedly occurred about the turn of the sixteenth century when Ottaviano Petrucci was able for the first time to use Gutenberg's epochal invention for the printing of musical notes. It surely marked the beginning of a new era in musical life. What had up to that time been available only in very few manuscripts which, besides, frequently differed from one another and were faulty, could now be produced in many identical copies. This immediately multiplied the circulation of a work, since it was made available to practically all music lovers, provided, of course, that they were skilled enough either to read or reproduce by means of an instrument the tone images painted by the composer. How many truly important compositions may have been lost or forgotten, just because their creators happened to live prior to that decisive year!

The world of our day is once more faced with a technical invention whose influence upon music is of the utmost importance. When, in 1878, Edison for the first time heard his own voice come softly out of a metal horn, he was, so he said, seized with a cold shudder. Had he a vision of the new world about to be unfolded? Could he have foreseen what two generations of inventors and technicians would make of his work? When he first displayed his talking machine before an international congress of scientific men, he caused an incredulous shaking of heads. One renowned physicist seriously thought that Edison had hidden a ventriloquist somewhere in the hall and was playing a trick on his colleagues.

From Edison's wax cylinder developed the phonograph record, the recording tape, the sound track, and the magnetic wire able to absorb an unlimited wealth of sound. The electrical transmission of sound followed as a logical development of the mechanical system, immeasurably expanding the already vast regions of newly discovered land. We do not propose to say much in this book about the technical side of the new inventions, of the manifold problems of sound recording and reproduction, of the construction of the microphones, record cutters, pick-ups; of the mechanical, optical, or electrical processes for fixing sound waves on records, ribbons, wires, and sound tracks; and of the reconversion of such impulses into sound, of its amplification in loudspeakers, of the tone filtering, blending, and of the many other aspects of the subject. These are scientific matters, for the technician, not for the musician. We are mainly concerned with what these new inventions—sound transmission over no matter what distances, sound storage for no matter how long a time—mean in connection with art, with musical activities, with musical life. Perhaps there is still another, and partly unconscious, reason why a detailed treatment of these questions within the framework of this book seems inappropriate: the series of inventions that started with Thomas Alva Edison's primitive talking machine is not concluded. Further, and perhaps undreamt-of, developments are in store for us.

Let us first consider the phonograph record, which started the train of developments leading into new land. The trade-mark of a firm making phonographs and records shows a dog on his haunches before the trumpet of a phonograph, his head cocked to one side, as if in surprise. He hears his master's voice, caught, confined, detached from the living figure, and independent of its presence. In penning this sentence, I am merely trying to recall to those of our generation, to whom all this has become as familiar as railways and street lighting, what their grandparents and parents felt.

To hear oneself! That is as mysterious as hearing one who is absent, or even one who is dead. Nobody knows his own voice, no orator or singer would ever have heard it had it not been for the phonograph record. This points the way to the appliance's first practical use: tuition. Not only is the vocal student able to hear the voices of great singers, but he can also make comparisons with his own ability, correct his faults, and observe his progress. The disciple of song is not the only one to be benefited by the record; every student of music finds in it an invaluable aid. All the things that formerly had to be read from the pages of rather dry treatises, that had been but "gray theory," are suddenly turned into sounding reality. The student of instrumentation, who had to acquaint himself with a vast number of sound mixtures, can now actually hear the magic charm of a horn solo, the effect of violin harmonics, or of a harp glissando. The budding conductor, too, can learn much from orchestral recordings.

Exact knowledge of a work can never be acquired through listening to it at a concert. The record, however, points an ideal way to thorough understanding. The lover of music is able to listen to masterly performances within his own four walls, in absolute seclusion and utmost concentration, under conditions, that is, which are unattainable at public hearings. The record has made permanent the utmost of perfection, which even the recording artists are but rarely able to achieve at concerts. To reach such a point of perfection, the process of recording may have had to be repeated a number of times, a procedure naturally impossible at a public performance. The record enables the true lover of music to indulge in conscientious study. He may listen to certain difficult passages of a symphony any number of times. He may at his leisure make observations, imprint upon his memory certain sound colorings, attempt to anlayze forms—all of which is not only impossible at a concert but also undesirable. The enjoyment of a work at a live production will be redoubled if a preparatory study of recordings has preceded it. Thus the record is not here an end in itself, but an ideal means to an ideal end.

Only now can musical appreciation be taught in the schools with any prospect of success. The beauty of good music in all its forms may reach the children's hearts by way of their ears. The same applies to mass education. In this connection, too, the value of the record, if properly used, is immense.

Let us now touch upon a second function of the phonograph record, hardly less important than the first: that of sound storing. What would we not give today if in addition to a verbal account of the musical production of far-off centuries we had also its actual sound! Take the artistry of a Chopin, the virtuosity of a Liszt, the witchery of a Paganini! Barely a century separates us from them, and yet we do not actually know whether or not they towered above the performers of our day. Neither do we know how Bach interpreted his organ works; and there are differences of opinion even in connection with the execution of many a passage in Mozart's operas. Such doubts about our music will not exist in the future. Coming generations will be able to refer to archives in which the living sound of our works and our artists have been stored.

No longer will there be any heated discussions among learned musical men concerning questions of style and interpretation. From a general cultural standpoint, an archive in which the events and voices of the past have been registered and stored represents a priceless possession.

Some reference to objections to the phonograph record may be in order. It has been pointed out that a piece is played over and over again in exactly the same manner and without giving an account of certain differences in mood and detail that distinguish a live interpretation. True. But a music lover is free to listen to different interpretations of the same work. Besides, are not the great masterpieces of painting and sculpture unchanging too? What about technical imperfections? No doubt, they exist. Today the record is still handicapped by certain time limitations, and there is the annoying scraping of the needle. But even these short-comings are rapidly being eliminated by long-playing records and spe-cially-processed "permanent" needles. A much more difficult problem is posed by those who inquire if the invention of mechanical means of presenting music will further or retard, stimulate or render unnecessary, the layman's efforts. Even at the risk of starting a discussion (or rather, of adding fuel to an already existing discussion) it may be stated that the optimistic alternative should be supported. Mechanical means of music, if properly used, are bound powerfully to stimulate the study and execution of music. Have boys ever stopped playing baseball after wit-nessing the contest of champion teams?

Printed music was the means of transmitting the intentions of the composer to a large number of interested persons. But, as we saw, it was of service only to those who know how to interpret it. The record goes an important step farther. It delivers to the lover of music the work in a superlative interpretation. (We may leave aside the possibility of a poor recording, a mutilation of a work of art, and similar contingencies.)

And now for the radio and television. Their spheres of influence are far larger even than that of the phonograph record. The number of radios in the world runs into the millions. This means that countless millions of people are now able to listen to music after the removal of all the obstacles which formerly had blocked its progress, obstacles of a social, geographic, or purely physical nature. The radio may bring about a true democratization of art, for it carries identically the same sounds into the homes of the rich and the poor. It offers an opportunity for the enjoyment and, what is even more essential, the understanding of art to classes which had formerly been prevented from attending theaters and concerts. Another highly important point: until recent times, musical life had been confined almost entirely to the cities. Rural districts had to content themselves with the cultivation of folk-like music. Now, the radio carries its sounds over land and sea, over mountains and plains. For the first time, the music of the great classics may be heard in the village, the farm dwelling, the mountain hut, the lighthouse. And for the first time music is able to reach the sick, the aged, the lonely. If radio were able to do no more than that, its existence would be justified a hundredfold.

In the days when printed music was invented, a handful of people were able to enjoy a musical work. This grew into thousands as musical life became more active, concerts were opened to the public, and the cities of the world received their share of musical presentations. With the coming of the radio, the number of the listeners was once more multiplied. Now there are millions of them spread all over the civilized world. In 1937, a certain performance was broadcast from the Festival Playhouse in Salzburg over a network of thousands of stations in almost all the countries of the world. The sounds which, at the actual performance, reached the ears of but a few hundred people, were made available to millions upon millions who, at the same moment, were in a kind of mystical communion with Salzburg and its atmosphre.

Let us pick out two dates from the history of the radio: March 28, 1914, and August 26, 1920. The former date marked the first musical broadcasting in Brussels. The selection was an excerpt from Wagner's *Parsifal*. On the evening of the second date, a group of young music lovers and self-taught radio mechanics for the first time broadcast the music performed at a theater. They had to do it secretly, for the head of the theater would never have given his permission. That happened in Buenos Aires, and, by a strange coincidence, the music was again that of *Parsifal*.

The immensity of radio's effective radius after but a few years' existence naturally started a keen competition for the control of the broadcasting stations and also placed a tremendous burden of responsibility on the shoulders of those in charge. In principle, radio activity may be regulated in one of two ways: it may either be government-owned or run by private interests. If government-owned, as is the case in almost all European countries, it represents a monopoly. America has from the very beginning considered radio a matter of private enterprise and placed its exploitation on a par with journalism. This attitude has led to strange results. The American radio is not being supported by the listeners' contributions, as is done in Europe, or by state subsidies, but by the amounts spent by commercial firms who are thus paying for the privilege of having their products advertised on the air.

It can hardly be doubted that radio and television are making their influences felt not only in the increased number of listeners. Music itself is undergoing changes; new forms are being evolved for special use over the air. The laws applicable to performances in concert halls and theaters are not valid for radio and television, whose tasks, too, are quite different. Just as in times gone by the playing of music in palaces was productive of new forms, and just as the lyric drama learned how to adapt itself to the opera house, so the radio and television will in the course of time assign to composers new tasks, different from anything heretofore practiced.

New fields of endeavor have been opened to music also by the third invention to be discussed here: the sound film. Music in the sound film is already being used for a great variety of purposes. There are even instances in which it has been made the chief ingredient of the comparatively new art. Remember Walt Disney's particularly daring attempt in his *Fantasia*, when he poured over his drawings and figures—products of his richly creative and brilliant imagination—a flood of the world's most famous music? Even those who doubt the admissibility of a pictorial—and especially a grotesquely pictorial—interpretation of serious music will have to admit that the experiment was highly interesting. There are a great many other uses to which music is put in the film of our day. Hardly any film is made today that does not have the occasional support of music. Invariably, certain moods and situations, pauses in the acting or the dialogue, call for a definite type of illustrative music. A song, or some other piece of music, may be used as a kind of leitmotif for a film. Or, the film version of a literary masterpiece may be accompanied by the corresponding score from the pen of a kindred spirit in the realm of music. A striking example of such a "'cooperation" was Reinhardt's filming of *A Midsummer Night's Dream* with Mendelssohn's scintillating music. Today, most films have a supporting score written expressly for them. This offers undreamt-of possibilities to composers whose work may well be a deciding factor in the success or failure of a screen product. Finally, there is the large number of musical films, ranging all the way from the biographies of great composers, depicting some of the more important and romantic scenes of their lives with the accompaniment of their own works, to the filming of musical revues, cabaret scenes, and music-hall acts.

A considerable number of eminent contemporary composers have felt drawn to film music and inspired by its possibilities. The following are but a few out of a great many: Milhaud, Prokofiev, Korngold, Copland, Silvestre Revueltas, Mossolov, Shostakovitch, and Jacques Ibert. And let us not forget that this third invention, too, has been the means of attracting further millions of spectators, of listeners. Let us not forget either that in the course of the past twenty years a considerable part of melodies that achieved popularity had their origin in films and that quite a few of the great masters' scores would never have gained general public acclaim and appreciation had it not been for the film.

What has been said in this chapter about mechanical music is by no means exhaustive. It should be mentioned, for instance, that in addition to the enumerated methods of sound transmission by mechanical or electrical means there also exist instruments that not only transmit sound but even produce it. These entirely novel instruments were demonstrated to the public in most of the large cities of the world and seemed to draw magically beautiful sounds out of the very air. Among the constructors of these new sound producers were men like Theremin, Trautwein, and Nernst. The fact that these contrivances are not used today does not mean that they may not play a part in the more or less distant future. Let us at least keep pace with the times by pointing out this new development and suggesting its possibilities in connection with musical history. Technical science, the driving power of our epoch, is taking giant steps forward. For all we know, it may not be long before a history of music will appear equipped with some films, strips, or tapes which by a simple device will reproduce the sound and by means of which the reader will hear the world's music. The word, the picture, and the music—all at the same time!

Appendix

THE INSTRUMENTS OF THE MODERN ORCHESTRA

In the sequence of their notation in the conductor's score:
- A. Wind Instruments
  - a) Wood-winds b) Brass-winds
- B. Percussion Instruments
- C. Keyboard Instruments and Harp
- D. Stringed Instruments

(The following tabulation corresponds in its numbers to those accompanying the instruments illustrated on Plate 216.)

GROUP A. (Wind Instruments)

a) *Wood-winds*

1. *Flute*
2. *Small Flute* or *Piccolo*. About half the size of a flute and sounding an octave higher with a shrill, piercing tone quality.
3. *Oboe*. Unlike the flute and other wood winds, it has a double-reed mouthpiece.
4. *English Horn*. Variety of the oboe used only exceptionally in the symphonic orchestra and then nearly always in characteristic solo passages, as for instance in the slow movement of Dvořák's *New World Symphony*, in Sibelius's *Swan of Tuonela*, and in the third act (Shepherd's melody) of Wagner's *Tristan und Isolde*. The English horn is one of the "transposing" instruments, which is to say that its actual sound does not coincide with its written notation, the variance in the case of the English horn being a fifth downward. Thus, to obtain a C, the composer must write a G.
5. *Clarinet*. A transposing instrument in various basic keys. Most frequently used in the symphonic orchestra are clarinets in A and B-flat; but there are also those in C, D, and E-flat. The A clarinet, according to the above explanation, must be read a minor third, and the B-flat clarinet a whole tone, deeper than written, etc.
6. *Bass Clarinet*. Used only in very large orchestras and in connection with modern works. Sounds an octave deeper than the clarinet.
7. *Soprano Saxophone*. 8. *Alto Saxophone*. 9. *Tenor Saxophone*. 10. *Bass Saxophone*. The saxophone was invented by the Belgian, Adolphe Sax, in 1838. Though hailed enthusiastically by Berlioz,

it has not been able to maintain itself in the symphonic orchestra. Appears only in exceptional instances, mostly in solo passages, but has been adopted by military bands in various countries and is one of the principal jazz instruments. Its playing technique is similar to that of the clarinet. The saxophone is another of the transposing instruments, occurring mostly in E-flat and B-flat.

11. *Bassoon.* Similar in playing technique to the oboe. While very expressive in its lower range, its high tones have a rather humorous effect. Used in this manner by Wagner in his *Meistersinger* and by Dukas in his *Sorcerer's Apprentice.*

12. *Contra-Bassoon.* Used only in very large orchestras and in connection with modern works. One octave deeper in range than the bassoon.

  b) *Brass-winds*

13. *French Horn.* Transposing instrument of noble sound. One of the most important instruments in the symphonic orchestra.

14. *French Horn.* In this older type of the instrument, chromatic playing was still impossible.

15. *Trumpet.*

16. *Cornet.* A kind of trumpet no longer in orchestral use.

17. *Trombone.* Occurring mostly in groups of three: Alto, Tenor, and Bass.

18. *Wagner Tuba.* Variety of the French horn devised by Wagner and occurring almost exclusively in his works and in those of his followers (Bruckner, for instance). Has a mellow and noble sound.

19. *Bass Tuba.* The largest and deepest sounding of the brass-winds.

GROUP B. (Percussion Instruments)

20. *Kettledrum* (*Timpano*). Used always in pairs (or threes). In contrast to most other percussion instruments can be tuned exactly and the pitch changed as need occurs.

21. *Bass Drum.*

22. *Military Drum.* Used only exceptionally in the symphonic orchestra.

23. *Snare Drum.* Used principally in dance and operetta music.

24. *Gong.*
25. *Triangle*
26. *Cymbals.*   }   Instruments for the production of special effects, without definite pitch.
27. *Castanets.*
28. *Tambourine.*

. 399

29. *Xylophone*. Made of parallel wooden bars of graduated length which are struck with flexible mallets.

29a. *Tubular Bells* or *Vertical Chimes* (not illustrated). A series of suspended metal tubes of graduated length, and therefore different pitch, which, when struck with a mallet, reproduce the sound of church bells.

GROUP C. (Keyboard Instruments and Harp)

30. *Harp*.

31. *Celesta*. Consisting of a series of steel plates struck by small hammers and producing a soft, bell-like tone. Quite effective in the symphonic orchestra (highly characteristic, for instance, in the second act of Richard Strauss's *Rosenkavalier*).

The piano also belongs in this group. It is used but rarely in the symphonic orchestra, but frequently is the solo instrument accompanied by and cooperating with the latter. The organ, which also occurs only rarely as an orchestral instrument, stands midway between this group and the winds.

GROUP D. (Stringed Instruments)

32. *Violin*. The largest group in the symphonic orchestra. In the classic epoch, the chief carrier of the melodies.

33. *Viola*. Somewhat larger than the violin and tuned a fifth lower.

34. *Cello*.

35. *Contrabass*.

N.B. While the old descriptive terms of wood-winds and brass-winds are still maintained, they have actually become meaningless, since almost all wind instruments are today made of metal.

THE DEVELOPMENT OF THE SYMPHONIC ORCHESTRA

City and Year	Violins	Violas	Celli	Contrabasses	Flutes	Oboes	Clarinets	Bassoons	French Horns	Trumpets	Trombones	Timpani (Pairs)	Total
Leipzig, 1730 (Bach's orchestra)	5	2	2	—	—	2	—	2	—	3	—	1	17
Mannheim, 1756	20	4	4	4	2	2	2	2	4	1	—	1	46
Milan, 1770 (First performance of a Mozart opera)	28	6	2	6	2	2	2	2	4	2	—	1	57
Esterhazy, 1783 (Hadyn's orchestra)	11	2	2	2	—	2	—	2	2	—	—	1	24
Paris Opera, 1788	28	6	12	5	2	4	2	4	?	?	?	1	64
Vienna, 1844	20	10	6	4	2	2	2	2	4	2	3	1	58
Bayreuth, 1880 (Wagner's orchestra)	32	12	12	8	4	4	4	4	8	4	6	2	100
Modern Orchestra [1]	32	12	10	8	4	4	4	4	8	6	3	2	97

[1] In addition to the instruments listed, the modern orchestra makes use of the following: English horn, bass clarinet, saxophone, contra-bassoon, tuba, celesta, harp, piano, and any number of percussion instruments, so that a total of from 100 to 120 musicians may be reached.

The figures here given—taken partly from works by Haas and Gassner—are average values, with the exception of the Milan entry, which refers to a one-time event.

As early as the eighteenth and nineteenth centuries, large sound masses were mobilized for special occasions, as for instance for the London concert in memory of the twenty-fifth anniversary of Handel's death. On November 5 and 9, 1843, Haydn's *Creation* was performed by 118 violins, 40 violas, 41 celli, 25 contrabasses, 13 flutes, 12 oboes, 12 clarinets, 12 bassoons, 4 contra-bassons (!), 12 French horns, 8 trumpets, 9 drums, 4 kettledrums, while 660 singers constituted the chorus. In 1844, Berlioz collected an ensemble of 1,000 musicians. Mahler did the same in Munich, when he first performed his Eighth Symphony, in 1908. Then there was the monster concert conducted by Johann Strauss in Boston, on the occasion of the 100th anniversary of Independence Day. 20,000 singers were accompanied by almost 10,000 musicians. 100 assistant conductors were required to communicate the conductor's tempi to this vast army of performers.

Index of Compositions and Their Composers

INDEX OF COMPOSITIONS